THE LETTERS
OF DOROTHY L. SAYERS

VOLUME TWO

THE LETTERS OF DOROTHY L. SAYERS

VOLUME TWO

1937 – 1943
From novelist to playwright

CHOSEN AND EDITED BY
BARBARA REYNOLDS

WITH A PREFACE BY
P. D. JAMES

PR
6037
.A95Z482
50-6

The United Library
Garrett-Evangelical/Seabury-Western Seminaries
Evanston, IL 60201

THE DOROTHY L. SAYERS SOCIETY

V H :   117674

ALSO BY BARBARA REYNOLDS

The Passionate Intellect:
Dorothy L. Sayers' Encounter with Dante
(obtainable direct from the author)

Dorothy L. Sayers: Her Life and Soul
(Hodder and Stoughton)

The Letters of Dorothy L. Sayers 1899–1936:
The Making of a Detective Novelist
(Hodder and Stoughton)

Translations (Penguin Classics)

Dante, *Paradise* (with Dorothy L. Sayers)
Dante, *La Vita Nuova*
Ariosto, *Orlando Furioso*

Introduction and notes Copyright © 1997 by Barbara Reynolds
Preface Copyright © 1997 by P. D. James
Letters Copyright © 1997 The Trustees of Anthony Fleming deceased

First published in Great Britain in 1997 by The Dorothy L. Sayers Society
Carole Green Publishing, 10 Market Street, Swavesey, Cambridge CB4 5QG

The right of the authors to be identified as the Authors of the Work has been
asserted in accordance with the Copyright, Design and Patents Act 1988.

All rights reserved. No part of this publication may be reproduced,
stored in a retrieval system or transmitted at any time or by any means, electronic,
mechanical, photographic, recording or otherwise, without prior permission
of the copyright holders

ISBN 0 95180 004 3

British Library Cataloguing in Publication Data
A catalogue record of this book is available from the British Library

Designed and produced by Geoff Green
at Geoff Green Book Design, Swavesey Cambridge CB4 5RA
Typeset in Baskerville
Printed in Great Britain by
St Edmundsbury Press
Bury St Edmunds, Suffolk

Contents

εγεγεγ

Preface

✑✑✑✑

P. D. JAMES

For most readers, particularly of crime fiction, the name of Dorothy L. Sayers is primarily associated with the well-crafted traditional detective story, and in particular with her aristocratic detective, Lord Peter Wimsey. It is doubtful whether she herself would be gratified by a posthumous reputation so focused on one aspect – and perhaps in her eyes the least important – of a literary life which is one of the most versatile, controversial and fascinating of her generation; novelist, poet, playwright, translator and Christian apologist. But it was with the publication in 1995 of the first volume of her letters, sensitively edited by her friend, the Italian scholar Dr Barbara Reynolds, that Dorothy L. Sayers became recognised in a new capacity, as one of the most remarkable letter-writers of her time. This second volume, again edited by Dr Reynolds, will enhance that reputation.

It should not surprise us that Dorothy L. Sayers was so remarkable a correspondent. A good letter requires a writer who has wide interests, a lively and original intelligence, humour which is not without an occasional trace of acerbity, honesty, moral courage and good writing. In brief, the writer should be a person with plenty to say and the talent to say it persuasively. Dorothy L. Sayers, as a letter-writer and as a woman, had all these qualities.

The second volume covers the years 1937–1943, and most of the letters are written from Sayers' home at 24 Newland Street, Witham, Essex, where she was living with her husband, Mac. The year 1937 opened well. Sayers had established herself as a successful novelist and her first play, *Busman's Honeymoon*, was a West End success. The worst of her emotional troubles were behind her, in particular her ill-fated and unconsummated love affair with the writer John Cournos and the birth of a son by a man who was to prove unsupportive and rejecting, both emotionally and financially. She had coped with these traumas with characteristic courage and

now looked forward to a period of stability. Her son, John Anthony, was
still in the care of her cousin, Ivy Shrimpton, when not at school, and was
healthy and doing well.

On 6th October 1936 Margaret Babington, organiser of the Festival of
the Friends of Canterbury Cathedral, had written a letter which was to
change Dorothy L. Sayers's life, and not only as a playwright. It was an
invitation to write a play for the 1937 Festival. This play, later named *The
Zeal of Thy House* on the inspiration of the set designer, Laurence Irving,
was to move Sayers into a new field of creativity which was to provide her
with intellectual stimulation, controversy and the comradeship of a joint
theatrical enterprise which she had already enjoyed when working on
Busman's Honeymoon. Her commitment to any undertaking was always
whole-hearted, not surprisingly in a woman who believed in the almost
sacramental importance of work and of intellectual integrity. The letters
show that she was closely involved in every aspect of *The Zeal of Thy House*
and the subsequent religious plays; production, casting, music, costumes
and the design of the set. This was a world in which her exuberant personality could feel naturally at home. And it was in the speech of the
Archangel Michael at the end of *The Zeal of Thy House* that Dorothy L.
Sayers first articulated her understanding of the Christian doctrine of the
Trinity in terms of creativity which she was to develop in *The Mind of the
Maker*, published in July 1941. A work of creation was three-fold, an earthly trinity to match the heavenly; the Creative Idea, timeless and passionate, which is the image of the Father; the Creative Energy begotten of the
idea and working in time, which is the image of the Word; the Creative
Power, the meaning of the work and its response in the individual soul,
which is the image of the Indwelling Spirit. It is on *The Mind of the Maker*
that Sayers's reputation as a lay theologian chiefly rests.

In February 1940 Dr James Welch, in charge of religious broadcasting
at the BBC, approached Sayers suggesting that she should write a drama-
tised life of Christ in half-hour episodes to be broadcast on the
"Children's Hour" programme. She had already written a religious radio
play, *He That Should Come*, but this new and more ambitious enterprise had
an inauspicious start. Dorothy L. Sayers had from the beginning set out
the conditions under which she would begin what would inevitably be a
long, challenging and poorly-paid task. She insisted that there must be no
writing down to a child audience which, in her view, was capable of
responding both to ideas and to elevated language. Unfortunately the
assistant to the producer suggested in a tactfully-worded letter that the
BBC should discreetly edit a few passages which she felt were "right above
the heads of the children" and too difficult for the audience. This suggestion provoked an immediate response from Sayers in some of the most
uncompromising and pugnacious letters which the BBC must ever have
received from a commissioned writer. Dorothy L. Sayers was always a

bonny fighter and here she was on sure ground: the sole responsibility of the creator for her creation. At one point Sayers even cancelled the contract, but Dr Welch was determined that the plays should not be lost, and the BBC capitulated. A producer acceptable to Sayers was appointed and the work continued with the author's usual energy and enthusiasm. The result, as might be expected at that time, provoked outrage from people and religious bodies who saw the depiction of Christ by an actor as sacrilege. The BBC stood firm in support of its author and the enterprise was fully vindicated by its success.

The religious plays and the broadcast of *The Man Born to be King* established Dorothy L. Sayers's reputation as a Christian apologist, and one senses from some of the letters that this was a role in which she was not altogether at ease, and one that involved her in an immense volume of correspondence. Some of the most fascinating and the longest letters in this volume are those in which she expounds her theological theories in replies to a wide range of correspondents seeking her views and advice on moral and ethical questions, particularly those relating to the war.

These letters will be interesting to more than amateur theologians or practising Christians. Dr Reynolds' judicious footnotes are helpful in explaining the doctrine which the non-theologian might otherwise find obscure. Sayers's own religion was devoid of emotion, religious enthusiasm or the outward signs of devotional life. Christianity, for her, was a passionate intellectual commitment to the formal creeds of the Church. In a long letter on 7th October 1941 to Cound Michael de la Bedoyère of the *Catholic Herald*, a letter which must have taken the best part of a day to write, she states: "I haven't got a pastoral mind or a passion to convert people; but I hate having my intellect outraged by imbecile ignorance and by the monstrous distortions of fact which the average heathen accepts as being Christianity (and from which he most naturally revolts)." Inevitably her reputation as a lay theologian and Christian apologist grew, and there is no doubt that, through her writing and her lectures, she had a greater personal influence on her time than we readers today often recognise.

She was certainly over-working, trying to reconcile this increasing public commitment with the need to earn a living and the daily problems of running a house in wartime. She was coping with, and fully supporting, an increasingly difficult husband. This overwork cannot have made relations with her son any easier. Without his side of the correspondence we cannot guess how far he resented his exclusion from much of his mother's life, but in a letter dated 17th March 1937 she writes that she is "nearly dead with tiredness every night". Most of her letters to him mention how busy she is. She never acknowledged him as her natural son but she was a generous, responsible and supportive parent. School fees were met and money for extras and occasional treats was found from a tight budget. The letters to her son are at their most interesting when they deal with intellectual questions he occasionally raised. She discusses the value of a university education, his ideas for his career and the nature of scientific creativity in letters which any son would have been proud and happy to have received. She couldn't give him maternal love in its fullest sense; a mother does not bond with a baby if she relinquishes him to another woman within days of his birth. But what she could give Dorothy L. Sayers gave, and one suspects that, as a parent, her reputation deserves better than it has received.

Although for many readers the most interesting letters will be those dealing with her theological theories and her career as a playwright, the range of her interests as a correspondent was wide. She wrote to the Editor of the *New Statesman* to disagree with the critic Desmond MacCarthy's views on Chekhov's *Uncle Vanya*; she corresponded about Lord Peter Wimsey's history and the purchase of his shirts; she wrote to the Editor of the *Daily Telegraph* in support of P. G. Wodehouse who had attracted odium by a broadcast while held in occupied France; she gave freely of her time in responding to queries from amateurs or professionals about the staging of her plays. The variety of her correspondents is as wide as her subject matter, ranging from statesmen, university professors and archbishops to fellow-writers and members of the public seeking her advice or her opinions. Always the voice is uniquely her own. In reading we feel ourselves in touch with a courageous, original and remarkable woman who, despite great difficulties, lived life with exuberant enthusiasm and has left a legacy of work which will endure.

P. D. JAMES

List of illustrations

ぐうぐうぐう

Introduction

❦❦❦

This second volume of *The Letters of Dorothy L. Sayers* brings to light an unknown dimension of her personality and writings. As she grew older and became established, her sense of involvement in society increased. This new focus was sharpened and strengthened by the Second World War. By 1943, the year with which this volume closes, Dorothy L. Sayers had come to be a figure of national influence and importance. The creative medium in which this development took shape was no longer fiction but drama.

She had begun writing plays in her childhood. The earliest recorded, entitled "Such is Fame" and written when she was 13 years old, concerns a young author (herself) who has imprudently based one of her characters on a combined portrait of two of her aunts.[1] With the help of her French governess she produced and acted scenes from plays by Molière. Enthusiastically she made costumes, props and programmes. Her parents enjoyed the theatre and encouraged her interest. She became, as the expresssion was, "stage-struck", idolizing actors. She acted out roles in her imagination, impersonating Athos, the gallant swordsman in Alexandre Dumas' novels. Such imaginative play was elaborate and sustained, involving her compliant family and friends for several years. A photograph taken when she was 14 shows her as Athos splendidly apparelled.[2]

At school, drama continued to play an important part in her life. Performances by a company of French actors are described ecstatically in her letters home. A melodrama of her own was considered good enough to be performed. In a school production of *The Merchant of Venice* she was cast as Shylock. She sent home continually for costumes, swords, wigs, a

---

1 See *The Letters of Dorothy L. Sayers: 1899–1936*, p. 4.
2 See Barbara Reynolds, *Dorothy L. Sayers: Her Life and Soul*, p. 20.

false beard, even a false nose. At the age of 17 she announced that she would like to go on the stage. With admirable foresight her Headmistress said she would be more of a success as a playwright than as an actress.

Her enthusiasm continued during her Oxford years but her earliest experience of the professional theatre came only in 1936, at the age of 43, when her play *Busman's Honeymoon*, written in collaboration with Muriel St Clare Byrne, was put on first at the Birmingham Theatre Royal, the Theatre Royal, Brighton and then in London at the Comedy. Her enjoyment of the camaraderie of theatrical life is vividly communicated in several of her letters. While this play was still in its early stages, even before it had gone into rehearsal, she received an invitation to write a drama for the 1937 festival of Canterbury Cathedral. This was the turning point in her career: Dorothy L. Sayers the playwright took over from the novelist.

By the end of the seven years covered by this volume she had written seventeen plays,[3] all of which were performed on stage, in cathedral or on radio. Two more religious dramas were written and performed in 1946 and 1951.[4] A secular play, *Where Do We Go From Here?*, was broadcast in 1948. Other plays, incomplete, are also to be found among her manuscripts.[5]

The height of her achievement as a playwright was reached with the twelve plays on the life of Christ, *The Man Born to be King*, a series which made broadcasting history in Britain. It also marked the apex of her recognition by the Church. The letters which form the climax of this volume concern an offer made by the Archbishop of Canterbury of a Lambeth doctorate in divinity, an offer which, after careful consideration, she declined. Her reasons for doing so included her wish to remain independent as a secular writer. The label "Doctor of Divinity" attached to her name would, she thought, lessen any influence she had as a commentator on social matters or as an expounder of the Christian faith. It might also, she feared, act as a constraint on the range and nature of her secular writing.

The letters in this volume provide glimpses behind the scenes, not only of the writing and producing of plays but also of the growth of her ideas. It is already known that her published works – plays, lectures, articles and the two books *Begin Here* and *The Mind of the Maker* – have had extensive

3 In chronological order: *Busman's Honeymoon*, *The Zeal of Thy House*, *He That Should Come*, *Love All*, *The Devil to Pay*, *The Man Born to be King* (consisting of 12 plays). In addition, her short story "The Unsolved Puzzle of the Man with No Face" was adapted as a play and broadcast on 3 April 1943, the first in the new series, "Saturday Night Theatre".

4 *The Just Vengeance* and *The Emperor Constantine*.

5 Including a play on Herod the Great and another on Admiral Darlan.

influence. What is not known is the part she played in shaping the creative thinking of the 1940s and '50s by means of her vast correspondence.

The exchange of substantial letters, some nearly as long as articles, was a regular, almost a daily, part of her activity. Among the topics discussed are the reconstruction of society after the war, the maintenance of peace, the importance of vocation in work (by which she did not mean vocational training), the position of women, the opportunities missed by the B.B.C., the need for a national theatre, the fallacy of 19th-century liberalism, the collapse of materialism, the limitations of the theory of "economic man", the ephemeral nature of many scientific concepts, the confusion of Church leaders on social matters and their inadequate preaching on Christian doctrine, the need for the young to be kept in touch with the past, the danger of society's failure to recognize the importance of creativity. Despite the profound nature of these topics, her lively humour and talent for dialogue make many of the letters as compelling and entertaining as anything she ever wrote.

The range of her correspondents is striking: archbishops, bishops, (not to mention many minor clergy), fellow writers, politicians, members of government departments, directors of the B.B.C., University teachers, students, leading personalities in the world of the theatre, publishing and journalism. There is scarcely an area of public life on which she did not bring some influence to bear. Remarkable too are the generous and time-consuming letters she wrote in reply to strangers who asked for clarification and guidance in matters concerning religion. In this respect she resembled C. S. Lewis, to whom she wrote an amusing letter of wry self-mockery, saying how much she begrudged the time. Yet, although she grumbled, she continued to take trouble, courteously explaining and advising whenever she felt that a correspondent's enquiries were genuine and sincere. She could be curt with those whom she suspected of being otherwise.

Threaded among the public letters are personal ones, showing her maturing relationship with her son, her contacts with friends, her delight in absurdity. Though she is writing no more novels, the Wimsey saga still lives on in her imagination and there are tantalizing mentions of Lord Peter and Harriet. Though bells were silenced in war-time, echoes of *The Nine Tailors* chime in the background with her election as an honorary member of bell-ringing societies. Air-raids, the shortage of food, the difficulty of obtaining domestic help are referred to with a characteristic lightness of touch: the time-bomb which falls in the garden of the pork-butcher across the road and the local excitement it causes, the arrival of a lemon, sent as a precious gift, packed like a rare gem in a jeweller's box, conversation in a London restaurant with members of the Metropolitan police summoned to investigate suspected Fifth-columnists; reactions to

The Man Born to be King: abusive letters from the public at the outset, later outnumbered by letters of gratitude, her husband, the "gruff warrior", being moved to tears as he listened to one of the plays, the evacuated school-children clustered round the radio, fascinated by the story of Jesus ("I know He didn't stay dead," said one, "because I've been reading on ahead") – there are many such moments which bring back the sound of voices talking, the gestures of people who, long dead, seem still alive.

Ideas take time. The realization that Dorothy L. Sayers was far more than an author of brilliant detective novels is gaining ground. The claim is being made increasingly that she was a creative force in the intellectual life of the twentieth century. We are a long way yet from assessing the full measure of her mind. These letters and those which follow in succeeding volumes reveal a Dorothy L. Sayers who lives on, more than can ever be estimated, in the work of those whose minds she enlivened.

"What we make is more important than what we are," she wrote in a letter to her son, "particularly if 'making' is our professsion." It will be seen that her letters are themselves a form of making.

BARBARA REYNOLDS
13 June 1997

NOTE

EDITIONS OF WORKS BY DOROTHY L. SAYERS TO WHICH LETTERS IN THIS VOLUME REFER

Plays

Busman's Honeymoon (Gollancz, 1937; Kent State University Press, 1984)

He That Should Come (*Four Sacred Plays*, Gollancz, 1948)

The Zeal of Thy House (Gollancz, 1937; repub. *Four Sacred Plays*, Gollancz, 1948)

The Devil to Pay (Gollancz, 1939; Harcourt Brace, 1939; repub. *Four Sacred Plays*, Gollancz, 1948)

The Man Born to be King (Gollancz, 1943; Harper and Brothers, 1949; Eerdmans, 1976)

Love All (Kent State University Press, 1984)

Books

Begin Here (Gollancz, 1940)

The Mind of the Maker (Methuen, 1941; Harper San Francisco, 1979; Mowbray, 1994)

The Letters of Dorothy L. Sayers: 1899–1936 (Hodder & Stoughton, 1995; St Martin's, 1996)

Articles and Lectures

Unpopular Opinions (Gollancz, 1946)

Creed or Chaos? (Methuen, 1947)

Christian Letters to a Post-Christian World (ed. Roderick Jellema, Eerdmans, 1969; repub. as *The Whimsical Christian*, Macmillan 1978)

Are Women Human? (including also "The Human-Not-Quite-Human", intro. by M. McDermott Shideler, Eerdmans, 1971)

A Matter of Eternity (ed. Rosamond Sprague, Eerdmans, 1973)

Dorothy L. Sayers: Spiritual Writings (ed. Ann Loades, Cowley Publications, 1993)

Acknowledgements

ഗ౩ഗ౩ഗ౩

My first expression of gratitude must be to Baroness James of Holland Park (the novelist P. D. James) for her continuing encouragement. As for the first volume, so now for the second she has provided an illuminating and discerning Preface.

Once again, my heartfelt thanks are due to the Marion E. Wade Center at Wheaton College, Illinois, where the originals of most of the letters in this second volume are held. I am much indebted to the research facilities which have been granted me there by the Wheaton College Board of Trustees, to the unfailing help provided by the Associate Director, Mrs Marjorie Lamp Mead, as well as by all members of staff. As previously, I thank Mr Tony Dawson for his accurate typing of the letters onto disc.

I thank Mr Laurence Harbottle, executor of the estate of Anthony Fleming, and Mr Bruce Hunter of David Higham Associates for authorizing me to enter into negotiations with the Dorothy L. Sayers Society and with Carole Green Publishing for the production of this and the next two volumes. I further thank Mr Hunter for much patient advice and encouragement. I also express my grateful appreciation of the generous sponsorship which has helped to make this project possible.

I am grateful to the many people who have answered questions, looked up information, identified persons and tracked down quotations, particularly Mr Andrew Lewis, who helped me with innumerable learned references. I also thank the staff of the Cambridge University Library for their patience and courtesy. Mr Jack Reading, Secretary of the Society for Theatre Research, has pursued the dates of birth and death of numerous actors. To him I owe also the inclusion of several delightful letters to Muriel St Clare Byrne and Marjorie Barber. Mr David G. Humphreys most kindly supplied three letters to Dennis Arundell and two photographs relating to *Busman's Honeymoon*. Mr Giles Watson drew my attention to a letter relating to the Theological Literature Association; I thank the Archbishop of Canterbury and the Trustees of Lambeth Palace Library for allowing me to publish it. I also thank the University of Sussex for permission to publish several letters addressed to Maurice B. Reckitt (from the Reckitts Papers, SxMs44, Manuscripts Section, University of Sussex Library); the University of Michigan (the Van Volkeburg-Browne Papers, Special Collections Library) for permission to print a letter to Maurice E. Browne; the Victoria and Albert Picture Library for permission to reproduce three photographs; and Constable Publishers for permission to reproduce the clerihew and cartoon by E. C. and Nicolas Bentley from *Baseless Biography*, thank the C. S. Lewis estate for permission to publish a letter and Mr Walter Hooper for a quotation from *C. S. Lewis: a Companion and Guide*. Mr Jeremy Stevenson supplied information about recordings and productions of *The Man Born to be King*. Miss Pauline Adams, Librarian of Somerville College, has again helped me with identities and dates. Mrs Penelope Hatfield, Archivist of Eton College, kindly sent me information concerning one of the masters, Mr J. D. Upcott. Mr Charles Noon, archivist of Blundell's School, provided information about the former Headmaster, the Rev. Neville Gorton. Mr James Pailing traced a rare pamphlet by G. F. Woodhouse, inventor of a change-ringing machine. Canon J. A. Thurmer helpfully clarified a note on a difficult theological phrase. Miss Anne Scott-James enabled me to be precise in my note concerning her father R. A. Scott-James, author, editor and literary critic. Dr Geoffrey Lee clarified the identity for me of certain members of the Leigh family. Mr Joseph Pearce instantly placed two quotations from G. K. Chesterton. Mr John Wagstaff, Acting Senior Reference Librarian of the B.B.C. Music Library, provided me with a copy of the once famous but now forgotten song "Hybrias the Cretan". In my search for a quotation from Greening Lamborn I was kindly helped by Mr C. B. L. Barr, Dr Donald Nicolson and Mr J. S. G. Simmons; in this connection I thank also Miss Ursula Bickersteth and Dr Jennifer March. Special thanks are due to Mrs Valerie Napier for the particulars concerning the birth of her half-brother, John Anthony Fleming, published here for the first time in the Appendix.

Mrs Simon Phipps has kindly allowed me to reproduce a photograph of her late husband the Rev. Dr James Welch. The Marion E. Wade Center has authorized me to publish a photograph of a portrait of Val Gielgud by Sayers' husband, Atherton Fleming. Two photographs already published in Ralph E. Hone's *Dorothy L. Sayers: A Literary Biography* are here reproduced by his kind permission.

I am grateful to three members of the Dorothy L. Sayers Society who checked the proofs of this volume and verified the notes: Mr Christopher

Dean (Chairman), Mr Philip L. Scowcroft (Research Officer) and Mrs Chris Simpson (Publications Officer). I am grateful also to Mr Pat Mills for his helpful sub-editing.

Finally, I express appreciation to Mr Geoff Green for his elegant design of this book.

BARBARA REYNOLDS

1937

Behind the scenes

෭ෲෲෲ

At the beginning of 1937, Dorothy L. Sayers was still involved with the reception of her play, Busman's Honeymoon, *and with the timing of the publication of the novel she had made of it. Gradually her commitment to the play for Canterbury Cathedral was to demand more and more of her attention.*[1]

24 Newland Street
Witham
Essex

TO MURIEL ST CLARE BYRNE[2]

4 January 1937

Dear Muriel,

To set against the pronouncements of some of our London critics,[3] who complain that they do not know whether we meant to write farce, melodrama, or sentimental comedy, here is the considered judgement of my gardener. I may say that this came out of him entirely unsolicited and unprompted, and that I have reproduced his words as exactly as I can remember them:

"What I thought was, it was meted out just right. There was a bit of everything – a bit of a thrill and then a bit of a laugh and then a bit of what I call the sob-stuff. That's what I like – not the same thing all the time, but go on just so long and then you're off on to something else. It's

---

1 The terms of the contract had been settled in November 1936.

2 Muriel St Clare Byrne (1895–1983), O.B.E., a contemporary at Somerville and close friend, part-author with D. L. S. of the play *Busman's Honeymoon*. See *The Letters of Dorothy L. Sayers: 1899–1936*.

3 "The play seems to have made some of the critics very cross indeed." (From her letter to Maurice Browne, 31 December 1936, *The Letters of Dorothy L. Sayers: 1899–1936*, p. 414.)

natural, ain't it? because life's always a mix-up. You may say, 'I've had seven years' good luck, or seven years' bad luck' – but when you come to look at it in detail, like, even those years have been a mix-up. Something sad, and then something funny comes along of it – that's how life is."

I really do not think, if we had tried with both hands for a fortnight, we could have stated our own theory – or Will Shakespeare's practice – very much more forcibly or concisely.

I hope you're having a good rest. Mine was a dose of flu, all right. It didn't hurt much at the time, but it's left me curiously shaky, and not altogether eager to tackle 120 Somervillians[4] at the end of the week. However, London will probably cheer up the old system, and so long as the cast escape the Scourge I don't much mind what happens. In the meantime I have asked various people to various meals – nobody replies to my letters or tells me anything!![5]

Bless you, dear, and all the best,
Dorothy

4 She was about to attend a meeting of the Somerville College Council.
5 An echo of John Galsworthy's James Forsyte: "Nobody tells me anything."

[24 Newland Street
Witham
Essex]

TO VICTOR GOLLANCZ[1]
17 January 1937

Dear Mr Gollancz,

We were all very sorry that you were unable, after all, to join us on Monday night. As I said to you on the telephone, I can see no objection to the distribution of advance copies of *Busman's Honeymoon*[2] to the booksellers; the only danger I foresee, would arise if there were too much advance publicity to the public so as to disappoint them when they could not get the book. Thank you for sending Mr Cadness Page's[3] letter; he wrote me one himself in somewhat similar terms. I am very much pleased

1 Victor Gollancz (1893–1967), her publisher, knighted in 1965. For further particulars, see *The Letters of Dorothy L. Sayers: 1899–1936.*, pp. 262–263.
2 The novel *Busman's Honeymoon* was first published in New York by Harcourt Brace on 18 February 1937. Gollancz published the play in February and the novel in June of the same year.
3 Cadness Page wrote: "I have been an ardent follower of Miss Sayers from the beginning but I am sure that in this book she has far surpassed anything she has written before. The humanity and character drawing in the book are first-class and many sides of her talent as a writer are admirably illustrated in *Busman's Honeymoon*. I am sure it will be very successful".

to have approval of this novel from him and from one or two other men, since while the woman's side of a honeymoon novel would be easy for me to write, the man's side of it is bound to be more conjectural. I am so sorry that we are having to hold you up like this on the novel, but as I think Miss Pearn[4] explained to you, I feel deeply responsible to the management and to the cast, and have pledged myself to do nothing that might hamper the run of the play. I do feel that at this moment publication would be a mistake; for one thing there would be people like my Aunt, who, having read the novel beforehand, felt a little bewildered by the play, feeling that a great deal had been left out of it. For another thing, one has to reckon with the critics, who may very well say that here is the novelist doing her own proper business, which is novels, and that therefore the novel is better than the play. If the play succeeds in establishing itself, then I think its objections will disappear. In any case we will keep our fingers firmly on the pulse of the thing and give you good warning when the time comes for publishing.

What has particularly interested me in the writing of the novel has been the problem of rethinking the story in terms of narrative, and of writing a book which should not be the ordinary novel of the play, but a distinct novel of the same [name]. I know that it would probably not fit in with your publicity scheme to tackle the thing along those lines, but I suggest that if the play should run, it might become desirable to look at the thing from this point of view in order to protect ourselves against the general feeling that there doubtless is about "the novel of the play". Of course we do not yet know how long the present business is going to keep up,[5] but we are at present playing to extraordinarily steady sheets, especially taking into consideration the influenza epidemic.

Yours very sincerely,
[Dorothy L. Sayers]

4 Her literary agent, Nancy Pearn (nicknamed "Bun"), of the firm of Pearn, Pollinger and Higham.
5 The play ran for nine months at the Comedy Theatre and was then transferred to the Victoria Palace.

[24 Newland Street
Witham
Essex]

TO ELIZABETH HAFFENDEN[1]

17 January 1937

Dear Miss Haffenden,
    I was at Canterbury last week talking over with Miss Babington[2] and

Mr Laurence Irving[3] the matter of the Canterbury Play, and they felt that the time had come when I ought to get into touch with you about the designs for the costumes. I have so far only sketched out the first section of the play, and the pageant which ends it,[4] but as this pageant contains most of the really difficult problems of stage management and design, the bits I have done will perhaps afford us sufficient basis for discussion. Mr Irving was very keen that we should have a final tableau full of colour and splendour bringing in all the various craftsmen[5] and so on who contribute to the building and furnishing of the church, and I feel that we ought to be able to have some fun over planning the costumes for this. There is also a matter of certain gigantic angelic figures forming a kind of chorus to the play about which we shall have to talk. I understand from Mr Irving that there are some costumes in existence which could be adapted for these angels. What I particularly want is to find out from you how far one may go in the matter of fantastic design, and how far angels could be expected to move about when encumbered by, what I understand will be, large quantities of gold american cloth!

I have to be in Town next Wednesday the 20th, and it would be very convenient if we could manage to meet on that date, or if it does not suit you I could manage to stay over until Thursday. Perhaps you could come along to my flat either morning or afternoon as suits you best, when I could show you the bits of the play I have done and go into all these questions. As I shall be away from home on Tuesday, would you very kindly either write to me at 24, Great James Street, Bloomsbury, W.C.1. or ring me up there on Wednesday morning – HOLborn 9156.

Yours very truly,

    [Dorothy L. Sayers]

---

1 Elizabeth Haffenden had designed the costumes for Charles Williams' play *Thomas Cranmer of Canterbury*, written for the Festival of 1936. She was also to design the costumes for D. L. S.' second Canterbury drama, *The Devil to Pay* (see illustrations). She later became well known as a designer of costume for films.

2 See following letter.

3 Laurence Irving (1897–1988) designed the permanent sets in the Chapter House of the Cathedral against which the play was performed. He was the son of H. B. Irving and the grandson of Sir Henry.

4 The pageant was later omitted.

5 The Canterbury Festival of 1937 was designed to celebrate Arts and Crafts.

[24 Newland Street
Witham
Essex]

TO MARGARET BABINGTON[1]
18 January 1937

Dear Miss Babington,

Thank you so much for your letter. I am so glad you like the title "The Zeal of Thy House":[2] it was Mr Irving's inspiration, and though I sat grinding my teeth with jealousy for two hours, I could not think of anything half as good! I am delighted to confirm it, since it has your approval; as you say, it is the imaginative touch about it which is so delightful. By all means get the postcards out at once.

I have already written to Miss Haffenden suggesting an appointment in Town for next Wednesday or Thursday; I hope we shall be able to make good progress and get your embroiderers on to the job without delay.

I had, in a half jesting manner – and explaining of course that casting did not come within my province – mentioned the subject of archangels to Mr Alan Napier.[3] I have now heard from him and he says that he would seriously be delighted to be Michael if called upon. This is, of course, just a suggestion, but if you did think of strengthening the cast with one or two professionals, I do think we could not possibly find a more suitable leading archangel. He is, as I told you, six foot four, and magnificently built; good-looking in rather a severe way with a very fine voice, and excellent training in the speaking of verse. He is a young man, and has a considerable reputation as a rising actor. I do not think, however, that he would be out of the way as regards fees. A further recommendation, perhaps, is that having been brought up more or less in the bosom of the

---

1 Margaret Babington (d. 1958), Festival organizer and steward and treasurer of the Friends of Canterbury Cathedral, had written to D. L. S. on 6 October 1936 inviting her to write a play for 1937. She said that she did so at the suggestion of Charles Williams. See letters to her dated 7, 18 October, 14, 27 November 1936 (*Letters of Dorothy L. Sayers: 1899–1936*, pp. 400–401, 402, 405, 406). "The tall, trim figure of Margaret Babington on her ancient bicycle was likened to Boadicea. She had a genius for organization and for securing volunteers and always marked her letters to the Dean 'Urgent'....She held together the vast numbers of volunteers needed for the Festival for thirty years....By the time of her death Miss Babington had enrolled 6000 Friends of the Cathedral and had helped raise over £100,000 for the Restoration of the Building." (Kenneth W. Pickering, *Drama in the Cathedral: The Canterbury Festival Plays 1928–1948*, Churchman Publishing, 1985.)

2 The phrase is taken from Psalm 69, verse 9: "For the zeal of thine house hath eaten me up".

3 (Sir) Alan Napier (1903–1988), then best known in the roles of Captain Shotover in *Heartbreak House* and the Marquis of Shayne in *Bitter Sweet*. In 1937 the part of Michael was played by (Sir) Anthony Quayle (1913–1989). Alan Napier played the part in 1938 at the Westminster Theatre. (See letter to Maurice Browne, 5 March 1938.)

church and a highly intelligent man, he would act his part with understanding and in the right spirit. I am not, of course, trying in any way to force him on you; but if he should be free in June I think it would be worth while considering him. I see that he is opening early next month in London in a new play *Because We Must*,[4] with Howard Wyndham[5] and Bronson Albery; it is, however, possible that the play may not run for five months.

I am trying to get on now with the middle part of the play, though I have been unexpectedly interrupted this week by the B.B.C. who have suddenly arranged a broadcast of *Busman's Honeymoon* for tomorrow, so that I shall have to go up and see to it.

I hope, however, to be able to report progress before very long.

Yours sincerely,

[Dorothy L. Sayers]

4 By Ingaret Gifford, staged at Wyndham's Theatre from 5 to 20 February 1937. Vivien Leigh was also a member of the cast.
5 Howard Wyndham, theatre manager (1865–1949), son of Sir Charles Wyndham, associated with his father's theatres, the Criterion, Wyndham's and the New, which he managed with (Sir) Bronson Albery (1881–1971).

[24 Newland Street
Witham
Essex]

TO JAMES PASSANT[1]

19 January 1937

Dear Mr Passant,

Thank you for your letter. I am so much looking forward to our team's visit to Cambridge.

I am glad you enjoyed the play, in spite of an unsatisfactory Harriet; the part, though small, is a very difficult one. I think you would like the way Veronica Turleigh[2] plays it in Town, she is so distinguished and so sympathetic. I am sorry that the love scene made your bowels heave; I can imagine that in the wrong hands it probably would! I expect the wretched people started to act. Dennis Arundell[3] and Veronica Turleigh put over the serious part with the very minimum of acting and the

1 A Fellow of Sidney Sussex College, Cambridge, member of the Confraternitas Historica, the historical society which invited Dorothy L. Sayers, Helen Simpson, Muriel St Clare Byrne and Wilfrid Scott-Giles to read papers on the Wimsey family. The meeting was held on 7 March 1937. See Barbara Reynolds, *The Passionate Intellect: Dorothy L. Sayers' Encounter with Dante* (Kent State University Press, 1989), pp. 244–245.

Dennis Arundell and Veronica Turleigh as Lord and Lady Peter Wimsey
in *Busman's Honeymoon*

quietest possible intonation, and it never fails to hold the house. It was so good of you to write and let me know your reactions to the performance, which unfortunately, neither my collaborator[4] nor I was able to attend owing to pressure of business and flu in our respective circles.

Yours sincerely,

[Dorothy L. Sayers]

2 Veronica Turleigh (1903–1971) also played the part of Helena in *The Emperor Constantine*.
3 Dennis Arundell (1898–1988) was the first Lord Peter Wimsey. See D. L. S.' comments on the interpretation of the role by Basil Foster in her letter to Muriel St Clare Byrne, 13 September 1937.
4 Muriel St Clare Byrne.

[24 Newland Street
Witham
Essex]

TO MRS K. L. R. MOLYNEUX[1]

19 January 1937

Dear Bella Donna,

Thank you so much for your two letters. I had put aside the first one meaning to answer it, but day after day went by, and I seemed to be in such a rush that I really have done no private correspondence at all for the last twelve months. I had sent a card to Japan, but I expect you had returned before it got there. So you are back in Oxford again! I rush down there from time to time to attend meetings of the Somerville College Council; we must certainly contrive to meet one day this term or next. At the moment I am spending most of my time tearing up and down to Town over theatrical business. Having just, more or less coped with the agitations of *Busman's Honeymoon* (have you seen it yet? It is really doing extraordinarily good business), I find myself plunged into work for this year's Canterbury play which I have rashly undertaken to write. We are going to have great fun with a lot of musical and scenic effects.

It was nice of you to be so forgiving and write again after my long silence.

Looking forward to seeing you,

Yours affectionately,

[Dorothy L. Sayers]

1 A voice from the past. Mrs Molyneux, a violinist, was a friend of D. L. S. during her Oxford days. (See *Letters of Dorothy L. Sayers: 1899–1936*, Index.)

[24 Newland Street
Witham
Essex]

TO MARGARET BABINGTON

23 January 1937

Dear Miss Babington,

Many thanks for your letter; I am so glad you feel that it would be a good thing to approach Mr Alan Napier about being the archangel Michael; I really think he would be an excellent choice, and in the hope of getting him, I am allowing myself to give some importance to the part.

Miss Haffenden and I had a long and most fruitful interview; she seems to be immensely keen on the idea of the thing, and I feel sure we shall see eye to eye about the costumes. I have given her a copy of the last section of the play so that she may get started at once on the pageant material which will, of course, mean the heaviest work.

In accordance with Mr Irving's suggestions, I have now added two extra pageants, that of the Sailors and that of the Royal Gifts, and I am enclosing a copy of this section with these additions. It is now getting pretty long, and I don't think we ought to put in anything more until the composer[1] and producer have seen what they can do with it. Have we had any reply yet from Mr Harcourt Williams?[2] It would be a good thing if I could get into touch early with the producer and if Mr Williams has accepted, it might be possible for me to see him when I am in Town at the beginning of the week after next.

Yours very sincerely,
[Dorothy L. Sayers]

1 G. H. Knight, the Cathedral organist.
2 Harcourt Williams (1888–1957) created the part of William of Sens in *The Zeal of Thy House*. It was recognized as one of his finest achievements. He also produced the play, with the assistance of Frank Napier. In addition he produced D. L. S.' second Canterbury drama, *The Devil to Pay*, in which he played the part of Faustus.

[24 Newland Street
Witham
Essex]

TO G. F. WOODHOUSE[1]

25 January 1937

Dear Mr Woodhouse,

Thank you so much for your letter and for your most interesting booklet about the change-ringing machine. I remain overwhelmed with astonishment at anybody who could work out a thing like that. It is also exceedingly good of you to let me have the list of errors in *The Nine Tailors*, and some time, if there is a new edition, I shall hope to go through it with a view to putting these details right.

I only wish I could take up ringing, but the fact is it appears to be such an enthralling pursuit that I am sure if I once started on it I should neglect all my work! It has been a great gratification to me to know that ringers have enjoyed the book, which I so rashly wrote without knowing anything about the subject, and have been so kind to the errors I have fallen into by the way.

Wishing every success to you and your band,[2]

Yours very truly,

[Dorothy L. Sayers]

1 George Fraser Woodhouse (1875–1952), a science master at Sedbergh School from 1897 to 1930, was a first-class ringer and conductor of hand- and tower-bells. He constructed three ringing machines in all. The booklet to which D. L. S. refers is *Change-Ringing Machine: Invented by G. F. Woodhouse of Sedbergh*. It contains diagrams and a photograph of the machine. Consisting of 8 pages, it was printed by Came and Cave of Bristol, no date, but presumably 1937. An obituary notice of the inventor was published in *The Ringing World*, 22 March 1957.

2 As part of his service to Sedbergh Church he trained a band up to Surprise Major standard.

The Detection Club
31 Garrard Street
W.1

TO THE EDITOR OF THE NEW STATESMAN

17 February 1937[1]

Dear Sir,

CHEKHOV AT THE WESTMINSTER

A losing bout with the flu germ put me out of action over the week-end, but I hope it is not too late to argue a little with Mr Desmond MacCarthy[2] about *Uncle Vanya*.[3]

1 Published on 27 February.
2 (Sir) Desmond MacCarthy (1877–1952), critic on *The Sunday Times*.
3 By Anton Chekhov (1860–1904). *Uncle Vanya*, his second play, was published in 1900.

I attended the first night at the Westminster under stimulating and, for anyone of my age,[4] unusual circumstances. I had never previously seen the play, read the play, or heard a single word of discussion about this or any other production of it. Through this strange gap in my education I thus viewed the performance as a stage-play, and not as a venerable institution. This probably accounts for some of the differences between my impressions and those of the seasoned critic.

I find, for instance, that I ought not to have come away filled with enthusiasm for Mr Cecil Trouncer's[5] interpretation of Astrov. But I remain impenitent about this. His reading may not be true to tradition, but if it is not true both to human nature and to what Chekhov actually wrote, I will eat my hat. I do not know what the "orthodox" reading may be, but if one goes by the text of the play it is clear that Astrov is not a man who has "lost his soul and looks like it". He is that far more disconcerting figure: the man who has lost his driving-power and does not look like it. All the exterior apparatus of strength is still there: the bodily energy (he does not merely chatter about trees, he plants them); the infectious enthusiasm; the physical attraction which "gets" not merely Sonia but the unintellectual and unmaternal Elena; what is lost is the inner cohesion and sustained courage to defy circumstance.[6] His tragi-comedy is that he still has his moments of believing in himself. At the end of the play he returns to his trees – under the comforting illusion that this time, perhaps, something will really come of it. We know that nothing ever will – and in his moments of self-knowledge, so does he. Incidentally, in the scene where Astrov shows the maps to Elena, Mr Trouncer triumphantly succeeded in convincing me that here was a man genuinely in love with an idea – for the first time on any stage, by any actor, in any part whatsoever.

There are other points on which the "fresh mind" would like to break a lance with Mr MacCarthy; but I believe that where he and I differ fundamentally is in our respective ideas of what the play is about. He thinks that in the final scene the reiteration of the words "they've gone" should affect us like a passing-bell, and that the laughter which greets them at the Westminster destroys the spirit of this drama of futility. That is, in spite of the end of the third act and other plain indications of the playwright's purpose, he insists on seeing the play as a tragedy. But the whole tragedy of futility is that it never succeeds in achieving tragedy. In its blackest moments it is inevitably doomed to the comic gesture. The sadder, the

4 She was 43.
5 Cecil Trouncer (1898–1953).
6 These were qualities which D. L. S. herself possessed. It is interesting that she defined them as absent in Astrov.

funnier; and conversely, in the long run, the funnier, the sadder. The English are at one with the Russians in their ability to understand and create this inextricable mingling of the tragic and the absurd, which is the base of Shakespeare's human (and box-office) appeal. Mr MacCarthy warns us against the conceit of thinking of ourselves first as "English" in relation to foreigners; but on this particular point we English are far closer in feeling to the "foreign" Russian than (let us say) the Irishman can ever be to either of us.

I am,
Yours faithfully,
[Dorothy L. Sayers]

[24 Newland Street
Witham
Essex]

TO LAURENCE IRVING

24 February 1937

Dear Mr Irving,

I am sending herewith, copies of the second and third sections of the play. Can you and Miss Babington and the musical director[1] do with two copies between you, as I want to send one to Mr Harcourt Williams, and I only have four? I am afraid these sections offer a good many difficulties to the producer, but when these have been coped with, the rest will be easy going. I am sorry to have been so long about all this, but the delay was not caused only by my dissipations in Town. I found a good many difficulties in the writing, not only as regards the sequence of the episodes, but also as regards making the relations of William and the Lady Ursula sufficiently defined to be interesting without offending the Dean and Chapter. I hope we may be able to get away with it as it is. I apologise for the frivolity of Simon's song; my own impression is, that it was probably really something much more rowdy and mediaeval. It does not, by the way, go to any tune that I know of, since the refrain is different from that usually associated with the Noah's Ark songs; but no doubt the composer can cope with this. Have we got a composer yet, by the way?

I am at work on the fourth section, and hope to be able to let you have this by the end of the week. Mr Williams said something about wanting a read-through in March; could you suggest any sort of date for this? I expect you would like me to come down. At present my engagements for

1 See letter to Margaret Babington, 23 January 1937, note 1.

March are for the 7th, when I shall be at Cambridge,[2] and the 15th and 16th when I have to be in Town. At any other time I could be at your disposal.

With kindest regards to you all,
Yours very sincerely,
[Dorothy L. Sayers]

2 See letter to James Passant, 19 January 1937, note 1.

[24 Newland Street
Witham
Essex]

TO HELEN SIMPSON[1]

25 February 1937

Dear Helen,

Many thanks for your letter; I will make Hubert[2] an Oblate as this seems a very suitable thing for him to be.

I enclose the undertaking for the Society of Authors, duly signed; it seems to be, by the way, a method of undertaking cases on spec. which keeps on the windy side of the law. However, that is not our affair.

Herewith the American *Busman's Honeymoon*;[3] I have corrected the misprint on page 112, and Tullia's Tomb[4] is printed on the wrong page, but I trust you will overlook these defects.

Looking forward to hearing from you about the New Zealand Wimseys.[5]

Yours ever,
[Dorothy]

1 Helen Simpson (1897–1940), novelist, playwright and historian.
2 A character in *The Zeal of Thy House*. An oblate is a member of a monastic order assigned to specific work. In the play Hubert is Superintendent of the Rough Masons.
3 See letter to Victor Gollancz, 17 January 1937, note 2
4 Poem by John Donne, beginning "Now, as in Tullia's tomb one lamp burnt clear...", quoted at the end of the novel *Busman's Honeymoon*. Tullia was the wife of Tarquinius Superbus.
5 Helen Simpson was to read a spoof paper on this subject at the meeting of the Confraternitas Historica held at Sidney Sussex College, Cambridge on 7 March.

[24 Newland Street
Witham
Essex]

TO LAURENCE IRVING

26 February 1937

Dear Mr Irving,

Many thanks for your letter. I enclose the fourth section of the play, which with the pageant, completes the job.[1] Perhaps when you have read it you will pass the copies on to Miss Babington.

In view of what you say about wanting to get on quickly to the end, I am alarmed to find that this section is five minutes longer than any of the others! It is, however, from the doctrinal point of view, at any rate, the most important of the lot. From a dramatic point of view also, William's spiritual conflict is the turning point of the action, and this has had to be worked out. Although his speech "We are the master-craftsmen" does in a sense express the theme of the Festival, it is, after all, rank blasphemy, and ends with an explosion of spiritual pride that is about as awkward a lurch in the direction of hell's gate as anything could very well be. You should have heard Charles Williams[2] reading this passage aloud in Simpsons,[3] bouncing a great deal upon his chair and saying: "Of course, you know, it is all quite true" – here the waiter brought us cold lobster – "Ah! now! it really is blasphemy!" – much to my embarrassment. I am sending you also a speech for Michael which, from my point of view, does sum up the theological side of the theme, and contains the plea for which you asked, that the people of Canterbury should look after their Cathedral. The proper place for this is at the opening of the pageant, but I shall not be at all surprised if we are obliged to leave it out for lack of time.[4] Having, as a dramatist, become enamoured of my own work, I am inclined to urge the cutting down of the pageant rather than of the four Acts of the play proper; but you will use your own judgement about this. The only bit of Act IV which could come out, lock, stock and barrel, is the little comedy interlude with Ernulphus and Paul, but this will only play about a minute, and I feel that it is helpful as lightening the rather sombre and supernatural atmosphere of this Act.[5]

I have had to be a little firm with Miss Babington, who wants the whole

1 She had written *The Zeal of Thy House* in 9 weeks.
2 For the influence of Charles Williams (1886–1945) on the life and writings of D. L. S., see Barbara Reynolds, *Dorothy L. Sayers: Her Life and Soul* and *The Passionate Intellect: Dorothy L. Sayers' Encounter with Dante.*
3 A prestigious restaurant in the Strand.
4 It was omitted.
5 This charming scene was retained.

play got into proof before it is even read to the actors; while I see that this solves for her the difficulty of providing copies, I have had to point out that the play is bound to be much altered in production, and that if I have to make many alterations on the proofs I shall be let in for an enormous printers' bill. Also the actors will need more detailed stage directions than I should be likely to put into the printed version. I have suggested that the whole thing might be roneo'd[6] for the cast at the expense of a few pounds.

I am sending a copy of everything to Mr Harcourt Williams, and will get into touch with him about a date for a reading.

I am so glad you like the play as far as you have seen it, and also that you enjoyed *Busman's Honeymoon* with whatever reservations about the acting and production.

It is so kind of you and your wife to ask me to stay with you when I come down; I shall be delighted to do so.

With best wishes,
Yours very sincerely,
[Dorothy L. Sayers]

6 A method of reproducing copies of text before the days of photocopying.

[24 Newland Street
Witham
Essex]

TO JOHN DICKSON CARR[1]

3 March 1937

Dear Mr Carr,
Many thanks for the photographs; I think they are really extraordinarily good, especially John Rhode's[2] which is superbly characteristic. I am sorry the groups did not come out well, but for some reason you cannot get people to stand still without giggling for six seconds.

I am astonished that you never came across any account of the Wallace murder; it certainly is a grand case and, like you, I find it very difficult to believe that he was guilty, though most people assume that he was, just, I suppose, because they cannot think of anybody else to fix the murder on. I am sending you the only full published account there is; don't trouble to

1 John Dickson Carr (1906–1977), detective novelist.
2 Pseudonym of Major C. J. C. Street, detective novelist (1884–1965). D. L. S. acknowledges his help "with all the hard bits" in *Have His Carcase*.

return this copy as I happen to have an extra one. I have had one or two interesting letters since the publication of *Anatomy of Murder*[3] from people who knew Wallace, all agreeing that he was probably innocent. One of them makes the interesting comment that, if Wallace had been the murderer, it would have been better for him to fix up a genuine appointment for the Tuesday night rather than trust to an imaginary one.

With all good wishes,

Yours very sincerely,

[Dorothy L. Sayers]

3 *The Anatomy of Murder, Famous Crimes Considered Critically by Members of the Detection Club*, first published by John Lane, Bodley Head, November 1936. D. L. S. contributed "The Murder of Julia Wallace", pp. 157–211.

> 24 Newland Street
> Witham
> Essex

TO MAURICE BROWNE[1]

12 March 1937

Dear Mr Browne,

Thank you so much for your letter. Pray assure everybody that there is not the slightest truth in the suggestion that I am leaving Mr Gollancz. In these cases the wish is always the father to the rumour. Console Mr Pinker by reminding him that his firm turned down my first book![2]

Yours very sincerely,

Dorothy L. Sayers

1 Maurice Browne (1881–1955), actor-manager and dramatist. See also letters to him, 4 May, 31 December 1936, *Letters of Dorothy L. Sayers: 1899–1936*, pp. 389–391, 414.
2 i.e. her first novel, *Whose Body?*. Her first book, *Op. I*, a volume of poetry, was published by Basil Blackwell.

> as from 24 Newland Street
> Witham
> Essex

TO HER SON

17 March 1937

Dear John,

I have been dreadfully neglectful all this term. But there has been nothing to tell you about, except that I have been having a terribly busy time, running about the place, coping with business connected with the play and one thing and another, and nearly dead with tiredness every night.

How have things been? Is the tiresome History getting any better? I hoped to be able to come down and see Mr Tendall this term, but I simply can't manage it – not even the party; I have to be at the other end of the country that day. I shall just have to write.[1]

I hope it hasn't been so bitterly cold with you as it has here. Nothing but rain, snow, sleet and frightful winds – and now the floods out all over the Fens where I used to live. I had to be at Cambridge[2] the other day – it was snowing heavily and melting off the roofs. Wherever one went, wet avalanches fell off the roofs onto one's only respectable hat! I think we had all better go to bed and hibernate for a twelvemonth.

I can't think of anything really amusing that has happened – except that on the 100th performance of the play,[3] the management invited a number of more or less safe and respectable "crooks" to see the show; and I am told that in the second interval, a couple of skilled pickpockets cleverly removed Mr Arundell's braces from his body without his knowledge, so that he had to play the last act in the horrid expectation of suddenly becoming undressed in public! Fortunately, nothing so alarming happened, but we all sat upon tenterhooks!

With love,
    Your affectionate Mother,
        D. L. Fleming

1 John Anthony was now 13 years old and at a preparatory school in Kent. Plans for his entry to a public school were in hand.
2 See letter to James Passant, 19 January 1937, note 1.
3 i.e. *Busman's Honeymoon*.

[24 Newland Street
Witham
Essex]

TO MARGARET BABINGTON

30 March 1937

Dear Miss Babington,

Many thanks for your letter and for the various proofs; the galleys of the play I have corrected and sent back to Mr Goulden. The corrections I have made are chiefly literals, together with one or two minor alterations and cuts. I have not tried to make any important modifications since I understand that Mr Goulden is only printing page galleys for use by the actors, and will wait to get the cuts decided upon in rehearsal before putting his galleys into forme. The preliminary announcement for the

Pickpocket and cast of *Busman's Honeymoon*

Chronicle seems to me excellent, although I should hesitate to lay claim to inspiration! The only point which does strike me is this: I wonder whether it is wise, from the point of view of dramatic effect, to let people know beforehand too much about the details of the last scene. When Mr Irving was discussing the play with me on my last visit, he was very anxious that no earlier scene should anticipate Michael's speech in scene 4 about the sin of pride. He felt, I think, that it would be more interesting for the audience to work out for themselves what sin it was for which William was punished amid the conflicting theories put forward by Theodatus and the other characters. I do not know how far this point of view is justified, but one or two theatrically minded people have said that they thought the play gained some advantage as a play from the fact that the majority of people would not know the whole ending beforehand as they did in the case of Becket[1] and Cranmer.[2] In fact, Mr Harcourt Williams went so far, at the reading, as to say he thought it a pity to remind people beforehand about William's accident – but this we can scarcely do anything about, since the account is printed and is known to all the Friends of Canterbury. However, since these suggestions have been made to me, I put them before you without prejudice. Perhaps it might be a good thing to ask Mr Irving whether he feels that the inclusion in the extracts of William's speech about pride is advisable or not.

I hope you have had a pleasant Easter in spite of the miscellaneous kind of weather we have had, and that you are beginning to see to the end of your casting difficulties. I am looking forward to seeing you all on the 12th; Mrs Irving has very kindly promised to give me hospitality at the Black Windmill.

Yours very sincerely,
[Dorothy L. Sayers]

P.S. I am looking forward to seeing the photograph of the Choir.

---

1 A reference to T. S. Eliot's *Murder in the Cathedral*.
2 A reference to Charles Williams' *Thomas Cranmer of Canterbury*.

24 Newland Street
Witham
Essex

TO SIR ĐONALD TOVEY[1]

3 April 1937

Dear Sir Donald,

I hope you will accept, as some small return for the many charming gifts you have made me, this copy of a little exercise in pastiche done by my friend Helen Simpson and myself.[2]

Peter and Harriet are still holding their honeymoon at the Comedy Theatre, and the book on the same theme will be out probably towards the end of next month.[3]

With best wishes,
    Yours sincerely,
        Dorothy L. Sayers

1 Professor Sir Donald Tovey (1875–1940), musicologist and composer. He much admired the Wimsey novels. (See *The Letters of Dorothy L. Sayers: 1899–1936*, pp. 317–318, 340–341, 361–362, 388–389.)
2 *Papers Relating to the Family of Wimsey*, privately printed December 1936.
3 See letter to Victor Gollancz, 17 January 1937, note 2.

24 Newland Street
Witham
Essex

TO B.S. STURGIS[1]

9 April 1937

Dear Miss Sturgis...

I do not think, in view of Harriet's financial position and Peter's, a gift of body linen would be altogether appropriate, at any rate before marriage. You cannot – or at least you do not – purchase ready-made shirts in the Burlington Arcade[2] unless it is from that rather peculiar shop at the upper end to which Peter's sort of person does not go. Peter would always have his shirts made for him, and one could not very well go to his shirt maker and offer to pay his bill. Harriet's shirt maker, on the other hand, would not be so startled by the paying of cash, since I imagine that she had only very recently taken to purchasing that kind of shirt. To buy them

1 A correspondent in Toronto, identity unknown.
2 A smart and expensive shopping area off Piccadilly.

and pay cash in these conditions would merely mean that one would solemnly inspect about five dozen patterns of material, tell them to make up the same as the last lot, and write a cheque. Even this would horrify them quite sufficiently, but I do not suppose that Harriet had ever ventured to order so large a quantity before, and the satisfaction of writing a cheque for about forty pounds would soothe Harriet's soul.... The shop is Lord's on the right hand side as you go up from Piccadilly, but Peter's shirts come, I fancy, from Drew's just opposite, where those two nice little old-fashioned men dodder respectfully about you and where you can also get remarkably good ties.

No; there is no connection between Mr. Tallboy[3] and Talboys. It was, as a matter of fact, Miss Byrne who christened the house Talboys,[4] and I had forgotten that there was a man of similar name in any of the books. Talboys is quite a common sort of name for an Elizabethan property.

In strict chronological fact the Wimsey second generation has already appeared. The marriage took place on October 8th, 1935, and Bredon Delagardie Peter was born on October 15th, 1936. As, however, his birth occurred[5] while we were all struggling with production difficulties and rehearsals, no announcement was made of this at the time, especially as the play might have confused people's minds by making it appear that the birth appeared before the honeymoon! By an entertaining coincidence we cast Dennis Arundell for Peter on the anniversary of the wedding, and finished casting on the anniversary of the birth.

I am so glad your colleague made acquaintance with the 5 Red Herring country,[6] it is a very pretty part of Scotland. Eighty miles an hour along the Kirkcudbright–Gatehouse road is quite correct; my husband has done it, but I can assure you that it is not comfortable to be the passenger on such an occasion.

You will have heard from Christine[7] that the *Busman* is still going strong and everybody seems very happy about it. Her performance has received so much praise from everybody; we were terribly lucky to get her to do that part, which very few people could pull off.

It is very kind of you to write, and I am so glad that Lord Peter and his Harriet have found so many friends in the University.

Yours sincerely,
  Dorothy L. Sayers

3 The murderer in *Murder Must Advertise*.
4 The house where Lord Peter and Harriet spend their honeymoon (in *Busman's Honeymoon*).
5 See "The Haunted Policeman", short story first published in *Harper's Bazaar* (New York), vol. 73, February 1938, pp. 62–63, 130–135; and in U.K. in *The Strand Magazine*, March 1938, pp. 483–494.
6 i.e. the setting of the novel, *The Five Red Herrings*.
7 Christine Silver (1883–1960), who played the part of Miss Twitterton in *Busman's Honeymoon*.

[24 Newland Street
Witham
Essex]

TO M. MOSLEY[1]

18 April 1937

Dear Miss Mosley,
    Nothing will induce me to pretend that there is anything unpleasant about making a success of one's books, or about making money from them. The writer's job is a soft one, and success in it entails no crucifixion of any kind. The only thing that is sometimes tiresome about it is, that people usually think you are a great deal richer than you are; I am not rich, I wish I were, but so long as my work provides me with a "genteel sufficiency", I have no quarrel with it.
        Yours faithfully,
            [Dorothy L. Sayers]

1 Identity unknown.

[24 Newland Street
Witham
Essex]

TO ÐOROTHY ROWE[1]

25 April 1937

Dear Dorothy,
    Thank you ever so much for your letter. I am frightfully glad you really think well of the Canterbury play, in spite or because of its "logic".[2] I do feel that if one has to write a play on a religious subject, the only way to do it is to avoid wistful emotionalism, and get as much drama as one can out of sheer hard dogma. After all, nothing can be more essentially dramatic than Catholic doctrine; but it is all lost if one surrounds it with

1 Dorothy Hanbury Rowe (1892–1988), a contemporary of D. L. S. at Somerville. She taught English at Bournemouth High School and directed an amateur theatre. See letter, 8 October 1915, *The Letters of Dorothy L. Sayers: 1899–1936*, pp. 113–115; also Index.
2 D. L. S. had sent her a copy of the typescript of *The Zeal of Thy House*, seeking her opinion as an expert on drama. Dorothy Rowe had replied: "Oh, how comely it is and how reviving to the spirits of just men long oppressed to find a plot based on inexorable logic...." She was one of the few who immediately perceived the connecting link between *Gaudy Night* and the play: integrity and selfless dedication to one's work. (See also Barbara Reynolds, *Dorothy L. Sayers: Her Life and Soul*, p. 286.)

a vague cloud of let-us-all-feel-good-and-loving-and-God-won't-mind-anything-much.

I hope the action will arrange itself effectively on the steps and stage as they stand, since the Chapter House was built in the 14th century. I suppose we can scarcely blame the architects for not having provided suitable back-stage accommodation, but I do think that when people come to build things like the Hall at Bedford College,[3] they might give one reasonable exits, a passage behind the back cloth and electrical equipment which does not have to be manipulated by a workman standing on his head beneath the stage, and unable to see or hear either the action on the stage or the frantic signals of the A.S.M.[4]

Poor Muriel[5] has wrestled with Bedford's frightful conditions for some years. In her production of *Tobias*,[6] a black-out could only be obtained by signalling from the back of the hall to a person down a passage, who then waved a handkerchief to a person standing by the switch at the end of another passage. On the occasion when I was there, it was not obtained.

Reassure yourself about the screens; they are permanent structures of wood and canvas designed and built in by Laurence Irving. On the left-hand side is a cramped space where half a dozen people can easily stand together if they are thin and hold their breaths; on the right-hand side, a narrow passage and awkward staircase lead to something which I have not yet dared to investigate, but where, I believe, performers can be got on and off in sufficient numbers, and from which they can, by running very hard, escape, to appear again at the bottom of the building, after traversing most of the Cathedral and Cloisters.

I got Theodatus's litany from a little book of Roman devotions; I agree that *Parce nos*[7] sounds all wrong, but it may be a mediaeval construction. I will have it looked up again.

We have started rehearsing, and performances begin on June 18th, extending over a week as you will see by the enclosed circular. I do hope you will be able to come and see the thing. I shall be attending the first performance on Saturday afternoon, together with a number of friends and sympathisers, so do join us if you possibly can.

---

3 One of the colleges of London University, then in Regent's Park and for women students only. Now merged with Royal Holloway College in Egham, Surrey, and co-educational.

4 Assistant Stage Manager.

5 Muriel St Clare Byrne, who was Lecturer in Drama at Bedford College.

6 *Tobias and the Angel*, a play by James Bridie (pseudonym of Osborne Henry Mavor, 1888–1951).

7 Latin: "Have mercy upon us", words which Theodatus recites while testing the rope. Dorothy Rowe had pointed out that it should be *Parce nobis*, since the verb *parcere* is followed by the dative. In the printed version of the play the words were altered to *parce nobis*.

Our Peter[8] is still bothered by ill health, but seems to be keeping his end up and giving very good performances. I will give your message to Mr. Arneil,[9] who will, I am sure, be most grateful for your kindness.

Wishing you all the best, and hoping to see you at Canterbury or elsewhere before long,

Yours ever, with love,

[J. G.][10]

8 i. e. Dennis Arundell. See letter to James Passant, 19 January 1937, note 3.
9 Theatre manager.
10 D. L. S. usually signed herself John Gaunt, or J. G., in her letters to Dorothy Rowe, in memory of the part she played at Somerville in *Admiral Guinea* by R. L. Stevenson and W. E. Henley.

[24 Newland Street
Witham
Essex]

TO MARGARET BABINGTON

18 May 1937

Dear Miss Babington,

Many thanks for your letter. Please do not bother about hospitality for me if it is difficult to fit it in; I can always quite easily go to an hotel, and so long as *Busman's Honeymoon* keeps running, can stand the financial strain! Then I shall feel free to run down whenever the producer wants me, and not make myself more of a burden than the author is bound to be in any case! As regards the Festival week, I do not know how many performances I shall be able to attend; I know that I am bound to be in Oxford for part of the time, in any case. I will let you know nearer the time, but please do not bother about me.

I am writing to the Railway Company to book seats for all my guests on the special train, and they and I should be grateful indeed if you could possibly manage to give them and me seats together for the performance, and in the Cathedral. I ought, perhaps, to have told you that nearly all of them are eligible for the Arts and Crafts Service on their own merits, quite apart from being friends of mine. Miss Byrne, in addition to being my collaborator in *Busman's Honeymoon* and the author of various books and plays of her own, is an amateur theatrical producer of considerable experience. Mr. Michael Mac Owan[1] is producer at the Westminster Theatre, and his

1 Michael Macowan (b. 1906) was to produce Christopher Hassall's *Christ's Comet* at Canterbury Cathedral in 1938.

wife, Alexis France, is an actress. Mr. Scott-Giles[2] is at the Institution of Municipal and County Engineers, of which he is the Secretary, and is a very fine heraldic draftsman and authority on heraldic art; and his wife is an artist. Mr. Denis Browne the surgeon does not, perhaps, quite fall into the category, but his wife is Helen Simpson the novelist, and certainly fits the bill. Miss Lake is my secretary, and certainly needs a certain amount of art and craft in dealing with me. Miss Dorothy Rowe, who wrote to you separately from Bournemouth has, I think, already explained that she is producer there at one of the most important amateur theatres in the kingdom. If it is possible for her also to be seated with us, I should be exceedingly glad. I am waiting to hear from another friend of mine, Miss Barber,[3] whether she can join us, but she will not know her arrangements for certain until Thursday. Would it be possible to squeeze her in if she can come?

With many thanks for all the trouble you are taking,

Yours very sincerely,

[Dorothy L. Sayers]

2 Wilfrid Scott-Giles (1893–1982), Fitzalan Pursuivant of Arms Extraordinary. See *The Letters of Dorothy L. Sayers: 1899–1936*, p. 368 and letters to him.

3 Marjorie Maud Barber (1894–1976) was at Somerville College from 1914 to 1917. She taught English at South Hampstead High School for Girls and shared a home with Muriel St Clare Byrne.

[24 Newland Street
Witham
Essex]

TO THE HON. JOHN F. A. BROWNE[1]

19 May 1937

Dear Mr. Browne,

Many thanks for your letter. Being distracted at the moment with theatrical business, I have not fully planned out what I mean to say to the women students on the 25th; but roughly speaking, I intend to follow the lines you suggest, saying really much the same things that I have said previously about the value of a University education. Roughly, I imagine it will work out as follows:

(1) For the pure scholar, the value of knowledge for its own sake and its increasing value as life goes on. (2) For those who are bound to think of

1 An undergraduate at Oxford, Secretary of the Oxford Society.

practical affairs, the actual advantage one finds, even in ordinary business, of having the right attitude to the tools of one's trade, i.e. willingness to learn, generosity of mind, and so forth. (3) The importance of a single-minded attitude to one's job, whatever the job is; with special application to the common charge against women, that they put personal feelings before the job. A charge which is not true of those who carry the University attitude of mind into their work. (4) In public affairs especially, the advantage of having been trained to think accurately and not be at the mercy of words and slogans. After this, I propose to pass on to the two-fold duty of the University graduate: (a) to apply to life in general the trained habits of thought which she has learnt to apply to scholarship, and (b) the duty of not only keeping the world in touch with Oxford, but of keeping Oxford in touch with the world. If the Universities are not to become desiccated and insular, then her old members must be perpetually revivifying her by contacts with the outside world. I shall then add those practical details about membership with which you have been kind enough to furnish me.

It is quite possible that I may give some offence at Oxford by what I may have to say about this subject of insularity; but it is my experience, and I believe that of many other University people, that this kind of insularity does exist, and forms a sort of barrier against those who return to their Universities from the outside world. The academic mind seems to find a good deal of difficulty in facing material facts with the same honesty with which it would face a fact of scholarship. There is a tendency to regard Oxford as a closed system into which ordinary considerations of public policy – and I will say frankly, even of business honesty – do not penetrate. People who come back from other jobs are disheartened by finding in Oxford a curious lack of sympathy for interests and problems in a community where so much is regulated by tradition and by personal influence; but the barrier certainly does exist and can, I think, be got over only if those who have gone down will exert themselves to keep in touch with the Universities. I do not mean, of course, that I want Oxford to be modernised into a school of commerce, God forbid! but only that she should be able to receive as well as give, and that the students' concern with the University should not end with the taking of the M.A. degree.

I have expressed all this very badly; I will try to do it better on the 25th.

Will you be good enough to let me know for what length of time you would like me to speak?[2]

    Yours sincerely,

       [Dorothy L. Sayers]

---

2 Cf. her article "What is Right with Oxford?", *Oxford*, No.1 Summer 1935, vol. 2.

24 Newland Street
Witham
Essex

TO HER SON

23 May 1937

Dear John,

Oh, yes! – I think the exchequer will run to riding-lessons, if you would like them;[1] please ask Mr Tendall (or whoever is the appropriate authority) to get you your kit and say that I hope to run down and see him one day before long – not this week, when I am engaged every day, but possibly next week or the week after.

I saw the Coronation procession,[2] which was a magnificent show. I tried to take some coloured photographs of it, but unhappily the rain came down just as it started, and by the time the King and Queen came by, the light was about 1 candle-power! By the way, the stamps on this letter are, as you will notice, King George V and his two sons[3] – a thing which apparently is the proper thing to have on one's letters nowadays. Or so your Father[4] says, who put these on for me, extravagantly busting one extra halfpenny in the process, as his supply of Edward VIII halfpennies had run out!

Hope you will have a good term.
    With best love,
        Mother

1 A moment of gratification for D. L. S. in being able to afford riding lessons for John Anthony.
2 Of George VI.
3 Edward VIII and George VI.
4 Atherton Fleming, his father by adoption.

[24 Newland Street
Witham
Essex]

TO MRS WILFRID SCOTT-GILES

7 June 1937

Dear Mrs. Scott-Giles,

This is just to remind you of the Canterbury play on Saturday, and to tell you about the arrangements. I shall not be going down myself that day since I shall have to be in Canterbury for the dress rehearsal, but my secretary, Miss Lake, will be at Victoria at ten minutes to twelve standing by the barrier from which the Canterbury train departs. She will carry and display conspicuously the novel of *Busman's Honeymoon*;[1] she will have got all the tickets with her including those for the train. I expect, perhaps, there will be rather a crowd at the barrier, but with this indication I do not think you can miss her even if you do not immediately recognise her. I do not know what arrangements are made at the other end for transporting pilgrims to the Cathedral; but no doubt plenty of conveyance will be provided for pilgrims, since Canterbury is organised to that end during the Festival week. Lunch is provided on the train and included in the price of the tickets, and I imagine from the station you will go direct to the Cathedral.

I hope we shall have a good performance; everything seemed to be going pretty well last time I was there.

Yours very sincerely,

[Dorothy L. Sayers]

1 The Gollancz edition had a bright yellow dust-jacket.

24 Newland Street
Witham
Essex

TO DENNIS ARUNDELL

7 June 1937

Dear Dennis,

Isn't it scandalous? Your 200th performance tomorrow, and I shan't be there to congratulate you, having basely deserted to Canterbury, to follow the fortunes of your Uncle Bill! (He is doing us proud – how I should get along without your family I can't think!) I'm sorry you can't get down and be photographed too, but Tuesday was the only possible afternoon, and we didn't think we should be able to manage that, since a number of the costumes seemed to have vanished into Limbo. However, they turned up on Friday night, per Carter Paterson[1], after a dawdling progress through the Garden of England.

How are you bearing up? I saw in the cards the other day that you didn't seem to be feeling too good – but the trouble looked like a passing one, and the future was full of good trumps, so I put it down to the heat. I wish you could get down to see one of the performances, but it would be frightfully exhausting, rushing down and back again. Anyhow, wish us

1 A firm of furniture removers.

luck for Saturday, and in the meantime all the best to you all and to your lordship in particular.

Yours ever,
Dorothy L. Sayers

London

TO DENNIS ARUNDELL

23 June 1937

Dear Dennis,

I was so sorry I couldn't stop to see you and Veronica[1] yesterday. I had to gallop round to my agent and then rush home to succour Frank Napier,[2] who was shut up in my flat with nothing to eat but a telephone, and unable to move till I got back, because I had given him my keys! *The Zeal of Thy House* is (touch wood!) coming to London at the end of July, and we are all in a grand kerfluffle[3] of casting and costings – "back to the old grind"[4] – but all great fun.

I've got to go back to Witham today and to Oxford on Friday for a Gaudy (save the mark!), but next week I shall be up and will bring you your signed copy of the *Busman* novel, which is waiting down in Essex.

How are you getting on? And how is the inside? I'm glad business is picking up – that's a comfort – I thought it would about now. I gather that the balance of "straight" and "low-comedy" is getting a little disturbed, so I am suggesting that Beatrice[5] and Harold Arneil should get together and do a spot of re-polishing, with your co-operation, and see if we can't get back to the standard of our earlier performances; things are apt to come a bit unstuck after a long run, aren't they?

With all good wishes,
yours ever,
Dorothy L. Sayers

1 Veronica Turleigh. See p. 8. note 2.
2 Producer, with Harcourt Williams, of *The Zeal of Thy House*.
3 Slang for confusion.
4 Words spoken by Lord Peter in *Busman's Honeymoon*.
5 Beatrice Wilson, the producer.

[24 Newland Street
Witham
Essex]

24 June 1937

Dear Dorothy,

I was terribly sorry not to see you at Canterbury, we had a most lovely production and a very fine reception. We are now all thrilled by the hope that the play will be produced in London at the Duchess within the next few weeks; if so, I hope you will be able to come and see it there.

Forgive a short letter; as you can understand, I am all in a kerfluffle with this tremendous excitement.

With love,
Yours affectionately,
[J. G.]

24 Newland Street
Witham
Essex

6 July 1937

Dear Sir Donald,

Thank you so much for your letter; I am delighted to know that you thought so well of *The Zeal of Thy House*. It really was a most beautiful production at Canterbury, and I am very much hoping that the play will come to Town some day or other. The musical interludes had to be a good deal cut in the acting version, because the whole thing had to be got into an hour and forty minutes, and Mr. Knight, the Cathedral organist, set everything very simply but, I think, very effectively. I expect if you had done the music, which would have been delightful, you would have wanted to let yourself go, especially on the John Donne choruses! We only had a small and rather inexperienced unaccompanied choir, among whom I caused consternation at rehearsal by exhorting them to cut out their "faint ecclesiastical rejoicing" and try and feel like the morning stars singing together and all the sons of God shouting for joy! Poor dears!

I will think over what you say about a volume of memoirs for the

Dowager Duchess;[1] in view of the lady's loquacity it would probably be a work in several volumes!

Wishing you a good stay at Aix-Les-Bains and a "good deliverance"[2] from the clutches of gout.

Yours very sincerely,
　　Dorothy L. Sayers

1　i.e. Lord Peter Wimsey's mother.
2　An echo of the Book of Common Prayer.

　　　　　　　　　　　　　　　　　　[24 Newland Street
　　　　　　　　　　　　　　　　　　Witham
　　　　　　　　　　　　　　　　　　Essex]

TO CANON F. J. SHIRLEY[1]

6 July 1937

Dear Dr. Shirley,

Thank you very much indeed for your kind letter. It was good of you to let me know Canon Lanchester's opinion[2] of the play; I feel it would be a great help to us if he would either write something about it for a Church paper, or let us have something that we can quote when sending out publicity for a London production. Just at the moment we have been disappointed in our hopes since the managements who were interested in the play have wanted either to put it on straight away in the slack season for a few weeks to fill up time, or to postpone production until Christmas. The first plan was impossible, since some of our actors have other engagements, and it also seemed unadvisable to start at such a bad time of the year with no prospects of an assured run. The second plan creates again enormous difficulties with the actors, who naturally have to live in the interval, and as I am determined not to put the play on without Harcourt Williams at any rate, we are faced with a good many difficulties. Both I and my agents feel, however, that the play ought to be seen in London, and that it has a very good chance of success, so the only thing to do is to hope for the best, and in the meantime to get together as much advance interest as possible. Whatever happens, we can never hope for anything like the same atmosphere which we had at Canterbury; but Canterbury

1　The Rev. Canon F. J. J. Shirley, Ph.D. (1890–1967), Headmaster of King's School, Canterbury.
2　Canon Shirley had written: "Canon Lanchester – who dined on the 'last night' with us, and who is really one of the most learned men in our Church – was much moved by your play, and said it was the work of a genius. If ever you want the critique of a cleric, let him do it." The Rev. Canon Henry Craven Lanchester was a scholar in Old Testament studies.

is, of course, a unique experience quite outside the range of the commercial theatre. I feel sure that we can count on the help of our Canterbury friends to interest people in the play both before and after production....

> [24 Newland Street
> Witham
> Essex]

TO MARJORIE BARBER

17 July 1937

Dear Bar,

I have found the top copy of the article[1] on *Gaudy Night*, so there is no hurry about sending back the carbon. I should be glad though, to know if Muriel or you have any comment to make about it. I am not sure that any of these revelations are really wise, but I undertook to do it, and there you are!

Could you let me have Muriel's address in case anything turns up? I hear from Mrs. Allen[2] that *Busman's Honeymoon* had a good try-out in some place near New York with the incredible name of 'Kisco',[3] which sounds like an advertisement for lipstick! According to the cable, it had a very good reception; we may get a New York production after all.

Yesterday I went and bought two cotton frocks and ordered two cotton coats and skirts; I also bought a hat box, got a passport application form from the bank and had my photograph taken. As you see I am trying to leave no room for repentance.[4]

Yours ever,
[Dorothy]

---

1 "Gaudy Night", article published in *Titles to Fame*, edited by Denys Kilham Roberts, Nelson, 8 November 1937, pp. 73–95.
2 Dorothy Allen, her dramatic agent.
3 Mount Kisco, Westchester, New York.
4 Marjorie Barber had persuaded D. L. S. to go on holiday with her to Venice and the Adriatic.

[24 Newland Street
Witham
Essex]

TO E. C. BENTLEY[1]

20 July 1937

Dear Jack,

Ever so many thanks for the book;[2] I am sure I shall enjoy it enormously. I am glad you liked *Zeal* ; it has greatly disconcerted the critics who seem to think it quite indecent that a detective story writer would deal in religion! I am reminded of your clerihew about Belloc:[3]

> He seems to think that nobody minds
> His books being all of different kinds.

By the way, I hope you spotted the influence of G. K. C. in the passage about Peter and John.[4]

With love,
   Yours ever,
      [D. L. S.]

---

1 Edmund Clerihew Bentley (1875–1956), detective novelist, author of *Trent's Last Case* and inventor of the "clerihew".

2 This may have been an advance copy of *Trent Intervenes*, a collection of short stories, published in 1938. See her letter to him dated 17 April 1936, expressing admiration for *Trent's Own Case* (*The Letters of Dorothy L. Sayers: 1899–1936*, pp. 387–388).

3 Hilaire Belloc (1870–1953), poet, novelist, biographer, historian, travel-writer.

4 *The Zeal of Thy House*, scene 3, the words of the Prior: "...God founded His Church, not upon John,\The loved disciple, that lay so close to His heart\ And knew His mind – not upon John, but Peter;\ Peter the liar, Peter the coward, Peter\ The rock, the common man. John was all gold,\ And gold is rare; the work might wait while God\ Ransacked the corners of the earth to find\ Another John; but Peter is the stone\ Whereof the earth is made." G. K. Chesterton said: "When Christ at a symbolic moment was establishing His great society, He chose for its corner-stone neither the brilliant Paul nor the mystic John, but a shuffler, a snob, a coward – in a word, a man. And upon this rock He has built His Church." (*Heretics*)

Miss Dorothy Sayers
Never cared about the Himalayas.
The height that gave her a thrill
Was Primrose Hill.

Clerihew and Caricature of Dorothy L. Sayers by E. C. and Nicolas Bentley

[24 Newland Street
Witham
Essex]

TO MARGARET BABINGTON

30 July 1937

Dear Miss Babington,

Thank you so much for the *Chronicle*; I think it was a very good idea to reprint the T.L.S.[1] review. If I should need any more copies I will certainly ask you; just at the present, however, I am packing up for a holiday in the Adriatic, and mean to abandon all thoughts of work, even of *The Zeal of Thy House*, for a month! I was talking to Mr. Harcourt Williams the other day, who had been spending a happy half hour over the financial statement of the Festival; all the cast are rejoiced to see that *Zeal* was responsible for so large a share in the profits. It seems to me, that taking everything all round, you did extraordinarily well, seeing what heavy expenses you had to face over the London Symphony Orchestra.

With kindest and best wishes for all my friends in Canterbury,

   Yours very sincerely,
      [Dorothy L. Sayers]

---

1 *The Times Literary Supplement*, 3 July 1937, p. 493; a very favourable review, praising the "flexible and natural" blank verse and the "rhythmical and alive" prose parts of the dialogue and calling the play "her finest perception" and "her finest art". The review was quoted in the *Canterbury Cathedral Chronicle*, No. 27, 1937, p. 22.

[24 Newland Street
Witham
Essex]

TO J. ROWDON[1]

4 August 1937

Dear Mr Rowdon,

For your information, as also for that of the Great British Public if it is interested, I propose to start my summer holiday on August 9th, going first to Venice, and after that for a short trip down the Dalmatian coast, returning at the end of the month to spend a few days in Paris and see any theatrical shows that may be going. My idea is to take a complete rest after a fairly strenuous year, though of course, if you like to suggest that I

---

1 Publicity agent.

am going to come back with two or three new plays and a novel I shall probably not trouble to contradict you! If anything agitating should happen at the Comedy during my absence, no doubt Dorothy Allen's office will let you know; Mrs. Allen herself will be in America, where *Busman* has just had a very successful try-out at Mount Kisco and West Point, and is hoping to place the film contract[2] for it; also to interest managers in *The Zeal of Thy House*, Miss Vosper,[3] however, will still be in London.

HOW ABOUT THE PHOTOGRAPHS YOU PROMISED ME????

Yours sincerely,

[Dorothy L. Sayers]

2 The film of *Busman's Honeymoon* (screen play by Moncton Hoffe, Angus MacPhail and Harold Goldman, American title "Haunted Honeymoon") was released in August 1940. (Robert Montgomery played Lord Peter, Constance Cummings played Harriet and Sir Seymour Hicks played Bunter)

3 Marjorie Vosper, a theatrical agent.

[24 Newland Street
Witham
Essex]

TO NANCY PEARN[1]

4 August 1937

Dear Bun,

Here is the other copy of "The Haunted Policeman";[2] I am not fearfully thrilled about getting this story published because it all happens after the action of my next novel which I have not written yet,[3] but I don't suppose this matters frightfully as it is only a short story and very few people read short stories, and the people who do are not the same people who read novels. I shall only be in Town next Monday and Tuesday morning, but I will try to give you a ring some time or other; I cannot promise to get round as I shall be full of last minute packing etc.

Yours ever,

[D.L.S.]

1 See letter to Victor Gollancz, 17 January 1937, note 5.

2 See letter to Miss Sturgis, 9 April 1937, note 4.

3 *Thrones, Dominations*, left unfinished by D. L. S., completed by Jill Paton Walsh, C.B.E. (London, Hodder and Stoughton, 1998).

24 Newland Street
Witham
Essex

TO IVY SHRIMPTON[1]

8 August 1937

Dearest Ivy,

Here is John's report – very good all round, don't you think? He is disappointed a little at not being first again in maths, but this is nothing to
worry about, as his average place in form is so high. We had a very pleasant, though rather hither and thither day in Town – I hope you got him
off to camp without too much trouble, and that his bedding reached him
safely.

Just off to Venice. Address, till August 24th – (36 hour post) – Hotel
Bauer-Grünwald, Venice, Italy –

Love,
D. L. S.

1 D. L. S.' cousin, who brought up her son John Anthony Fleming. See Barbara Reynolds,
Dorothy L. Sayers: Her Life and Soul and *The Letters of Dorothy L. Sayers: 1899–1936.*

Venezia

POSTCARD[1]

TO DENNIS ARUNDELL

Comedy Theatre
Panton Street
London S.W. 1
Inghilterra

26 August 1937

How are you getting along? We thought of you with deep sympathy
during all that frightful heat-wave and hoped you were bearing up pretty
well. We had a lovely trip down the Dalmatian coast in a tiny coasting

1 On the reverse, a view of Korkula, Dalmatia.

steamer – no other English-speaking people aboard; I had to try and speak German, which I hadn't done for 20 years! Back to Paris tomorrow, and then, after about a week, back to England, home and the Comedy. Glad to learn business picked up last week *"in* the cooler weather".[2] Love to you all –

Dorothy L. Sayers

2 A quotation from *Busman's Honeymoon.*

24 Newland Street
Witham

TO MURIEL ST CLARE BYRNE

13 September 1937

Dearest Muriel,

I got your letter this morning, and it made me laugh like hell to reflect that just about the very time you were writing to me to say you were glad everything was so nicely settled, Harold[1] and Roger[2] were frantically telephoning me to say it had all come unstuck; and that while I was reading your comforting approval of one leading lady, you were reading my hopeful apologia for a totally different leading lady! There is a magnificent lack of hidebound monotony about the stage which makes it a most invigorating atmosphere to plunge into on returning from holiday; though to be sure one might appreciate it less if one hadn't had the holiday first.

Well (as Kirk[3] says) to resume: your conscientious collaborator duly turned up on Saturday morning shortly after 10.30, to find a rehearsal in full blast in the Comedy bar; and was again roped in to read the odd parts. In this way we did the first two acts in the morning and Act 3 in the afternoon; so that before staggering home to my deserted family I had been through the whole thing with them. We all think (I mean, Harold and Roger and I) that Glendinning[4] is going to be much better than Branch.[5] It is true that her ankles are more meaty, but so is her personality. (I have not so far had any further message from Rog. or Harold, so I suppose she is still in the cast, but as you know, I never believe anything till the curtain goes up.)

They worked extremely hard – indeed, I have never seen people toil so energetically as they did over the Quarrel Scene, and I believe it is going to be really good. Harold said it was quite a revelation to him, how much

1 Harold Arneil.
2 Roger Maxwell, who played the part of Mr Puffett in *Busman's Honeymoon.*
3 Superintendent Kirk, a character in *Busman's Honeymoon.*
4 Ethel Glendinning (1910–1996), who played the part of Harriet Vane.
5 Eileen Branch (b. 1911).

they were contriving to get into it, it all seemed to take [on] a new life. The
fact is, darling, that we are at least going to get some HAM in the leading
parts, and while I admit Basil Foster[6] hasn't got Dennis's delicate and
melancholy distinction, he has got a proper leading man's temperament,
which is rather a good thing, if you ask me, especially at the Vic-Palace.[7]
It was interesting to see him take firm hold and tell the girl how to give
him what he wanted; and she seems quite able and very intelligent. It was
a joy watching them really tackle the TIMING of the poker-scene,
which has never yet been right, but possibly may be before next week!
Also he will undoubtedly get far more zip and honeymoon pep into the
opening of Act 1. Of course, he has got a bit of the musical-comedy touch
about him, but I hope it won't give you too much pain – what we lose on
the swings of distinction we make up (I hope and trust) on the round-
abouts of vigour – and people may say what they like, but I can't help feeling it's an advantage to an actor to have his glands in the right place for a
change!

Foster definitely wants to put in the "Hamlet" quotation[8] – and if Kirk
goes and gets a laugh there, there'll probably be a spot of trouble for Kirk!
In some places (opening of Act 1, parts of Act 2 and the love-scene opening) Basil Foster wants to alter the positions a bit. Harold and I are being
as tactful as possible, most of our reactions falling under one or other of
three heads:

(1) (*When it really doesn't matter a darn*): But of course, it's your own reading
we want – do just as you like.
(2) (*When we can find a good excuse for firmness*): I quite see your point, but I'm
afraid it's got to be done the old way, because of (the exigencies of the
plot, Goodacre's entrance, there being so little room behind the settle,
Bunter's being so slow on the ladder, what is coming later – or what
not).
(3) (*When we are sure it is ill-advised but can't think of any objection quickly enough*):
Well, let's try it your way, and when Miss Byrne and/or the producer
are here, we'll ask them.

One or two trifling alterations I have already allowed – e.g. Basil Foster
doesn't like the reference to "the management" in the "fruit-trees" passage. On the other hand, when there is something you and I want done
which has never been done before, I have an infallible recipe which always

6 Basil S. Foster (1882–1959), actor and singer, known in the role of Prince Danilo in *The Merry
Widow*.
7 *Busman's Honeymoon* was about to be transferred from the Comedy Theatre to the Victoria
Palace.
8 In Act 2 of *Busman's Honeymoon* Lord Peter quotes, "There are more things in heaven and
earth, Horatio…"

produces the goods, and that is: "Oh, Mr Foster, just one moment – forgive me! I wonder, while we are about it, if we could get that bit done the way we always wanted – you know, Harold! Darling Dennis took a dislike to it for some reason, we never knew quite why – but perhaps we might just try it that way – what do you think, Roger? – Yes, I know you agreed at the time, but Dennis never quite got the hang of it, did he? – Yes, that's it, Mr Foster - of course it went quite well the other way, but – you prefer it this way? Well, that is what Miss Byrne and I meant when we wrote it – Right! then we'll try it our way." And our way it is.

I have got back the *pas de deux* round the Prickly Pear, and am hoping for a more convincing duet in "She sings of luckless ladies"[9] – Glendinning has quite a strong voice and picked up the line instantly – Foster, needless to say, being a singer, couldn't pick it up by ear at all – they never can – but I wrote it down on paper for him and shall hope for the best.

I trust the new people will get on well with the rest of the cast. Foster is said to be unpopular in the theatre – I don't know why. He is vain and opinionated, of course, but they are all of them that; possibly he insists too much on taking centre stage, but from our point of view that will be a welcome change. Anyhow, he has had a long experience and knows all the stage tricks inside-out. Like Dennis and every one else, he is incapable of recognising a line of Shakespeare when he sees it or getting it correct – he will say "Take these bodies away" for "Take up the bodies!"[10] All actors should do their 9 months at the Old Vic., to save other people trouble.

In all this turmoil, I haven't had time to write Bar[11] a proper letter about Paris or anything. I expect now I'd better leave all casual chat till we meet. I am sending this to London, since I don't know whether you are starting off tomorrow or Wednesday. Give me a ring when you arrive and let me know how you find things. They are rehearsing at the Theatre – on the stage, I mean, – Monday, Friday, and Saturday this week and next, and the other days in the bar. I think Harold will be deeply thankful to see you turn up there, as in my absence he may find Basil Foster apt to get out of hand. He can't shove everything off on the absent authors, especially as time is short and decisions have to be made.

I hope you'll be more or less satisfied with the way things are turning out. I am sorry to say we are losing Macintyre,[12] who has been offered a

---

9 A line from D. L. S.' translation of "Auprès de ma blonde". See *Poetry of Dorothy L. Sayers*, ed. Ralph E. Hone (The Dorothy L. Sayers Society in association with the Marion E. Wade Center, 1996).

10 *Hamlet*, Act V, scene ii.

11 Marjorie Barber.

12 Alastair Macintyre, who played the part of Constable Sellon.

job at a higher salary by Limpus[13] in the Lucie Mannheim[14] show – but Denham[15] is pretty good, and playing Sellon will console him for not stepping into the lead.

Basil Foster thinks Peter a perfectly *wonderful* part – or so he says, anyhow, so snooks to those who said it wasn't a proper leading part!!...

Looking forward to our next (probably highly humorous) meeting,
    With best love,
       Dorothy

Mac[16] most amiable and sympathetic about all this - he is now convinced that *Busman* is (for some reason or other) the goods! I have had a kindly review[17] of *Zeal* in the *New Statesman*!!!!!

13 Alban Brownlow Limpus (1878–1941), producing manager.

14 Lucie Mannheim (1905–1976), German actress. She played as Sonia Duveen in *The Last Straw* at the Comedy Theatre in September 1937.

15 Maurice Denham (b.1909), who played the minor part of George at the Comedy Theatre and was promoted to play Sellon at the Victoria Palace.

16 D. L. S.' husband, Atherton Fleming, known as "Mac". See Barbara Reynolds, *Dorothy L. Sayers: Her Life and Soul*, chapter 11.

17 *The New Statesman and Nation*, 11 September 1937, pp. 384, column 1 and 386, column 2. The reviewer, William Buchan, described the play as "interesting and exciting"..."a straightforward, balanced, and tidy piece of work, with no loose ends about it. The good sense and astringent humour which makes Miss Sayers' novels so engaging are here to advantage."

                          [24 Newland Street
                          Witham
                          Essex]

TO JOHN DICKSON CARR
17 September 1937

Dear Mr. Carr,

Of course, do please make any reference you like to *Gaudy Night;* I shall be honoured by the interest and approbation of Dr. Fell.[1]

1 John Dickson Carr's detective. No novel by John Dickson Carr is found to contain a reference to *Gaudy Night*, but there is a reference to *The Nine Tailors* in *The Hollow Man* (Hamish Hamilton, 1935, chapter 17), where Gideon Fell says in the course of a lecture on locked room mysteries: "I do not care to hear the hum of everyday life, I much prefer to listen to...the deadly bells of Fenchurch St Paul."

I, too, should have enjoyed a more prolonged discussion at the last meeting;[2] as you know, I am a confirmed sitter-up, but one cannot expect everybody to share these morbid tastes.

Life is full of activity at the moment, since as you may have seen in the *Daily Mail*, *Busman's Honeymoon* is transferring to the Victoria Palace on Monday week with two new leads, Basil Foster as Peter; I think he is going to be very good, and so is the new girl, but all this means extra agitation and rehearsals.

With best wishes for the new book (mine[3] is suffering sadly from theatrical competition!)

Very sincerely yours,

[Dorothy L. Sayers]

2 Of the Detection Club.
3 i.e. "*Thrones, Dominations*".

Herbert Hamilton Kelly (1860–1950), founder of the Society of the Sacred Mission at Kelham Hall, Nottinghamshire had considerable influence on the Church of England, partly through his own writing, partly through the community's missionary work and the training of ordinands. The Zeal of Thy House *was first published by Gollancz in June 1937. The final speech of the archangel Michael, which had been omitted from the performance, was there included.[1] It caught the eye of Father Kelly who was moved to write D. L. S. a letter destined to have important consequences. He began by saying how wonderful and delightful it was to find a writer "of your influence who actually realizes and can state the vital force of a Christian faith in God and His Christ, not in the abstract fashion which is all we theologians can teach, but in a living, pictorial fashion which common people can follow". He then asked: "I wonder if you recognize, or are interested in recognizing, how closely your book images the principles of the Athanasian Creed – the two-fold necessity of faith in the Trinity of God, and the Incarnation". Thus Father Kelly was the first theologian to recognize the relevance of the play and in particular of the archangel's speech to Trinitarian theology. The correspondence which developed between them constitutes much of the substance of articles which D. L. S. was soon to write, and especially of her book* The Mind of the Maker.

1 It was restored by Christopher Hassall in his production of the play in 1949.

[24 Newland Street
Witham
Essex]

TO FATHER HERBERT KELLY

4 October 1937

Dear Father Kelly,

Before I attempt, in the mediaeval manner, to "defend my thesis", let me thank you most sincerely for your kind and sympathetic understanding of what I was trying to do in *The Zeal of Thy House*. I have been pleased, touched, and also amused by many friendly reviews, announcing that the play was "about" this, that, or the other; but it is with a deep chuckle of delight that I greet the discovery, by an isolated person here and there, that this is actually a play "about" that dusty and disagreeable thing, Christian Dogma. The neglect of dogma is the curse of nearly all religious plays, from the playwright's point of view. The dogma of the Incarnation is the most dramatic thing about Christianity, and indeed, the most dramatic thing that ever entered into the mind of man; but if you tell people so, they stare at you in bewilderment. Yet one would think (to adapt Voltaire) that if the Incarnation had never happened, it would have been necessary for some dramatist to invent it.[2] However, since it is not the playwright's business to argue but to present, the only thing one can do is to put it on the stage (in any form the Censor of Plays will permit) and let it speak for itself.

In this case, there was no doubt at all about the dramatic effect of the final scene in which Michael argues the matter out with William. It held the house attentive and excited, though there is absolutely no movement on the stage and the whole drama is contained in the dogmatic argument. But it was interesting to discover, as I did, how many people (whether nominal Christians or not) either were Arians,[3] or believed that the Church taught a purely Arian doctrine. However often they had heard or recited the Creeds, it had obviously never sunk into their minds that Christ was supposed to be God in any real sense of the word. The Good and Suffering Man was a familiar idea to them; but the idea of a Suffering God was a staggering novelty. This isn't exaggeration – some of them quite simply and innocently told me so – especially some of my own actors, who, having seen the play through two months of rehearsal and

2 Voltaire said: "Si Dieu n'existait pas, il faudrait l'inventer." (If God did not exist it would be necessary to invent Him.) (*Epîtres*, 96)

3 Referring to the Arian heresy, preached by Arius in the 4th century, who denied that Christ was consubstantial with God. (See D. L. S.' play *The Emperor Constantine*.)

ten performances, had had plenty of time in which to chew it over. I explained as much as I could (doing my best to steer clear of Sabellianism,[4] Patripassianism[5] and all the other terrifying heresies which lie in wait for amateurs who try to explain things over the lunch-table), assuring them that the doctrine really was that Christ was always and equally God and Man. But I had to remind them that I was a playwright and not a theological expert and should certainly go wrong if I tried to express the matter otherwise than in terms of my own craft, and beg them, if they really wanted to know, to go to somebody better qualified. I took the line that I wasn't asking them to believe anything (because earnest middle-aged females imploring young men to believe things do more harm than good) but that the play was meant to be a statement of what the doctrine really was, after which they could take it or leave it. It does seem just as well, if you're going to disbelieve a thing, to find out exactly what you are disbelieving. And I do honestly think we have heard a great deal too much lately about the "Human Jesus". That attractive and picturesque figure has almost succeeded in pushing the Divine Logos off the stage altogether, with the result that God the Father appears as the villain of the piece, which isn't orthodox. For my Angel Cassiel – a young professional actor, who had been brought up a Unitarian – the play was a most peculiar experience! Being condemned, poor dear, to stand and listen for an hour-and-three-quarters, immovably trussed up in a pair of wings, while the characters argued about the nature of Christ, he could at first make neither head nor tail of what was going on. But, having a very sensitive and intelligent mind, he applied himself to working the thing out, and found it most surprising and interesting.

One thing that interested me was to discover a new application of that much-disputed Athanasian statement that "this is the Catholic faith, which except a man believe faithfully, he cannot be saved". Artistically speaking, it turns out to be a plain statement of fact. I mean that, unless you keep the God-Man idea properly balanced, your play, as a mere piece of dramatic structure, falls to pieces and makes no artistic sense:[6] which brings me to the defence of my thesis; because the play is really chiefly "about" the Christian dogma as it presents itself to the creative artist.

And therefore 1. The speech about the Trinity. This isn't meant to be a re-statement of St. Augustine (whose illustration, if I ever knew it, I had

---

4 Referring to the heresy of Sabellius of the 3rd century, who preached that Father, Son and Holy Ghost were merely aspects of one Divine Person.
5 The heresy according to which God the Father suffered with or in the Person of the Son.
6 Cf. Introduction to *The Man Born to be King* (Gollancz, 1943, p. 19): "From the purely dramatic point of view the theology is enormously advantageous...never was there a truer word than that 'except a man believe rightly he cannot' – at any rate, his artistic structure cannot possibly – 'be saved'."

forgotten). It is, I'm afraid, only an effort of my own to make an illustration of three-in-oneness familiar to every creative artist and drawn from his own experience. (The play, by the way, was written to fit in with the Festival of Arts and Crafts at Canterbury, and that is why it is all about craftsmen.) St. Augustine says that God, in making Man, made an image of the Triune. I am trying to say that Man (made a craftsman in the image of the Master-Craftsman) in making a work of art presents also an image of the Triune, because *"every work of creation"* is three-fold.[7] Now, it is a *fact* that when you set out to make a book (or anything else, of course, but I naturally tend to think in terms of books), you are simultaneously making three books, which are all the same book:

(a) *The Book as You Think It*, which I have called the Idea (in the ordinary, not the philosophic sense). This presents itself all at once, in a dispassionate kind of way, with the end and the beginning all there together, a timeless sort of thing with no distinguishable parts, just existing (here, I suppose one links up with St. Augustine) as if it had always been there and always would be.

(b) *The Book as You Write It*. You can't have the Idea without, *at the same time* seeing it as a sequence in time and a struggle with the material. This I have called the Energy, and it is, quite literally, "begotten of that Idea" *from the beginning*, because the one without the other is unthinkable. The Energy produces, of course, a visible "incarnation" of the book in material form, but it exists before that and goes on after, so that it and the Idea co-exist inevitably and are still the same book.

(c) *The Book as You and They Read It*. This is the most difficult to explain. I have called it the Power. It isn't the same thing as the Energy, though it proceeds (in the most orthodox manner) from the Idea and the Energy together. It is the thing that you give out to your readers and your readers give back to you; and it, too, exists from the beginning, because every book is written for somebody, so that

[Added at foot of page]
Of course, to make the analogy go on all-fours, the artist should have created his own public, but that is only true metaphorically. Still, all analogies break down somewhere, because if anything were *exactly* like another thing at all points it would *be* the thing. Even St. Athanasius' illustration about "the reasonable soul and flesh" lands you in awful difficulties about human reason if you take it literally.

---

7 This sentence and the following four paragraphs constitute the essential thesis of *The Mind of the Maker*. She had then no intention of writing this book, which only came into existence after the project "Bridgeheads" was formed in September 1939.

there is a perpetual exchange of Power going on. I mean, you can't write a book *in vacuo*; even if every other person in the world were annihilated, the writer would always be his own reader, so to speak. So that your book comes back to you, as it were, from the minds to which it is addressed – still the same book, but with a different personality, "neither compounding the persons nor dividing the substance".

But Idea, Energy, Power – it is always the same book; at least, it would be in an ideally perfect book, though, as William truly observes, "no man's work is perfect,"[8] and often the Idea is feeble, the Energy ill-directed and the Power conspicuously lacking.[9] But the writer would, I think, recognize the illustration as being sufficiently expressive of his own experience to serve as an illustration – no more, of course than that. And if you were to ask him which of the three was "the real Book" – as Thought, Written or as Read – he could only say, "each and all of them," because you can't really separate them, even in thought.

Perhaps this explanation sounds even feebler than the original statement, but I did want to make it clear that I wasn't just jumbling up St. Augustine but trying to work out a little picture of my own – very limited, naturally – of an earthly three-in-oneness which I know by experience to exist and which may therefore serve as an inadequate analogy of the Divine Three-in-Oneness. There may be several illustrations for the same thing, mayn't there? – though I absolutely refuse to accept St. Patrick's shamrock! Each leaflet of the shamrock isn't equally by itself the whole leaf, and you can't reasonably say that any one of them is begotten of, or proceeds from, another, because they all proceed alike from something quite different!

2. Mr. Laurence Irving, bless his heart! Oh, dear – well, there you are! I've told him a hundred times that the play was about DOGMA, but, you see, he won't believe it.[10] He thinks it's terrifically dramatic, but he cannot understand that Dogma IS the Drama. He probably thinks it's dramatic in spite of the dogma – and when people write prefaces to your book for you, you can't very well say, "Hi! that's not what it means to me". He may reply, "Well, that's what it means to me". (Apparently "the Power" hasn't provoked quite the right response in the living soul in his case!) His kindly intention was, I'm sure, to keep readers from being put off by the notion that the play might be about DOGMA. No doubt he feels that the world will accept God more easily if you call him something else (like the editor in G. K. C.'s story, who crossed out the word "God" wherever it

---

8 Words of William to the archangel Michael, *The Zeal of Thy House*, 4.

9 Examples of such deficiencies are entertainingly illustrated in the chapter entitled "Scalene Trinities" in *The Mind of the Maker*.

10 In his Preface, Laurence Irving omits all reference to the dogma of the Incarnation, which is the main theme of the play.

occurred and substituted "Circumstances").[11] I didn't expostulate with him (though I should enjoy it immensely if somebody else did). For one thing, my sense of humour got the better of me. For another, that book will go to theatrical managers, who will be much more inclined to give the play a London production if they don't think it's about that dreadful DOGMA. This consideration is highly immoral, but this is the point where, like William, one "damns one's soul for the good of the work".[12]

3. The Cherub and 4. Michael. These two points are part of the same thing. For dramatic purposes I've adopted the very idea you mention, viz: that, to the Angels, the whole business of Man's creation and Redemption is a puzzle. But they know it isn't their business to solve puzzles. I have tried to depict them as perfect but limited beings, each doing his own specialised job obediently without speculation or question. Raphael occupies himself with prayer; he can distinguish between true and false (William's devoted craftsmanship is recognised by him as having more of the true spirit of prayer than Theodatus's self-righteous litanies) – but his function does not extend further. Gabriel, the Heavenly Messenger, intervenes in human affairs from time to time (as when he speaks in the ear of Ernulphus, or as in the "rope-scene"), and he has a touch of that heavenly humour which makes the non-conformist mind so indignant. Cassiel records with austere impartiality, and can distinguish between the sin itself and the good use to which God may turn it. Michael's job is to deal out rewards and punishments and "justify the ways of God to Man".[13] Therefore, when he is deputed to deal faithfully with William, he knows how to give him the appropriate theological instruction. But if William had gone further and asked, as the Young Cherub asks, "Why did God create man at all, and with this particular nature?" Michael could only say: "I don't know. I am a soldier; I take my orders, and my orders are to deal with man as I find him. If you want to know anything outside revealed religion, you must not ask me. Possibly the College of Seraphim may know, but I do not, and I am not supposed to ask". Hence the rebuke to the Young Cherub: Angels must not ask that kind of question: that leads to the fall of Lucifer; man, indeed, asked questions, and that (for some inscrutable reason) led to the Incarnation, but Angels are angels and Men are men and it would never do for an angel to behave like a man. As a matter of fact, William never asks the Cherub's question; it would never occur to him, the artist, to ask *why* another Artist chose to create anything, however fantastic or unusual. The love of making things for their own

11 See the final paragraph of "The Purple Wig" in *The Wisdom of Father Brown.*

12 William's words to Gervase (*The Zeal of Thy House*, 1) are: "...sometimes one has to damn one's soul for the sake of the work".

13 John Milton, *Paradise Lost,* Book 1, line 6. The line is often misquoted, as here. Milton wrote "And justifie the wayes of God to men" (Oxford University Press, 1921).

sakes is to him a perfectly sufficient and self-evident reason.

5. Your last point is about the Prior. It has to be Michael, not the Prior, who finally copes with William's trouble, because Michael knows, as the Prior does not, what the trouble is. The Prior, you see, never heard William's outburst of hubris. He does not, like the rest of them, commit himself to the easy assertion that the fall is a judgement for the Ursula affair. He knows God is usually a bit more subtle than that, so he puts the blame where, humanly speaking, it belongs and leaves it at that. But he feels a spiritual snag in William, only, as he says, he "cannot read the heart" and isn't very sure where it is. And William is by this time incapable of telling him. (Ursula knew it at the time, of course; but her own sense of guilt over the accident has made her lose sight of it.) William quite honestly doesn't see what the Prior is getting at. It is true there was an accident, due to somebody's perfectly plain carelessness, and in spite of it, here he is – crippled, certainly, but still able to work, obviously preserved because he is indispensable and carrying on very creditably under great difficulties – he really cannot see how anybody can find anything to blame him for (except, of course, those cheerful faults on which the Church is always so severe and which he is sorry for). And since William really does seem to feel no conviction of sin, the Prior feels he can't refuse him Absolution merely because he (the Prior) only thinks there is something else behind. He can only exhort him to self-examination, and when this fails, absolve him and hope for the best, adding at the same time a warning that the Sacraments are not magic, acting independently of the will of the penitent. The Prior isn't really absolving him "in bits", though I admit that the thought is rather condensed; he is only reminding him of the conditions under which any Sacrament is valid. (I don't think the Prior thinks William is making a bad confession; I think he recognises that he is only in a state of complete ignorance himself.) The confession scene is already rather long in performance, and there isn't room for a detailed discussion about Sacraments, and since there is a deeply-rooted conviction in most people's minds that Sacraments are magic, working *ex opere operato*,[14] possibly a slight over-emphasis in the other direction may do no harm. But I might try to get this clearer. If it can be done in a line and a half! – Of course, the minute Michael puts his finger on the seat of the trouble,

14 This Latin tag, which cannot be translated neatly, means literally "from the work done", and is designed to safeguard the objectivity of the sacraments; that is, their reality does not depend on the state of mind of the participants. The alternative doctrine, that they are so dependent, can be expressed by the parallel phrase *ex opere operantis*, literally "from the work of the worker". Broadly speaking the first phrase is "catholic", the second "protestant". But since it is also catholic teaching that sacraments are not beneficial to the participants without some response on their part, the difference expressed by the two phrases is less than is sometimes supposed, as D. L. S., with characteristic insight, realizes.

William is up in arms. God has no right to take that attitude. And, after all, if it wasn't for the Incarnation, I don't know that He would have the right. But if God has really been through the whole grim business Himself, then He's fairly won the right and one must give in – and that's why it's so exciting and dramatic, and why anybody should think that sort of doctrine DULL passes my comprehension. You may call it a fairy-tale, but it's ridiculous to call it *dull*.[15]

I didn't mean this letter to draw out into such a fearful great screed. Such is the vanity of craftsmen that any expression of interest or approval provokes them to shocking outbursts of egotism. And I can't tell you how glad I am that you (on the whole) think well of the play and were kind enough to write and say so. It's always perilous for laymen to meddle with theology; but I gather you find the Incarnation part of it reasonably sound, and I hope you will allow the Trinity illustration, even though it's not St. Augustine's, but only a sort of marginal note on my own copy-book. I gave myself a fairly free hand over the Angels, because we don't seem to know much about them that's necessary to faith, so I gave them those attributes which seemed most useful dramatically.

If the play is performed in London after Christmas, will you come and see it? Harcourt Williams[16] (William) and Anthony Quayle[17] (Michael) have promised to play in it again, and they are simply magnificent. I think you would like my angels – they stand eleven feet high in their wings and blaze with gold and colour. And with all its faults, the play does come off as a play. People come away from it with the idea that religion is interesting and exciting and practical, and not just a kind of dreary and sloppy emotion about something that has nothing to do with life. I'm sure it's full of theological slips, but it can't be worse for people than the perfectly incredible accounts of the Christian religion one gets in so many books and plays. The great thing is to get people interested, and then they can ask their questions in the right quarter. They are all asking questions – especially the young men – and it's a funny thing, but practically any play that has so much as a whiff of any sort of religion about it can get an

15 Cf. "The Greatest Drama Ever Staged is the Official Creed of Christendom" (first published in *The Sunday Times*, 3 April 1938): "If this is dull [i.e. "the terrifying drama of which God is the victim and the hero"], then what in Heaven's name, is worthy to be called exciting?"... "Now, we may call [the Christian] doctrine exhilarating or we may call it devastating; we may call it revelation or we may call it rubbish; but if we call it dull, then words have no meaning at all." See also letter to Mrs Stevenson, 6 April 1938, note 2.
16 See letter to Margaret Babington, 23 January 1937, note 2.
17 See letter to Margaret Babington, 18 January 1939, note 3.

audience in London. Look at *Murder in the Cathedral*[18] – look even at *The First Legion*[19] which is all about Jesuits and miracles and hasn't a woman-character in it, and which everybody said would be off in a week, and it did quite well at Daly's (of all places) and is carrying on cheerfully at the Cambridge, which is a beastly theatre to play in.

Well, please forgive my inflicting all this upon you, and thank you very much.

> Most gratefully yours,
> [Dorothy L. Sayers]

18 Drama by T. S. Eliot, produced at Canterbury Cathedral, 1935.
19 Drama by Emmet Godfrey Lavery, first produced in London, 1934.

> [24 Newland Street
> Witham
> Essex]

TO H. L. LORIMER[1]

6 October 1937

Dear Miss Lorimer,

I am most terribly sorry; yes, it was to me you lent *The Common Reader*[2] and I had clean forgotten the fact. There it sat on my book-shelf, and the other day I actually looked at it in a vague kind of way and wondered why I had bought it in that edition and not to match Series I! I really am most terribly ashamed of myself.

I am afraid I can tell you very little about *Hybrias the Cretan*[3], except that it was a baritone song of the full-blooded sort much performed by

1 Hilda Lockhart Lorimer, a classical tutor and Fellow of Somerville, described by Vera Brittain as "one of the most brilliantly eccentric of women dons" (V. Brittain, *The Women at Oxford: A Fragment of History*, London, 1960, p. 91).
2 By Virginia Woolf, first published 1925.
3 Hybrias of Crete, a warrior poet, is supposed to have lived in the 7th century B.C. All that exists of his work is a poem of two strophes expressing the scorn of Dorian warriors for tillers of the soil. (See *Paulys Real-Encyclopädie der Classischen Altertumswissenschaft*; H. W. Smythe, *Greek Melic Poets*.) Translated into English verse by Thomas Campbell (1777–1814) and set to music by James William Elliott (1833–1915), a church organist and composer of several anthems and cantatas. The song is mentioned in *Busman's Honeymoon* (novel), chapter 5. It was "generally considered one of the finest bass songs ever written". *Musical Times*, 1 March 1915. An edition "entirely revised by the composer in the year 1897" was published by Edwin Ashdown, Ltd. for both baritone and bass voice. It was advertised as sung by "Signor Foli", a celebrated Irish bass, A. J. Foley (1835–1899). Orchestral parts were available from Messrs Goodwin and Tabb.

parsons at village concerts at the end of the 19th century and beginning of the 20th. My Father used to sing it, and it had a powerful crescendo passage, if I recollect rightly, about "with my good sword I plough, I reap"; I thought I still had my Father's copy here, but it seems to have disappeared. I will make enquiries about it.

I'm glad you had your account of the Appeal Meeting from so sympathetic a source as Helen Waddell;[4] I felt I was being very rude and making myself highly unpopular, but I really was exasperated by the real incompetence with which that literature was sent out. And it seems so difficult to make Oxford people understand how the non-academic world lives – always in a hurry, always worried by a thousand other things, and so often troubled, not by immediate poverty, but by insecurity of income. Then the lack of central organisation – different bodies sending out different times and overlapping one another so that people received the Appeal either three times over or not at all. I felt in my bones that I was going to misbehave myself, and that was why I retired to the Clarendon instead of asking for a room in College! I was very sorry to miss a glass of sherry with you, but when one's temper is unreliable, it is well to avoid opportunities of saying things that one might afterwards regret.

With again very many apologies about the book,
 Ever yours sincerely,
  [Dorothy L. Sayers]

4 Helen Waddell (1889–1965), novelist, mediaeval scholar and translator.

[24 Newland Street
Witham
Essex]

TO FATHER HERBERT KELLY

19 October 1937

Dear Father Kelly,

Thank you very much indeed for your long and friendly and most stimulating letter. I was really ashamed when I thought what a fearful great screed I had sent you to wrestle with.

One thing I expressed badly. I am all for encouraging laymen to meddle with theology on their own account – the more they go in for a little hard thinking as a change from woolly emotionalism the better. I should have said, "it is perilous for laymen to meddle with *expounding* theology" – it is so easy to get confused and give a totally wrong impression, owing to lack of practice in handling technical terms.[1]

That is one of the reasons why I feel sure that the artist's business is to present and not to expound. (I'd back Shakespeare against Shaw every time!) Another is, that when the dramatist abandons his own technique and starts to argue, he is apt to lose grip on the thing, and become so eager to split hairs and justify himself that he fetters his own work. And thirdly, I believe people are more ready to be persuaded by a religious drama if it is not preceded by anything that looks like preachment.

Actually, in practice, I don't think any of the people who saw *Zeal of Thy House* acted were in much doubt about what I was trying to say as regards the Incarnation doctrine. What they found great difficulty in believing was that the doctrine as presented was orthodox C. of E.[2] Their attitude was, not so much "this is too good to be true" as "this is too exciting to be orthodox". Even if the book were prefaced by a certificate of orthodoxy signed by the entire bench of Bishops, they would probably not be persuaded.

Arians:[3] Yes – I think Arians is about right – or let us say that the *highest* point most of them get to is to imagine that the Church's position is Arian. They range from a wholly "human Jesus" up to a position in which they allow that "some unique kind of divineness" is to be imputed to Jesus. What *exactly* they mean by this latter I don't know. One woman said: "Isn't it the sort of divine spark that there is in all of us, only in a unique degree – the same thing only more so?" I said I thought that wasn't quite what was meant, because Christ was held to be the same – here the word "Person" loomed up like a trap, but I avoided it, since she *might* remember the Athanasian Creed and convict me of heresy – "the same *personality* as God the Creator – the same *Thing* – this sounded merely irreverent – "in fact the same God and just as much God – *really* God, in a very different way from you and me". Which is where explanations land you. As a dramatist, of course, one just puts the idea over, not by explanation at

---

1 E. L. Mascall said in *The Secularisation of Christianity* (Darton, Longman and Todd, 1965, p. 107): "Popular theological writing is one of the most difficult of all forms of communication, and its practitioner needs to be careful and self-critical to a degree; like marriage, it is not by any to be enterprised, nor taken in hand, unadvisedly, lightly, or wantonly, like brute beasts that have no understanding, but reverently, discreetly, advisedly, soberly and in the fear of God; I can vividly remember how impressed I was many years ago by the extreme trouble which that great Christian apologist the late Dorothy Sayers took in her popular writings on religion to ensure that what she was trying to express in contemporary idiom was the authentic teaching of Christianity and that the technique which she had worked out was neither ambiguous nor misleading". See also p.158, note 2.
2 Church of England.
3 See letter to Father Herbert Kelly, 4 October 1937, note 2.

all, but by re-iterated statement; "Crucify God", "Those . . . . . Hands that bear the sharp nails' imprint and uphold the axis of the Spheres". "God bore this too", "God died", and so on – leaving them to draw the conclusion, "if it was God who was crucified, then Christ = God". But it isn't really the dramatist's job to say "this is orthodox"; that's the parson's job.

I'm afraid I haven't read your books, but I will, especially as "my" theology turns out (and I am very happy to know it) to be "your" theology also. I didn't think it was "my" theology exactly; I thought it was the Church's, so far as it went, and am a little startled to hear that your "brothers" find such a personal flavour about it. Bits of my *expression* of it (notably the Prior's speech about John and Peter) are indebted to G. K. Chesterton;[4] but I think the body of it emerges quite simply from the Creeds – always provided that one starts by supposing that the Creeds were intended to mean something sensible and are not just a lovely rumbling of hypnotic sound, suitable for stupefying congregations – "the Father incomprehensible, the Son incomprehensible and the Whole Thing incomprehensible", as the old tale has it.

De Trinitate:[5] I admit that my use of the word "Idea" is a little confusing – but only, I think, to theologians, not to the ordinary person, for whom it has no special metaphysical connotation. The artist uses it as I use it – you will notice that William is made to use it twice: "I've had an idea about this." – thus "planting" it (as we say) for later use in the Trinity speech. The word you use, "expression", would do admirably for the Second Person, but that, of late years, it has become horribly contaminated by "expressionism" and "self-expression", used to convey the pouring-out of one's feelings higgledy-piggledy, without regard either to form or to "good form" – a meaning as far removed as possible from the blood and sweat and discipline of the genuine craftsman's "energy".

Prior. I'm glad that, on the main point, your Prior feels I've got hold of the right end of the stick. (The actor, by putting the right emphasis here, can help a lot to give the right sense.) Most Protestants labour under the delusion that: "It must be nice to be a Catholic, because you can get all your sins cleaned off by the priest every Saturday and start again". (Or alternatively, of course, it must be dreadful, because the priest has a high old time licking his lips over your sins in the Confessional and then pursuing them into your private life and brandishing them in your face so as to "get a hold over" you.)

Crucifixion: In a *play* (which only takes about two hours and has a story to tell) one can't give a complete exposition of Christian doctrine. One has to take the bit that is important *for the story* and concentrate on getting

4 See letter to E. C. Bentley, 20 July 1937, note 4.
5 Latin: concerning the Trinity.

that "planted" all through, so as to make its effect when the time comes. For *William*, the point where he comes smack up against it is that line "For lo! God died, and still His work goes on". Everything else has to be subordinated to that dramatic effect. But you'll notice I've left out all those disgusting ideas about "satisfaction" and "paying-off". I've tied it up with the "knowledge" question all through. Man says, "You say I mustn't know – but I intend to know". God replies, "Very well. If you insist, I shall not prevent you; nor shall I annihilate My creation or stop My work on that account. But I have to inform you that the price of that particular kind of knowledge is toil, suffering, renunciation and death. And since I made you with free-will, (and what we make we love), I will stand by you. I will go every step of the way with you. Further, I will turn your evil to good, so that, in the end, and by holding on to Me, you will attain all, and more than all, I originally intended for you, and a 'crown such as the angels know not'".[6]

Angels: That is why, dramatically, the Angels are made to stand so far apart from this business of "wanting to know". I quite agree that it is a pity for man to obey man implicitly; but for an Angel to take God's orders for granted isn't quite the same as for Tommy Atkins[7] to take Colonel Blimp's[8] orders for granted. (My professional actors, trained to display human passion, had a shattering task! "You've got to imagine", said I, "that you are beings who have never known passion, grief, remorse, rebellion, irritability, doubt, hesitation, pain, sickness, fatigue, poverty, anxiety or any of the ills flesh is heir to; you may show a divine anger, but you mustn't sound cross; you may be tender, but on no account emotional; you may be joyful but not excitable; and although you have to stand for two mortal hours on a very hot day in heavy robes and uncomfortable wings, you must try and imagine that you have no bodies to speak of, that your legs do not ache, that your harness is not digging into your shoulders, that the sweat is not rolling down your faces and that two of you are not, in fact, sodden and streaming with hay-fever!" And very nobly they did it, poor lambs!)

Well, I do hope the play will come to Town, and that you may yet be able to see it – it *looks* so beautiful. I will see that you have the centre of the front row of the stalls, if you do come, and perhaps, with the electric contraption, you might hear some of it. My Michael has the grandest voice, like a silver trumpet – when he says "all the Sons of God shouting for joy" it sounds like it! It is good of you to say you will send people and

6 From a speech by the archangel Michael, *The Zeal of Thy House*, part 4: "They that bear\ The cross with Him, with Him shall wear a crown\ Such as the angels know not."
7 Non-commissioned soldier.
8 A stout, blustering, mustachioed officer, from a cartoon figure.

William of Sens and Archangels in *The Zeal of Thy House*

will try to get Toc H[9] interested – that would be a tremendous help. Of course, it's a great job trying to get managers to do anything about a "religious" play – the very word fills them with dreary discomfort and sends their financial spirits down to the soles of their boots. They don't like Christ very much (since half of them are Jews, that is not so very surprising). They only know two versions of Him. There is "gentle-Jesus-meek-and-mild" (dull, and suitable for Christian plays for amateurs); and there is "Suppose-Christ-came-again-today" (usually strongly Communistic and all about working-class prophets in drab surroundings). But a Christianity with colour and humour and suitable for use under ordinary conditions of life is a very queer thing, for which they feel nobody is likely to pay good money. As Lord Melbourne[10] is once said to have

9 Toc H (morse signallers' language for Talbot House) was a movement founded by Philip Thomas Byard Clayton (1885–1972). Known as "Tubby" Clayton, he was chaplain to Talbot House in London and the promoter in both World Wars of ideals of Christian service and fellowship.
10 William Lamb Melbourne, 2nd Viscount (1779–1848), Prime Minister, adviser to the young Queen Victoria, husband of Lady Caroline Lamb. Charles Parker reminds himself of this saying in *Clouds of Witness*, chapter 2.

remarked, "Nobody has a greater respect for the Christian religion than I have, but really, when it comes to intruding it into a gentleman's private life …!"

Again, a thousand thanks for your great kindness and interest. I am truly and deeply grateful.

Yours very sincerely,
[Dorothy L. Sayers]

P.S. "Gentle-Jesus-meek-and-mild"[11] has probably made more apostates than any other single phrase of the language. And what a phrase! About as adequate as calling a man-eating tiger "poor pussy"!

---

11 From the hymn by Charles Wesley (1707–1788): " Gentle Jesus, meek and mild\ Look upon a little child;\ Pity my simplicity;\ Suffer me to come to thee."

24 Newland Street
Witham
Essex

TO IVY SHRIMPTON
20 October 1937

Dearest Ivy,

So sorry – I left your accounts locked away in a drawer while I was away. I enclose cheque £17 for bills and board and lodging. Is this O.K.?

I asked Mr Tendall to have John overhauled by the doctor, who says there seems to be nothing serious wrong with him except the onset of puberty, but he will have an eye kept on him. Everyone has to go through this kind of bother both ends of the business, and it really is nothing to worry about though bumping hearts and tummy upsets are very worrying at the time.

John told me you were having a bother with the mamma and papa of your youngsters – especially papa. I gather papa was having the legal screw put on him at the time, which is all right provided there is anything to screw out! John, with the peculiar values incidental to youth, seemed to feel that to be pounced on for not paying was more disgraceful than failure to meet one's obligations. I endeavoured to disabuse him of this error – which indeed is shared by many persons better informed than himself!

I expect things are very wearing and worrying for you – especially now that you have lost Isobel.[1] It does seem very sad, when she meant so much to you and was repaying your care with so much help and affection. Anyhow, there seems to be nothing much wrong with John, so far; and he appears cheerful enough.

My days have been strenuous as usual. The show is doing remarkably well in its new home at the Victoria Palace; but all these changes and transfers take time and trouble, and put one badly behind with one's other work. I am hoping to get the Canterbury Play on in London some time next year. That will be a terrific gamble, but it may do well, though you never know, with a serious play, whether it may not be a dead flop from the start!

Mac keeps much the same. Aunt Maud[2] is away for the moment – she is becoming quite a gad-about in her old age.

With best love,
    yours affectionately,
        Dorothy

1 Isobel Tovey, who had died of endocarditis. Ivy Shrimpton had fostered her from early child-hood and she had been like an elder sister to John Anthony.
2 Alice Maud Leigh (née Bayliss), the widow of Henry Leigh, brother of D. L. S.' mother. She lived for a time with D. L. S. and her husband in Witham, after the death of Aunt Mabel Leigh.

24 Newland Street
Witham
Essex

TO HER SON
20 October 1937

Dear John,
    Many thanks for your letter. Glad you are getting on all right. I hope Mr Wyn-Werdink is able to give you interesting sidelights on the German nation, in addition to the act of playing the piano. He is probably preju-diced one way or the other, as most people are in speaking of the Germans; but in either case, he ought to be interesting, if he has been in Germany recently. The great difficulty with a country that keeps such a careful censorship on its books and newspapers, is to find out what life is really like for the average person. I am glad History is improving – it is a difficult subject to make much of, or take much interest in, until one grows up – and then it suddenly becomes enthralling, and one wishes one had done more about it in one's school-days. The hard thing to realise is that

today's politics are history, and that "history" is just the politics of so many hundred years ago, and just as vital and exciting to people *then* as our politics are to us. And *always* the same difficulties, the same questions and the same confusions cropping up in every age. Our trouble over Edward VIII's abdication was so curiously like Henry VIII's difficulties about Anne Boleyn, for instance; and the difficulties of the Church in Germany are now so oddly like our own quarrels between Church and State at the Reformation. Only in the history-books it sounds all so dead and settled – as though everything was done by "tendencies" and political theories, instead of by the usual bunch of worried human beings, grappling hastily with all kinds of situations they didn't understand, any more than *we* understand *ours*. But the great thing is to grasp that those people felt exactly as we do ourselves, though of course they had a different sort of knowledge and different facts to go on. Here endeth the History Lecture! I shall not offer a lecture on trigonometry, for maths in every branch is a sealed book to me!

I don't *expect* I shall be able to get down at half-term. Week-ends are always a bad time for me. But I shall come some day this term. Mr Tendall has the business of the new school well in mind; I expect he will tell you about it before long. It'll be a question of exams and things, no doubt.

I hope the old knee is all right now, and that you haven't had any more tummy-upsets.

Busman is doing well at the new theatre – much to everybody's astonishment. There's life, apparently, in the old play yet!

With best love,
    Mother

No – I'm afraid we know practically nobody in Witham. Father's health is so shaky, we don't have people in much – and I am so much in Town. When I come here, I just shut myself up and try to get some work done!

[24 Newland Street
Witham
Essex]

TO M. CHANNING-PEARCE[1]

20 October 1937

Dear Sir,

I believe you have now received from my agent, Mrs. Dorothy Allen, permission to go ahead with the performance of my play *The Zeal of Thy House*. I hope you will understand and forgive the caution with which, at the present moment, we are obliged to surround permission for amateur production. In the case of an ordinary play, it is unusual to permit amateur performance in advance of London production, and we are obliged to make it clear that a solitary permission for educational purposes does not involve the general release of amateur rights.

I am personally delighted to give permission in a case like yours, where the aim is to arouse interest in the subject of the play, and where there is no question of a performance to the general public. The play was seriously conceived as a presentation of Christian doctrine, and I should not wish to stand in the way of anyone who is anxious to present it, as simply and sincerely as possible, to young people. The only thing one has to be careful about is that the performance is not such as to put obstacles in the way of its presentation to a wider public.

As regards the presentation, I feel that I can safely leave this matter in your hands. Simplicity is, I believe, the key to success. As regards costume, the only thing that is likely to present serious difficulty is that of the angels. As regards visual effect, they are the crux of the production, and "ineffectual angels" would give an ineffectual air to the performance. Our angels at Canterbury were enormously effective – but only at the price of being both elaborate and extremely expensive. We had (as I think you know) four well-matched, young, six-foot men, with rigid gold draperies of solid material; and they cost the earth, from the management's point of view. In fact, we set rather a high standard in heavenly beings! I feel that, where economy has to be considered (as it must be, for a single private performance) it would be unwise to attempt elaboration. Generally speaking, the amateur wing has a tendency to wobble, and I would infinitely rather have my angels wingless than wobbly. Plain but good robes in gold, white or colours, without wings, would not be subject to any objection; or, if the production was without costume or with very simple costume, the angels might perhaps appear in plain albs.

---

1 A master at Southleigh College, Oxfordshire.

I am very busy at present, and doubt whether I shall be able to run down and see you as you so kindly suggest. I am, however, very much interested in your production, and shall be very glad to hear from you how you intend to tackle it, and to assist you as best I can in any difficulties.

Yours very truly,
[Dorothy L. Sayers]

[24 Newland Street
Witham
Essex]

TO E. K. FLETCHER

30 October 1937

Dear Mrs. Fletcher,

Thank you so much for your letter and for the copy of *The Ringing World* in which we are all so handsomely reported.[1] I was just about to write to you to thank you and the Ladies' Guild for my delightful evening and for the great honour you have done me in electing me an honorary member of the Guild. I think you are indeed to be congratulated on the way in which the dinner went off.

I have written to the Manager at the Victoria Palace for tickets for either Monday, Tuesday or Wednesday, November 8th–10th whichever evening they can most easily spare. The tickets come in pairs, so that I shall be sending you four; perhaps you will be able to find a fourth friend to go with you.

With again many thanks and best wishes to the Guild,

Yours sincerely,
[Dorothy L. Sayers]

---

1 *The Ringing World*, 29 October 1937, pp. 719–721, published a detailed account of the celebration of the silver jubilee of the Ladies' Guild of Ringers by a dinner held on 23 October at Anderton's Hotel, Fleet Street. D. L. S., elected an honorary member, replied to the toast to "The Visitors". Her speech is reported in full.

[24 Newland Street
Witham
Essex]

TO DAVID HIGHAM[1]

24 November 1937

Dear Mr. Higham,

I really haven't the faintest idea what would be the value of an "original Sayers manuscript", and in any case it feels rather like selling my skin
before I am dead. It might be interesting to make inquiries as to price, but
my impression is, that modern mss. are not likely to fetch very much at the
moment, and that it would be more profitable to my heirs as well as more
seemly for myself to await my decease.

Yours sincerely,
[Dorothy L. Sayers]

---

1 A partner of the firm of literary agents, Pearn, Pollinger and Higham, now David Higham
Associates. See also *The Letters of Dorothy L. Sayers: 1899–1936*, Index.

24 Newland Street
Witham
Essex

TO THE EDITOR OF THE TIMES

2 December 1937[1]

THE WIMSEY CHIN

Sir,

By comparison with the Wimsey nose, any chin may indeed appear
relatively unobtrusive; but there is no member of the family at present
living in which that feature can properly be said to recede, with the possible exception of the Lady Winifred Wimsey, only daughter to the present
Duke. The Duke's own chin is squarish, a contour repeated in a softened
and more elegant form in the physiognomies of his sister, the Lady Mary,
and his son, Viscount Saint-George. Of Lord Peter Wimsey it has been
authoritatively stated that he possesses "a long, narrow chin, and a long,
receding forehead . . . Labour papers, softening down the chin, carica-
tured him as a typical aristocrat" (*Whose Body?* 1923 edition, p. 48).[2] A

---

1 Published on 4 December.   2 Chapter 3.

The Tenth Duke of Denver

typical example of such a caricature may be seen in the cartoon[3] execut-
ed a couple of years ago in the *Evening Standard* by Mr. David Low,[4] whose
political sympathies are well known.

The narrow chin and high receding forehead may be observed in the
portrait of the tenth Duke, Thomas (b. 1703), by Thomas Hudson, which
hangs in the Long Gallery at Bredon Hall; see the collotype reproduction
by the Zoffany Society, and the photograph of the artist's original sketch
in charcoal crayon which appears in the privately printed collection of
"Papers Relating to the Wimsey Family", edited by myself (Humphrey
Milford [1936]). The chin of the tenth Duke is cleft, and this peculiarity
reappears in the chin of the present Lord Saint-George. It will be seen

3 Reproduced in *The Letters of Dorothy L. Sayers: 1899–1936*, between pages 236 and 237.
4 David Low (b. New Zealand 1963), cartoonis t.

Lord Peter Wimsey

that in this family the chin tends to be a variable structure, unlike the nose, whose characteristic outline is already clearly traceable in the tomb-effigy of the fifth Baron, Gerald (1307–1370), although its tip has sustained some damage at the hands of time and iconoclasts.

I am,
    dear sir,
        yours obediently,

MATTHEW WIMSEY,[4]
pp. DOROTHY L. SAYERS

4 See *Busman's Honeymoon* (novel), "Epithalamion", 2.

[24 Newland street
Witham
Essex]

TO FREEMAN WILLS CROFTS[1]

20 December 1937

Dear Mr. Crofts,

Thank you so much for your letter. I am afraid I cannot see my way to being one of the signatories; while I am quite ready to agree that the solution for our present difficulties is chiefly spiritual, I must admit frankly that there are aspects of the Group Movement[2] which to me, as an English Catholic, are distasteful. I am sorry, but there it is! I expect you will find many people whose signatures will be of more value to you than mine, and who will be able to identify themselves sincerely with your cause.

With regrets,

Yours very sincerely,

[Dorothy L. Sayers]

1 Freeman Wills Crofts, detective novelist (1879–1957).
2 The Oxford Group Movement (not to be confused with the Oxford Movement or Tractarian Movement prevalent in the 19th century) was a cult which began among Oxford undergraduates, known as "Groupists", who encouraged the confession of sins at group meetings. Cf. *Gaudy Night*, chapter 7.

[24 Newland Street
Witham
Essex]

TO JOHN DICKSON CARR

28 December 1937

Dear Mr. Carr,

Thank you very much indeed for the Lizzie Borden[1] volume which arrived in good time to give me a happily blood-stained Christmas Day.

1 Lizzie Borden was born at Fall River, Massachusetts, on 19 July 1860 and died there on 1 June 1927. The bodies of her father and stepmother were discovered on 4 August 1892, both having been struck repeatedly with a sharp instrument, possibly an axe. She was tried for both murders in June 1893 but was acquitted, the evidence being circumstantial and inconclusive. Surprisingly, she continued to live in Fall River until her death. She is the subject of the jingle, "Lizzie Borden took an axe\ And gave her mother forty whacks.\ When she saw what she had done\ She gave her father forty-one".

It is the most extraordinary story, and I do wish they had put that woman on the stand, though I quite agree that it would have been extremely unwise to do so, but I feel she would have been a most interesting witness. There are points in it which curiously remind one of the Wallace case;[2] the manner of the murder, the apparent lack of any immediate provocation, the theory that the assassin was naked, the suggestion of the fake appointment and so forth, but the evidence against her is much stronger than the evidence against him, and there being two victims at such a distance of time apart gives a touch of extravagance to the whole thing. And in broad daylight too! It was most charming of you to send me the book, and thank you very much indeed.

Looking forward to seeing you on January 12th, and with best wishes to you both for the New Year,

Yours very sincerely,

[Dorothy L. Sayers]

2 See letter to John Dickson Carr, 3 March 1937.

1938

Response to a new public

ↄ₰ↄↄↄ₰

24 Great James Street[1]
W.C.1

TO IVY SHRIMPTON

15 January 1938

Dearest Ivy,

Many thanks for your letters. Glad to hear John's flu is better. Let me
know to this address whether he is coming up on Tuesday and by which
train. If he is only just over flu he had better not come by an early train,
had he? There is no point in exhausting him by trailing him round Town.
He could either arrive just in time to have some lunch, or he could lunch
on the train and I could meet him and take him across. However I leave
it to you to decide what he will be up to doing. Just send me a card to
reach me Tuesday morning.

Love,

D. L. S.

1 The address of D. L. S.' flat in London.

[24 Newland Street
Witham
Essex]

TO MARGARET BABINGTON

31 January 1938

Dear Miss Babington,

Many thanks for your letter. I am so glad you have got a good play this
year after all your agitations. I have not read *Christ's Comet*,[1] but I have

Marie Ney, who played the Lady Ursula in *The Zeal of Thy House* at the
Westminster Theatre. (See p.78)

heard favourable reports of it in theatrical circles. I do hope it will be a
very great success; I shall certainly try to come and see it.

Zeal of Thy House will come on at the Westminster at the end of March,
so I don't suppose Miss Haffenden will come down about the costumes
before February 12th; but she may at any time ask to have one or two
items, including the angels' wings, sent up to her for alteration. We hope
you will be kind enough to hold the costumes and props for me, if you can
possibly find the room, until we are able to have them sent direct to the
Westminster theatre. It is difficult to find storage room in London, and it
is not good for things to be continually carted about. I do hope you will
not find this inconvenient.

We have all been very excited about the production, and have been
through some anxious moments; but all appears to be now well, although
the contract is not actually signed. I am hoping very much to have quite
a number of my original professional actors; Mr. Williams and Mr.
Napier[2] are with us, of course, and I have great hopes that we shall have
also Mr. Quayle, Mr. Winter[3] and possibly Michael Gough[4] and Tom
Morgan[5] if they can get back from America.

A little nearer the time, may I send down a few posters and leaflets for
distribution in Canterbury? I know that I may rely on my friends there to
come and support us in Town, and give us as much publicity as possible.

With best wishes to yourself and all the Friends of the Cathedral,

Yours very sincerely,

[Dorothy L. Sayers]

---

1 By Christopher Hassall, the play chosen for the Canterbury Festival of 1938. See Kenneth
   Pickering, *Drama in the Cathedral*, Churchman Publishing, 1985, chapter 8.
2 Frank Napier, who played the part of Theodatus and assisted in the production.
3 Cecil Winter, who played the part of Cassiel.
4 Michael Gough (b. 1917), who played the part of Simon.
5 Thomas Morgan, who played the part of Gervase.

[24 Newland Street
Witham
Essex]

TO FATHER HERBERT KELLY

7 February 1938

Dear Father Kelly,

I know you will be glad to hear that *Zeal of Thy House* is coming to London at the end of March; it is being put on by Mr. Anmer Hall[1] at the Westminster theatre for a run of one month with Mr. Harcourt Williams as William of Sens, and Mr. Anthony Quayle as Michael and one or two others of my original Canterbury cast. I do hope you will be able to come and see it and send as many friends as you can persuade. It is a little unfortunate that we have to begin in Lent and so close to Holy Week, since the first two weeks of a short run are so very important; we hope, however, that in view of its being a religious play, some good Christian people may be able to reconcile their consciences to going in Lent, and we shall, in any case, run on over Easter week, which ought to be a good one. Perhaps later on, I may send you one or two posters and leaflets to display at Kelham. It is all very exciting, and I do hope we shall do well with the show.

I continue to make interesting discoveries about Christian doctrine as understood by the Laity; a young man of my acquaintance, brought up in some kind of Christianity, was astonished to hear that the Church considered pride to be a sin at all, having always been under the impression that sins of the flesh were the only sins that counted.[2] He seemed to think that the main outline of the Faith, as I endeavoured to explain them over a glass of sherry in a pub (I always seem to be expounding the Faith in pubs!), was something quite revolutionary and unheard of, though interesting.

1 Anmer Hall (Alderson Burrell Horne), actor, producer and manager (1863–1953).
2 Possibly the young man quoted in "The Other Six Deadly Sins" as asking: "I did not know there were seven deadly sins: please tell me the names of the other six". The talk, given to the Public Morality Council, Caxton Hall, Westminster on 23 October 1941, was published in *Creed or Chaos?* (Methuen, March 1943).

I had a very kind letter from Mr. Eric Fenn,[3] asking permission to give an amateur performance of the play at a Student Conference; in view of the London production I had to refuse this permission, but he has very kindly undertaken to do all he can to help in getting publicity for our production.

With kindest remembrances,
Yours very sincerely,
[Dorothy L. Sayers]

3 The Rev. Eric Fenn, Presbyterian Minister, Secretary of the H.Q. of the Student Christian Movement from 1926 to 1937, later Assistant Director of Religious Broadcasting, B.B.C.

24 Newland Street
Witham
Essex

TO IVY SHRIMPTON
28 February 1938

Dearest Ivy,

It has just come to me that I have forgotten to send you the money for John's last holiday – I enclose £5 to cover his bed and board and the little account you enclosed.

He goes up for his scholarship exam[1] at the beginning of the month, as you know, and Mr Tendall has arranged for him to stay with friends in Town, as I have nowhere to put him and shall be down at the theatre all day. Then he will have told you about his holiday trip abroad. I think this will be a good thing for him, as he is now old enough to remember what he sees. I don't know where I shall be on April 5th when they break up, but I suggest it would be nice if you could contrive to come up to Town that day (if you can find somewhere to park the youngsters) and then you and he could meet and go to see *Zeal of Thy House* at the Westminster. Of course I would pay for the tickets and your railway-fares etc. This would give you an opportunity of seeing him before he starts off abroad. Mr Tendall can put him up in Broadstairs for the 2 or 3 nights before they set out as it obviously isn't worth while for him to trail to Oxford and back for a couple of nights.

It has been very hard work getting the play arrangements going, but I think it's going to be all right now and a good show. We start rehearsals etc. on Tuesday. Aunt Maud is better but not yet really right after the

1 For Malvern College, a boys' public school. He was then at a preparatory boarding school in Broadstairs, Kent. He won the scholarship.

nasty attack she had at Christmas. She is going away for a couple of weeks tomorrow – not, thank goodness, to Cornwall – I hope she won't pick up anything fresh.

I had a depressing letter from Shirley the other day, asking for money. She said she had had an operation in the breast and that Aunt Lil² was ill – I don't know with what. I sent her £50, which was as much as I thought I could well spare under all the circumstances. After all, I never actually met any of them.

Best love,
　　Dorothy

2　Lilian Sarah Leigh (her mother's sister), married to Norman Logan, who lived in California. Shirley was their daughter. They also had a son named Kenneth, who came to London with his wife later that year. See letters to Ivy Shrimpton, 18 June and 6 November 1938, and letter to her son, 27 June 1938.

[24 Newland Street
Witham
Essex]

TO MAURICE BROWNE¹

5 March 1938

Dear Maurice,

I am so sorry you should have had to wait to see the announcement of *Zeal* in the papers. The minute it was fixed up with A. B. H.² – about a fortnight ago, I think, or more – I dashed in to 10 Golden Square and told Marjorie,³ adding messages of regret and affection for you. She must have forgotten to tell you; but my intentions were good!

We are rehearsing and I think it's going to pan out very well, despite a certain cramping of the angels here and there by theatrical conditions. Tony Quayle, the little beast, backed out at the last moment to go to the Gate, of all places; so Michael is being played by Alan Napier – his robes have had to be let down 8 inches! One actor is returning from America to play for us – his ship has caught fire and he can't now sail till Wednesday – I only hope the Queen Mary doesn't now blow up or hit an iceberg! So we have our little ups and downs, you see. Nevertheless, we hope to open on March 29th and to see you there to wish us luck.

Love,
　　[Dorothy L. S.]

1　See letter to him, 12 March 1937, note 1.
2　i.e. Anmer Hall. See letter to Father Kelly, 7 February 1938, note 1.
3　Marjorie Vosper, her dramatic agent.

[24 Newland Street
Witham
Essex]

TO MRS STEVENSON[1]

6 April 1938

Dear Mrs. Stevenson,

Many thanks for your letter. I am glad you liked the article[2] in the *Sunday Times*, and I hope you also liked the play, *The Zeal of Thy House*; I gather that you saw it at Canterbury. I should like very much to come down and speak to you at Tewkesbury on one of the dates you mention, especially as my friend, Frank Napier, who produced *Zeal* for me, is producing *Saint Joan*[3] for you, and I should have wanted in any case to come and see the production, so if you will let me know which day you prefer, I will endeavour to think out something to say. I must warn you, however, that I have a way of upsetting people by what I do say – I have just been accused of heresy in the pages of *Punch* of all papers! However, if you are ready to take the risk, so am I. (The *Punch* man is, in my opinion, a vile agnostic, and I have written and told him so!)

I hope your Festival at Tewkesbury[4] will be a very great success. The business for *Zeal* is building up slowly in London, and we hope that all those who are interested will come and see the show before it is too late, since it is only on for a limited run. I wonder whether you will help us by distributing the enclosed leaflets to anybody who may be interested.

Thank you so much for your kind invitation.

Yours sincerely,
[Dorothy L. Sayers]

---

1 A member of the Religious Drama Society.
2 "The Greatest Drama Ever Staged is the Official Creed of Christendom", first published in *The Sunday Times*, 3 April 1938. Later published, with the shorter title, "The Greatest Drama Ever Staged", as a pamphlet together with "The Triumph of Easter" (Hodder and Stoughton, 2 June 1938). Subsequently included in *Creed or Chaos?* (Methuen 1947).
3 By George Bernard Shaw.
4 Tewkesbury was planning an appeal to raise funds for the repair of the tower and east chapel of the Abbey. The Religious Drama Society was organizing lectures on "The Meaning and Purpose of Religious Drama Today". D. L. S. agreed to give one on 11 July. The title was "Author, Actor and Audience".

[24 Newland Street
Witham
Essex]

TO S. DARK[1]

6 April 1938

Dear Mr. Dark,

I am glad to hear from Miss King that you liked my article[2] in the *Sunday Times*; it was written in a rather bludgeoning style, because it was originally intended for the *Daily Mail*, who asked for an article on that subject, but when they saw it were afraid to print it!

In the meantime I have been accused of heresy in the pages of *Punch*; I have drafted an answer to the editor, though, of course, they allow one no opportunity for public rejoinder. I enclose a copy of that reply, in the hope that possibly you might be interested in raising the same question in the columns of the *Church Times*. It is, of course, always dangerous to put forward any theological statement, particularly in paradoxical form and expression, but it seemed to me so important to stress the reality of Christ's human suffering and His participation in that suffering with His Divine Personality, that I was ready to take the risk. To keep the exact middle course between Arianism[3] and Docetism[4] is always difficult, but one has to try and do it if one is not to lose the whole meaning for us of the Incarnation.

Thank you for your kindly interest in the play.

Yours sincerely,
[Dorothy L. Sayers]

1 Editor of *The Church Times*.
2 See letter to Mrs Stevenson, dated 6 April 1938, note 2
3 See letter to Father Herbert Kelly, 4 October 1937, note 3.
4 The heretical belief that Christ's body was either a phantom or of celestial substance.

[24 Newland Street
Witham
Essex]

TO THE EDITOR OF PUNCH

6 April 1938

Dear Sir,

It is seldom wise to answer the observations of critics, and in the present case, as I am aware, useless, since the pages of *Punch* are not open to correspondence and an attack from that quarter permits no public rejoinder. Nevertheless, since your dramatic critic[1] has seen fit to accuse me of "free and easy theology",[2] I feel that I must enter an objection privately, and I should be obliged if you would pass it on to the right quarter. The theology of the last scene of *The Zeal of Thy House* is strict enough, and "High Church Divines", so far from demurring, have endorsed it.

There is no question of denying the operation of the Holy Ghost; on the contrary, Michael mentions it specifically: "For you the task, for you the tongues of fire."[3] But unless we are to fall into the Docetic heresy of supposing the Humanity of Christ to have been a mere phantasm, we must allow all the temptations and sufferings of that Humanity to have been a reality. The first great temptation and the last great temptation are, significantly, almost identical: "If Thou be the Son of God, cast Thyself down."[4] "If Thou be the Son of God, come down;"[5] and the answer to both is a refusal. To deny the reality of the temptation and the refusal is to deny the reality of the Humanity.

I have made William of Sens say: "Could God, being God, do this?" (i.e. suffer the agony of human frustration) and the reply is: "Christ, being Man, did this." But that which was done by Christ's Humanity on the Cross was done once and for all: "But this man, after He had offered one sacrifice for sins for ever, sat down on the right hand of God."[6] The rest is indeed for the Holy Ghost, "qui et semper aderat generi humano;"[7] but it will not do to confound the Persons of the Holy Trinity; that way lies heresy indeed.

Yours faithfully

[Dorothy L. Sayers]

---

1 Douglas Woodruff (1897–1978), editor of *The Tablet* (1936–1967), on the editorial staff of *The Times* (1926–1938) and on the staff of the B.B.C. (1934–1936).

2 The tone of the review was condescending and the actual words used were "very free and easy theology" (*Punch*, 6 April 1938, p. 384).

3 *The Zeal of Thy House*, the archangel's words to William, scene 4, in the speech beginning, "Christ, being man, did this..."

4 Matthew, chapter 4, verse 6.

5 Matthew, chapter 27, verse 42.

6 Epistle to the Hebrews, chapter 10, verse 12.

7 Latin: who likewise has ever sustained the human race. D. L. S. quotes these words in her Introduction to *The Man Born to be King* (Gollancz, 1943, pp. 27–28).

24 Newland Street
Witham
Essex

TO HER SON
7 April 1938

Dear John,

I hope this will catch you before you leave tomorrow. I meant to write yesterday, but I got the dates mixed.

I'm so glad you've had such a good term and distinguished yourself all over the place and now I hope you'll have a really grand trip. It sounds a most delightful tour. I enclose £1 tip for you to spend on this and that as you go.

I have had a very hard month or so working on the play. Did you and Aunt Ivy get to it all right and enjoy yourselves? And did you think the angels handsome?

Best love and have a good time.
    Your loving
        Mother

[24 Newland Street
Witham
Essex]

TO CLIFFORD MATTHEWS[1]
7 April 1938

Dear Mr. Matthews,

Your sister, Irene, has passed me on your letter; thank you for saying that the authors' names shall be given correctly in your future announcements. I am very busy at present, and afraid have not time to write out a clear cut description of all the characters in *Busman's Honeymoon*. I did do this once, and handed the ms.[2] to my collaborator, who is now frantically searching for it; if she finds it, I will send it on to you. The great thing to remember about *Peter* is that the presentment of his character and appearance should be taken from the later books, e.g. *Gaudy Night* and the novel of *Busman's Honeymoon*, and not from the earlier ones, since he is twelve years older in the *Honeymoon* than in *Whose Body?* and has developed considerably in the intervening period. Physically, he should ideally be five

---

[1] Identity unknown.
[2] It is now in the library of the Marion E. Wade Center, Wheaton College, Illinois.

feet nine and a half inches, clean shaven, fair hair brushed straight back, hawk-nosed, fine hands, nervously energetic and with rather a light, not booming sort of voice. At the time of the play he was forty-five. *Harriet* is dark, with an interesting rather than beautiful face, sparely made, physically and mentally sturdier than Peter, with a rather beautiful voice; she is about thirty-three. *Bunter* should be a couple of years older than Peter, and precise rather than pompous in manner; slight, not paunchy. This may help you to go on with unless and until the original character sketches can be found. The other people in the play do not appear in any of the other books, and the producer may use his imagination. Barrie Livesey[3] was, to my mind, the ideal Crutchley, because he had both the attractive physical appearance, which accounts for Miss Twitterton's infatuation, and also that touch of something uncontrolled, which suggests the possible murderer.

Wishing you the best of luck with your production,

    Yours very truly,

        [Dorothy L. Sayers]

---

3 Barrie Livesey, b. 1904.

           [24 Newland Street
           Witham
           Essex]

TO DAME CHRISTABEL PANKHURST[1]

19 April 1938

Dear Dame Christabel,

Thank you very much for your letter; I am so glad that you liked the *Sunday Times* article.[2] I do not really feel that the Press is my proper pulpit; I think myself that my Canterbury play now running at the Westminster represents my ideas better; perhaps it would entertain you to see that. It really is a beautiful performance, or I would not urge anybody to go to it.

    With many thanks,

        Yours very truly,

           [Dorothy L. Sayers]

---

1 Daughter of Emmeline Pankhurst, the British suffragist.
2 See letter to Mrs Stevenson, dated 6 April 1938, note 2.

Dame Christabel replied on 24 April:

Dear Miss Sayers,

Thank you so much for your letter and for telling me about your play which yesterday I saw with admiration.

I think, however, that it is not a question of or play or press, but that both are your proper pulpit.

The press brings your message straight to your readers in their homes while they are yet unready to go out in search of it.

Also a newspaper article makes them understand the better that you believe that what you say in your plays is true for ordinary people, in real life, at the present day.

Each of your two modes of appeal to the public strengthens the other; plays and newspapers alike being written that they may believe that Jesus is the Son of God and believing may have life through His Name.

So I hope to see more both of your articles and your plays.[1]

Yours very truly,

Christabel Pankhurst.

1 Dame Christabel's hope was to be fulfilled.

> [24 Newland Street
> Witham
> Essex]

TO FATHER HERBERT KELLY

1 May 1938

Dear Father Kelly,

I feel very discourteous at not having replied to your letter or come to see you, but last week was one prolonged and purgatorial agitation. We were reduced to desperation by the fact that although the business for *Zeal* was building up at the Westminster, we could not carry on there, and could see no prospect either of transferring or of raising money to finance a tour. In this hopeless situation we implored God for a miracle, to which He responded with His accustomed sense of humour by arousing the interest of the hardest headed and the hardest hearted management in town! We had nearly a week of frantic negotiations, during which they wanted first to make all the cast play for pittances, secondly to cut down half the cast, and thirdly to make the author give her work for nothing. After agitated bargaining on all these points, we at last succeeded in screwing out of them mean, though just barely adequate terms, and this Shylock bargain was finally clinched at midnight on Friday. The result is, that the play reopens at the Garrick Theatre on Tuesday week, May 10th. Amid all the whirling of the dust of conflict, I fear I quite lost touch with my friends and my correspondence; I hope you will forgive me.

I am so glad you liked the play; I am immensely pleased with the production and the acting that my company have given me. I have not yet heard from Mr. Clayton,[1] but as soon as I am in a more coherent frame of mind, I will write to him.

With very many thanks,
 Yours sincerely,
  [Dorothy L. Sayers]

---

1 See letter to Father Kelly, dated 19 October 1937, note 9.

[24 Newland Street
Witham
Essex]

TO R. ELLIS ROBERTS[1]

3 May 1938

Dear Mr. Roberts,

I am afraid I had to reply rather hastily to Mr. Housman's[2] criticisms on Saturday afternoon; I hope he did not think I was discourteous. I had a very old friend who had seen the play just hurrying off to catch a train; another very old friend trying to convey to me a message from the Duke of Bedford; a new Ursula[3] waiting upstairs in Harcourt Williams's room to be vetted and a conference about archangels to be undertaken with the producers, one of whom was hurrying away to an appointment!

In addition to this we were all thoroughly worked up at getting the transfer at last signed, sealed and delivered. We are opening on Tuesday, May 10th at the Garrick and shall, I believe, be playing three matinées a week, with no performance on Monday evenings. We shall be exceedingly grateful to you for all the publicity you can get us in the religious and

---

1 R. Ellis Roberts and his wife were in Carmel, California when war broke out. In December 1940 they sent as a Christmas and New Year greeting a little pamphlet of poems, privately printed, entitled *In Exile: to Those in Exile*. The first line of the first poem would have been to the liking of D. L. S.: "This is a war of minds, of faiths, of gods." In 1939 R. Ellis Roberts published *Portrait of Stella Benson*.

2 Laurence Housman (1865–1959), poet and dramatist. It is not known what the occasion was.

3 A character in *The Zeal of Thy House*.

other weeklies; the managers of the Garrick will not, themselves, spend much money on newspaper publicity, though they will probably arrange for a good display on the theatre itself. Thus, anything we can get in the way of editorial mention will be extremely valuable to us.

We are all exceedingly happy to have got the transfer; we are all accepting very small salaries and microscopic royalties, gambling on the opportunities for a tour later on, which will, we hope, bring us back our money. The transfer means that we shall (a) go out with the prestige of having played at two theatres in town (b) that we shall have more time in which to collect money for the tour, and (c) that the company will be kept together during these arrangements. The cast will be practically the same as at the Westminster, except that Marie Ney's[4] part will be played by Ailsa Grahame, and Alan Napier's by Raf de la Torre.[5]

With many thanks for all your kind sympathy and help,

    Yours very sincerely,

        [Dorothy L. Sayers]

4 Marie Ney (1895–1981), who played the part of Lady Ursula. It was played by Vera Coburn Findlay at Canterbury. (see p. 66).
5 Raf de la Torre also played the part of the Persona Dei in *The Just Vengeance* at Lichfield Cathedral in 1946.

                    [24 Newland Street
                    Witham
                    Essex]

TO A.MURE MACKENZIE[1]

15 May 1938

Dear Miss Mackenzie,

Thank you so much for your very kind letter about *The Zeal of Thy House*. We were a little hurt that the *Times*, which had given us two such magnificent notices from Charles Morgan,[2] should then send their second critic to damn us at the Garrick. I do not think this gentleman knows the meaning of the word "rhetoric" – unless, indeed, he takes it in the mediaeval sense, viz: the art of presenting arguments by word of mouth. I hope this notice will not damage the play too much, it is difficult enough to get West End audiences to go and see anything which can be called religious or intellectual. I hope we may count on your personal support, and

1 A colleague of the dramatic critic on *The Times*.
2 Charles (Langbridge) Morgan (1894–1958), novelist and playwright. He was the dramatic critic for *The Times* from 1926 to 1939.

you will send as many friends as possible to see the show despite your colleague's bad opinion.

I am so glad you and your sister enjoy the Peter Wimsey books.

Gratefully yours,

[Dorothy L. Sayers]

[24 Newland Street
Witham
Essex]

TO FATHER HERBERT KELLY

16 May 1938

Dear Father Kelly,

Many thanks for your letter. We are hoping to do well with the show at the Garrick, though, of course, it will again take a little time to build up business. I should be rather afraid of what the films might do to it; I fear the theology would be likely to suffer.

I am exceedingly interested to learn that I am about to join the Roman Catholic Church; if your informant had heard the things I said about that institution the other day (stimulated by Douglas Woodruff's[1] disagreeable criticism of *Zeal* in *Punch*) he might reconsider his prophecy. There are moments when I feel that the Inquisition was one of the least dishonest of its activities.

I went to see Tubby Clayton[2] the other day, who was very agreeable though somewhat preoccupied; he seems to have got into a curious habit of saying: "Good, good; well done!" at intervals throughout the conversation, with curiously little relevance to the context. It must come of having so much to do with Boy Scouts and Leagues of Youth. However, I was inveigled by one of his young men into promising to go and talk about Religious Drama to Toc H, on the understanding, of course, that they would give me publicity for *Zeal*. I get to feel more and more like the unjust steward every day. I ought to be getting on with my new novel,[3] instead I am impelled to write a play about Herod the Great;[4] it will probably turn out to be another version of the downfall of the proud.

With all good wishes, Yours sincerely, [Dorothy L. Sayers]

---

1 See letter to Editor of *Punch*, 6 April 1938, notes 1 and 2.
2 See letter to Father Kelly, 19 October 1937, note 9.   3 *Thrones, Dominations*.
4 The first act of this play exists in manuscript and is in the possession of the Marion E. Wade Center, Wheaton College, Illinois. It is significant that she had begun a play about Herod before introducing him into *The Man Born to be King*. See also the following letter to Herbert Kelly.

[24 Newland Street
Witham
Essex]

TO FATHER HERBERT KELLY

24 May 1938

Dear Father Kelly...

John Middleton Murry[1] is an author and critic, editor of *The Athenaeum*
for some time after the War. He has written a number of books, includ-
ing a *Life of Christ*[2] (which I haven't read, but which is probably what you
connected him with – I should think it would be awful); according to
Frank Swinnerton,[3] he "turned first Christian and then Christian
Communist", whatever that means exactly. He was the husband of
Katherine Mansfield[4] and a friend of D. H. Lawrence[5] (at least, until
Lawrence took to calling him "Judas", having indeed every reason to cry
"Save me from my friends!") and wrote a very emotional sort of biography of him, called *Son of Woman*. I should think he was probably quite
right about Dick Sheppard.[6] I only met D. S. twice. He possessed an
astonishing amount of personal charm, but he made me feel a little
uncomfortable. I think he was sincere, but he seemed to me over-anxious
for the affection of all and sundry. He impressed me as being restless,
feverish and essentially unhappy, always in quest of reassurance, and, I
am sure, lacking in intellect – but then, I always tend to rate intellect too
high and to be embarrassed by magnetic personality and that kind of
thing.

Herod (confound him) is becoming very insistent, trampling
ferociously into my mind over the heads of all the other things it is my
duty to do. Can you or any of your brethren guide me to a book (not too
learned and difficult) about the position of the Jews under the Roman
Empire, between Maccabees and St. Matthew? I want to know how they
carried on their daily life and institutions under that alien but tolerant
despotism. Herod seems to have had a bad time with them, because,

---

1 John Middleton Murry (1889–1957), was the editor of *The Athenaeum* from 1919 to 1921. His
  Son of Woman, published in 1931, is a study of D. H. Lawrence's sexuality. See also her letter
  to Maurice B. Reckitt, dated 14 May 1941.

2 *Life of Jesus*, published in 1926.

3 Frank (Arthur) Swinnerton (1884–1982), novelist, critic and publisher.

4 Katherine Mansfield Beauchamp (1888–1923), writer of short stories, born in New Zealand.
  She was first married to George Bowden, whom she left. She married John Middleton Murry
  in 1918.

5 D. H. Lawrence (1885–1930) lived near Mansfield and Murry for a time in Cornwall.

6 The Rev. Dick Sheppard (1880–1937), Vicar of St Martin-in-the-Fields from 1914 to 1917,
  Dean of Canterbury from 1929 to 1931, a popular and charismatic preacher.

though he got back Jerusalem from the Parthians and rebuilt the Temple and did quite a lot of the enlightened-monarch business, they hated and despised him for being Rome's nominee, and for building a wicked heathen amphitheatre, and especially for being a Philistine and not "hundred-per-cent Jewish" (thus the whirligig of time brings in its revenges!)[7]. I expect he had it pretty well dinned into his ears about the expected "pure-Jewish" Messiah and the "pure-Jewish" kingdom-to-be, and all the rest of it – his wife's family apparently lost no opportunity of rubbing [it] in about his low antecedents. I don't wonder that after a long lifetime of disappointments in his own offspring he lost his (always precarious) hold on his temper and determined to do away with Messianic pretenders. I can see the development of his character very clearly, but where I'm stuck is on domestic and political details – what sort of people he would have in his household, how far he could administer the province off his own bat and how much he had to act for Rome, what were the relations between the Jewish Church and the Roman State, and so forth. I am extremely ignorant of the history of that – and indeed of any – period. I imagine that to Rome he would appear very oriental and barbaric and to the Jews sadly occidental and internationalized – rather like an Indian maharajah who had been educated at Oxford, neither flesh, fowl nor good red herring.

I too, you see, am bursting over with ideas, and seem to have no time to deal with them. But it's great fun. It would be awful to come to the end of one's ideas. Good luck to the Inquisition. As to blasphemy – the R.C.'s seem to me to specialise in blasphemous explanations. Some well-wisher (anxious to keep me out of the Roman fold) favoured me with a revolting little R.C. pamphlet on Purgatory, full of stuff about Hell which I shouldn't have thought anybody would have the face to publish at this time of day.[8] Anyway, the Vatican seems to be in rather bad odour to-day, even among its own people, for its political dishonesty and the pruriency of its sexual ethics. R.C. theology seems to me to be chiefly dialectics – though I suppose some of the really important writers attach some meaning to the terms they bandy about so freely – even if Douglas Woodruff doesn't!

Lord! what a long letter to bore you with –

Very sincerely yours,

[Dorothy L Sayers]

---

7 Shakespeare, *Twelfth Night* V 1.
8 See her Introductions to her translations of Dante's *Inferno* and *Purgatorio* (Penguin Classics).

[24 Newland Street
Witham
Essex]

TO M. N. WHITELAW[1]

8 June 1938

Dear Miss Whitelaw,

Thank you so much for your letter; I am very glad you enjoyed *The Zeal of Thy House* so much. Your suggestion about "The Keys of Canterbury"[2] is interesting and ingenious, though in most versions I think the song is called "The Keys of Heaven"; I do not know what gave it the local application.

As regards the Peter Wimsey story of the "Copper Fingers",[3] I think it is mentioned there somewhere that the modelling seemed inferior to that of the sculptor's usual work. The story actually derived from an astonishing advertisement by an American firm of morticians who demanded: "Why lay your loved ones in the cold earth? Let us electroplate them for you in gold and silver". So apparently the thing has been done.

Yours sincerely,
　　[Dorothy L. Sayers]

---

1 Identity unknown.
2 "The Keys of Canterbury" is included in *Folk-Songs from Somerset*, collected and edited by Cecil J. Sharp, Set 1, Novello's School Songs, Book 201, pp. 18–19. The tune and words are not the same as those of "The Keys of Heaven".
3 "The Abominable History of the Man with Copper Fingers", first published in *Lord Peter Views the Body*, Gollancz, 12 November 1928.

24 Great James Street
W.C.1

TO IVY SHRIMPTON

18 June 1938

Dearest Ivy,

I learnt with horror from John that I had forgotten to send you his report. So sorry. This play of mine seems to preoccupy my mind to the exclusion of all memory and common sense.

I enclose £10 for bills etc. Will this be O.K., as he wasn't at home for very long?

I have received warning of the American invasion,[1] and now await the

---

1 The visit of her cousin Kenneth Logan and his wife from California.

assault. By a Special Providence and my own slackness, there is no spare room fit to occupy at Witham, so I shall do my entertaining in Town, packing them off to see *Zeal* at the earliest opportunity! What in the world is one to do with people one has never seen, all bursting with family enthusiasm?

Hope your cold is now all right. John seemed very fit when I saw him, and said nothing about a bad foot.

Best love,
  Dorothy

        [24 Newland Street
        Witham
        Essex]

TO THE SECRETARY

Advisory Committee on Spoken English
British Broadcasting Corporation

27 June 1938

Dear Sir,
 I pronounce my name to rhyme with "stairs".
  Yours faithfully,
   [Dorothy L. Sayers]

        24 Newland Street
        Witham
        Essex

TO HER SON
27 June 1938

Dear John,
 As usual I have to apologise for being so slow in thanking you for my nice birthday present. As usual, the excuse is that I have had a very heavy fortnight, full of theatrical business interspersed with dashing about the place to speak at places and open things. Next week is going to be worse! – so I seize the day when I've contrived to land up at home. I was away the day of your half-term, and now again it's quite impossible for me to get along tomorrow to see the Geographical Exhibition at the school. I didn't get Mr Tendall's message till yesterday, by which time it was too late

to make any arrangement for today – and tomorrow I have a date in Town – and on Wednesday. It's all rather tiring! The other day I had to go and open a garden fête at Bluntisham, where I used to live – very exhausting, with lots [of] people coming up to say, "Do you remember me?" (which I never did) and "I knew you when you were so high" (a thing which ought not to be permitted – no one should ever have known one at such a time, or be allowed to make any allusion to it!). Well, anyway, thank you very much for thinking of my birthday, and congratulations on your contributions to the exhibition, which Mr T. tells me are very good indeed. Perhaps I may get down one day to see them in the school.

The play still survives[1] – 100th performance on Thursday – but last week we did rather poor business and all feared the worst. I hope it will be all right, but one is kept in a perpetual state of anxiety and fidgets. Mr Tendall has asked me whether you could go camping again this summer, and I said, by all means, if you would like to. So you just tell him and arrange with Aunt Ivy.

I dealt firmly and competently with the Logans – giving them a cocktail party, dinner and seats for the show, and they departed satisfied, having bored everybody to death. A dull, well-intentioned pair!

    With love,
        Mother

1 i.e. *The Zeal of Thy House.*

[24 Newland Street
Witham
Essex]

TO MARGERY VOSPER
4 July 1938

Dear Margery,

As you will have seen, we departed from the Duke of York's[1] on Saturday in a blaze of glory; the staff, both backstage and front of house, weeping gallons of angry tears over us, and having to hold the curtain for ten minutes at the matinée because of the crowds fighting in the foyer. Westminster history repeats itself. Guy Charles is trying to get his touring dates pencilled, and I shall be up next week and will go into the situation with you and him. In the meantime, I enclose copies of two letters which have come in about amateur performances. Father Kelly's application for

1 *Zeal* had moved to the Duke of York's, where it played from 13 June to 2 July 1938.

the theological students is in rather a different category from the ordinary amateur show, and it might be possible to give him permission for what he wants, if you thought well. In any case, please treat him with peculiar tenderness, as he is some fantastic age, 84 or something![1] My company left on Saturday in a fighting spirit, and I think most of them will be ready to do the tour unless they get very tempting engagements in the meantime. The scenery and props have gone to the Westminster for storage, the costumes are with Frank Napier and the scripts will come to me, so that everything can be reassembled promptly when required.

I am hoping to get through all necessary work this month, so as to be able to take a holiday in August, so let us hope Guy Charles will be able to stimulate his managers. I have told him to arrange with you about the financial terms for himself.

Yours ever,
[D. L. S.]

1 Father Kelly was then 78 years old.

[24 Newland Street
Witham
Essex]

TO HENRY WADE[1]

11 July 1938

Dear Henry,

Don't bother about the Children's Hospital at Highbury unless you feel like it; what happened was, that this bloke wrote asking would I endow a cot to be named after me? I said I neither would nor could, but that if he was able to collect sufficient subscriptions from detective writers, I would contribute to a detective writers' cot. I also gave him a few names and addresses, saying that he might mention what I had said, but was not, on any account, to make himself a nuisance. I think a number of Club[2] members have contributed various sums from one guinea upwards, but there is absolutely no obligation on you, nor any special interest so far as I am concerned, other than the interest one has generally in children's hospitals.

I am so glad the family enjoyed the play; they were most sweet about it, and we had a merry tea with some of the actors afterwards.

Yours ever,
[D. L. S.]

1 Henry Wade (1887–1969), the pen-name of Major Sir Henry Aubrey-Fletcher, was an author of detective stories.
2 i.e. the Detection Club.

24 Newland Street
Witham
Essex

24 July 1938

Dearest Ivy,

I fear we are again faced with the bother of school outfits. I enclose list for Malvern. Will you cope and let me know the result.

Life has been strenuous as usual lately – culminating last week and the week before in a mild dose of flu followed by a small and foolish burglary at my flat.[1] Just as I had tottered back to sanity, I was obliged to spend a wearisome night interviewing the police. The men didn't get very much – only a camera and a few rugs and a pound or two in cash, and I'm insured – but it was a bore and a waste of time. I'm struggling now to get the arrangements through for a tour of *Zeal of Thy House* in September, before going to Venice on August 3. Hope you are all right – I'll send you my Venice address as soon as I know it.

Yours ever with love,
   Dorothy

---

1 An incident mentioned in her article "How Free is the Press?", first published in *World Review*, June 1941, later republished in *Unpopular Opinions*, Gollancz, 1946; see p. 130.

940 Calle Dei Frati
San Trovaso
Venice[1]

10 August 1938

Dear John,

I think your house[2] is No. 4; but I am not quite certain. I left all the particulars with my solicitor who is dealing with the business side of things while I am abroad. He could tell you for certain – his name is Mr C. Kelly, Hargrave, Son and Barrett, 24, John St., Bedford Row, W.C.1.

---

1 This was D. L. S.' second holiday in Venice. Once again she was accompanied by Marjorie Barber. By the time she returned she had written the play *Love All*, which is partly set in Venice.
2 John Anthony had won a scholarship to Malvern College. The reference is to the house to which he had been assigned.

I enclose your altogether admirable report for Aunt Ivy.

Having a pleasant time here. Venice is as beautiful as usual, but rather subject to thunderstorms at the moment. It is cooler than it was, but one feels pretty lazy all the same.

Glad you enjoy Eddington.[3] He isn't exactly easy reading, but he does end up with an attempt to deal with what you were speaking of – from how few assumptions one can build up a coherent universe.

I didn't have time before I left to look out the Dante[4] – so sorry. You shall have it for next term....[5]

3 Sir Arthur Stanley Eddington, O.M. (1882–1944), astronomer. John Anthony was probably reading *The Nature of the Physical World*, first published in 1928. He was then 14 years old.
4 Six years were to pass before D. L. S. began to read Dante herself. She was to bring Eddington and Dante together in an amusing dialogue in "Dante's Cosmos", a paper she read to the Royal Institution in 1951. (See *Further Papers on Dante*, Methuen, 1957, pp. 78–101.) She also mentions Eddington in *The Documents in the Case* and in the short story, "Absolutely Elsewhere", first published with the title "Impossible Alibi", in *Mystery*, vol. 9, no. 1, January 1934, later republished in *In the Teeth of the Evidence*, November 1939.
5 The letter is unsigned.

On 15 September 1938 John Dickson Carr wrote as follows:

...what do you think of having a genuine Viennese psychologist to talk to the Detection Club on murder? One has been unearthed...

[24 Newland Street
Witham
Essex]

TO JOHN ÐICKSON CARR
18 September 1938

Dear Mr. Carr,

I should think a genuine Viennese psychoanalyst would be very interesting, provided he was not embarrassingly earnest, if you know what I mean. That is to say, if he will set forth a thesis rather than preach a gospel! I may add that there is in me a devilish tendency to fight psychoanalysts whenever I may[1], though as far as I am concerned it ought to be great fun.

1 In an unpublished draft of notes for a *curriculum vitae*, undated but probably 1928, D. L. S. had listed under *Views*: "bored with Freudians, psycho-analysts, Russians and people who exploit adolescence".

Very many thanks again for honouring me with the dedication of *The Crooked Hinge*.[2] I look forward immensely to reading it, but then I always look forward to your books, dedication or no dedication.

With best wishes for a grand holiday,

    Yours ever,

        [Dorothy L. Sayers]

2 Published by Hamish Hamilton, 1938. The dedication reads: "To Dorothy L. Sayers in Friendship and Esteem".

24 Great James Street
W.C.1

TO THE EDITOR OF THE TIMES

24 September 1938[1]

"TROILUS AND CRESSIDA" AT THE WESTMINSTER

Sir,

    Your Dramatic Critic seems a little surprised to discover that *Troilus and Cressida* is a play about a war and not about a love affair. Modern-dress productions frequently have this merit of restoring the emphasis to the place where Shakespeare put it. The Greek swords and helmets of a period production distract attention from the actuality of the fighting; but one thing that strikes one in even a cursory reading of this most difficult work is that here is the great "war-debunking" play, whose savage bitterness has never been equalled before or since. Troilus is, indeed, a fool, with the pathetic folly of all young and generous spirits who idealize wantons. And Cressid, like the great wanton War, bestows her favours on the brute Diomedes, who demands and takes. If ever there was a play for the times it is this.

    Yours, &c.,

        Dorothy L. Sayers

1 The date of publication.

[24 Newland Street
Witham
Essex]

TO LADY FLORENCE CECIL

4 October 1938

Dear Lady Florence,

Forgive my delay in answering your letter; I have been very busy as you will realise when I tell you that the provincial tour¹ of *The Zeal of Thy House* opened last Monday week in Norwich in the very middle of the war scare.² We had three very upsetting financially disastrous days, after which things pulled themselves together a bit. I was in Norwich until Wednesday, and then had to come back to London to deal with the financial situation caused by all these alarms. Since I am, to some extent, involved in backing the tour, I am afraid I am not very flush of cash, but I have pleasure in sending a cheque for £3 for the Clergy's widows wishing that it could be more.

With kindest regards and all good wishes,
    Yours very sincerely,
        [Dorothy L. Sayers]

1 The tour of *Zeal*, with Harcourt Williams in the part of William of Sens, opened in September. John Hotchkiss directed the music. Cf. letter to her son, 6 November 1938.
2 See letter to Ivy Shrimpton, 6 November 1938, note 1.

[24 Newland Street
Witham
Essex]

TO MARGARET BABINGTON

25 October 1938

Dear Miss Babington,

It is rather difficult for me, at the moment, to say "Yes" or "No" to your very flattering request that I should again write the Canterbury play for you.¹ From the point of view of personal pleasure, nothing would delight me more; on the other hand, I have to bear in mind that these plays are

1 D. L. S. eventually said "Yes" and the play she wrote was *The Devil to Pay*, performed at Canterbury in 1939 and subsequently at His Majesty's Theatre that same year.

not a very lucrative business. I have, in fact, lost a good deal of money on taking *Zeal* to London, and I do not think I shall get it back on tour, since at the moment, it seems very difficult to get people to come and see plays on religion. On the other hand, if one does not take the play to London, it means putting in a vast amount of work and time for very small compensation, so that I should have to think it over carefully, and see whether I can afford it. Also, I hope you will forgive me if I once again draw attention to the amount of physical and mental suffering caused to the actors and myself by the acoustics of the Chapter House! They add greatly to the difficulty of writing the dialogue, and it is depressing for the actors to know that however well they act it is difficult to make themselves heard, and also (on account of the seats not being raked) difficult for them to be seen by a great part of the audience. If only something could be done to overcome these difficulties it would add greatly to my enthusiasm in setting about a new play.

Do believe me that I am not trying to be tiresome; I so greatly enjoyed my connection with Canterbury in 1937 that it is quite difficult for me not to say "Yes" at once, and let the practical considerations go hang. I am sure you will understand how I am placed. In the meantime, I will look through the literature about Archbishop Sudbury, and see how it appeals to me as a play.

I am very glad indeed you liked the articles, "The Greatest Drama Ever Staged" [etc.]; they have let me in for a terrible lot of correspondence with bishops and Baptist ministers, and an astonishing number of requests to address religious bodies and open flower shows!

I will write to you again when I have had time to think the matter of the play over.

With kindest regards to all my friends at Canterbury,

    Yours very sincerely,

      [Dorothy L. Sayers]

P.S. I shall be in London on Wednesday and Thursday, November 2nd and 3rd, and shall be free in the mornings if you could manage to come up for a talk, which perhaps would be the best way of getting the thing thrashed out.

[24 Newland Street
Witham
Essex]

TO VAL GIELGUD[1]

26 October 1938

Dear Mr Gielgud,

I have completed the draft of the Nativity play,[2] and enclose a copy for you to look at. I expect trouble from Mr. Iremonger's[3] end, on the score of levity, and this will probably be another of the occasions when your liking for lively comedy will conflict with the official caution! In my first interview with Mr. Iremonger, he did not seem very sure whether he wanted the play to last forty minutes or sixty minutes; in any case, some cuts can be made, and if necessary we can dispense with the Prologue. I thought it advisable to keep remarks made by the sacred personages to the minimum; after all, in the circumstances, there was not very much for them to say.

If, by any chance, we succeed in getting the play through, you will see that a certain amount of music will need to be composed:[4] (1) Melchior's song, "High upon the holy tree", this should be written in ballad style. (2) Song of the Legionaires: this is a marching song with one of those refrains, "Bread and cheese", which go on and on in march time "till ready". (3) Greek Gentleman's song, "Golden Apollo", this should be in the manner of an Elizabethan madrigal. (4) Jewish Gentleman's song, "Adam and Eve", this is one of those cumulative songs in the folk-song manner after the fashion of "The Tree in the Wood", in which two lines are added in every verse. (5) Angels' chorus, "Glory to God", anything you like. (6) Our Lady's carol presents no difficulties, being a plain carol melody.

I am looking forward to seeing you at four o'clock on Friday, and hope that by that time you and Mr. Iremonger will have got over the preliminary ground of the combat.

Yours very sincerely,
[Dorothy L. Sayers]

1 Val Gielgud (1900–1981), producer, brother of the actor Sir John Gielgud. This is the beginning of a happy collaboration with D. L. S. which led ultimately to his triumphant production of *The Man Born to be King*.
2 *He That Should Come*, broadcast on Christmas Day 1938 and first published in *Four Sacred Plays*, Gollancz, November 1939.
3 See following letter.
4 It was composed by Robert Chignell (1882–1939), who composed operas and many songs.

Portrait of Val Gielgud by Atherton Fleming

[24 Newland Street
Witham
Essex]

TO REV. DR F. A. IREMONGER[1]

26 October 1938

Dear Mr. Iremonger,

I enclose the Nativity play; it is probable that you will think it is too long, but no doubt we can make some cuts here and there, and if necessary, dispense with the Prologue.

I have treated the story realistically, and therefore, as I said over the telephone, there may be trouble from the pious, who prefer religion and reality kept in separate compartments. I feel, myself, that it is of some importance to get people to realize that the Gospel story was enacted against an ordinary human and political background. This means, of course, that for the other characters concerned, the events appeared of very trifling importance, whatever they may seem to us now. I have tried to sketch in the complicated political background in Judaea, and to make it plain that what was expected of the Messiah was that he should be a military dictator. The idea of a spiritual kingdom was, after all, not hammered into the minds, even of the Disciples, until after the Ascension, if the first chapter of Acts is to be trusted.

I shall be seeing Mr. Gielgud on Friday at four o'clock, and hope you will be able to join us . . . .

Trusting your bronchitis is better,
    Yours sincerely,
        [Dorothy L. Sayers]

---

1 The Director of Religious Broadcasting, B.B.C. (1878–1952). In 1939 he became Dean of Lichfield Cathedral and was succeeded at the B.B.C. by Dr James Welch.

[24 Newland Street
Witham
Essex]

TO NANCY PEARN

5 November 1938

Dear Bun,

I am passing on to you a number of things to turn down; I know you are already being firm, and I think we shall have to be quite firm even with the Bishop of Lichfield[1], but I should like you to write him a personal note, explaining that I really am obliged to cut out these evenings of public speaking, because it exhausts time and energy. He is a nice man, and I started to write to him myself, and then decided, perhaps, it would be better for you to do it, for you can put up a better and more pathetic story about the burdens on the flesh.

Would you say to the Women's Employment Federation that I refuse to be a patron of anything with which I am not intimately and personally connected; I am opposed to this whole business of patronage, which seems to me to be one of the most insincere ramps ever invented.

In reply to your letter, I think it would be an excellent thing for you and Dorothy Allen's office to get together in the matter of the subsidiary rights of the Nativity play; so far as I can make out, the correspondence as it stands leaves us in an excellent position with full control, and since the B.B.C. say they do not want a contract, they will probably find themselves left with the short end of the legal bargain. We do not want to stir them into making a contract, lest they should suddenly discover this fact! I think the best thing is to keep as quiet as possible until after the broadcast, lest the minds of the producer, the director of religion, the actors and myself be cast into confusion by the uproar of controversy raging about us. On the other hand, I am all for snatching any advantage we can get out of the thing, and we shall, of course, have to face this question of publication, both in serial and in book form, but I really do think the best way is for my two Agents to settle their plan of campaign between them. The date suggested for the play is either December 23rd or Christmas day; Christmas eve is held to be impossible, because listeners are too much engaged in doing their domestic stuff. Val Gielgud wants Christmas day, and I agree with him, and he is fighting the governors for us.

As regards "Thrones, Dominations" – I cannot tell you anything yet; the fact is that I have taken a dislike to the story, and have great difficulty in doing anything about it.

Yours ever,

[D. L. S.]

---

1 Rt Rev. Edward Sydney Woods, (1877–1953) who was Bishop of Lichfield also when *The Just Vengeance* was performed there in June 1946.

24 Newland Street
Witham
Essex

TO IVY SHRIMPTON

6 November 1938

Dearest Ivy,

Here you are – I'm so sorry to have been all this long time. I've been dashing about all over the place, coping with the tour of *Zeal*, which was very nearly killed off dead by the crisis.[1] We opened at Norwich in the crisis week, and with that and the next week lost practically every penny we had, before things began to pull themselves together. Fortunately I was able to get another backer in, and matters are a bit more cheerful now. But the whole thing was so depressing and unnerving, never knowing what was going to happen at any minute – whether all my actors would be called up, or only some of them, whether theatres were expected to close or stay open, and, worst of all, whether, when the crisis had blown over, we shouldn't get a fresh series of crises to upset everything further. There were moments when one would positively have welcomed a war as being a definite decision. However, London seems a bit quieter in its mind at the moment – but for these weeks after the crisis itself, everybody was so played out and on edge that it seemed absolutely impossible to settle down to work.

John seems pretty cheerful at Malvern – everybody has to face the change from top-dog to bottom-dog some time. Congratulations on Rosemary's success.[2] Your youngsters always seem to do well.

Mac is much the same as usual. Aunt Maud is in Ireland with Margaret[3] – of all dreary times of the year for an old lady to go trotting off to that damp hole. But apparently Margaret has taken it into her head that Ireland is the one spot in which she can finish a book. She has given up the Cornish farm, I believe, and what comes next I know not – nor does anybody, so far as I can make out. I saw her in London with

1 Known as the Munich crisis. Following Hitler's demands that Czechoslovakia should cede the Sudeten territories, Neville Chamberlain, then Prime Minister, flew three times to Germany in an attempt to prevent war. There was general expectation that war would be declared but on 30 September the Munich agreement was signed, which conceded almost all Hitler's demands and left Czechoslovakia defenceless. The Sudeten territories were seized and in March 1939 Germany occupied the rest of Czechoslovakia. Military conscription in the U.K. was introduced in April and preparations for war began. Gas-masks were issued to the civilian population; volunteers filled sand-bags and dug trenches in Hyde Park and elsewhere.

2 Another child fostered by Ivy Shrimpton, who had won a scholarship to a grammar school.

3 Margaret Leigh (1894–1973), D. L. S.' cousin and contemporary at Somerville.

Aunt Maud, looking rather thin and tired.

I don't think I've written to you since seeing Kenneth Logan and his wife. I rather liked her – K. seemed to me a fairly dull sort of hearty. However, I asked them to a theatrical party, and gave them dinner and tickets for *Zeal*, and they expressed themselves as pleased with their entertainment.

Very glad to hear that Mrs. Spiller is better after her operation. She is a good soul.

I'm all right, but dreadfully tired with rushing about speaking at all kinds of places. I think I'm getting too old for this kind of thing – and what is the good of it? The passion people have for hearing speeches is quite beyond me!

Best love and heartfelt thanks,
    Dorothy

24 Newland Street.
Witham
Essex

TO HER SON
6 November 1938

Dear John,

Many thanks for your two letters, which I was very glad to get, though you mightn't think so from the time I have taken to answer. Curse this pen – I'll try another.

Glad you seem to be settling down pretty well at Malvern. It's quite all right about the Fives equipment. It won't really blow me out of the water, though your guess about a theatre co. having gone pop came painfully near the truth! Still, we're not in such straits that eight shillings and sixpence will either make or mar us. Actually, we did have an awful time during the crisis. We opened our tour[1] at Norwich the very week that the whole affair pooped off, and of course business was killed stone dead. The second week we played Southport, and then, as though Hitler & co. weren't trouble enough, the Lord saw fit to afflict us with a record gale and a flood on the Monday night that laid the street in which the theatre stands axle-deep in water for 200 yards. Our leading man[2] took off his shoes and socks and paddled in! The audience (with some excuse) mostly

---

1 Of *The Zeal of Thy House*, in association with the Religious Drama Society.
2 Harcourt Williams.

stayed at home. Those two weeks ate up all our reserve funds, and we were afraid we should have to pack up altogether, since I certainly couldn't afford to put in any more money. However, by great good fortune we succeeded in getting hold of a kindly backer, and have since played to good business at Newcastle and Brighton and rather less good at Southsea. So we hope for the best and are in any case carrying on till just before Christmas.

The beastly thing about the crisis was not knowing what one was expected to do in case anything did happen. I wish to goodness they would get on with the blooming National Register and get these matters clear. You can't think how jolly it is to be more or less in charge of 40 people, of whom over 30 are men, and not know whether one is supposed to carry on or stop, whether one's men will all be called up, or only some of them, or when, and whether one is to report one's self where, or for what, when! However, things do seem a little calmer now, if only some other botheration doesn't boil up in the next few weeks. I think anyhow it's time we stopped making ugly faces at Germany and calling rude names. There are only two safe ways of dealing with people whose goings-on one doesn't like – one is to try and see their point of view and straighten matters out; and the other is to hit them extremely hard on the head and stop them. The fatal thing, which we've been doing for years, is to say "Oh-you-nasty-horrid-wicked-man-if-you-do-that-again-I'll-hit-you", and not hit them. Actually, I think the Germans were abominably treated at Versailles and afterwards – not so much by anybody's fault as by stupidity and being afraid to do the right thing – and have been driven into a sort of psychological persecution-mania from which they can only be coaxed by sweet reasonableness; only we've put it off so damned late. There's a book you ought to read, if you haven't already, by E. Wingfield-Stratford, called "The Harvest of Victory",[3] which shows better than anything I know just how we came to involve ourselves and each other in this ghastly muddle. I'll try and get a copy in London and send it down to you. I think you would like it, because it is written with great fairness, and doesn't try to solve the whole complicated question by just blaming one set of people, or shouting slogans about democracy or civilisation and that sort of thing.

How is the Baruka?[4] I never heard of it before, but I'll take your word for it! I hope it is better, anyway.

With love and best wishes,
Mother

---

3 Esmé Cecil Wingfield-Stratford, *The Harvest of Victory: 1918–26*, 1935.
4 This must be a mistake for verruca, a contagious wart-like growth, caught at swimming pools and other public places.

In November 1938, in order to raise money to help the tour of The Zeal of Thy House, *D. L. S. lent her name to an advertisement for Horlicks Malted Milk. The editor of* The Times *commented humorously in the fourth leader on 21 November:*

There can be few people nowadays who are not conversant with the perils of Night Starvation. The format and technique of advertisements in which these and other perils are graphically set forth are almost as firmly established, and much more widely apprehended, than the structure of a sonnet.

In the esteem of large sections of the populace these advertisements hold a high place; and their devotees have been electrified by the appearances of the latest of the series under the title "Tight-Rope: a true-life story told by Dorothy L. Sayers"... and in literary circles there has been much praise for the skill with which the gifted creatrix of Lord Peter has adapted herself to a new and special medium. A certain disappointment, it is true, has been caused by the fact that Lord Peter himself does not figure in her latest *tour de force*, which is concerned with a Mr and Mrs Bob Brown. Noblemen, so far as is known, are not immune from night starvation and often wake up tired....

To this D. L. S. replied as follows:

> [24 Newland Street
> Witham
> Essex]

TO THE EDITOR OF THE TIMES

22 November 1938

Dear Sir,

My attention has been drawn to your leader of yesterday, "Whither Wimsey?" You are curiously out-of-date in your information if you suppose that this is the first time that either Peter Wimsey or myself have been connected with the advertising profession. Peter was himself an advertising copy-writer for a short time with the firm of "Pym's Publicity" – (is it not written in the book called "Murder Must Advertise"?), while I for nine years held a similar position with Messrs. S. H. Benson, Limited.

I heartily agree that the style of advertisement in question is not up to Peter's standard or mine – but then, the advertisers refused to make use of the elegant copy I prepared for them and re-wrote it according to their own notion of what was fitting. This is what invariably happens to copy-writers.

It may be of interest if I add that I undertook this advertising job when a small amount of capital was needed to finance the provincial tour of my play *The Zeal of Thy House*, and I had already invested in it as much as I could justifiably contribute from my revenue as a writer. Since no assistance was forthcoming from the Church for a play written and performed for her honour, I unblushingly soaked Mammon for what I could get in that quarter. *Et laudavit Dominus villicum iniquitatis.*[1]

Yours faithfully,

[Dorothy L. Sayers]

---

1 And the Lord commended the unjust steward (Luke, chapter 16, verse 8).

[24 Newland Street
Witham
Essex]

TO JOHN DICKSON CARR
22 November 1938

Dear Mr. Carr,

Thank you so much for your letter. I did not see the paragraph in question, but it would be just as well to have it corrected, since a very odd thing happened about *Gaudy Night*. I invented both parts of the plot off my own bat: (a) There were the disturbances in College. No sooner had I started about these, than St. Hilda's at Oxford promptly started on a series of poltergeist shocks played by some of the students, and I spent my time altering the book as I went to avoid reproducing any of the actual facts. (b) There was the story of the man who had falsified something in a thesis, and been deprived of his doctorate and degrees through the action of a woman scholar. Having invented this situation, I wrote to one of the Somerville dons to ask whether such a thing could possibly occur; she replied that it not only could occur but had occurred in Dublin, and gave me the names of the man and woman concerned, and the result was that I had to alter the plot again so as to avoid coming too close to the facts, which just shows how closely, as Oscar Wilde pointed out, "Nature copies art". So that under the circumstances, it is just as well that the reporter should be made to eat his words, though I do not blame you in the least, since I know that reporters will always put down the precise opposite of what one has said if they can think of it quickly enough. Curse the whole race of them!...

Yours ever,

[Dorothy L. Sayers]

24 Newland Street
Witham
Essex

TO R. A. SCOTT-JAMES[1]
22 November 1938

Dear Mr. Scott-James,
 Please forgive my long delay in acknowledging your very kind letter
about *The Zeal of Thy House*, which gave great pleasure to myself and to
my Company. We are particularly pleased by what you say about the way
in which we all work together in the spirit of the play. Having seen the
show right through at every stage from its first beginnings at Canterbury,
I know better than anyone how astonishingly that original spirit has been
maintained through the various professional productions in London and
on tour, and I attribute it chiefly to Harcourt Williams and Frank Napier,
who have been with us all the time as actors and producers and have
never allowed the thing to get out of shape. We have been trying very
hard to get back to London for a series of Christmas matinées, but it is
very difficult to get managers interested, though I still have one faint hope
that something may be done about it.
 It is sad that the National theatre[2] will not be built in time; I do feel that
there is need of an endowed theatre where this kind of play can get a
showing. As you doubtless know, the great difficulty is the reluctance of
commercial managers to take a courageous line with serious plays that
need nursing and, of course, the reluctance of the public to come to anything which looks like doing them good or making them think, even
though they may like it very much when they do get there. Anyhow,
believe me that I am deeply gratified by the kind things you have said
about the show.
 Yours very truly,
  Dorothy L. Sayers

---

1 R. A. Scott-James, O.B.E., M.C. (1878–1959), author, editor and literary critic.
2 As a schoolgirl D. L. S. discussed the need for a National Theatre with her friend Molly
 Edmondson. (See letter to her mother, 19 June 1910, *The Letters of Dorothy L. Sayers: 1899–1936*,
 p. 46.)

On 26 November 1938, The Times published the following letter from H.E. Cainan:

WHITHER WIMSEY?

Sir – Miss Dorothy L. Sayers mildly remarks that certain advertisers rewrote her elegant copy. Have you done it again? Or does her elegant copy sometimes need rewriting?

"Et laudavit Dominus villicum iniquitatis"! Not a bit of it! "Laudavit dominus villicum iniquitatis", please. The words were spoken by the "Dominus". And He was speaking of the steward's employer. See the context.

Miss Sayers will surely repudiate such a bad example....

To which D. L. S. replied:

> [24 Newland Street
> Witham
> Essex]

TO THE EDITOR OF THE TIMES

28 November 1938

Dear Sir,

ET LAUDAVIT DOMINUS[1]

Alas! it was the Dominus Himself who identified Himself with the dominus. "*And* I say unto you, Make to yourselves friends . . . . ." The word is "and" – though I have heard it misquoted as "but" by an agitated child of light, who sought thus to darken a counsel unexpected and possibly unwelcome.

Yours faithfully,
   [Dorothy L. Sayers]

---

1 The words in the Vulgate are as quoted by D. L. S.

24 Newland Street
Witham
Essex

10 December 1938

Dear John –

"Rich be thy habit as thy purse can buy, but not displayed in fancy –
neat, not gaudy."[1] All right, but use a suitable discretion in the purchase.

Glad to hear all your news, and know that things are going well and you
find life interesting. I gather – was it from you or from Aunt Ivy, I haven't
the letter handy – that your English style finds more favour at Malvern
than it did at Broadstairs. A little tendency to the ornate in early years is
one which time corrects, and is not a bad symptom in itself. At any rate,
I suffered from similar criticisms, but the result has not been so bad in the
end.

I haven't forgotten *The Harvest of Victory*,[2] but they had run out of copies
at the Times Book Club. I'll try Smith's when I'm back in Town.

Love.
        Mother

1 The quotation from *Hamlet*, I, 3, echoed here, is: "Costly thy habit as thy purse can buy,\ But
   not express'd in fancy; rich, not gaudy".
2 See letter to John Anthony, 6 November 1938.

[24 Newland Street
Witham
Essex]

12 December 1938

Dear Mr. Waldman,

It was most delightful to get a letter from you, and I hope you will forgive my not having answered it earlier; I was away from home dashing
about in hotels and had not the leisure to deal with it properly at the time.
As a matter of interest I should be most delighted to hear the facts about
the Elizabethan spy murder, though I would not, with my very small historical knowledge, very readily undertake the task of embodying it in a
Chronicle. You are perfectly right in supposing that there was a Wimsey
among Walsingham's young men; he was one of the innumerable sons of

1 Milton Waldman (1895–1976), American-born author and publisher.

the Elizabethan duke, whose family rapacity was so wittily rebuked by the Queen (see a hitherto entirely unedited paragraph of Harington)[2]. There has always been a certain strain of detective talent in the Wimsey family; witness Duke Peregrine, who, in the reign of Charles II, boldly undertook the defence of a pair of Norfolk witches and triumphantly secured their acquittal, not without a certain amount of peril to himself. He was an early Fellow of the Royal Society, and did some useful investigations into the action of arsenic; his adventures I propose to write some day, if I can find the time and the ability. I am most anxious to hear more about the Elizabethan one; it may have been Piers, who was a son of the first wife, or one of the two hopelessly indistinguishable Jocelyns! or even the mysterious Nicholas, whose existence is only attested by a mutilated brass in Duke's Denver Church. What with the duke's many wives and his wives' many husbands and the inextricable confusion in which their separate and combined families have involved the genealogical trees of that period, even Cousin Matthew[3] is at the moment totally unable to say definitely which Wimsey was which, and would be immensely grateful for any light on the subject.

May I take this opportunity of saying what I have always wanted to say, of the enormous delight I have had from your books, especially the two about Elizabeth.[4] They are among the books which I read and re-read for sheer delight.

With many thanks, and hoping to hear more from you about this most exciting Wimsey episode.

Yours sincerely,

[Dorothy L. Sayers]

P.S.

It is quite true that there have been sixteen Dukes of Denver; the duchy is an old one, taking seniority after Norfolk. I have some of the early genealogy worked out, and shall be happy to show it to you at any time. The first Duke (not the third, as Peter inaccurately says in one passage) was that notorious "cat's paw", who was a friend of Warwick the King-maker and of whom it was said:

> "When the cat sits on the bear's shoulder
> Craft doth make treason bolder."[5]

2 Sir John Harington (?1560–1612), translator of Ariosto's *Orlando Furioso*. The reference is an example of the spoof historicity which D. L. S. so much enjoyed.
3 See *Busman's Honeymoon*, "Epithalamion, 2".
4 Probably *King, Queen, Jack: Philip of Spain Courts Elizabeth*, 1931 and *Elizabeth, Queen of England*, 1933.
5 See letter to Wilfrid Scott-Giles, 18 February 1936, *The Letters of Dorothy L. Sayers: 1899–1936*, pp. 368–369.

1939

The crisis of war

c/oc/oc/o

[24 Newland Street
Witham
Essex]

TO VAL GIELGUD

2 January 1939

Dear Val Gielgud,
    How is the British public re-acting to the show?[1] Has the B.B.C. been buried under a shower of brick-bats? I have received a dozen or so bouquets, and enclose the relevant portions of those which might interest you. I am particularly pleased by the letter from Mr. John Rhode[2] (the detective writer) describing the effect on his village audience, and I like also the one from the vicarage family, who have previously suffered from Nativity plays!
    May I again say how very much I appreciate the fine cast and production you gave me, and the sympathy and patience which you extended to the author.
    With best wishes for the New Year,
        Yours very sincerely,
            [Dorothy L. Sayers]

---

1 The Nativity play, *He That Should Come*, which had been broadcast on radio on Christmas day.
2 See letter to John Dickson Carr, 3 March 1937, note 2.

[24 Newland Street
Witham
Essex]

TO JOHN RHODE[1]

2 January 1939

Dear John Rhode,

Thank you so much for your letter; it was very kind of you to write. I am very glad you enjoyed the Nativity play, and also that it had the effect you described on your pub audience. I was particularly pleased to hear this, because I had a mild struggle with the gentleman at the B.B.C.[2] who is humorously described as the Director of Religion, and had told him in almost the very words of your village elder that I felt it important to get people to believe that the characters in the Bible were real people like ourselves, and not just "sacred Personages" apart from common humanity. So it was extremely gratifying to hear that in one case at least the desired effect had come off.

With best wishes to you both for the New Year, and again many thanks,
Yours very sincerely,
[Dorothy L. Sayers]

1 See letter to John Dickson Carr, 3 March 1937, note 2.
2 The Rev. Dr F. A. Iremonger. See letter to him, 26 October 1938.

[24 Newland Street
Witham
Essex]

TO THE EDITOR OF THE GLASGOW HERALD

2 January 1939

Dear Sir,

In his very kind notice of my broadcast play, *He That Should Come*, your critic "A. P. S." makes especially favourable mention of Robert Adams[1] in the role of Balthazar; "the little Irish lilt in his voice being", he says, "for no apparent reason in perfect keeping with the part of an Ethiopian monarch". He will, I think, be interested to have this little mystery explained and the reason made apparent. Mr. Adams is, in fact, not an Irishman but a man of colour, and what your critic's ear, with so sure an

1 Robert Adams, b.1906, in British Guiana. His early films included *Sanders of the River* and *King Solomon's Mines*.

instinct, seized upon and recognised as appropriate, was the very beautiful and characteristic quality of a genuine negro voice. I am greatly indebted to Mr. Val Gielgud, the producer, for the great care and trouble he took in the casting, and, in this particular instance, for giving me "the real thing", and I am very glad that the excellence of Mr. Adams's performance in this small part should have received the praise it deserved.

I am, Sir,
    Yours faithfully,
        [Dorothy L. Sayers]

> [24 Newland Street
> Witham
> Essex]

TO DOROTHY ALLEN

2 January 1939

Dear Dorothy...

It seems to be now definitely agreed that the tour of *Zeal* is to start on February 6th, [and] letters have been sent out to that effect. We have had a period of alarm over the weekend, due to the fact that Ben[n] Levy[1] had offered Billie Williams[2] a magnificent part in London, and Billie Williams had got agitated owing to the fact that the tour dates were not settled; the excitement has now, however, died down, and Billie is with us. You should have heard me being managerial and firm to Mr. Levy on the phone.

I have had quite a number of fan letters about *He That Should Come*, many of them saying that they hope to see the play either in print, on the stage or broadcast again. I have decided not to print the broadcast version, but to wait until I can find time to make a stage adaptation when we can print that.[3] We seem to have got away with it all right in the Press. For next Christmas it would be, I think, a good thing to get into touch with some of the American broadcasting companies and see if there is any chance of getting a good broadcast over there.

I am coming up to Town on the 5th, so that if I am needed for anything, I shall be available.

With best wishes,
    Yours ever,
        [Dorothy L. Sayers]

---

1 Benn Wolfe Levy (1900–1973), playwright.   2 i.e. Harcourt Williams.

3 She did so and the stage version was included in *Four Sacred Plays*, Gollancz, 1948.

Ever since the production of The Zeal of Thy House *and the publication of her articles "The Greatest Drama Ever Staged", "The Dogma is the Drama" and "The Triumph of Easter", religious bodies had been seeking D. L. S.' help. One of these was the Church Social Action Group, who set themselves to keep a watch on newspapers and journals in order to seize opportunities of combating anti-Christian views. D. L. S. agreed to help them and was assigned the task of keeping an eye on* John o' London's Weekly.[1] *Her first action was to challenge an article by Professor Julian Huxley entitled "Life Can be Worth Living".*

1 The journal ceased its independent existence in 1962, becoming incorporated with *Time and Tide*, which itself ceased to exist in 1986.

[24 Newland Street
Witham
Essex]

TO THE EDITOR OF JOHN O'LONDON'S WEEKLY

2 January 1939

Dear Sir,

PROFESSOR HUXLEY'S ARTICLE

One ought not, perhaps, to expect a scientist to be a logician; nevertheless, it is a little surprising to find Professor Huxley[1] committing himself to the pronouncement: "Even if a god does exist behind and above the universe as we experience it, we can have no knowledge of such a power." This kind of reasoning is known as *petitio principii*, or "begging the question" – that is, it assumes in advance the truth of the very conclusion it sets out to prove.

The statement makes, in fact, a double assumption: first, that if God exists, He does so only "behind and above" the universe of human experience, and not also within it – a premise which no Christian theologian would accept for a moment. This highly disputable assumption forms the basis for another, namely: that in whatever mode God exists, man can have no knowledge of Him. Here we have one of those universal negatives that are so notoriously awkward to prove.

Professor Huxley is perfectly entitled to rebut evidence as to God's existence, or man's knowledge by any arguments that may seem good to him, but not to sweep the whole matter out of court by an assertion which, however confidently advanced as a self-evident proposition, is, in fact, no more than an expression of personal opinion.

Yours faithfully,
[Dorothy L. Sayers]

1 Sir Julian Huxley (1887–1975), biologist and writer, brother of the novelist Aldous Huxley.

[24 Newland Street
Witham
Essex]

TO MARGARET BABINGTON

3 January 1939

Dear Miss Babington,

Thank you so much for your beautiful little book, which is one of the most charming series of drawings I have ever seen. Thank you, also, for your letter; I am very glad indeed to hear that the acoustics of the Chapter House are being firmly tackled, it will make a very great difference to the comfort of the actors if something can be done about it. I believe Mr. Williams is going to approach you in any case, to see whether it is possible to get the use of a room for some of the early rehearsals, as it is easier for the actors to get together in the comedy parts in a smaller space where they are not swamped, so to speak, by their surroundings.

I am getting on as fast as possible with *Faustus*,[1] but have been held up very much by the work necessary on the broadcast Christmas play; as soon as I have anything ready, I will send it along to you.

With best wishes for the New Year,

Yours very sincerely,
    [Dorothy L. Sayers]

1 Her second play for Canterbury, later entitled "The Devil to Pay". Among other titles she considered were "Pact with the Devil", "The Devil's Bargain", "Dr Cheat-the-Devil", "The Sale of a Soul", "Seller of Souls".

On 28 December 1938 J. D. S. Hunt of the Amalgamated Press Ltd wrote to inform D. L. S. that the B.B.C. intended to include Sexton Blake[1] in a new programme at the end of January. To coincide with the first week of this broadcast, he planned to bring out a special issue of The Detective Weekly[2] *in which Blake was to feature. He asked D. L. S. if she would send a few lines for publication.*

[24 Newland Street
Witham
Essex]

TO J. D. S. HUNT
3 January 1939

Dear Sir,

In reply to your letter, I am hoping to send Sexton Blake my cordial good wishes for a prolonged and successful career. I enjoyed his adventures greatly in my childhood, and even at a very much later age might have been found a little sheepishly demanding his latest adventure from the local newspaper shop. You may remember that when I published the short adventure of Sexton Blake in the *Evening Standard* series of Great Detective Stories, I wrote a brief introduction,[3] which sums up what in a more serious and scholarly manner I might have to say about this. I enclose a copy of this, and if the *Evening Standard* has no objection, you might like to reproduce it in your special issue.

Yours faithfully,
[Dorothy L. Sayers]

1 The stories about Sexton Blake, over 3500, were written by a syndicate of nearly 200 authors. The first story, "The Missing Millionaire", by Harry Blythe (1852–1898, pseudonym Hal Meredith), appeared in December 1893 in a boys' weekly paper, *The Halfpenny Marvel*, launched by Harmsworth the previous month. *The Union Jack*, another Harmsworth weekly for boys, which lasted from 1894 to 1933, carried many other Sexton Blake stories, as did other magazines. In 1915 the Sexton Blake Library initiated a full-length novel, published in instalments, between 1915 and 1925. The last novel, *Sexton Blake and the Demon God*, was published in 1978.

2 This journal has not been traced.

3 A feature entitled "Detective Cavalcade", consisting of a daily series of detective stories, edited by D. L. S., ran from 29 July to 1 September 1936. No story by Sexton Blake was included.

[24 Newland Street
Witham
Essex]

TO R. STOKES[1]

3 January 1939

Dear Mr. Stokes,

I fear I have been rather late, owing to pressure of work, in coping with Professor Julian Huxley's article in the Christmas number of *John o' London's Weekly*, which I enclose in case you have not seen it. I have, however, despatched the enclosed letter, which I hope they will print; I was careful not to enter into argument with Professor Huxley, thinking it better to point out the monstrous assumption made in the marked paragraph and leave it at that. It is, I fear, precisely these *obiter dicta*[2] of scientists, which are dangerous to the uneducated mind, since they insidiously take for granted propositions which never have formed part of orthodox doctrine, and then proceed to refute them with a remarkable air of plausibility.

I suggest that it would now be a good thing for someone to pounce on the interesting statement made on December 23rd by "Enquiring Layman", that old-fashioned orthodoxy was bankrupt long ago, and ask what precisely he means, if anything, by old-fashioned orthodoxy. These are the wounds with which we are wounded in the house of our friends. It is, at any rate, a statement which again takes a great deal for granted, and one would like to know what. I must leave "Enquiring Layman" to you, since I cannot write a second letter; a vigorous high-Churchman with a sense of humour would probably tackle it best.

Yours faithfully,

[Dorothy L. Sayers]

1 A member of the Church Social Action Group.
2 Latin: things said incidentally.

as from 24 Newland Street
Witham
Essex

TO HER SON

8 January 1939

Dear John,

Your question is a complicated one; and that is why I have had to take a little time to answer it.

First of all, this question of being "really" a mathematician, writer, or what not.

I imagine that what both you and Mr Cosgrove mean by "real" is what I prefer to call "creative". There are creative mathematicians, who are mentally as much unlike the merely clever worker in figures as the great musical composers are unlike the brilliant executants. In the same way, the true creative writer is quite unlike the man of letters, whose talent is critical or interpretative.

Of one thing you can be sure: if you are a creator in any particular medium, you will end by discovering the fact. Nothing can prevent the genuine creator from creating or from creating in his own proper medium. All that education can do is to make matters more or less easy for him. If, by somebody's mistake, he gets started off with the wrong equipment, or shoved into the wrong job, he will (if he has the essential guts of the creative artist) eventually equip himself and get himself out into the right job, but he may waste a lot of time and energy by the way.

On the other hand, you may quite possibly not be creative in that irresistible and self-determining way; you may be only a brilliant executant in one form or other. In that case, it is much more important that you should start off in the right direction, because you will have less power to put yourself right again.

In any case, I agree entirely with Mr Cosgrove that the pursuit of mathematics, or indeed of any pure science, is deadening and narrowing to the mind, unless contact is kept up with the "humanities". I don't mean this merely from the point of view of personal relationships. The thing that (in my opinion) tends to hamper the work of scientists in these days, and to diminish its value, is that they tend to work in isolation from the general body of thought. At present, those scientists who try to relate their work to a comprehensive scheme of philosophy are distrusted, both by philosophers and by their fellow-scientists. The reason, I think, for this unfortunate state of things is, precisely, that they are too strictly specialised; so that the philosophic side of their work is amateurish and bad. I believe there will be a reaction, in the next few generations, to a synthesis of science and philosophy,[1] which will help to correct the present disjunction of these two activities.

On the other hand, I agree with you that it is going to be far easier for you to study the humanities on your own than mathematics on your own – from the purely practical point of view, that is. If it is possible to keep both sides of the thing working together for a little longer, the time will –

---

1 Such as, for example A. R. Peacocke, *Creation and the World of Science: The Bampton Lectures, 1978* (Clarendon Press, Oxford, 1979).

or should – shortly arrive when you will know without question which is the right side for you to come out on.

There is also, of course, the very mundane question, whether there is better opportunity for getting a job in the one subject or the other. This is a particularly important point if you should turn out not to be creative. I should not advise anyone to "go in for literature" if he is not to some extent creative.

I doubt whether I shall be able to see Mr Cosgrove in Town this week; but he shall be written to, at any rate.

Thank you very much for your Christmas present, which is very pretty and will come in most useful.

With love and best wishes,
  Mother

On 6 January 1939 the Manchester Guardian *published an item under "Our London Correspondence Column" taking D. L. S. to task for using the phrase "words are actually a kind of high explosive" in the course of a talk she gave at a Conference of Educational Associations on the careless and inaccurate use of English in newspapers. This was followed on 13 January by a paragraph entitled "She ought to know better". D. L. S. replied as follows:*

    [24 Newland Street
    Witham
    Essex]

TO THE EDITOR OF THE GUARDIAN

15 January 1939

Dear Sir,

The writer of the paragraph "She Ought to Know Better" in your issue of January 13th. seems to be a little confused in his mind. There is nothing whatever to prevent one from saying "Words are actually a kind of high explosive". The "kind" in question is, of course, a mental kind, and the whole expression figurative. The word "actually" means "in actual fact; really" (see O.E.D.),[1] and its antonym is "supposedly".

Similarly, one may say, if one is so minded, "Religion is actually a kind of opiate" – the implication being, "and not, as you seem to suppose, a valuable mental stimulant".

---

1 *Oxford English Dictionary.*

What one may not say is: "Words are literally trinitrotoluol" or, "Religion is literally morphia". These expressions would be incorrect, since the word "literally" specifically excludes a figurative interpretation, as the word "actually" does not, even where the metaphorical nature of the phrase is not further pointed by the use of the words "a kind of".

Yours faithfully,

[Dorothy L. Sayers]

[24 Newland Street
Witham
Essex]

TO VAL GIELGUD

16 January 1939

Dear Val Gielgud,

Thank you ever so much for your letter; I am so glad you enjoyed working on the show. I shall be delighted to come some time to talk over fresh plans. At present I have no engagements to take me to Town until the 25th of this month when we start rehearsals for the *Zeal* tour. I shall be free all day on Friday the 27th and the following week I shall be there every day, though I expect lunch time will be an affair of a hasty chop in Baker Street between the morning and afternoon calls. However, I expect we can fix up something if you are free at any time during that period.

After I had written to you I received a great bunch of letters forwarded by the B.B.C., all favourable; I am having some of these copied for American propaganda, so that if you would like to see them they will be available. The half-wits and hysterics seem to have left me alone and concentrated on you, praise God!

Yours very sincerely,

[Dorothy L. Sayers]

[24 Newland Street
Witham
Essex]

TO VAL GIELGUD

20 January 1939

Dear Val Gielgud,

Many thanks for your letter; I shall be delighted to lunch with you one day during my rehearsal; shall we say Wednesday, if that would suit you?

We usually finish rehearsal about one o'clock. We shall be at the Portman Arms in Baker Street, so if you could suggest a meeting-place at some point between there and Langham Place it would be easier for me than getting down to Soho. How about Pagani's in Great Portland Street? Perhaps I should warn you that I am a little apt in the heat of rehearsal to forget other engagements, so that it might be as well if your secretary would kindly send me a reminding postcard to reach me at Great James Street on that morning!

People are still writing about *He That Should Come*, and I have now had one disgruntled letter from an agitated old lady; but as she is the only one out of about thirty-three, I think I may take it that the protests represent no more than three per cent of the listening population.

Looking forward to seeing you,
    Yours very sincerely,
        [Dorothy L. Sayers]

                                        [24 Newland Street
                                        Witham
                                        Essex]

TO G. C. PIPER[1]

24 January 1939

My dear Sir,
    Nothing would induce me to "set down my religious beliefs and convictions". Setting down what I understand to be the Church's beliefs and convictions is a different matter; but in any case the place for the novelist is not in the pulpit, and if anybody asked me to preach in St. Martin-in-the-Fields, I should promptly refuse.[2]
    Yours faithfully,
        [Dorothy L. Sayers]

---

1 Of Messrs Skeffington and Son, Ltd., Publishers.
2 But see her letter to Muriel St Clare Byrne, 11 February 1942, in which she says that she has just arrived from delivering a sermon in St Martin-in-the-Fields!

A. H. Sleight, Editor of Modern Languages, *the journal published by the Modern Language Association, of which D. L. S. was President, asked her to let him have a copy of her Presidential Address in a form in which she would wish it to appear in the journal. She replied:*

[24 Newland Street
Witham
Essex]

TO A. H. SLEIGHT

24 January 1939

My dear Sir,

I weep for you, the Walrus said, I deeply sympathise,¹ but I'm afraid you have about as much chance of getting that address as a snowball in Hades!

I start rehearsals tomorrow for the Spring Tour of *Zeal of Thy House*, which opens at Wimbledon on February 6th. As soon as that is off my mind, I shall have to work full-time on my new play for Canterbury, which is already badly in arrears. I simply cannot spare the time to do all over again a job that is done and dismissed from my mind. I am afraid you will have to fall back on the *Times* report,² which is probably more or less accurate so far as it goes.

Speaking in public is one thing, and the reading of papers is another. The extraordinary modern habit of writing out public speeches in extenso and reading them from the platform accounts for the dreary level to which public speaking has fallen, and also for the badness and slackness of present-day reporting. Upon my soul, I don't know why speeches should be delivered at all, if they are to consist of written papers, which might just as well be multigraphed and handed round, to the great saving of the audience's time and convenience. To save my life, I couldn't recap-

---

1 Quotation from Lewis Carroll, *Through the Looking-Glass and What Alice Found There.*
2 In the issue of March 1939 of *Modern Languages*, p. 7, the editor wrote: "Our readers will notice the omission of the Presidential address from this number, but Miss Sayers spoke from notes only, and owing to the pressure of work in attending rehearsals of her plays at Wimbledon and Canterbury, and in fulfilling similar demands upon her energies, our new President has not been able to send us the full written address. We hope, however, to include the address in the June number but cannot be certain of doing so." Alas, the hope was not fulfilled. The address, given on 5 January 1939 and entitled "The Dictatorship of Words", was reported in *The Times* of the following day, p. 7. She took the opportunity to attack propaganda, which had made possible "Germany's bloodless conquest in Austria and the Sudetenland", and expressed her opposition to the muzzling of the Press.

ture the rhythm of the spoken word – and as for turning the thing into a printed essay, it would need a week's work.

I'm sorry – but things should be reported as spoken, or left to the happy oblivion that enfolds – thank God! – the ephemeral utterances of the human voice.

I don't blame you for not having the stuff reported. The same thing happens continually. Newspaper-men besiege me to hand them speeches before they are delivered, and flatly refuse to believe that the "speech" is represented by a dozen headings on a half-sheet of paper. Such are the times we live in.

Yours sympathetically,
    [Dorothy L. Sayers]

                                        [24 Newland Street
                                        Witham
                                        Essex]

TO THE BISHOP OF NOTTINGHAM[1]

25 January 1939

Dear Lord Bishop,

I do not quite know what to say to your suggestion. I have tried for various reasons – as, that speaking is not a writer's job, that religious instruction is not my job, that such activities interfere with my work and that my perpetual appearance in the pulpit will only detract from the force of whatever I might say about Christianity – to get out of invitations to speak on any subject connected with religion. Speaking to the clergy is, however, rather a different proposition from speaking to the "Youth of this Country".[2] I suppose if the laity do not sometimes tell the clergy what it is they would like to hear from them, they cannot blame the clergy for being perplexed about the response of the laity, in their ministrations. I think, perhaps, I had better say I will come on the strict understanding that I am not required to hold forth about "What God means to me" or "Spiritual Communion with the Unseen" or "Avenues of Prayer" or anything of that kind. I shall be happy to tell you at some length and with some force a number of extraordinary ideas which anti-Christians, un-Christians and semi-Christians have contrived to get into their heads, and possibly suggestions of a few ways of countering the prevalent impression

---

1   The Rt Rev. Neville S. Talbot, of the Roman Catholic diocese.
2   See her talk to the Presbyterean Fellowship of Youth "Worship in the Anglican Church", published in *Seven: An Anglo-American Literary Review*, vol. 12, 1995, pp. 31–48

that the Christian religion is unreal, depressing and fit only for very stupid people. The latter are sentiments which I should happily oppose even if I were a Mohammedan or a worshipper of Odin. Perhaps I can take the misconceptions before lunch and the suggestions for combating them after lunch when we are refreshed and put into good spirits.

Yours very sincerely,
[Dorothy L. Sayers]

[24 Newland Street
Witham
Essex]

TO LADY FLORENCE CECIL

8 February 1939

Dear Lady Florence,

Many thanks for your letter. I do not know that I had any particular solution in mind when I wrote the first chapter of *Double Death*[1]. The idea is that each writer should lay down a certain number of clues for the other writers to elucidate and add to so as to arrive at some sort of logical solution to the problem. Actually, I believe the writers who carried on after myself and Mr. Crofts[2] did not pay very much attention to the logical development of the detection.

We played this game once before in *The Floating Admiral*[3] and there the writers were all members of the Detection Club and, therefore, were conscientious about sticking to the facts supplied to them; but this particular bunch did not, I think, take their responsibilities so seriously! I am afraid in the end the result was rather disappointing.

I am hoping to get on with another Peter story[4] before long, but I have been exceedingly busy just lately with theatrical work.

With kindest regards,
Yours very sincerely,
[Dorothy L. Sayers]

---

1 *Double Death: A Murder Story*, by Dorothy L. Sayers, Freeman Wills Crofts, Valentine Williams, F. Tennyson Jesse, Anthony Armstrong, David Hume (Gollancz, 19 January 1939). D. L. S. wrote Part I, "The Riddle of the Poisoned Nurse", pp. 21–61.

2 Freeman Wills Crofts (1879–1957).

3 By G. K .Chesterton, Dorothy L. Sayers, V. L. Whitechurch, G. D. H. and M. Cole, Henry Wade, Agatha Christie, John Rhode, Milward Kennedy, Ronald A. Knox, F. Wills Crofts, Edgar Jepson, Clemence Dane and Anthony Berkeley; published by Hodder and Stoughton, 2 December 1931.

4 This may refer to *Thrones, Dominations*.

[24 Newland Street
Witham
Essex]

TO THE BISHOP OF NOTTINGHAM
7 March 1939

Dear Lord Bishop,

Alas, too well do I know that keen parson with the glowing eye! He turned up last at Oxford, and I meet him continually in other parts of the country; his influence is mesmeric, one shrivels beneath the glance and only escapes by murmuring that if he will write one will give him an answer after consulting one's engagement book!

Since I shall be coming to Nottingham in any case, I don't mind doing a second job while I am there; but you are right in assuming that I refuse to be a Christian evangelist. I could not attempt to "kindle the younger generation with the Gospel", the most I could do would be to suggest to them that the Christian Faith is a logical explanation of the Universe well worth their attention, and neither an irrational myth nor a system of ethics which will stand by itself when the dogmatic foundation has been removed from beneath it. The only point which I am at pains to hammer home to people is that the Christian belief is not a kind of intellectual weakness for which any reasonable person should feel bound to apologise. Further than this I am not inclined to go on the lecture platform; the only medium in which I am fitted to communicate enthusiasm is the novel or the stage. If you do not mind this somewhat chilly approach to the subject, I will tackle the young people, only I do hope that this precedent will not set in motion an interminable procession of hypnotic parsons, because after all one has one's daily work to do.

Yours sincerely,
[Dorothy L. Sayers]

[24 Newland Street
Witham
Essex]

TO REV. A. R. JAMES
10 March 1939

Dear Mr. James,

Many thanks for your letter; I am afraid Good Friday is quite an impossible date for me to come to Shanklin[1] – and besides, you know I am

1 On the Isle of Wight.

really a novelist and dramatist and not a Christian evangelist. In fact, I think that too much direct preaching from people in my position does more harm than good in some ways. I mean, that any imaginative treatment of the Christian faith comes with less force from anybody who has become an official apologist.

I am sorry, but not surprised to hear of the prevalence of paganism in Shanklin; as a matter of fact nine people out of ten in this country are ignorant heathens. I do not so much mind the heathendom, but the ignorance is really alarming. Nevertheless, I feel that the business of writers like myself is primarily to show rather than to exhort.

Yours sincerely,
[Dorothy L. Sayers]

[24 Newland Street
Witham
Essex]

TO DOROTHY ROWE

? March 1939

. . . You can't expect decent work, if somebody has to sit down there and then [and] bung it off, regardless of whether he's had time to think of either theme or plot. I told Mr. Bartlett that whether the proposition attracted me or not would chiefly depend on whether I happened to have something I really wanted to say in that form, and I'll swear that's the only way to get an honest play written. So one really ought to be able to allow three months for brooding and three months for hatching. It's not an easy proposition: one set, small cast, lashings of females, vigorous action, clearly-drawn characters that don't demand enormous technical range in the performance, and a theme equally important and comprehensible to the rustics of Little-Doddering-under-the-Wallop and the sophisticated ladies and gentlemen of Highbrow-End Garden City.

Meanwhile, I am struggling with Acts 2 and 3 of *Faustus*. Having invented a tender, wise, unworldly and finely symbolical Pope for dramatic technological purposes, and written him a tender, wise etc. speech, I was fool enough to consult the Encyclopaedia in an idle way to see who the contemporary Pope actually was. He turns out to have been the notorious Alexander VI − the most flagrantly vicious and corrupt Borgia that ever defiled a family or the Vatican. This seemed a little too thick − I mean, symbolism is all very well, but nobody could accept Alexander VI as a symbol of anything but putrefaction. I shall have to make it Julius II, and turn the battle of Pavia into the Sack of Rome. Oh, dear!

Yours distractedly,
[D. L.]

[24 Newland Street
Witham
Essex]

TO MARGARET BABINGTON

17 March 1939

Dear Miss Babington,

Here, at last, is the complete Faustus, or rather *The Devil to Pay*, (how did you get along with the Dean?).[1] I hope you will like the play; as you see, it is going to make greater demands on the production and stage management, but I feel sure Mr. Williams and Mr. Napier will manage to cope with it. I have tried, in the Preface, to explain something of what I wanted to do in this play, especially in the passage which deals with time and the problem of evil, pages 9 and 10.[2] The bits of the play which I think most important, if you are thinking of quoting them in the *Chronicle*, are (1) The Judge's speech on page 67,[3] "All things God can do . . . . ."; (2) Mephistopheles' speech on page 72,[4] "I am the price that all things pay for being . . ."; and, perhaps, if there is room for it, part of the Pope's speech on page 29,[5] from "Hard it is, very hard", to "so all damnation is." Theologically speaking, these are the cardinal points of the play.

You will see from the cast list what we shall need: I propose to bring actors for the two Faustus', Mephistopheles, Helen and the Judge. You will see, by the way, that we shall need a Lisa who can sing the little song, "Five silver fishes" on pages 32 and 33;[6] I shall have to ask Mr. Knight[7] to compose this as well as the recitatives and chorus at the end of the play, and also to suggest some sort of diabolical melody for Mephistopheles' verse on page 58,[8] "Jump little man". I do not know how the play will work out for time, but I think really the easiest way is to print it as it stands without bothering about the cuts made in production, as this only creates confusion and holds up the printer. I shall be very glad if Mr. Goulden can give us, as he did before, page galleys with good wide margins at both sides and bottom, stamped together to form acting scripts; he will remember how this was done for *Zeal*.

With all good wishes to the Festival and yourself,
Yours very sincerely,
[Dorothy L. Sayers]

1 The Very Rev. Hewlett Johnson, Dean of Canterbury from 1931. He was known as "the Red Dean" because of his Marxist views.
2 pp. 25 and 27 in edition by Gollancz, 1939.   3 p. 100 in ed. cit.
4 p. 106 in ed. cit.   5 pp. 54–55 in ed. cit.   6 p. 58 in ed. cit.
7 Gerald H. Knight, the Cathedral Organist, who also composed the music for *The Zeal of Thy House*.
8 p. 102 in ed. cit.

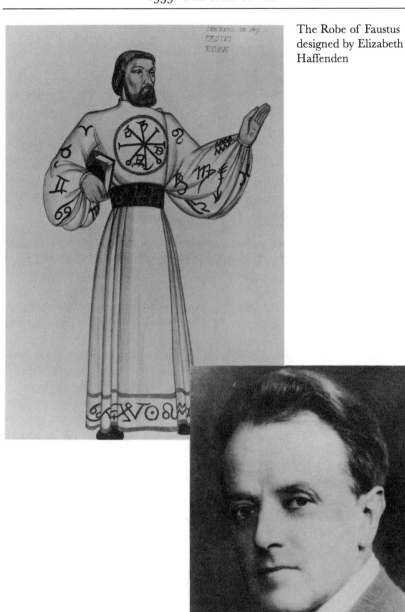

The Robe of Faustus
designed by Elizabeth
Haffenden

Harcourt Williams who played
Faustus

Costume for Mephistopheles designed by Elizabeth Haffenden

24 Great James Street
W.C.1

TO HER SON

22 March 1939

Dear John,

Well, you are a one! What with Hitler blowing off steam in Central Europe,[1] and you busting your collar-bone[2] at Malvern, and every possible agitation boiling up every five minutes about the play, and Canterbury screaming for the script of the new play there, and clergymen writing by every post imploring one to open bazaars at Penzance or South Shields – oh, gosh!

I'm frightfully sorry about the collar-bone – I hope they've now tied it up securely, and that it won't go wrong again. You will probably have to abandon the idea of becoming rugger centre-forward for England (or do centre-forwards only come in soccer? I forget, never having been at all intelligent about football!).

I will try, when the telephone stops ringing, (which it has done twice since I started, curse it!) to go forth and collect some reading for you. It's very difficult to tell "what to read", just like that. I've always had one of those snipe-like minds myself, which dart off in all directions, pursuing now this and now that, as one thing leads to another. I'll send down a bunch of "Penguin" sixpennies – good print and light to handle – of various sorts of things ranging from philosophy to fiction, which you can browse about in and see if there's anything you take a fancy [too] to (can't spell!). I'm sure the best rule is just to follow one's immediate fancy and see where it goes to. Sometimes one happens to read a book at the wrong moment and it says nothing to one, whereas a few years earlier or later it would have seemed a direct revelation from Heaven – but one can't legislate for these things. Nobody of my generation has or can have the faintest idea what's going to appeal to a person of your generation and it's no good pretending we can. Poetry which to us looks like clotted madness is clear as daylight to you, and the stuff you find dull and old-fashioned is prized by us because it once seemed new and exciting. We talk a different language, though I think it's very important that each generation should know what has been said in previous generations – otherwise they may discover that somebody's brand-new philosophy is really only an old one that has been tried and found wanting for centuries. Also, of course, it's

---

1 On 16 March 1939 Hitler proclaimed from Prague the dissolution of the State of Czechoslovakia.

2 This was the second time he had broken a collar-bone. See letter to Ivy Shrimpton, 13 May 1927, *The Letters of Dorothy L. Sayers: 1899–1936*, p. 261.

always much easier to get the hang of a thing if one knows what led up to it. (The jargon for that is "historical perspective" – an excellent thing if not overdone.)

I'm here in Town for a day or two. All next week I shall be at the Palace Court Hotel, Bournemouth – unless anything unexpected happens.

Best love and good luck with the shoulder.

> Your loving
> Mother

[24 Newland Street
Witham
Essex]

TO JOHN DICKSON CARR

3 April 1939

Dear Mr. Carr,

I enclose the Order of Initiation[1] which I have adapted so as to make as few repetitions as may be. The promises upon the skull must, I think, be made by each candidate separately. If I am to be the Proposer, will you see that I have a copy with the full names of the candidates and their works clearly written out, as it is not easy to read hasty pencillings by the light of one candle.

> With best wishes,
> Yours ever,
> [Dorothy L. Sayers]

P.S. Forgive delay; I have been away at Bournemouth.

---

1 Of the Detection Club. This letter is evidence of D. L. S.' authorship (at least as reviser) of the Order of Initiation. (See Brabazon, pp. 144–145.)

[24 Newland Street
Witham
Essex]

TO T. S. ELIOT
4 April 1939

Dear Mr. Eliot,

I have taken the liberty of quoting from *The Family Reunion* in an article for the Leader page of the *Sunday Times*[1] on Easter Day; I hope you do not mind, and that you will feel you can approve of the way I have interpreted the very small part of the play's meaning, which I have been able to get into this restricted space. Also I must apologise because in order to cram what I wanted to say into their confounded columns, I have been obliged to string the verse all together as though it were prose. I have done my best by inserting capital letters at the beginnings of lines (to the great confusion of the printer) and by using a semi-colon for a full stop in a place where the capital I was ambiguous. Please forgive me for taking these liberties.

May I take this opportunity to say what a magnificent play I think it; I took with me to the theatre a friend of very agnostic views, who was further prejudiced against the play by the fact that she did not care for *Murder in the Cathedral*; she was profoundly moved, and said it was the most exciting evening she had spent in the theatre for very many years.

I expect Michael Mac Owan[2] has told you that I tried with some other friends to get a letter about the play into *The Times*, but we were crowded out by National Conscription. I hope business is picking up.

With best wishes,
    Yours sincerely,
        [Dorothy L. Sayers]

T. S. Eliot replied that he himself had no very high opinion of Murder in the Cathedral.

---

1 "The Food of the Full-Grown", published in *The Sunday Times*, 9 April 1939. Re-titled "Strong Meat" and published as a pamphlet by Hodder and Stoughton, June 1939. Later included in *Creed or Chaos?*, Methuen, 1947.
2 Michael Macowan, producer at the Westminster Theatre, at which the play was later put on.

The White House
St Peter's Lane
Canterbury

TO HAROLD ARNEIL

17 May 1939

Dear Harold,

I always said *Love All*[1] would burst into song at the most agitated and inconvenient moment possible! I believe you and Dorothy Allen have done it on purpose!

Of course I would love you to do it, dear, and I know you are just the person to make a first-class job of it. The really tiresome thing is the date. As you know, I am settled down here for a month, looking after *Devil to Pay*, which is a hell of a big, complicated production; and even if I were to kill myself rushing backwards and forwards between Canterbury and Cambridge, I shouldn't be able to give an awful lot of time and thought to *Love All*. Not that the production couldn't get along perfectly well without me; but I wrote that play some time ago, and in a rather irresponsible mood, and I'm quite sure there are a thousand things I ought to alter and improve, which will only be discovered in rehearsal.

Of course, if you can get Cecil Parker[2] to produce and cast, that would be the best possible arrangement, because I know he likes the play, and would get the right angle on it. It is such a light little trifle that everything depends on getting just the right touch in the acting and production.

I wired to you this morning to ask whether you could possibly get up to Town tomorrow afternoon or Friday morning to talk it over. I have an appointment at the War Office on Friday at eleven, and an R.D.S.[3] Committee-meeting at two, after which I dash back to Canterbury for a rehearsal; but I could give you all Thursday afternoon or Friday lunch-time. We might possibly arrange that I could get over to Cambridge for, say, one rehearsal and conference and for the dress rehearsal and first night.

1 A light-hearted comedy written by D. L. S. during her second visit to Venice in August 1938; ed. Alzina Stone Dale, Kent State University Press, 1984.
2 Cecil Parker (1897–1971), actor, best known at the time for his interpretation of the role of Mark Antony.
3 Religious Drama Society, also known as RADIUS.

How are you getting on at Cambridge?[4] I hope all is going well. I haven't been able to get any news of you, as there has been no one at the flat, and Muriel hadn't heard from you.

With all love,[5]

    Yours affectionately,

      [D. L. S.]

4 Harold Arneil was hoping to put on *Love All* at the Festival Theatre in Cambridge.
5 A nice play of words.

The White House
St. Peter's Lane
Canterbury

TO MURIEL ST CLARE BYRNE

20 May 1939

My dear Muriel,

Thank you so much for your very encouraging and enthusiastic welcome to the Sonnet[1] – it was frightfully good of you to bother to write. I rang you up yesterday morning, but there was no voice nor any that answered, so I concluded you were out of Town. (I was up for the night, calling at the War Office, etc.) I'm much relieved that you like the thing and think it nice and tough and dignified; one is always haunted by the fear that in paying a man a public tribute one may only succeed in making a public fool of him. Billy is going to be just as grand in Faustus as he was in William. That last act suits him down to the ground, as I knew it would. He's marvellous, of course, [in] that queer, incoherent speech he has to make on waking – you remember –

> Christ! Christ! Christ!
> They have taken away my Lord these many years,
> And I know not where they have laid Him. Sir, if you know,
> Tell me, for I denied Him, and just now
> I heard the crowing of the cock. How long
> The night has been! And now the dawn is red,
> And a great storm coming . . .[2]

And he's charming, too, in the little love-scene with Lisa – about the

1 Her sonnet to Harcourt Williams, "To the Interpreter", published as a dedication in *The Devil to Pay*. See also *Poetry of Dorothy L. Sayers*, edited by Ralph E. Hone, who calls it "this magnificent sonnet, one of the best poems Sayers ever wrote" (ed. cit., p. 119).
2 Scene 4.

swallows building and the "peace in those quiet streets, cool and deep beneath the leaning gables."[3] And Frank[4] is a grand Mephisto, and I think is going to get the hardness and cruelty into the last act, which was the thing I was a little afraid about, with his highly sympathetic personality. Raf[5] is at present wrestling with a fancy for all the kinds of symbolic gestures and what-not, which we feel destroy the immobile awfulness of God, and from which we are weaning him with what tenderness we can. He will be all right, though. He always starts off with a lot of fads which have to be quietly eliminated! Betty Douglas excellent as Lisa – a bit of inspired casting on Bill's[6] part – Alastair Bannerman[7] coming on nicely in his "dog" act. (The bloody dog itself is going to be a difficulty; if you get a frenzied wire for Bunter,[8] don't be surprised. Barking is, of course, the thing one has to fear – but surely the dog could wear a light muzzle which would prevent that. Whimpering would be tiresome, too, but at any rate in character!)

We have at last got a Helen of Troy, one Mary Alexander, with a very beautiful voice and the right unearthly touch about her. We thought we were having Vera Lindsay, but she cried off after the try-out – not enough in the part for her, I imagine. I'm not sure this girl won't be even better, though not so astonishing in appearance.

Our one agony now is that we have had to sack the local Emperor. A very nice man, and very keen – 25 years on the stage and runs a School of Drama, and we placed great reliance on him. Unhappily, he is, without any exception at all, the worst actor I have seen on any stage, in any part. Not only were all his gestures ridiculous and all his intonations false, but also he could never remember a line, nor repeat it correctly when it was given him, nor recognize a cue, nor come in on it! This, as you may guess, rather destroyed the zip and oompah of the siege of Rome! Another bloke is promised for Monday – if he's no good, we must have another pro. The set is going to be good, I think, judging from Frank's drawings; he starts building Hell-mouth with his own hands on Monday. (That's the kind of company we are – all hands to the capstan-bars, and we should like to see "that gentleman that will not set hand to a rope"!)

Life was complicated on Wednesday by Dorothy Allen, who put it into Harold Arneil's head that he might do *Love All* at Cambridge. He

---

3 Scene 2.
4 Frank Napier.
5 Raf de la Torre, who played the Judge (God).
6 i.e. Harcourt Williams.
7 Alastair Bannerman played the part of Young Faustus. He married Betty Douglas, a niece of Miss A. M. Douglas, founder of the Godolphin School.
8 Muriel St Clare Byrne had a dog named Bunter.

promptly suggested doing it in May Week[9] – June 5th of all dates! – five days before we open here. I dashed up to Town, and persuaded him to postpone it till July – out-of-term, but giving more time for production and allowing me to get there and do any necessary alterations and repairs. He is trying to get Cecil Parker to produce, and London actors for the three chief parts. It may or may not come to anything; I have rather made it a condition that he shall get Parker.

A further distraction is that Robert Atkins[10] has asked me to join the committee of the Open-Air Theatre.[11] I have said yes, because I thought it might be a useful thing to do. But I wish everything didn't happen at once!...

    With love and many thanks,
      D.

9 The name given to a week of festivity at Cambridge University, previously in May but now in June.
10 Robert Atkins (1886–1972), actor and stage director. He acted in the companies of Tree, Benson and Forbes-Robertson before World War I. He was director of the Old Vic from 1921 to 1925 and of the Open Air Theatre, Regent's Park from 1938 to 1960. He was made C.B.E. in 1949.
11 Productions were put on in Regent's Park, London, near Queen Mary's Rose Garden.

                    [24 Newland Street
                    Witham
                    Essex]

TO FATHER HERBERT KELLY

2 July 1939

Dear Father Kelly,

I was so terribly sorry not to be able to come and see you after all at Nottingham; it was really a great disappointment, but as I think my secretary explained to you, I was suddenly thrown into a great turmoil of business over the arrangements to produce *The Devil to Pay* in London, and could only dash up to Nottingham, speak my speeches and hurry back by the next train. I hope very much that I shall, before long, be able to visit Kelham.

I am glad you found *The Devil to Pay* interesting, and could approve of it on main lines; its theology is, of course, not so straightforward as that of *Zeal*; in fact, it is, perhaps, a little obscure in places, and this, I think, has been an advantage to it with the Press, who always treat obscurity with respect. It has irritated the *New English Weekly*, who, having no good answer themselves to the problem of evil, very much dislike anybody else's attempt to find one. The entertaining thing is, the number of people who think it would be so nice to be turned into a little innocent dog, and do not see that they are exactly the people against whom the play conveys a warning. Anyway, I hope we may do well with it in town, though I feel we should have more chance if it would please God to call Adolf Hitler to Himself; perhaps He does not want him!

With best wishes and with again very many regrets that I was not able to accept your invitation,

    Yours very sincerely,
       [Dorothy L. Sayers]

                           24 Great James Street
                           W.C.1

TO HER SON

23 July 1939

Dear John,

Now that the intolerable uproar surrounding two successive productions of *The Devil to Pay* has subsided, or at least eased off a trifle, I can look round and find out what is happening elsewhere.

So you have been mumping – I gather, and fervently hope that you are now de-mumped. It is a dreary and unbecoming disease. I had it in France, a good many years ago, and thought poorly of it as an entertainment. How does this affect the question of holiday camps and things? I can't remember anything about the length of quarantine and so on.

About your History Vth question – I think I must get your Head to write me a full report on the matter, since I see no possible chance of getting away from this dashed play for a little time yet. I had a letter from Mr Whats-his-name at Dumpton House about holiday cruises, but it all seemed (a) a bit expensive, (b) dubious, in the present state of things abroad. What with Musso in the Mediterranean, the Danzig confusion in the Baltic, Japan in the Pacific, unrest in the Balkans, mystery in Russia, settlement in Spain, and confusion on the Alps (where, I am told, German troops have arrived to keep the French out of Italy – a position that must be extremely mortifying to the Italians) – I can think of no spot, except perhaps the Arctic Circle, to which it would be agreeable to go.

Music – I am inclined to agree with you that if one isn't going to do anything much with it, it's rather a waste of time and energy. I'll take this up with Mr Cosgrove.

I hope the collar-bone is now satisfactory, and ready to stand up to life's requirements.

In the midst of everything else, the Government chose this moment to haul me up on the question of what will you do in the next Great War, Mummy.[1] I have written them a bright set of suggestions, which will either impress them very much or make them decide that I am too uncontrollable for their purposes![2] Drat them. I hear from people who have been in Germany that the man in the street there has been rather staggered by our appearance of determination, and is deeply disinclined to have any sort of row with us, so that poor Goebbels and Goering and Co. have to set out and work up their anti-British stuff all over again, which must be very tiresome for them. I also heard a good tale, which didn't, I think, get into the papers, that a short time ago, there occurred an inexplicable and apparently irreplaceable failure in the electric light supply at Milan, which plunged the whole city in darkness for the night – and that in the morning a perfect rash of anti-German propaganda was found to have broken out all over the walls. I hope it is true. The Italians have a grand knack of stage-craft in political matters!

Love and best wishes,
Mother

---

1 An echo of the recruiting slogan and cartoon published during the first World War, showing a child asking its father: "What did you do in the Great War, Daddy?"
2 See James Brabazon, *Dorothy L. Sayers: The Life of a Courageous Woman* (Gollancz, 1981), pp. 175–176.

[24 Newland Street
Witham
Essex]

TO MARGARET BABINGTON
28 July 1939

Dear Babs,

Thank you very much for your letter; I am so glad you enjoyed the show.[1] We have not yet heard from Queen Mary, but are still hoping that she may turn up one night.

We seem to have annoyed some of the atheists and agnostics considerably, to judge by the papers. However, we are hoping for the best, but do push along any well-wisher you can find, because it is vitally necessary to get money into the theatre during the coming week.

With many thanks,
Yours ever,
[D. L. S.]

---

1 The performance of *The Devil to Pay* at His Majesty's Theatre.

[24 Newland Street
Witham
Essex]

TO THE EDITOR OF THE CHURCH TIMES

1 August 1939

Dear Sir,

It is usually unwise for a writer to undertake the defence of his own work; but when your dramatic critic complained that, in *The Devil to Pay*, the Devil's claim is not answered "on its own plane" he raised a question of more general importance than the merits or defects of my play.[1]

The objection is a natural one; but *The Church Times* is the last quarter from which I expected it to come. Anybody rash enough to contend with the Devil on the Devil's plane is bound to yield his adversary "the best of the argument" – just as anybody who attempts to answer the famous question, "what does poetry prove?" is lost before he begins.

That the possibility of evil is implicit in Good, so soon as Good is expressed in Time-Space-Matter, and that the knowledge of Evil is therefore implicit in the self-conscious knowledge of Good within the expression of Time-Space-Matter, are facts to which the only possible answer is the Time-Space-Matter expression of the Incarnate Good. This the Judge asserts, the Devil admits and Faustus finally accepts; as the result of that acceptance, the resolution of the problem is found to be

...in the person of the very Christ
In Whom stands all the meaning of creation.[2]

It is true that this solution removes the argument from the Devil's plane altogether; how should it not? That is what the whole Christian doctrine is about.

The subject is very suggestively treated by Charles Williams in *He Came Down from Heaven* (Heinemann, 5 shillings), in Chapter 2, "The Myth of the Alteration in Knowledge" and Chapter 7, "The City". If I had read this little book before writing my play, I should have suspected myself of thinking under its influence; as it is, I am happy to find myself groping, by a very different path, to a similar conclusion.

Yours faithfully,
[Dorothy L. Sayers]

1 In *The Church Times*, 28 July 1939, p. 88, under the heading "From a Journalist's Note-Book: The Week's Jottings", *The Devil to Pay* was defined as "a play of high ambition and inspiration". The critic went on to say: "The devilish claim that the world is 'the work of a mad brain, cruel and blind and stupid' is amplified by Mephistopheles with great gusto, but neither the subsequent rebuke of the Pope, nor the speech of the celestial judge, seemed to me to answer it on its own plane. One left the theatre with the uncomfortable feeling that the devil had the best of the argument."

2 Scene 4.

*On Sunday 3 September 1939 the Prime Minister, Neville Chamberlain,
announced that Hitler had invaded Poland and that consequently Great Britain
was at war with Germany.*

> [24 Newland street
> Witham
> Essex]

TO DR J. H. OLDHAM[1]

10 September 1939

Dear Dr. Oldham,

Thank you for your letter of the 7th. I expect to be in Town some time
this week – I am not sure of the exact day, because it depends, among
other things, upon when I can get hold of my dentist, but I should think
it would be towards the end of the week. I will find out tomorrow and let
you know.

I shall be happy to see you and do what I can about all this. But I don't
think it's going to be enough merely to keep the Christian flag flying; I
fancy that now or never is the time to bring it out and carry it ostenta-
tiously down the street. In a sense Christianity is in a good position – even
if it is only that of being able to say, "I told you so". Materialism is dead,
and the people who have been busy for the last fifty years secularising
everything are now thoroughly frightened by the results when they see
the idea carried to its full conclusion. Even the intellectuals, whom
the Church was foolish enough to lose, seem to be wavering in their self-
confidence, though most of them still dislike the Church, and prefer fancy
brands of Christianity of their own. There are a good many complaints
from those who ask why "the Churches" don't say something loud and
definite, and I think the Church has got to do it.

On the other hand, I do think it very important that Christianity
shouldn't make the mistake of identifying itself with any political or economic panacea. That is fatal – and incidentally, a thing that Christ was far
too shrewd to do. In any case, the panaceas are liable to be discredited by
hard facts just about the time that one arrives at adopting them.

But I do think it is necessary to bring the statement of Christian
doctrine into some sort of relation with reality. A lot of the stock phrase-
ology has become meaningless, so that people not merely don't know
what it means, but are unaware that it ever had any meaning.

---

1 Dr. J. H. Oldham, founder and editor of *The Christian News-Letter*, a weekly which ran from
1939 to 1957. See also her letter to him, 2 October 1939.

However, there's no point in writing what I can perfectly well say when we meet. As soon as I know my plans, we can fix a time. So far as I know, any day or hour will suit me, when once I have coped with the dentist problem. It is disconcerting these days not to know whether people are going to be there or evacuated or tied up with war-work. But I suppose somebody has to be about to deal with civilian teeth!

Yours very sincerely,
    [Dorothy L. Sayers]

                                              [24 Newland Street
                                              Witham
                                              Essex]

TO T. S. ELIOT
11 September 1939

Dear Mr. Eliot,

Thank you for your very kind letter about *The Devil to Pay* addressed to Alan Bland;[1] I do not think anything much could have been done about it. Despite my warnings, the management insisted upon putting it on at a hopeless time of year when all our special audience was out of London, while at the same time, they put off until far too late the publicity to Church congregations, which might have done us some good. I was not very much upset about it, because I had a very good reason at the time to suppose that there would be war, and that we should come off in any case; but I do thank you very much for your expression of sympathy and kind offer to help.

I have had a letter from Dr. Oldham about getting together and doing something to keep the flag of Christianity flying; I gather you are more or less connected with this movement. Could you tell me anything about it? I have said I will meet him in town on Friday to talk things over, though I do not know that there is very much that I can do.

I do not know what you are doing at the moment, so I address this c/o Faber and Faber; if you are likely to be in town at any time it would be very nice if we could meet. I shall be hovering between here and 24, Great James Street, W.C.1, and letters addressed to either place will reach me.

Yours very sincerely,
    [Dorothy L. Sayers]

---

1 Alan Bland (1897–1946), press representative with Sir Barry Jackson at the Birmingham Repertory Theatre and then for the Old Vic and Sadler's Wells Theatres.

[24 Newland Street
Witham
Essex]

TO J. H. JONAS[1]

26 September 1939

Dear Sir,

I must reply briefly to your long letter about my article "What Do We Believe?"[2]

(1) What I have written is a true statement of Christian belief as formulated by the Church. (Not a full statement, of course, but true as far as it goes.) That many Christians have a more limited conception of it is also true, nevertheless, that is the Faith.

(2) "No real comfort to the rank and file" – I said, and I repeat, that the creed is primarily not intended as a comfort but as a statement of truth.

(3) Free will – I have dealt with this question in another article, published in pamphlet form under the title *Strong Meat*.[3] In Christian theology the only uncaused Cause of will, or anything else, is God. The human will partakes of His freedom in so far that it is not caused (though it must, of course, be influenced) by anything within the framework of creation.

(4) God, being the source of all things, is the ultimate source of evil as well as good. He knows evil, that is, "by intelligence" (His intelligence being infinite) but without calling it into being. Man, being a finite intelligence, if he determines to know evil, can only do so by experience, i.e. by calling it into being, which, having free will, he can do, but at his own cost and the denial of his real nature, which is good. Having found the evil in good, he can thereafter only find good by bringing it again out of evil and thereby restoring his own reality.

(5) "Saved in danger and suffering" – If we are afraid of a thing, there are two kinds of assurance that may be given us. One, that the thing feared will not happen; two, that if it does happen, it is not to be feared. Christianity makes no promise whatever of the first, but only of the second. It is not, for instance, suggested that a Christian will not die; but only that death cannot harm him.

(6) The resurrection of the body is not the same thing as the survival of personality, which might very well survive without bodily expression. Nor is "survival" an altogether happy expression for the "life everlasting" or "eternal life", since it suggests mere duration, rather than something

1 Identity unknown.
2 First published in *The Sunday Times*, 10 September 1939. Later included in *Christian Letters to a Post-Christian World* (Eerdmans, Grand Rapids, Michigan, 1969).
3 See letter to T. S. Eliot, 4 April 1939, note 1.

apprehended now and untouchable by time. But in any case, I had already said that the truth was indestructible; what I was chiefly concerned with was the resurrection of its material expression – the "new creation". The indestructibility of matter within the time-space universe is a different thing and denied by nobody. Christian eschatology[4] deals with matters outside that continuum altogether.

Yours faithfully,

[Dorothy L. Sayers]

4 A theological term signifying the science of the four last things: death, judgment, heaven and hell.

[24 Newland Street
Witham
Essex]

TO DR. J. H. OLDHAM

2 October 1939

Dear Dr. Oldham,

I was so glad to hear from you. I was, in fact about to write to you myself on another, cognate, subject; so that one letter will now serve both ends.

I am, as I said to you, very willing to do anything I can to help you on the news-sheet, the general programme of which seems to me to be excellent.[1] I am particularly pleased to see sections (c) and (d) among the main fields for treatment, and also section (a); though I feel inclined to add that such is the astonishing ignorance of persons who ought to know better, that this section might well be widened to embrace "interpretation of the Christian faith in relation to experience", or even "interpretation of the Christian faith"– but it is obviously wise to proceed from the particular to the general, and scarcely possible to interpret it in any relation without interpreting it universally.

I should be quite ready to come and see you at Chipstead, if you think I can be useful to you, and can, as you kindly suggest, transport me; I shall

1 Dr Oldham invited her to contribute an article on the meaning of Christmas. She agreed to do so but warned: "I always get hauled over the coals for talking about Him as though He was somebody real". Her article, entitled "Is This He That Should Come?", was published as supplement No. 8, included in the Christmas issue. The archbishop of York (The Most Rev. Dr William Temple) wrote to Dr Oldham, "How magnificent Dorothy Sayers is!". The Rev. Dr James Parkes also wrote: "Dorothy Sayers is superb, magnificent. *The Christian Newsletter* would have justified its existence on that supplement alone".

be in London from time to time, and if you like to suggest a day, I can probably make my own appointments fit in with yours.

It occurs to me that a man who might be interested and willing to write for you is Prof. John Macmurray.[2] He has been writing for some years on the need for a revivified Christian philosophy, and can express himself so as to be understanded of the multitude. Like most people, he says he doesn't like dogma (probably because, like most people, he thinks dogma to be something quite other than what it is), and he used to have great hopes of Communism, though what he feels about it since the Russian business[3] I don't know. But he is an excellent writer, and has a following.

By the way, I see you have not yet scheduled the name of the bulletin. Are you still calling it "The New Christendom"? I'm not awfully sure I like that too well, I almost think we've had too much of "new" this and "new" that – "New Thought" and "New Art" and so on – some of them rather bogus; and we don't get the idea of continuity. On the other hand, it is still more fatal to suggest the "Return" of anything, as though we wanted to plunge back into the Middle Ages. This is rather negative criticism, I'm afraid. If you are still wanting suggestions, I will try to think of some.

The other subject[4] I was going to write about was this. A couple of friends and myself were at one time anxious to put our services as writers at the disposal of the Ministry of Information, hoping that we might thus get an opportunity for doing something to disseminate encouraging ideas about war aims, reconstruction and so forth. Having, however, penetrated as far as the Ministry, and realising that for the moment an honest writer had no hope of doing anything in that overcrowded monkey-house of graft and incompetence, we determined to do what we could off our own bat. We are trying to get together a little group of people who will write, lecture, etc., on anything that comes to hand, bearing in mind the general attitude towards the whole problem that we have endeavoured to set forth in the accompanying expression of our common aims and beliefs.[5] This is rather a verbose and pompous document, chiefly because its harassed author (me) had to invent long phrases to avoid the use of the brief and obvious, but controversial, word "God", and we wanted to enlist

2 John Macmurray (1891–1976), author and broadcaster. D. L. S. is probably referring to his book *Creative Society* (1935).

3 i.e. the Russo-German Pact of August 1939, or Russia's invasion of Poland on 17 September.

4 Namely, the project entitled collectively "Bridgeheads", a series of books intended to prepare readers' minds for post-war social reconstruction. The first of them was her own book *The Mind of the Maker* (Methuen, 1941).

5 This is the earliest mention of the Statement of Aims. (See James Brabazon, *Dorothy L. Sayers: The Life of a Courageous Woman*, Gollancz, 1981, Appendix, pp. 278–282.)

the help of people who, though agreeing about the extra-historical standard of values, might have a phobia about that useful word.

Our idea is that we should each and all get our stuff published as far as
possible through our usual channels, and not call ourselves anything in
particular, nor advertise ourselves as a "group", but just plug away and do
what we can whenever we can get a foot in. Here and there we shall try
and function as a team, where that may seem a good way of going to work
– e.g., we have in mind a series of half a dozen pamphlets on reconstruction, to be put out by one publisher under one editorship – but otherwise,
we don't propose to have any constitution.

Our difficulty, of course, will be to get platforms, with the present shortage of paper and difficulties about unemployment on newspapers and so
on, but we shall do our best to get people interested, though we shall have
to begin in a small way. It looks rather absurd for three women, without
any very special influence or qualifications, to embark on this kind of programme, but we have come to the conclusion that the most successful
efforts don't seem to start in palaces in Geneva, but in back-parlours and
coffee-houses and inn-stables in obscure villages; so we mean to do what
we can. Of the three of us who started it, one is R.C.,[6] the other C. of E.[7]
and the third[8] rather inclined to be anti-organised-religion of any kind,
so that we can scarcely be called sectarian – but we thought we might
possibly work in with you, if you would think kindly of us, and help
to spread the news-sheet, while on the other hand you might be able
to give us a platform from time to time, if you had room. We have got a
historian and a doctor[9] interested and several educationalists, and hope to
attract others. We only started last week, so it's all very much in the air.

Please forgive this long letter and this profusion of documents. When I
see you – soon I hope – I hope to have some more concrete suggestions to
offer.

Yours very sincerely,
    [Dorothy L. Sayers]

6 Helen Simpson.
7 D. L. S. herself.
8 Muriel St Clare Byrne.
9 Denis Browne, surgeon, husband of Helen Simpson.

24 Newland Street
Witham
Essex

TO MURIEL ST CLARE BYRNE

23 October 1939

Dearest Muriel,

Well, dash it, if it comes to that, how about A Day in the Life of an Inoffensive Citizen, anxious only to toil for the nation's good.

9.20 – Breakfast – 2 letters from persons applying for the situation.

9.30 – Invent new kind of batten, while waiting for husband to vacate bath.

9.40 – Bath and dress.

10.10 – Secretary arrives, dizzy with anti-cholera inoculation.

10.15 – Cook says another young person has called about situation.

10.19 – Interview young person.

10.25 – Send secretary out to buy screws to mend cigarette-box broken by outgoing housemaid. Order meals.

10.30 – Ring M.S.B. about W.E.A.[1]

10.45 – Start on letter to Sec. of W.E.A.

10.50 – Stop to mend cigarette-box – unsuccessful.

11.00 – Continue letter to W.E.A. Sec.

11.10 – Listen to Secretary's symptoms and say she had better go home till after lunch.

11.20 – Continue letter to W.E.A. Sec.

11.30 – Irritated by failure of cigarette-box to function. Mend it again (one of the automatic kind, made in Japan, with interior like intoxicated spider). Successful.

11.50 – Draft letter to W.E.A. Sec. & further letter to Sec. of C.S.U.[2] at Newnham, offering to lecture on Nov. 9.

12.30 – Feel it is too late to start on Christmas Message to Nation. Saw batten preparatory to experiment with new idea. (Mem: husband has borrowed best saw.)

1.00 – Lunch. Remind Cook prospective housemaid arriving 2.15 & will she meet her at station.

1.30 – Present housemaid says, can I tell Cook name of prospective housemaid. Tell her Dora Wybrook.

1.35 – Suddenly recollect, not Wybrook but Wymark. Convey correction to Cook.

1 Workers' Educational Association.
2 Christian Students' Union.

1.40 – Feel Disintegrated. Cut out & hem grey border.

2.00 – Front-door bell rings. Nobody to answer it. Cook at station, housemaid changing.

2.5 – Call housemaid down to answer door.

2.6 – Caller turns out to be Dora Wymark, train having arrived 16 mins. earlier than Passenger Enquiries (L'pool St.) said it would, so that Cook missed her at station.

2.8 – Explanations. Take D.W. to kitchen and leave her there.

2.10 – Uneasy feeling of expectation. Sew border.

2.30 – Hearing Cook return, apologise for error in information. Sew border. Cook and D.W. exploring avenues, and the house.

3.00 – D.W. returns. Interviews. Says she would like to come.

3.5 – Interview Cook separately. She is willing.

3.10 – Engage D.W.

3.12 – Hunt house for change to pay D.W.'s fare.

3.20 – Return to library. Secretary says she is feeling better.

3.25 – Telephone. Mysterious caller for husband. Fetch husband.

3.30 – Husband says message is from local baker, asking why we have changed to rival baker. Did not know we had. Refer husband to Cook.

3.35 – Return to library. Sign letters, & try to understand where everything is.

3.40 – Ring Bun, and tell her must urge Ed. Spectator make up his mind about Wimsey letters and must soothe Gollancz about blurb. Bun says Hodder and Stoughton interested in booklets provided they are (a) religious or educational & (b) edited under my supervision; hopes of really embracing scheme for getting stuff out. Say, Excellent – perfectly ready to edit anything provided others do most of the work.

3.45 – Return to library. Dismiss Secretary with good wishes & wedding-present.

3.55 – Try to think about Christmas message to nation.

4.10 – Local joiner arrives to ask what it was I wanted done about battens & fly-gallery. Explain model theatre to him and work the curtains. Place order. Ask about spot-lights and cleats. Local joiner says he has friend with diploma for making models of things, but he is in R.A.F. Reserve and may go any minute – also is "busy courting".

4.40 – Try to think about Christmas message to nation. Disintegrated.

4.45 – Disintegrated.

4.50 – Abandon message to nation. Try to put batten together.

4.57 – Joiner's friend arrives unexpectedly.

5.00 – Tea-bell rings. Tell husband I am engaged with joiner's friend. Explain too hurriedly and have to explain again.

5.5 – Joiner's friend very intelligent and voluble. Says he will explore avenues.

5.20 – Tea (cold).

5.50 – Come up to Library and write letter to M.S.B.

So there you are. At any rate, I have engaged the housemaid.

I enclose my letter to W.E.A. Sec. If you think it is all right, will you post it, if not, will you ring me. I was afraid of something too vague and idealistic, so put in all that stuff about education and housing, etc.; but it is difficult not having been able to get hold of Scott T.

    Love

     D.

I enclose copy of my previous letter to Coutts and his reply (original). Please hold on to these. I forgot to ask Miss Lake to do copies, and anyhow we were *both* disintegrated.

24, Great James Street
London, W.C.1
England

TO MISS JONES[1]

11 November 1939

Dear Miss Jones,

How delightful to hear from you after all this time! Of course I remember you very well! I am afraid I was always a most undesirable member of the sixth form, and especially hopeless at mathematics!

I am very glad you feel that my two Canterbury plays have enabled me to make good in your eyes. I had a very enjoyable time while they were being produced and run in London.

I remember that I once caused scandal at school by too great a liking for the company of actors, and that I disturbed the minds of the authorities by informing them that the Stage was my rightful place! Despite all attempts to hold me on the straight and narrow path, I have eventually found my way into the Theatre, though only as an author, and after a

---

1 Another voice from the past. Miss Jones was a mathematics mistress at the Godolphin School, Salisbury. She was not one of Dorothy's favourite teachers. See *The Letters of Dorothy L. Sayers: 1899–1936*, "School", pp. 44–45.

delay of thirty years; I regret to say that I was perfectly right, and that I enjoy the theatre enormously. Unhappily, of course, the war has rather interfered with that kind of activity for the moment.

I heard from Miss Douglas[2] a little time ago, and also from Miss White.[3]

I hope you are keeping fit and well. If your sister is with you, please remember me to her.

With kindest remembrances, and with many thanks for your charming letter,

Yours very sincerely,
[Dorothy L. Sayers]

2 The former Headmistress.
3 Miss F. M. White, who taught D. L. S. French and German. See *The Letters of Dorothy L. Sayers: 1899-1936*, "School".

24 Newland Street
Witham
Essex

TO IVY SHRIMPTON

27 November 1939

Dearest Ivy,

Please forgive (a) my using up on you portion of paper-supply on which diabolic agency (unidentifiable, but thought to be departed kitchen-maid) upset ink! (b) my delay over the account. For some time I was beginning to wonder whether there was going to be any money to pay any accounts! However, I have now got my activities with publishers taped for the next few months, and I imagine that things will carry on till the war is over; when that happens the whole nation will go bankrupt together, so it won't matter!

Yes, John must have been having some fun at Blenheim – though uncomfortable, probably, when the first excitement was over. He did well with his School Certificate[1]. Oh, yes, Aunt Lil and Co. *always* think England is being shattered into little pieces, whenever anything happens. People seem to get so excitable living in America. I believe it's the air of California, or something that goes to the head – hence the Hollywood glamour!...

Best love,
D. L. S.

1 Equivalent of G.C.S.E. (General Certificate of Secondary Education)

[24 Newland Street
Witham
Essex]

TO MRS G. HEDDERWICK[1]

1 December 1939

Dear Mrs. Hedderwick,

Thank you very much for your kind letter about the Wimsey papers.[2] I am so glad you enjoy them. It seemed a fairly good idea to try and push a little quite serious comment on the present times across in this rather frivolous way. The Editor tells me he intends to continue the series and I hope perhaps you will help both him and me by directing the attention of any Wimsey lovers to the *Spectator*, which, like most intelligent journals, is having a hard row to hoe under war conditions.

I quite agree with all you say about the series of mistakes we have made about peace, but it is so difficult to persuade people that there is no panacea for our troubles and that even peace can only be kept going by strenuous struggles.

Thanking you again very much for your encouragement,

Yours sincerely,

[Dorothy L. Sayers]

1 Identity unknown.
2 War-time letters and documents exchanged among members of the Wimsey family and their friends, published in *The Spectator* between 17 November 1939 and 26 January 1940.

1940

A false start

෨෬෨෬

24 Newland Street
Witham
Essex

TO SIR HUGH WALPOLE[1]

3 January 1940

Dear Sir Hugh,

By all means make use of my name on your books and manuscripts committee, if you feel that it is of any use. (Note: that I have a foolish fancy for always having it written with the "L" in the middle.)

I cannot promise to contribute money, because I am very short of it, nor yet skill and knowledge, of which I have none in this connection. I could, however, turn up occasionally at committee meetings and vote as I am instructed, which is, I take [it], all that is required.

How do you find yourself in the midst of all this shemozzle? I am trying to do a little mild propaganda in the way of articles and lectures, but I can't say I think the official people give us a very inspiring lead. If you are in Town, perhaps you would lunch with me one day when I am up. I am there fairly often, though less often now that I am not doing anything in the theatre.

With all good wishes,
   Yours very sincerely,
     Dorothy L. Sayers

---

1 Sir Hugh Walpole (1884–1941), author of over 40 novels, of which the best remembered are *Mr Perrin and Mr Traill* (1911) and *The Herries Chronicles* (1930–1933).

[24 Newland Street
Witham
Essex]

TO VAL GIELGUD
13 February 1940

Dear Val,

I clean forgot on Friday to thank you for my lovely lunch. It made me feel so much like a giant refreshed that I delivered a determined assault upon the searchlight position at Bethnal Green. It required great determination, because the whole place seemed shut up and deserted, with not even a sentry, nor nothing, but after walking round four times and peeping through the bars, I encountered an enormous sergeant who took me into the orderly room and allowed information to be extracted from him. I should never have persevered in a north-easterly wind if it had not been for your good burgundy.

I am sending a copy of *Begin Here*[1] with love and gratitude.

You will think about doing that article, won't you, on the need for constructive listening? I feel pretty sure the *Fortnightly* would rejoice to have it as part of the series they are now doing. In the meantime, I will promise to think hard about a detective play for radio.[2]

With all good wishes and again many thanks,

    Yours ever,
      [D. L. S.]

1 *Begin Here: A War-Time Essay* (Gollancz, 20 January 1940).
2 Nothing is known about a new radio play by D. L. S. around this date. She did adapt her short story, "The Unsolved Puzzle of the Man with No Face" as a play, which was broadcast on 3 April 1943, the first in the new series, "Saturday Night Theatre". (See also her letter to Stephen Hobhouse, 7 April 1943.) In 1948 her play *Where Do We Go From Here?* was broadcast on radio as part of a series of six 30-minute plays by members of the Detection Club. See also her letter to Val Gielgud, 24 February 1941, p. 236.

On 5 February 1940 the Rev. Dr James Welch, who had become Director of Religious Broadcasting at the B.B.C., wrote a letter to D. L. S. which was to have momentous consequences. It would appear that he was prompted to do so by the favourable reception of her Nativity play He That Should Come. *His letter began:*

Dear Madam,

I am writing to ask whether you could help us in our work of religious broadcasting for children....

I have long been conscious that some consistent Christian teaching

might be given in dramatic form and I have long wanted to find someone who could write a series of thirty-minute plays on the Life of Our
Lord. The children we have in mind are those between the ages of
seven and fourteen. I had thought either of a dramatic retelling of the
Gospel story, or even the dramatic imaginative telling of Our Lord on
earth today. I feel that we might rightly and reverently use direct speech,
but my mind is not quite made up about this yet. You may well
imagine the good that such a series of about twelve plays might do,
broadcast regularly to millions of children and adults. It seems to me a
wonderful opportunity which ought to be taken. I believe that you are
probably the only person who could take it....

D. L. S. replied:

> [24 Newland Street
> Witham
> Essex]

TO THE REV. DR JAMES WELCH
18 February 1940

Dear Sir,
Forgive my long delay in replying to your letter of the 5th February.
Just at present I have so much on hand that it is very difficult to see
when I shall be able to undertake any additional work; indeed, in the
matter of radio plays Mr Val Gielgud has been before you, clamouring for
a detective drama which I have weakly promised to write if I can possibly
manage it.
   The sort of series you suggest, of little dramas from the New
Testament, is a thing I have frequently thought I should like to do, but it
would, of course, entail a good deal of very careful thought and, consequently, a good deal of time. Your suggestion is exceedingly tempting, and
if you are not in a great hurry for the series is just the thing I should enjoy
attempting, but it would not be honest to accept it without warning you
that I should not be able to get down to it for the next two or three months
at the earliest.
   If I did do it, I should make it a condition that I was allowed to introduce the character of Our Lord Himself, and to present the play with the
same kind of realism that I used in the Nativity play *He That Should Come.*
I feel very strongly that the prohibition[1] against representing Our Lord
directly on the stage or in films (however necessary from certain points of

---

1 This prohibition ceased to be operative after 1965.

view) tends to produce a sense of unreality which is very damaging to the ordinary man's conception of Christianity. The device of indicating Christ's presence by a "voice off", or by a shaft of light, or a shadow, or what not, tends to suggest to people that He never was a real person at all, and this impression of unreality extends to all the other people in the drama, with the result that "Bible characters" are felt to be quite different from ordinary human beings.

It seems to me that in broadcasting we are freed from any of the obvious objections which attend the visual representation of Christ by an actor, and are protected from the vulgarities and incongruities which the ordinary theatrical or film producer might import into a stage or screen representation. Radio plays, therefore, seem to present an admirable medium through which to break down the convention of unreality surrounding Our Lord's person and might very well pave the way to a more vivid conception of the Divine Humanity which, at present, threatens to be lost in a kind of Apollinarian[2] mist. The only difficulty I foresee is in a right choice of language. It would not, of course, be suitable to give to Christ any speeches which do not appear in the Scriptures, but if all the other characters "talk Bible", the realism will be lost, whereas if they talk modern English we may get a patchwork effect. However, the difficulty is not really insuperable; it is just a question of choosing language which is neither slangy on the one hand, nor Wardour Street[3] on the other. This difficulty did not, of course, arise in the mediaeval mystery plays, whose authors were quite prepared to let Christ say anything that seemed natural and appropriate, but we could not go so far as this without arousing roars of disapproval among the pious.[4] It is not that the thing cannot be done but that it requires a good deal of careful consideration and cannot be done in a hurry. I should like, if I may, to think it over and perhaps discuss it with you at some time, always provided, of course, that you can contemplate putting off the series until, let us say, the Autumn. Perhaps you will let me know what you feel about this.

Yours sincerely,

[Dorothy L. Sayers]

---

2 Apollinarianism is a heresy which consists in a failure to admit the completeness of Christ's humanity. Apollinarius' own position changed over time: his fullest developed belief was that Jesus had a human body and an animal, not a human, soul and that He had but a single, divine nature. It has been said that the phrase of becoming incarnate "by the Holy Ghost of the Virgin Mary" was added to the Creed to combat this heresy.

3 See letter to May E. Jenkin, 22 November 1940, note 7.

4 Roars of disapproval were indeed raised after the press conference held on 10 December 1941. See Barbara Reynolds, *Dorothy L. Sayers: Her Life and Soul*, pp. 320–323.

[24 Newland Street
Witham
Essex]

TO REV. A. J. MORRIS[1]

19 February 1940

Dear Mr Morris,

Forgive my long delay in answering your letter and thanking you for sending me your fine hymn. Perhaps I may answer briefly some of your remarks about my *Christian News-Letter* article:[2]

1. I do not think there is any contradiction in saying that a man may be a genius though a savage in manners and temperament – Herod the Great was undoubtedly both. (I was referring to him – obviously not to Caesar Augustus who did not die until very much later.) Even in the eulogistic pages of Josephus, Herod bears all the marks of the semi-civilized savage, though a military and political genius beyond any question.

2. There is, of course, something to be said for the argument about the painless birth – it has been said by St Thomas Aquinas – but the Mediaevals were in little danger of being unreal about the Humanity. Nowadays, the difficulty is to convince anybody of its reality.

3. I don't believe in the "Gate" or "Rope" explanations of the camel going through the eye of a needle! I think it was a joke of the right Oriental flavour, just like the one about swallowing the camel.

4. I am charmed by your suggestion that the tables of the money-changers and of them that sold doves have a parallel in charity bazaars. I believe one of the   complaints was that the purchasers got very poor value for their money, so that the parallel is only too painfully exact – I have paid some wicked prices at church bazaars.

I have not read either of the books you mention but will take an early opportunity of doing so.

With many thanks for the kind things you say about the article,

     Yours very truly,

         [Dorothy L. Sayers]

---

1 Of University College, Oxford.
2 Supplement No. 8, 20 December 1939. The article was entitled "Is This He That Should Come?"

24 Newland Street
Witham
Essex

TO MAURICE B. RECKITT[1]

21 February 1940

Dear Mr Reckitt,

Thank you so much for your letter. I have written to Mr Gollancz, asking him to send a review copy of *Begin Here* to "Christendom". It ought to have been sent to you in due course, but I fear Mr Gollancz is not so knowledgeable about Christian journalism as about the other kind.

It is very good of you to be interested in the book – everybody seems to have hailed it as Christian propaganda, although I rather pointedly refrained from drawing any conclusion from my own premises!

Yours sincerely,
Dorothy L. Sayers

1 Maurice B. Reckitt (1888–1980), an influential figure in the development of Anglican thought. He founded a group known as Christendom and edited the quarterly journal of that name from 1931 to 1950. In 1968 he founded the Christendom Trust which endowed the M. B. Reckitt research fellowship at the University of Sussex. (See John S. Peart-Binns, *Maurice B. Reckitt: A Life*, The Bowerdean Press and Marshall Pickering, Basingstoke, 1988.)

[24 Newland Street
Witham
Essex]

TO THE BISHOP OF DERBY[1]

24 February 1940

My dear Lord Bishop,

Thank you very much for your letter. I shall be delighted to come and address your Association[2] on Saturday, 4th May.[3] It is very good of you and Mrs. Rawlinson to offer to put me up, and I accept your hospitality with pleasure for the Friday and Saturday nights. I am not quite sure just

1 The Rt Rev. Alfred Edward John Rawlinson.
2 The Church Tutorial Classes Association, which was holding a biennial festival.
3 The address, entitled "Creed or Chaos?", was published by Hodder and Stoughton on 10 June 1940. It was included in the book *Creed or Chaos? and Other Essays* published by Methuen on 27 February 1947.

at present what my engagements for the following week will be; if there is a Sunday train, I may have to leave by that in order to get back to London on the Monday, otherwise I shall be very grateful for your kind offer to allow me to stay the week-end. May I let you know a little later which day I shall be returning to Town?

Yours sincerely,
   [Dorothy L. Sayers]

                                                24 Newland Street
                                                Witham
                                                Essex

TO HELEN SIMPSON

27 February 1940

Dearest Helen,

What a blasted nuisance! I was rather afraid it might work out that way, because I'd noticed that your face, while retaining all its original charm, had gradually been getting smaller and smaller – a curious and interesting phenomenon which, according to my observation, usually presages a visit to the hospital. Never mind! I expect you will feel much better now you have got rid of the beastly thing. (Not your face, of course.) I rang up the hospital last night, and was told that your "condition was very satisfactory", which I took to mean, as usual, that the patient was feeling like death warmed up, and that the medicoes were gathered in the bar, congratulating one another, over a round of quick ones, on not having actually removed your liver by mistake for your kidneys.

Don't worry about the lectures and things; we shall manage somehow. It's tiresome, of course, and infuriating for you, but these things can't be helped. Thank you for having dealt with John Armitage; I will try to get on to him when I am in Town this week. I shall also do my best to be allowed to come and bring you the statutory grapes – I will promise not to eat them myself, because I do not care very much for grapes....

I have no particular news, except that the Friends of Canterbury Cathedral have decided to revive *Zeal* for the Festival, as Laurence Irving prognosticated. I shall therefore remove myself from the Lecture-list for June – and you can make up for your present inaction by delivering all my eloquence for me! Attagirl!

Well, good luck to it, my dear, and I'm most frightfully sorry and hope all will be well soon. Mac sends his best wishes. He went up to the War Office yesterday and returned in good spirits, having seen a general and two colonels, whereas his previous visit produced only a colonel and two majors. He hopes the next interview will be adorned by a field-marshal and two generals, after which he will only have to be presented to the King before being entered on a list for a job as 2nd. Loot[1] in a training camp.

That fool, Hilda Matheson, has written asking me to give a Wireless Talk to France on "some aspects of religious thought in England"! I replied that (a) all I know about religious thought in England was that it was in a state of great confusion, (b) that in any case, I should only offend French Lutherans by my Catholicism and Catholics by my ignorant Protestantism, (c) that if the French had ever heard of me (which was doubtful) it was as the author of "romans policiers" and not of *Zeal* or *Devil To Pay*, and finally, (d) that I would talk about detection or nothing. I feel like the Scotch minister who said to his wife: "I'm aye thinkin', Jeanie, the whole warld's daft except you an' me – an' whiles I doot ye're a wee thing daft yersel'".

Best love to you, and be good and get well quickly,[2]

Yours ever,
Dorothy

1 American pronunciation of Lieut[enant].
2 Sadly, Helen Simpson did not get well. She died soon afterwards in a convalescent home of inoperable cancer.

[24 Newland Street
Witham
Essex]

TO K. C. HARRISON[1]

4 March 1940

Dear Mr Harrison,

I am sorry you and your readers have been so much puzzled by Mr. Charles Williams' book, *He Came Down from Heaven*.[2] The particular chapter you quote either strikes people as being extremely illuminating, or else says nothing to them at all.

The sentence you ask about: "Men had determined to know good as evil", links up with the passage on page 17 about God's knowledge of evil: "Not by vision, but by simple intelligence" (St. Augustine).

1 Identity unknown.
2 Published by William Heinemann, 1938.

Possibly a very simple illustration may make the line of thought clearer:

I am standing on the Hampstead and Highgate platform of the Underground at Piccadilly. So far, all the trains which go through the station are morally indifferent to me. But the moment I make up my mind to go to Hampstead, the Hampstead train is the "right" train for me, and the Highgate train is the "wrong" train. That is to say, by my decision to create a rightness in the one, I have inevitably created a wrongness in the other; but the wrongness is a purely mental concept and does no harm to anybody; but if I then proceed to step into the Highgate train, I have called the wrongness into active existence, with evil results to myself, (I shall get to the wrong place); to my husband, (who is waiting for me at Hampstead to go to the Everyman Theatre); for the audience in the theatre (over whose feet we shall trample after the curtain goes up), and no doubt for the tempers of everybody concerned.

This illustration[3] is, of course, very much over-simplified, but it will serve to make the point Mr. Williams is dealing with. There are three things to notice:

(1) The wrongness is not in the trains themselves – to God or the Railway Company both are equally good trains.
(2) By my free choice to go to Hampstead I have created – I cannot help creating – a wrongness in all trains that go elsewhere, but I know this wrongness only by pure intelligence.
(3) But when I step into the wrong train, I know its wrongness, not as God knows it, by intelligence, but as man knows it, by experience, and the wrongness then becomes a real evil. That is to say, my ignorance, carelessness, or perversity, has caused me to know the perfectly good train as an evil train, and that is to create positive evil in the world.

That, roughly speaking, is what Mr. Williams means when he says that man had determined to know good as evil. I do not gather from your letter that you have yourself read the whole of the book, but if you will read the second chapter attentively, I think possibly my illustration may help you to an understanding of Mr. Williams' thesis, which he has of course elaborated with much more richness and profundity than my parable is capable of carrying.

Trusting this may be of some assistance to you,
　　Yours faithfully,
　　　　[Dorothy L. Sayers]

---

3 D. L. S. used this illustration again in a lecture on Dante: "The Meaning of Heaven and Hell", given at Jesus College, Cambridge at the Summer School of Italian, August 1948. (See *Introductory Papers on Dante*, Methuen, 1954, pp. 64–65.)

[24 Newland Street
Witham
Essex]

TO DR JAMES WELCH
4 March 1940

Dear Dr Welch,

Many thanks for your letter of the 1st March. I am very glad you feel able to take this line about the plays and about the presentation of Our Lord, and greatly welcome the courageous spirit which, in order to get the reality of the Gospel across, is prepared even to "give slight offence to some adult listeners"! Under these conditions, I should like very much to tackle the series of little plays, and think I ought to be able to get down to it about July, when I shall have finished with the revival of *The Zeal of Thy House* which is to be produced at the Canterbury Festival, June 24–29.[1] Between that time and this, I hope to be able to come and see you, to discuss details as to the episodes to be selected, and so forth. Between us, we should be able to think out something which shall be realistic in presentation, while giving as little offence as possible. . . .

1 The revival was cancelled owing to fears of a German invasion.

[24 Newland street
Witham
Essex]

TO LORD DAVID CECIL[1]
10 March 1940

Dear Lord David,

That's a grand article in the *Fortnightly*[2] – I whooped with joy when I saw it. And my God! how right you are about the hopeless attempt to abolish human passions by miracle! If only people would determine to use the existing machinery to deal with concrete evils they might get

1 Lord David Cecil (1902–1986), son of the Marquess of Salisbury; critic and biographer; Goldsmith's Professor of English Literature at Oxford University; known during this period for his *Early Victorian Novelists* (1934).
2 "True and False Values", March 1940, pp. 296–303. D. L. S. quoted it in "Creed or Chaos?" (Methuen, p. 40) and in *The Mind of the Maker* (Methuen, p. 13, note 1).

somewhere. But they will imagine that they can somehow devise a new kind of machinery which will automatically eliminate the devil without further effort.

Look! can you do anything to clear up a point that has been worrying me a lot lately, and that is the distinction which we find we have to make between men of intellect and the "intelligentzia"?[3] The current contempt of learning and reason which drives men of intellect out of the control of human affairs is a new and bastard growth in the body of society. But if you tell people that society needs the man of intellect, they point to the gutless "intelligentzia" and say, "Look at that!" – and can you blame them?

Is it that, just because the power of "money and push" has driven the intellectuals out of public affairs, the intellect has turned inwards to feed on itself and produced this set of detached and unpractical rabbits, who run away from any situation when they see it developing itself in life and action? Just as so many of the poets took recently to chattering to one another about the books they had read, in terms unintelligible to the common man, instead of transmuting experience into poetry, as was always supposed to be their job?

It seems to me there really is a profound division today between two sorts of people, both with some claims to intelligence. One lot, like the Auden[4] and Mitchison[5] crowd, retire to America, or to some sort of soul-solitude, and denounce society from a distance, refusing steadfastly to be mixed up with the War. The others (like, shall we say, you and me and a good many more), who seem to have a more earthy and vulgar constitution, remain angrily scolding in the midst of the uproar, crying, "We told you what would happen, you adjectival idiots! but since it has happened, we suppose we're all in it – give me that battle-axe!"

What I want to know is, what makes the difference? Is it just physiological make-up? Or is one lot really cleverer than the other? Or is it (as I am inclined to suppose) a difference of philosophy? And if so, is the

---

3 Lord David Cecil's article began: "To an ironical observer, the most curious feature of a hitherto uneventful war has been the collapse of the English intelligentzia – especially the intelligentzia of the left. Up till six months ago they seemed, with the exception of a few complete pacifists, to be united in a militant front against Fascism. To resist it was, in their view, the first obligation of every human being; their thinkers spoke with justified scorn of English weakness, their poets, headed by Mr Auden, adjured us to throw aside all other considerations and concentrate on 'the struggle'. Now the war against Fascism has at last begun; and within a few months their morale is broken...Some, Mr Auden himself among them, are in America; others, like Mrs Mitchison, clamour forlornly for peace on any terms;..."

4 W. H. Auden (1907–1973), the poet, who emigrated to the U.S.A. with Christopher Isherwood when war was declared.

5 Naomi Mitchison (b. 1897), novelist.

difference between the intellectual man and the "intelligentzia" in fact a conflict of philosophies?

This beautiful piece of confused thinking was started by your opening paragraph. Can you cope with it in something sometime? (How about that *book*?)[1]

Yours very sincerely,
    [Dorothy L. Sayers]

1 D. L S. had invited him to write a book for "Bridgeheads".

[24 Newland Street
Witham
Essex]

TO REV. T. A. O'NEIL AND REV. A. M. STACK[1]
21 March 1940

Reverend Fathers,

(This sounds rather like a speech at a public meeting, but the etiquette-books supply no handy formula for addressing two clergymen at once.)

Thank you very much for your kind letter, and for the somewhat alarming extract from *Home Words*. Well do I know that publication; it formed the internals of our own Parish Magazine many years ago, and was felt by my father, who introduced it there, to be a distinct improvement on its predecessor, called, if I remember rightly, *The Dawn of Day*. Its printing and paper were superior, and it was held to have a definitely "higher" flavour – without, of course, any whiff of Popery.

I can scarcely imagine anything more frightful than a competition in prayer-making under the liberal auspices of *The Spectator* – I may say, for your consolation, that I cannot at all imagine Wilson Harris lending his columns for any such purpose. Prayers should, in any case, appear anonymously – or at most attached to an author whose name is as remote and beautiful as St. Chrysostom's. And I must say that the efforts to produce modern prayers for national crises are as a rule so ghastly in their results as to send one fleeing back to the "liturgical experts" of the past. It isn't so much liturgical or theological knowledge that is lacking as the ability to write good English, and I refuse to believe that God is well served, or a spirit of worship promoted, by knock-kneed, broken-backed phrases that sound as though they were written by a tired journalist in a hurry. So far, the writer of the article is right – it takes a good writer to write good prayers; and they are, as a matter of fact, more difficult to write than

1 The "Reverend Fathers" had written from Clonroe Vale, Tinahely, Co. Wicklow, Eire.

anything in the world. T. S. Eliot or Charles Williams might manage it, though goodness knows what children would make of their petitions.

But it's very unwise to dogmatise about children – how does one know what they make of anything? They don't tell one. When I was a young-ster, I might have asked the meaning of the phrase, "there is no health in us", but what I should never have mentioned to any grown-up was the secret rapture with which I hailed the all-too-rare appearance in the pro-gramme of the Quicunque Vult.[2] I had a feeling that they would not approve of this fantastic preference, and I knew they would say, in their shy-making and unimaginative way, "Oh, but you can't possibly under-stand that!" Of course I couldn't understand it, but it was grand. So mys-terious and full of rumbling great words, and it made such a wonderful woven pattern. And it didn't talk down to me, like those embarrassing hymns about being but little children weak. It was queer and exciting, like the beasts full of eyes, and the people casting down their golden crowns around the glassy sea.

Children have a disconcerting knack of not liking the things intended for their liking. Christmas was nice, because of the presents, and the story of the shepherds and the wise men with their myrrh (what on earth is myrrh?) and frankincense (what a lovely word) – but it couldn't compare for fascination with the gloomy drama of Good Friday; besides, it too had that "children weak" touch about it. Some psalms were good ("sitteth between the cherubims", "Og the king of Bashan", "the mountains skipped like rams"), but not the 119th,[3] which was dreary beyond descrip-tion, or "The Lord is my shepherd", which was rather smarmy.

You can't generalise about children, except that talking-down is pretty well always fatal. And it's probably true that if they learn the solid meaty stuff when they are young, they won't have so much to blush for when they remember it later. I still enjoy the Quicunque, only now, instead of being magnificent and obscure it seems to be magnificent and lucid. But there are some morbidly sentimental hymns which I liked as a child and which now give me a stomach-ache to think of. They are just plumb bad,

---

2 Latin: "Whoever wishes...", the first two words of the Athanasian Creed. Her memory of her reactions to the Athanasian Creed varied. In a letter from school to her parents, dated 22 May 1910, she wrote: "What a peculiarly ugly sort of chant [the creed] is sung to...like a very dreary litany, with, I am really very much ashamed to observe, a certain amount of comic relief. It is very wrong, of course, but I really do think it is comic in parts..." (See *The Letters of Dorothy L. Sayers: 1899–1936*, p. 43.) In *The Mind of the Maker* she said: "In my childhood, I remember feeling that this verse formed a serious blot upon a fascinating and majestic mys-tery. It was, I felt, quite unnecessary to warn anybody that there was 'one Father, not three fathers; one Son, not three sons; one Holy Ghost, not three holy ghosts'....I found myself blushing faintly at the recitation of words so wildly unrelated to anything that the queerest heathen in his blindness was likely to fancy for himself." (Methuen, July 1941, p. 120)

3 Beginning: "Blessed are the undefiled in the way, who walk in the law of the Lord".

and whether they appeal to children or not, they have no business to be there. They produce a horrible reaction of loathing which the good stuff never does.

I agree to some extent about the archaic words and unreal sentiments, only I think this is rather a matter for explanation in sermons and instructions than for alterations in the liturgy. It's no good running anxiously out with new words, trying to keep pace with changes in language – it takes all the running we can do to make words stay in the same place.[4] We call a hospital for mad people a Bethlehem, and it soon becomes Bedlam, and a word of fear. We change the word to Asylum, and it goes the same way. We hastily abolish Asylum and call the thing a Home, and the same thing happens again. All we have got by the changes is that three beautiful words have become corrupted instead of one. It would be better to stick to Bedlam, and keep on reminding people of its original meaning. What have we gained by calling a dogma an ideology, except the totally false notion that an ideology is a more liberal thing than a dogma? I do think, though, that parsons and others might bear in mind that language does change, and that the meaning of words like Person, redemption, love, substance, worship and so on is not self-evident to the man in the street.

I seem to have rambled on at great length. Forgive me for being tedious. No, I don't think I will enter for the competition – I am quite sure that if I did, the result would not satisfy the writer in *Home Words*.

Yours sincerely,
[Dorothy L. Sayers]

4 Echo of Lewis Carroll's Red Queen in *Through the Looking-Glass and What Alice Found There*.

[24 Newland Street
Witham
Essex]

TO THE PROVOST OF DERBY[1]

21 March 1940

Dear Mr. Provost,

Thank you very much for your letter. I have received some further suggestions for titles from Miss Fone.

What I rather feel about all of them, including "Sound Doctrine for Critical Times", is that they scarcely somehow suggest a faith that any-

1 The Very Rev. P. A. Micklem, D.D.

body would be prepared to live or die for. They seem to lack a challenge. A more ringing note is struck by Eric Mascall[2] in the title of his book *Death or Dogma?*,[3] but we can't very well use that again. Christ (as usual) hit the nail on the head when he said "Ye worship ye know not what; we know what we worship".[4] The totalitarians do at least know what they worship, and that is their advantage; but Christians have too weakly acquiesced in a vague religiosity and the worship of nothing-in-particular. We have been so anxious to avoid the charge of dogmatism and heresy-hunting that we have rather lost sight of the idea that Christianity is supposed to be an interpretation of the universe.

Here are a few suggestions along these lines:

CREED OR CHAOS?
DO WE KNOW WHAT WE WORSHIP?
UNDERSTAND OR PERISH
A PEOPLE OF NO UNDERSTANDING
UNDERSTANDING AND ANSWERS (too subtle, perhaps)
THE ONLY WISE GOD

I don't feel that any of them is quite right – the first two perhaps come nearest to what we want.

I am sending a copy of this to Miss Fone, hoping I am not too late. I have been rather addle-headed this week with the fashionable influenza-throat. In any case, I am quite ready to accept whatever title you decide to use.[5]

Yours sincerely,
  [Dorothy L. Sayers]

2 The Rev. Eric L. Mascall, D.D., F.B.A. (1905–1993), theologian and mathematician, professor of Historical Theology at King's College, London University, 1962–1973. See his article
   "Whatever Happened to Dorothy L. Sayers that Good Friday?" in *SEVEN: An Anglo-American*
   Literary Review (published by Wheaton College, Illinois), vol. 3, 1982, pp. 9–18.
3 *Death or Dogma? Christian Faith and Social Theory*, 1937.
4 John, chapter 4, verse 22.
5 The title chosen was "Creed or Chaos?".

24 Newland Street
Witham
Essex

TO IVY SHRIMPTON

22 March 1940

Dearest Ivy,

No – I'm sorry – it was my fault. It was rather a job getting any money in this quarter. However, now it is in I can send the money for the Easter holidays as well.

This last six months seem to have been nothing but influenzas, burst pipes and confusion. My secretary started the flu in November, and everybody I know seems to have gone on having it in waves ever since. Some people put it down to black-outs and shut windows, but I think it's more likely to be camps and evacuation. However, by the time the War's over I daresay we shall be hardened to these things. I seem to have spent my time delivering lectures and writing articles which nobody can afford to pay for, in the hope of stimulating the morale of the nation and all the rest of it. We are lucky to have known one war already – our generation stands up to it better than the generation next below; which is all at sixes and sevens. In the intervals one knits socks, an agreeable exercise which I thought I had left behind for ever!

Glad you got your claim to the missing £20 settled – the posts have been quite potty lately. I wish they would contrive to lose some of the nonsense written to me by perfect strangers! But they prefer to lose important papers and such!

Love,
D. L .S.

[24 Newland Street
Witham
Essex]

TO ANMER HALL

15 April 1940

Dear A. B. H.,[1]

Thank you so much for your kind telegram of good wishes for *Love All*.[2] We had quite a good First Night, in spite of clashing with Mr. Hitler's gala performance in Norway and Denmark, and when I went in on Friday, I

---

1 See letter to Father Herbert Kelly, dated 7 February 1938, note 1.
2 The play had been put on at the Torch Theatre, Knightsbridge. It ran from 9 to 28 April.

found a very good house, all roaring with laughter, so I trust we shall not do too badly. I do hope that you and Miss Scaife will be able to get in some time to see our little show – it is running for three weeks, with matinées on Thursdays.

As a rule, I make a firm resolution not to give away school prizes, but in your case I think I must make an exception, and shall be happy to come on the 19th July, and say what I can. It is very good of you to offer to take me, and perhaps you will let me know later on all about the arrangements.

I expect you will have heard that they have decided to revive *The Zeal of Thy House* this year for the Canterbury Festival.[3] Harcourt Williams and Raf de la Torre will be playing their original parts, and by great good luck, most of the best amateurs are still available.

With affectionate regards,
    Yours ever,
        [D. L. S.]

3 See letter to Dr James Welch, 4 March 1940, note.

> [24 Newland Street
> Witham
> Essex]

TO SIR RICHARD ACLAND[1]

17 April 1940

Dear Sir Richard Acland,

Thank you very much for your letter, and for the copy of your book,[2] which, indeed, I had already read with much interest.

I am glad you liked *Begin Here*,[3] in spite of the fact that we do not see eye to eye about Russia! Capitalist or Communist, I cannot believe that salvation is to be found in any system which subordinates Man to Economics; but we need not quarrel about that, since there are so many things on which we can happily and fruitfully agree.

As to the "enforced leisure" which this rather odd kind of war has inflicted upon so many people, it is a very real problem, as you could not, I think, fail to realise if you did not yourself live a very active and busy life among those to whom war has naturally brought a great increase of work and activity. Some of the prevalent causes of boredom and discontent I have mentioned in my first chapter. Have you considered all the men and

1 Sir Richard Acland (1906–1990) Liberal M.P., author and social commentator.
2 *After the War: A Symposium of Peace Aims*, 1940, edited by William Teeling.
3 Published by Gollancz, January 1940.

women who have to pass long hours in A.R.P.[4] posts, or the hundreds of doctors and nurses immobilised in hospitals, deprived of their civilian patients and waiting interminably for casualties who, thank Heaven, have not yet materialized? The men who sit about all day and night looking after blimps[5] and searchlights, often in remote places, almost entirely cut off from other society? Then there are those who, in the winter months, are too old or too timid to venture out in the black-out to visit their friends or the cinema, those who have had to put down their cars, and are forced back for entertainment on their own minds, quite untrained for any such exercise; those whose income has been so reduced that, even now that the cinemas are open again, they cannot afford to go; those townspeople who have had to retire into the country, and are quite unfitted for that kind of life; and those who are now unemployed through the readjustments in industry, and have not yet been reabsorbed. It is quite true that they ought not to be idle and bored, but the fact remains that they are, simply because they are the produce of a standardised civilization which does their thinking and feeling for them, and because it is a very long and difficult job for them to learn, at this late hour of the day, to think for themselves.

These are the people who write passionately to me, begging for more detective stories, "to keep their minds off the war". I tell them, and have tried to tell them in this book, that they will be much happier, and much more useful citizens, if they will only put their minds *on* the war, and especially on the peace. Neither you, nor I, nor the Government, can do things for them – we have only too much to do already; they must learn to do things for themselves. There are plenty of people eager and anxious to do things – but what they chiefly need is to learn to think, and to be made to understand their own power. They need not be at the mercy of the bishops or the government or the press – they are the Church, they are the State, and they are the Public; but unless they are made to understand what they want and stimulated to go out and get it, they will remain a passive nation, ready to fall for the next Hitler or Quisling[6] who comes along.

This is what you say yourself – but you go on to ask, What do I propose to do? It isn't what *I* do that matters, but what I, and others who have done their "considering" can make the common man do. I can write and lecture and take the chair at committees, and in that way reach a number of people, but my political power is limited to a single vote, which has no

4 Air Raid Precautions.
5 Slang for barrage-balloons, so called after the non-rigid British airship of the first World War (B for British, limp for non-rigid).
6 Vidkun Quisling (1887–1945), the Norwegian traitor, appointed premier of the puppet government set up after the German occupation of Norway in April–June 1940.

more weight than that of the silliest nit-wit who can be cajoled into a polling-booth.

You say, xxxxxxxxxx the ways of doing the

(Sorry – something has happened to my type-writer ribbon!)

You say we must find ways of doing things "to force them to read and understand" – I only wish I knew any way of forcing people to read, let alone understand! If you have any plan for working that miracle I should be delighted to hear about it. I agree that the war has started a great out-burst of real mental activity, and that we ought to catch the tide while it is on the flow, hoping to heaven it is not too late. I hope to be in Town at the end of this week and the beginning of the next, and should like very much to meet you and talk over what ought to be "done". I will also tell you what small efforts my friends and I have already made to get in touch with people and fan the flame of their activities; we shall be very grateful if you can suggest ways in which we can help on the good work. On Monday evening, the 22nd., I have to be at Canterbury; otherwise I can come and see you almost any time. Will you send me a line, either to this address before Saturday morning or after that to 24, Great James St., W.C.1, suggesting an appointment?

Yours sincerely,

[Dorothy L. Sayers]

In 1940 the London Zoological Society offered the public the opportunity to "adopt" certain animals in the Regent Park Zoo for the duration of the war. D. L. S. chose two porcupines and was duly photographed feeding them, as the following letter discloses:

> [24 Newland Street
> Witham
> Essex]

TO THE SUPERINTENDENT

Zoological Society of London,
Regent's Park, N.W. 8
18 April 1940

Dear Mr. Vevers,

I have now arranged with Mr. Suschitzky to be photographed with the Porcupines on Saturday afternoon, meeting him at the Zoo Offices at 3 p.m. No doubt you will be kind enough to arrange with the keeper that my adoptees shall be ready with their faces washed and their nails cleaned at the appointed time.

Dorothy L. Sayers with Stickly-Prickly

In view of the slight obscurity which veils the subject of Sex, it will be better to give them non-committal names, so as not to be embarrassed by the sudden birth of a family to the wrong partner. Was it of the Porcupine that Kipling wrote:

> "Can curl up, but can't swim,
> Stickly-Prickly, that's him"?[1]

Because, if so, Stickly and Prickly would do very nicely. But I have mislaid my *Just So Stories* and am not sure of my biological data. Hedge-hogs curl, I know, but do porcupines?

I am hoping before long to get my christening party together. In the meantime I note that carrots, apples, and a simple vegetarian diet will be acceptable.

Yours sincerely,
        [Dorothy L. Sayers]

---

1 Kipling's words are: "Can't curl, but can swim –\ Slow-Solid, that's him!\ Curls up, but can't swim – \ Stickly-Prickly, that's him!" The first two lines refer to the tortoise, the last two to the hedgehog. (Recited by the Painted Jaguar in "The Beginning of Armadilloes", *Just So Stories*.)

                                            [24 Newland Street
                                            Witham
                                            Essex]

TO DR JAMES WELCH

29 April 1940

Dear Mr. Welch,

You will think I am very rude for not having suggested a meeting with you before this, to discuss the Children's Broadcasts. I have, however, had so much to do this month, that I felt it would be quite useless even to begin thinking about a new venture at the moment. Anything we arranged in discussion would have been driven out of my mind by pressure of other things. I hope, however, to be able to arrange a meeting with you either in May or June, if you are going to be in London during that period.

There is just one thing I want to make clear before we start. The reason why the rate of payment is less for plays broadcast in the Children's Hour than for plays performed to adults is, I understand, because it is customary to give the actors far less rehearsal when they are broadcasting to children. I think we shall have to say quite firmly that we are not going to allow these little plays to be rushed through without proper rehearsal. It is delicate and dangerous enough to introduce Our Lord speaking in person, without the additional complication of his having to be played by an actor who has only rushed through the part in a couple of readings. I feel sure that you will agree with me about this, and I think it would be as well to establish the point with the financial authorities before going any further. I will leave it to you to take the matter up, and if you require any support from me in the matter, I shall be glad if you will put me directly in touch with the Department responsible.

Yours sincerely,

[Dorothy L. Sayers]

> [24 Newland Street
> Witham
> Essex]

TO DR. J. H. OLDHAM

20 May 1940

Dear Dr. Oldham,

Thank you very much for your letter. I am very glad you were interested in the address[1] I gave at Derby, and so far as I am concerned, I am delighted that you should quote from it in the *Christian News-Letter*. It will, however, be necessary, or at any rate proper, to obtain the consent of Messrs. Hodder and Stoughton who are publishing the complete address in sixpenny pamphlet form in the course of the next few weeks.[2] If you will send them a line, saying how much you propose to quote, they will probably be happy to give their permission, on the understanding, of course, that you mention their name and the fact that they are publishing the pamphlet.

I must apologise to you for not having yet produced the promised paper on the Rights of Man.[3] Several things have happened to delay me. First, there was the production at the Torch Theatre of a little play[4] of mine which suspended my other activities for nearly a month while I was coping with rehearsals and production. Secondly, I found it, as I expected, very difficult to get my ideas into any sort of organised shape. The Derby address is, in fact, a preliminary effort in this direction and embodies, so far, the result of my cogitations on the subject. I gather that Mr. Wells's pamphlet has not made quite the effect that was expected of it and, there-

---

1 "Creed or Chaos?"
2 It was published on 10 June 1940.
3 Nothing is known of this paper.
4 *Love All.*

fore, there is perhaps the less necessity to publish an immediate counter-blast. Thirdly, owing to [these] various delays, I am very much behind-hand on a book[5] which I had already promised Methuens to deliver to them by the end of June, and which it is really my immediate duty to get on with, since there is here a contractual obligation to fulfil. Finally, of course, the very nerve-racking condition of things in Europe has acted as a brake upon intellectual output – I find it extraordinarily difficult to put my mind to questions of principle when the pressure of the practical situation is so heavy. In plain language, we have all been very much frightened[6] and one does not work well in fright.

All these circumstances make it difficult for me to give a definite promise of another News-Letter Supplement. I will, however, do my best. If it is going to be possible to carry on with one's prearranged plans during the next two months, I expect to be at Canterbury during June, dealing with the Festival revival of *The Zeal of Thy House*.[7] This will again occupy my mind to some extent, though it has enabled me to put off numerous other distractions in the way of outside engagements, and since the play has been done before, I ought to be able to get quite an amount of time free to do some writing while I am there.

I am sorry to hear that the production of the News-Letter has reached a critical stage – I feared that this might be the case, in view of the paper and postage question. I hope to hear shortly from you that you find yourself in a position to go ahead – which reminds me to send you the extra two shillings and sixpence to make up my subscription to the full amount to the end of the current year.

　　With best wishes,
　　　　Yours very sincerely,
　　　　　　[Dorothy L. Sayers]

5　*The Mind of the Maker*, which was published on 10 July 1941.
6　By the defeat of the French in the battle on the River Meuse. This was followed by the surrender of France in mid-June.
7　See letter to Dr James Welch, 4 March 1940, note.

[24 Newland Street
Witham
Essex]

TO REV. ERIC FENN

11 June 1940

Dear Mr. Fenn

I suppose I ought to undertake to do the broadcasts on the 11th and 18th August, though I am increasingly uneasy about these personal appearances in the role of Christian apologist. The plays about the life of Christ are a different matter – that sort of writing is my job. When I use the direct appeal, I am constantly haunted by the feeling that I am running counter to my proper calling. I know it is my own fault for ever having started it; one spreads a net, and immediately one becomes tied up in it.

Will you please note that I have to speak in Westminster at 6 o'clock on the evening of the 11th August, so I should be grateful if the B.B.C. talk¹ could be as early as possible, so that I may take a breath in between.

Yours sincerely,

[Dorothy L. Sayers]

1 The talks were entitled: "Creed or Chaos: Christ of the Creeds" and "Creed or Chaos: Sacrament of the Matter".

24 Newland Street
Witham
Essex

TO HER SON

23 June 1940

Dear John,

Thank you for your letters and birthday wishes. Events have been moving so fast that it is difficult to keep up with things.

As regards the Harvest Camp – of course, there ought to be no question of asking my permission. You must do whatever the Government wants you to do, as we all must, without delay or question. Tell your school authorities so. Harvest camps are asked for, and obviously every able-bodied citizen of school age must take part.

Apart from that: stay where you are. You are probably as safe in Oxfordshire as anywhere. This part of the country is more immediately threatened. If I should be killed in an air-raid, you and Aunt Ivy must at

once get into communication with my solicitors, Messrs. Hargrave Son
and Barrett, 24 John St., Bedford Row, London, W.C.1, who have my will
and know how to act. There will not be very much money, I am afraid –
nobody will have much money when this is over, even if all goes as well as
we can hope. It is not possible to plan out anything for the future. I shall
try to pay the school fees as long as is necessary. In the event of a German
occupation of this country, which is possible, though I think not probable,
be careful not to advertise your connection with me; writers of my sort
will not be popular with the Gestapo. If there should be any question of
evacuating to the Dominions, on the other hand, I will take what mea-
sures I can. But we are in the front of the battle now, and the great thing
is to stay put and work at whatever the defence requires. It may be that
your next object should be to make your mathematics useful in connection with engineering or something of that sort. Keep this possibility in
mind when the time comes.

Do not be troubled because you are afraid of being afraid. Everybody
feels like that. It doesn't matter, and is nothing to be ashamed of. Do what
is asked for – that is all that matters.

Look now at the history you used to find so difficult. England is back
now in the centre stream of her tradition – she is where she was in 1588
and in 1815. Spain held all Europe, France held all Europe, they broke
themselves upon England; we have got to see that the same thing happens
to Germany.[1] Foch[2] said towards the end of the last war that all would be
well, "pourvu que les civils tiennent".[3] That is the truth again, but this
time it means us. You have done well at school – do well in this business.
If we can stick it out, then, as the vision of Christ said to St. Julian of
Norwich: "All shall be well, and all shall be well, and all shall be very
well."[4]

> With love and best wishes,
>   Dorothy L. Fleming

---

1 Compare her poem "The English War", first published in *The Times Literary Supplement*, 7
  September 1940. (Included in *Poetry of Dorothy L. Sayers*, ed. cit., 1996, pp. 120–122.)
2 Marshal Ferdinand Foch (1851–1929), Generalissimo of Allied Forces in the First World War.
3 Provided the civilians hold out.
4 *Julian of Norwich: Showings*, ed. E. Colledge and James Walsh, "The Long Text", 29 (London,
  SPCK, and Paulist Press, New York, 1978).

The address which D. L. S. delivered in Derby on 4 May 1940, entitled "Creed or Chaos?" (see her letter to the Bishop of Derby, 24 February 1940), was published as a pamphlet by Hodder and Stoughton on 10 June 1940. Dr William Boothby Selbie, formerly Principal of Mansfield College, Oxford, had previously published an article in The Spectator, *entitled "The Army and the Churches", in which he had said:*

The rise of the new dogmatism, whether in its Calvinist or Thomist form, constitutes a fresh and serious threat to Christian unity. The tragedy is that all this, however interesting to theologians, is hopelessly irrelevant in the life and thought of the average man...

D. L. S. quoted this and another passage in her address, challenging his view. This prompted Dr Selbie to write to The Spectator *as follows:*

Doctrine is a Latin word, the root meaning of which is simply teaching, or that which is taught. Christian doctrine, therefore, is just Christian truth, that which is taught about the Christian facts. Dogma, on the other hand, is a Greek word, the root meaning of which is opinion. In theology a dogma is a religious opinion formally and authoritatively stated. Miss Sayers...[restates] some of the Christian fundamentals in a very interesting way and in terms more adapted to human needs than those of the ancient creeds. In other words she elaborates her own system of Christian teaching or doctrine. This is what she believes and how she believes it. Doubtless she would like others to believe it too, and to accept her statement of it, and she has every right to try and persuade them to do so. But she would probably hesitate to turn her teaching into dogma by making it an imposition of faith with the familiar words "This is the Catholic Faith: which except a man believe faithfully he cannot be saved"....

D. L. S. replied as follows:

> [24 Newland Street
> Witham
> Essex]

TO THE EDITOR OF THE SPECTATOR
13 July 1940

Dear Sir,
    With reference to Dr Selbie's letter: The dictionary meaning of "Dogma" (apart from its denigratory use) is: "Opinion; the body of

opinion formulated and authoritatively stated; a doctrinal system".¹ The relevance or otherwise of Christian doctrine to human life and thought depends precisely upon the dogma, i.e. upon what opinion is held concerning the person of Christ. That is what I have endeavoured to make clear. The Church has formulated and authoritatively stated her opinion – that is, her dogma; and that statement is the statement which sums up all her doctrine, or teaching.

I cannot repudiate too strongly the suggestion that I have "restated some of the Christian fundamentals...in terms more adapted to human needs than those of the ancient creeds", or that I have "elaborated my own system of Christian teaching or doctrine". The terms are not mine: they are the terms of the ancient creeds; the doctrinal system is not mine; it is that of the Church. All that I have done is to explain, to the best of my ability, what those terms mean, and what that doctrine is.

It is preposterous to talk about "my hesitating to turn my teaching into dogma". The teaching (which is not mine) is the teaching of the dogma – which is not mine either. As for the statement: "This is the Catholic faith, which except a man believe faithfully he cannot be saved", it is not usually realised that the operative word is "cannot". That is to say, the Church here brings her statement of opinion to the bar of fact, saying: "Believe or not as you choose, but what judges you will be the unalterable nature of the universe".

    Yours faithfully,
       [Dorothy L. Sayers]

---

1 The definition given in *The Shorter Oxford English Dictionary.*

                               [24 Newland Street
                               Witham
                               Essex]

TO THE REV. ERIC FENN

14 July 1940

Dear Mr. Fenn,

I hadn't even begun to consider thinking about the broadcast next month! I'm trying to finish a book on the Creative Mind,¹ and some tom-fool paper wants to know by next Friday "whether Hitlers have a place in the Divine scheme of things!"!! I know you wanted something on the lines of "Creed or Chaos?" but your letter is with my agents, and I can't

---

1 i.e. *The Mind of the Maker*, published by Methuen, July 1941.

remember whether it was the importance of dogma or the nature of sin you wanted me to talk about.

Curse the publicity anyway. It only encourages people to think I am putting over some new doctrine or interpretation of my own invention. This personal angle on religion is getting on my nerves, and I think I shall have to stop it, and go back to writing nonsense....

I will talk, if you like, about any of the following: The Christ of the Creeds; the Gospel of Sin; the Judgement of God; the Sacrament of Matter. You will find a convenient "summary" of anything I may have to say about them in "Creed or Chaos?". But do make it clear that all I propose to do is to explain, to the best of my ability, what the Church thinks about those subjects, and that I am not bringing any "new" lights of my own to bear upon them. I am not a prophet, but only a sort of painstaking explainer of official dogma – "this is the opinion of authority, and what it actually means is this"....

[24 Newland Street
Witham
Essex]

TO DR JAMES WELCH

23 July 1940

Dear Dr. Welch,

Forgive my delay in replying. Life has been full of complications, including, among other things, a wistful magazine editor, anxious to know, instantly, briefly, and at the shortest possible notice, what place Hitlers and such have in the Divine scheme of things, and why – one of those easy little questions to which anybody may be expected to rattle off a reply on the typewriter without thinking twice about it.

What I have been considering with regard to the Children's Hour plays on the Life of Christ is the general theme of the whole series. The thing must have a direction and unity as a complete work, apart from the unity of each separate play, so that [it] can build into a reasoned structure theologically as well as historically.

The theme I want to take is particularly that of the kingship of Christ. At this moment, even children can't help knowing that there is a great dispute going on about how the world should be governed, and to what end, and I think they are fully capable of understanding what the meaning of the quarrel is, if the situation and arguments are put before them in a simple and vivid way. I shall make this business of the Kingdom the framework of the series, and choose incidents that will bring out this aspect of the story – much on the same lines as in *He That Should Come*, which is also a play about the Kingdom.

The first play will probably be the most difficult to get going on, because it has to set the key for the rest, as regards style, language, treatment, etc. I am trying to get to work on this now; as I said to you the other day, I rather want to start off this theme with the Magi, because there I get the earthly ideal of government – Rome and Herod – brought right into conflict with the Kingdom of God at the beginning of the story. I don't want to do the Bethlehem shepherds again – partly because I find it difficult to do the same thing twice over, and because they may again repeat *He That Should Come* for the Christmas broadcast, and audiences would get rather fed up with having to hear me doing the same stuff a second time. But Herod would be breaking new ground; besides, I am rather strong on Herod, who was an engaging old ruffian, to whom the traditional mediaeval treatment has never done justice.

The real job, when the style etc. have been fixed, is making the separate episodes into coherent playlets, each with its own crisis and dramatic unity. I shall probably have to do a certain amount of rather bold dovetailing to get action and plot into each section. I mean, while one could make a pretty little piece of dialogue out of, say, Christ blessing the children, one couldn't exactly call it a drama, unless one could set it in relation to something else. Certain high-spots, of course, we have ready-made for our theme: the Nativity, the entry into Jerusalem, and so on; and when we come to the Trial and Crucifixion we are, dramatically speaking, on velvet; but there are all sorts of little twiddly bits – such as the tribute-money, and the disciples arguing about who should be the greatest, and the parables of the Kingdom, which, while very relevant to the subject, are just fragments of teaching and dialogue, unless they can be worked into some sort of sub-plot, so to speak. It looks as though I should have to pull myself together and really make up my mind about Judas; – what did that man imagine he was doing? Pilate and Caiaphas and the rest are quite understandable, and from their own point of view highly respectable – one sees exactly what they were after – but Judas is an insoluble riddle. He can't have been awful from the start, or Christ would never have called him – I mean, one can't suppose that He deliberately chose a traitor in order to get Himself betrayed – that savours too much of the *agent provocateur*, and isn't the kind of thing one would expect any decent man, let alone any decent God – to do. And He can't have been so stupid as to have been taken in by an obviously bad hat; quite apart from any doctrinal assumptions, He was far too good a psychologist. Judas must have been a case of *corruptio optimi pessima*;[1] but what corrupted him? Disappointment at finding that the earthly kingdom wasn't coming along? or defeatism, feeling that the war was lost, and one had better make terms quickly? Or just (as the Gospels seem rather unconvincingly to suggest) money and alarm for his own interests? If we can get a coherent Judas we can probably get a coherent plot.

Well, all that is my artistic funeral; I only mention it as an example of the kind of difficulty one comes up against. . . .

1 Latin: the corruption of the best, which is the worst corruption.

[24 Newland Street
Witham
Essex]

TO THE BISHOP OF CHICHESTER[1]

27 July 1940

My dear Lord Bishop,

Look! Here are the things I have contracted to do during the next three months or so:

Finish book on the Creative Mind (over-due);
Write and deliver two broadcasts on Christianity;
Ditto one broadcast on keeping up morale;
Choose, copy, and arrange vast religious Anthology (about one-third done);[2]
Write twelve broadcast plays on Life of Christ (not begun);
Write paper for Archbishop of York's Conference (ditto.);
(?) Write broadcast detective drama (may not be wanted, but has not been cancelled);
Two articles for *Guardian* (promised, but not yet tackled);
Write "Anti-Rumour" pamphlet for M.O.I.[3] (held up by violent quarrel

1 The Rt Rev. George Bell (1883–1958), who as Dean of Canterbury (1924–1929) had encouraged the re-introduction of drama into the Cathedral. He was Bishop of Chichester from 1929 to 1958.
2 This work has not been traced.
3 Ministry of Information.

with Ministry, but may be wanted);
Write and deliver talk at Chatham House on August 20th.[4]

I don't really think I can honestly take on anything more; especially as I have now no secretary. I had one, but she has now left the district, her husband having been lost on the Scotstoun.[5] (This accounts for my messy typing, for which I apologise.)

I would have liked to come to Brighton, but I think you will understand when I say that I simply cannot manage it.

With regrets,
    Yours sincerely,
        [Dorothy L. Sayers]

4 Not known.
3 The *Scotstoun*, 7,046 tons, was a liner built in 1925, converted in 1939 as a Royal Navy armed merchant cruiser. She was sunk in the North West approaches north of Ireland on 13 June 1940 by a torpedo from U25. (See *British Vessels Lost at Sea 1939–1945*, 2nd edition, 1983.)

                                        [24 Newland Street
                                        Witham
                                        Essex]

TO THE REV. ERIC FENN
28 August 1940

Dear Mr. Fenn,
    Many thanks for your letter. I am glad you thought the second talk came over all right. I have not yet seen the notice in the *Listener*,[1] but I am glad to find that I succeeded in satisfying the *Church Times*; I was afraid I might get trounced for making the basis of the Sacramental position too broad, but it is a job to address talks like these to all the various Christian sects, without offending any of them.

    I have offended some people, of course, but as a number of these appear to be candidates for the loony bin, I am not too much distressed.

1 15 August 1940. Under "The Spoken Word", p. 248, W. E. Williams wrote: "In the way of accomplished exposition I have seldom heard anything more admirable than Dorothy L. Sayers on the essentials of Christian belief (August 11). She tackled a most recalcitrant theological topic without making any concessions to mere piety. In one of his moods of elephantine obstinacy Dr Johnson once ridiculed the notion of a woman in the pulpit. I'd back Dorothy Sayers to put the case for Christianity better than many of our wireless padres; and if she will promise to abate a wayward high note in her voice I will gladly listen to her for a month of Sundays.". See letter to Eric Fenn, 11 June 1940, note. See also letter to Cardinal Heenan, 31 August 1940.

A number of people have written complaining that the talks were not published in the *Listener* and asking whether they are to appear in pamphlet form. I believe the *Listener* has the option on first publication, but if they are not going to take this up, I will turn the matter over to my agents and get them to approach the publishers.

I am afraid you have been seeing and hearing a good deal lately of Mr. Hitler's friends. They have looked us up once or twice lately, and the other day staged a very noisy dog-fight over our back garden. My husband was much affronted because it all took place above the clouds, where he could not see it. Personally, I don't want to see it and retired to the cellar with my knitting.

With best wishes,
    Yours sincerely,
        [Dorothy L. Sayers]

[24 Newland Street
Witham
Essex]

TO FATHER PATRICK MCLAUGHLIN[1]

28 August 1940

Dear Father McLaughlin,

Forgive my delay in answering your letter, I have been kept rather busy with preparing talks and speeches and also in struggling with a series of broadcast plays on the Life of Christ for children, which has got very much behind hand.

I should like to give a broadcast talk for you if possible, though I hate broadcasting and am always dried up by the atmosphere of Langham Place. My correspondents, by the way, seem to be getting quite annoyed (some of them), by the way the Church "ropes in", as they express it, the outsiders to talk about religion, the implication being that the Church consists only of the Clergy, and that the outsiders have no business to lift their voices.

I don't know whether the subject of Preparation for Death is one I should choose myself – I have a strong objection to dying – possibly you may feel that this is an excellent reason why I should talk about it, but I can't honestly pretend that I am of the stuff of which martyrs are made.

---

1 Father Patrick McLaughlin (1909–1988), Vicar of St Thomas' Church, Regent Street, with whom D. L. S. collaborated on the work of St Anne's House, Soho, a centre of discussion between Christians and agnostics.

I am, however, quite prepared to uphold the Chestertonian view about the time when

> death and hate and hell declare
> that men have found a thing to love[2]

and if you really want me to do it, I will do my best with it.

I am extremely glad to see that somebody is dealing with the heresy of economic man. I am always very much distressed by the total neglect by Socialists, as well as by Capitalists, of the question of the value of work done, as apart from the price paid for the work. There is certainly a screw loose somewhere in the economic aspect of society. We seem to have got as far as considering the importance of Man, but nobody seems to feel that they have any sort of duty towards Matter.

May I take this opportunity of saying how very highly I think of the Signposts series.[3] They all seem to me excellent, with the possible exception of Bentley's *Resurrection of the Bible*,[4] which seems to be unnecessarily fundamentalist. It has puzzled and bothered a good many people and is likely perhaps to lead us into further difficulties with the opponents of Jonah and the Whale.

I agree with you about the Writers' Guild.[5] I certainly think it would be a good thing to have more meetings, but like you I feel that we don't get on with the job as well as we might. I feel we need to do something rather more definitely. Perhaps some day when you and I are both in Town, we might meet and think up a few suggestions for getting the Guild to take a more active line. There is a little obscurity about our ends; if these are only to pray and eat lunch, all is well, but if we are also supposed to "bear witness" in our writings, then we ought to try and organize our efforts a little.

Perhaps you would send me a line telling me when you are likely to be available in London.

Yours sincerely,
[Dorothy L. Sayers]

---

2 *The Napoleon of Notting Hill*, from the dedicatory poem to Hilaire Belloc, stanza 4.
3 "Signposts" was the name of a series of books on Anglo-Catholic theory and doctrine, price one shilling.
4 Geoffrey Bryan Bentley. His book was published in 1940.
5 The Guild of Catholic Writers.

[24 Newland Street
Witham
Essex]
HIS GRACE THE ARCHBISHOP OF YORK[1]
York
30 August 1940

Your Grace,

Thank you very much for your letter and your suggestion that I should write a play for the Youth Council. Although as a rule I am ready to snatch at any opportunity of writing plays, I am in rather a difficulty about the next three months.

I have madly undertaken, in addition to my other work, to write a series of twelve short broadcast plays on the life of Christ for the Children's Hour. I am only just tackling the first of these in which Herod has to explain, in words of one syllable, the extremely complicated situation in Judaea and to rage characteristically in language suitable for the nursery! If this effort pleases the authorities I shall then have to write the eleven other plays, in which case I don't think I could honestly undertake to do anything about Wilfred or Alcuin this side of Christmas, even if I knew anything about Wilfred or Alcuin, which I can't say I do. Of course, if the religious powers at the B.B.C. don't like Herod, then I shall be released from the undertaking, but I cannot count on their disapproval, so I am afraid I shall have to say no, much as I should have otherwise enjoyed the task if it had come at a more convenient season.

I hope Herod will not get mixed up with the appalling questions with which I am faced at the conference in November![2] In spite of Mr. Kirk's pleading for practical suggestions, I don't know that I can offer much of a "solution". Everybody wants "solutions" to world problems, as though they were some kind of detective story and by some simple trick you can discover [one] and there you are. However, I will do my best about it.

I am, your Grace,
   Yours very sincerely,
      [Dorothy L. Sayers]

1 Dr William Temple (1881–1944), Archbishop of York from 1929 to 1942, Archbishop of Canterbury from 1942 to 1944; author of *Readings in St John's Gospel* (1939) and *Christianity and Social Order* (1942).
2 The Conference called by Archbishop Temple, deferred until January 1941 and held at Malvern to be out of the way of air-raids.

D. L. S. asked Dr. James Welch if it would be posssible for Val Gielgud to pro-
duce her plays on the life of Christ; she had enjoyed working with him on the
broadcast of her Nativity play He That Should Come. *Dr Welch replied that*
it would not be possible for Gielgud to produce the plays as they would be broad-
cast from Bristol by the Children's Hour Department. He thought it would be
appropriate to invite Derek McCulloch (known to listeners as "Uncle Mac") to
produce the plays as Head of that Department, "if after meeting him, you can
confidently trust the production to him". He asked if she would go to Bristol to
meet him.

                                              [24 Newland Street
                                              Witham
                                              Essex]

TO REV. DR JAMES WELCH

30 August 1940

Dear Dr. Welch,

Thank you so much for your letter. I am sorry about Val Gielgud, because, as you know, he and I understand each other's way of working. However, if it can't be I suppose it can't be.

To be quite plain with you I would really rather not come down to Bristol for discussions. Quite apart from the time and energy wasted on the long journey, it is my experience that to talk over any work which one is doing has the curious effect of destroying one's interest in the work itself. I will finish the first play, after which if you pass it from the religious and general point of view, as regards the subject matter, the only person I shall really want to see is the producer. If Mr. McCulloch can't get up to Town then I shall have to come and see him, but I must leave all this until the first play is done. I am taking it that I may allow myself on the average from eight to a dozen actors, plus crowd effects if required, with small musical effects, such as a sung hymn, or a little playing on the harp or lute, if it seems necessary. If later on I can manage to get down for rehearsals I shall try to do so, because there I may be able to make myself useful. It is only discussion beforehand that is apt to get in the way of the job.

I am getting on with the Magi and struggling at present with the difficult job of sketching in briefly, and in language which the children understand, the political situation in Judaea. This is very important, because in some ways Judaea was so much like Hitler's idea of a territory protected by the Reich, but the way in which the Christmas story is usually presented to school children, and indeed to grown-ups too, usually leaves out all the historical background. I never remember being at all clear about the position of Herod with regard to Rome, or what Augustus Caesar had to do with it, or why he was taxing people, or why Herod should have been in such a rage at hearing of the birth of a Messiah. When you come to think of it, the Magi must have thought that the heir whom they were sent to announce would be a Prince of Herod's house, or why did they go to Jerusalem and ask Herod to produce him? I have got the poor men hastening in, full of enthusiasm and expecting to be very well received with their gifts and what-not, and much taken aback by the consternation into which the Palace is thrown. If I can once get this idea about the earthly kingship properly fixed at the beginning of the series, then the later working out will be very much easier.

I am sure you will understand my reasons for not wishing to come to Bristol at the moment, and not consider me in any way ungracious.

Yours sincerely,

[Dorothy L. Sayers]

                                                  [24 Newland Street
                                                  Witham
                                                  Essex]

TO THE REV. J. C. HEENAN[1]

31 August 1940

Dear Dr. Heenan...

I enclose the scripts of the two broadcast talks. The one on Sacraments was difficult to do, because it had to be made reasonably acceptable to all sorts, from Catholics to Quakers. I expected to be roared at by the "spikes"[2] for making the sacramental basis of life too broad; but I got away with it in the *Church Times*, so I suppose it is all right. Oddly enough, no teetotallers have yet written to protest about the sacramental drinking of healths – they must have accepted the rubric about the permissive use of lemonade and tea! Also, to my surprise, the passage about praying with candles provoked no more violent opposition than the one pamphlet abusing "Infallible Popes" (the printing of which was undoubtedly a "sacrilegious abuse of matter" within the meaning of my last paragraphs).

I know, of course, that the foolish public would always rather hear about religion from a detective novelist than from an ex officio expert; I try to do as little as possible, for fear of being classed as a "religious writer"; but it's difficult to refuse. I think one of the troubles is that so few

---

1 Cardinal Heenan (1905–1975).
2 Slang, for people who are extreme in Anglo-Catholic belief and practice.

parsons are really trained in the use of words. They use the standard technical phrases without quite realising how they sound to the ordinary reader or listener. The result is that when the trained writer restates an old dogma in a new form of words, the reader mistakes it for a bright new idea of the writer's own. I spend half my time and a lot of stamps telling people that I have not been giving them fancy doctrine of my own, but only the same old doctrine that they have heard and ignored a thousand times. Typical of this is the woman who writes to say: "I can't agree with you that Christ is the same person as God the Creator". One can only say: "It isn't a question of agreeing with me – I have expressed no opinion. That is the opinion of the official Church, which you will find plainly stated in the Nicene Creed, whether or not you and I agree with it." I do wish, by the way, that the word hypostasis[3] had been translated by anything but *persona*, or that the word person had not acquired such a "personal" meaning in the vulgar tongue. It makes so many explanations necessary and lays so many traps for one's feet. But that is now past praying for. But who was the Anglican bloke who carried on that long correspondence with Haldane[4] about religion, during which they argued for many weeks about transubstantiation, or dividing the Substance, or some such subject, without any effort on the Christian's part to inform Haldane that "substance" in theology had no connection with material structure, or to ask him whether, by "the substance of a document" he really meant the ink and paper that composed it?

Forgive my rambling on so long. It is very kind of you to tell me how many people liked the talks. Most encouraging, after the gentleman from Oxford!

With many thanks,
    Yours sincerely,
        [Dorothy L. Sayers]

P.S. Got it! the "Anglican bloke" was Arnold Lunn.[5] He was in process of conveying himself over to Rome during the controversy – perhaps they will have taught him there a little polemical tactics.

---

3 She interprets this term as "mode of being" in her letter to D. G. Jarvis, 18 October 1940.
4 J. B. S. Haldane (1860–1936), physiologist, author of *The Sciences and Philosophy*, 1929 *The Philosophy of a Biologist*, second edition 1936.
5 Sir Arnold Lunn (1888–1974), writer and ski champion.

On 8 October 1940 Derek McCulloch made his first approach to D. L. S. about
the series of plays on the life of Christ. He began by asking if she had heard a
recent series on Paul of Tarsus by L. Du Garde Peach.[1] *He referred to an article of*
hers which he had read in The Guardian[2] *of 15 March, entitled "Divine*
Comedy"[3] *on the subject of Christian drama. It was crammed, he said "with*
irrefutable advice: I particularly like the line 'At the name of Jesus, every voice goes
plummy' – we have been on our guard against this danger of humbug for more
years than I care to remember.…Mutual confidence is everything between author
and producer. Your article, quite apart from all your other work, makes me feel sure
that we shall establish this at the outset. Thank you for writing it".

1 L. du Garde Peach (1890–1975), author of over 400 plays, mainly for radio, ranging from historical and Biblical pieces to contemporary comedies. He founded an amateur theatre group
  in Derbyshire, known as the Village Players. He was awarded an O.B.E. in 1972.
2 Anglican weekly which ran from 1846 to 1951
3 Later published in *Unpopular Opinions* (Gollancz, 30 September 1946).

The situation looked promising. D. L. S. replied:

> [24 Newland Street
> Witham
> Essex]

TO DEREK MCCULLOCH
11 October 1940

Dear Mr. McCulloch,
  Thank you so much for your very kind and most encouraging letter. I
was very glad to hear from you and to find that you as Producer and I as
Author were obviously going to see eye to eye over this series of plays. I
had been feeling very guilty for not having let you have the first one earlier, but I am now very thankful, as I had somehow gathered from Dr.
Welch that the time was only 30 minutes, probably it was my stupidity in
misunderstanding him. 45 minutes is a great improvement and I shall not
now have to cramp the Bethlehem scene so much by comparison with the
Herod scene.
  Unfortunately I missed the Paul of Tarsus plays. I wish I had heard
them. I am particularly interested to know from you that the children
found them enthralling and exciting, because Mr. Fenn suggested that
some people had thought them a little too advanced for youngsters, and I
was afraid the same criticism might be made of the one I am now doing.
When you are writing for children of all ages it is difficult to hit on the
highest common factor of their combined intelligence, but I always think

it is far better to write a little over the heads of the youngest rather than insult the older ones with something that they think babyish, and I believe Dr. Welch agrees about this. Also I gathered from him that one of the ideas is to catch adults in the net that we spread for the children, and if that is so, then we shall have to get a little above the quite simple and pretty-pretty. As I wrote to Dr. Welch, I am trying to base the whole series on the idea of the Kingdom and I have started by attempting to make real to the listener the complicated political position of Judaea under the Roman Empire. This is so very like that of a tributary state today, either under the British Empire, or in some cases under the Reich, that intelligent children of reasonable age should, I think, be able to grasp the awkwardness of Herod's position. I know that when I was a child it was never really explained to me why Herod should have been so angry about the birth of a Messiah and it would have made the whole story much more intelligible if somebody had told me. You will have to let me know whether you think, as I have written it, it will be comprehensible to the "middle-aged children": we cannot really address ourselves for 45 minutes to the toddlers.

As regards the cast: I have allowed for a cast of about 12, some of whom will double so that the bits and pieces of Herod's court can do duty as supporting characters in the Bethlehem scene. I hope you will not think this is too much of a company. In this play we are embarrassed with three Kings, which rather bulk out the number of actors required.

There are a few characters, of course, who will have to run through more or less the whole series of plays, though they may not appear in each one – such for example as the Blessed Virgin, St. Peter, St. John, and of course, Christ Himself; others will be character parts appearing only in one or two plays as occasion arises. I have also got in the first play a Roman Centurion, who is useful as symbolizing the power of Rome at Jerusalem, and I think he may run all through the series and become at the end the Centurion who said "Truly this was the Son of God". Gordon McLeod played this kind of part extremely well in *He That Should Come*. My Herod is a Cecil Trouncer part, but he I think is at Manchester and I don't know whether we could get him. Our big trouble will be to get a Christ; Raf de la Torre has some claims on this part and his voice is beautiful, but from the producer's point of view he is difficult. He is very slow at rehearsal and fearfully argumentative. Nobody would be better if one could work on each play for a month. Under present conditions you would perhaps prefer a quicker study. Of course, I don't know what scope they give you to engage real stars; if you have carte blanche, I think Michael Redgrave[3] would be quite a possibility, but of course I have no

3 (Sir) Michael Redgrave (1908–1985).

idea whether he would come and whether they would pay for him, but I do think if we are going to put on Christ that they will have to make an effort to get somebody really first-class. After all, it is a very experimental thing to do and we shall get into the most dreadful trouble if there is anything not quite first-class about the performance.

I have done the Herod scene and as soon as I have recast and expanded the Bethlehem scene and the final tail-piece in which Herod orders the Massacre of the Innocents, I will send the manuscript along for you to look at.

In the meantime may I say that after your letter I look forward very much to working with you.

Yours sincerely,
[Dorothy L. Sayers]

[24 Newland Street
Witham
Essex]

TO ANTHONY GILBERT[1]

17 October 1940

Dear Anthony Gilbert,

Many thanks for your letter, I enclose the cheques signed.

It is very sad about Helen Simpson. I had been afraid for a long time that things were going that way. I did not think it was much use doing anything about flowers, she died in the country, but they did not tell me when or where the funeral was to take place and I felt that by the time we had got the details and despatched a wreath, it would be too late, but there is no reason why we should not send something to be put on the grave if we can find out where this is. It was stupid of me not to ask her secretary at the time. She rang me up from London but had had some difficulty in getting through and I did not quite get my wits about me. It is a frightful job to get calls to Town from here[2] but if you would like to ring up the Children's Hospital, I expect they would be able to tell you about it.

I have just sent out a notice to the Club[3] saying that this does not seem a good time for Dinners, but that if anybody would like a Lunch, I should be glad if they would communicate with me. I am glad to know that you

---

1 Anthony Gilbert (1899–1973), a woman detective novelist. Her real name was Lucy Beatrice Malleson. She had two other pseudonyms: J. Kilmeny Keith and Anne Meredith.
2 Owing to war-time congestion on telephone lines.
3 The Detection Club.

are all right so far. I imagine that the Club premises are still standing since nobody has told us they are not. I don't know whether we ought to put the Minute book and some of those prints in a place of greater safety, and I don't quite know what place is of greater safety. We have a good cellar in Gt. James Street[4] but just at present I understand we are surrounded by time bombs,[5] but I will leave it to you to take any action you think desirable.

It might be a good thing to send the Minute book down here. We get a few bangs and bumps in the neighbourhood most nights but not in such profusion as London.

Wishing you safe and sound,
    Yours sincerely,
        [D. L. S.]

4 Beneath her London flat at No. 24.
5 This is the time of the Blitz on London.

                                                [24 Newland Street
                                                Witham
                                                Essex]

TO DR. W. W. GREG[1]
18 October 1940

Dear Dr. Greg,
    Thank you so much for your kind note. We shall feel the loss of Helen Simpson very much; she had one of the finest minds I know and an extraordinarily vivid personality. I don't think I ever met anybody who was so intensely interested in every kind of person and thing she encountered on her passage through life, and I feel that her death at this moment is a blow not only to her friends but also to the country; she would have taken a vigorous part in the post-war re-building.

Muriel Byrne, who is staying with me, I hope for some little time, thanks you very much for your message and asks me to send her love and say that she is writing to you and hopes very much to come and see you before very long. She is finding this place rather more peaceful than London, though to be sure we get a series of bumps and crashes most nights, but not quite so loudly or so persistently as they do in Town.

1 Sir Walter Wilson Greg (1875–1959), mediaevalist and Shakespearean scholar.

With again much gratitude for your kind thought and hoping that you are all keeping safe and well.

Yours sincerely,

[Dorothy L. Sayers]

[24 Newland Street
Witham
Essex]

TO D. G. JARVIS[1]

18 October 1940

Dear Miss Jarvis,

Thank you for your letter; I am glad you were interested in my little pamphlet, "Creed or Chaos?"

The doctrine of the Trinity is, I think, not nearly so puzzling as it sounds, but it would take rather a long time to expound it in a letter. (As it happens, I am writing a short book[2] which has some bearing on the subject, from the point of view of the creative artist, who keeps a kind of "working model" of the Trinity inside his own mind, forming a useful analogy to the Great Trinity that created the world.)

I think the two points about which one is most likely to get confused are: (a) the word "Person", which does not mean, theologically, what it means in every-day English – i.e. an entirely separate *character*, but is a (not very happy) translation of the Greek *hypostasis*, meaning, rather, a distinct *mode of being*; (b) the phrase "Son" of God, which tends to suggest that the Second Person of the Trinity begins and ends with the human Jesus. That, of course, is not what is meant at all – Jesus is God the Son manifested in human nature, but the Godhead of the Son existed and exists eternally, and is the Creator "by whom all things were made". In some ways I think St. John's phrase "the Word of God" is easier to understand than "the Son of God". If you try taking – let us say, any beautiful line of poetry in which the thought is perfectly expressed by the words, and try to *distinguish* in your mind between the thought and the word, you will probably get some idea of what is meant by saying that "the Father" and "the Son" are the same and yet distinct (or, as the theologians put it, two Persons but the same Substance). If you then try again to distinguish the Thought and the Word from the Meaning which they have for you, you will get some idea of what is meant by saying that the Spirit is also a distinct Person, but still the same Substance. Or take a book – any book – and ask yourself: which is the actual book – the general idea of the book

---

1 Identity unknown.
2 i.e. *The Mind of the Maker.*

in the author's mind, the succession of words and scenes that make up the book as he planned it all out, or the book as you read it yourself? You will probably find it hard to decide, and may end by saying: Each is the book, and the whole book, and all three together are one and the same book – and I can only know any of them because one of them (the second) has been manifested in material ink and paper (the second person incarnate).

The theory that Jesus was only a very good man is, of course, perfectly tenable – but, for the reasons given in "Creed or Chaos?" it gets one precisely nowhere, and can scarcely be called "Christianity" in the sense that the Christian Church understands the word.

Yours very truly,
[Dorothy L. Sayers]

[24 Newland Street
Witham
Essex]

TO DEREK MCCULLOCH
25 October 1940

Dear Mr. McCulloch,

Very many thanks for sending the St. Paul plays,[1] which I shall very much enjoy reading.

I am driving on with the Magi, who are getting rather talkative – owing no doubt to the sudden expansion of their Lebensraum[2] to twenty minutes instead of ten! I think Robert Donat[3] would probably be a very good choice; as it happens I don't know his work very well except on the films, but I believe he is a very intelligent and sympathetic actor, which is what we want. In addition to those qualities I feel that the third indispensable thing is a voice which is essentially alive and flexible. Technically the most exacting feature of the part is the immense range of expression it will demand, from the fieriest denunciation to the most compassionate tenderness all telescoped into a very few minutes.

The one kind of Christ I absolutely refuse to have at any price whatsoever, is a dull Christ; we have far too many of these in stained-glass windows.

I am so glad you can count on Robert Farquharson,[4] he is an excellent

---

1 By L. du Garde Peach. See introduction to letter to Derek McCulloch, 11 October 1940, note 1.
2 German: living space.
3 Robert Donat (1905–1958), stage and film star.
4 Robert Farquharson (1877–1966). He acted the part of Ephraim, a Gentleman of Herod's Bedchamber, in the first play.

actor and I am sure he will be sympathetic because he so much enjoyed being the Greek gentleman in *He That Should Come*. The Virgin Mary always presents a certain amount of difficulty – again in getting rid of the stained-glass window touch; that is, she has got to be sweet without being sentimental. The part itself presents difficulties in this way, especially as we have to cope with the feelings of Roman Catholics, to whom she is almost as divine as her Son, and deeply dyed Protestants, who regard everything about her with the deepest suspicion. However, that is my funeral. I hope to let you have the script of the first play next week.

　　With best wishes,
　　　　Yours very sincerely,
　　　　　　[Dorothy L. Sayers]

　　　　　　　　　　　　　　　　[24 Newland Street
　　　　　　　　　　　　　　　　Witham
　　　　　　　　　　　　　　　　Essex]

TO REV. DR JAMES WELCH

25 October 1940

Dear Dr Welch,

　　I am anxious to find out whether there is a regular Evening Hymn sung by Jewish families in their household devotions. I want it to finish off the Bethlehem scene in the Children's play. I think you told me you had a Jewish friend[1] who would be ready to furnish details of this kind and I should be very glad if you could ask him whether there is such a thing and whether he can supply the traditional words and music. If there is no such thing, I will write one myself.

　　I have been in communication with Derek McCulloch, who has been very nice, and it looks as though we should be able to work together very well.

　　Trusting you are carrying on in reasonable comfort, despite Hitler,
　　　Yours very sincerely,
　　　　[Dorothy L. Sayers]

1　Dr Welch enlisted the help of the Chief Rabbi, Dr Hertz, who supplied the traditional airs which are used in plays five and seven.

24 Newland Street
Witham
Essex

TO THE EDITOR OF TIME AND TIDE

26 October 1940[1]

Sir,

MR WINSTON CHURCHILL

I should like to voice my appreciation of Maurice Collis'[2] article on Winston Churchill. We cannot be told too loudly or too often of the need for restoring to the man of vision the control of public affairs. For a long time, many of us have watched with distress and alarm a growing tendency to entrust our national destinies to the heedless hands of the "plain man", while despising the man of vision as a visionary. That, when the inevitable doom was fulfilled and our agitated repentance took place, we should have found the right man ready and waiting seems almost more than we deserved.

Mr Churchill has reaffirmed in us the classic virtues; is it perhaps a little exaggerated to say that these are "very distinct from Christian virtues"? A certain sentimentality in our religious attitude sometimes leads us to forget that the four "natural" virtues, recognized by the Schoolmen as the Cardinal Virtues on which all the rest depend, are Justice, Prudence, Temperance (i.e. Measure), and Fortitude – and these have a strongly "classical" sound. We might do worse than adopt them as a national watchword. The three "theological" virtues of Faith, Hope, and Charity are more mystical and paradoxical – to believe when all is betrayed, to go forward when things are desperate, and to love the unlovable. Two of these, at any rate, are not altogether absent from our present leadership; and we shall probably need to learn the third, if the next European settlement is not to go the way of the last.

Finally, may I take this opportunity of congratulating *Time and Tide* on its careful observance of the cardinal virtue of Temperance in dealing with ministerial and other errors at the present time. Criticism is an excellent thing, and the corner-stone of our liberties; but when it degenerates into malignant and indiscriminate abuse, it not only outruns Prudence, overthrows Justice, and undermines Fortitude, but defeats its own ends by

---

1 The date of publication.
2 Maurice Collis' article on Winston Churchill was published in *Time and Tide* on 19 October 1940. D. L. S. evidently had it in mind when she wrote her own article on Churchill, "They Tried to be Good", first published in *World Review*, November 1943, pp. 30–34, later republished in *Unpopular Opinions* (1946).

evoking an obstinate and resentful antagonism to criticism of any kind. From this intemperate virulence, your paper has kept singularly free; and that is no small achievement.

I am, etc.,
Dorothy L. Sayers

24 Newland Street
Witham
Essex

TO J. E. SPICE
28 October 1940

Dear Mr. Spice,

Forgive my delay in answering your very kind letter of the 21st. I am, of course, greatly honoured by your invitation to become an Honorary member of the Oxford University Society of Change Ringers. I have pleasure in enclosing my cheque for half a guinea in payment of this year's subscription.

I am afraid it must be very difficult for Ringers Societies to carry on under present conditions, but one can only hope that the bells will not be silent too long.[1]

Wishing you all success,
Yours sincerely,
Dorothy L. Sayers

1 Church bells were not rung during the war until November 1942, in celebration of the Battle of Alamein.

[24 Newland Street
Witham
Essex]

TO DEREK MCCULLOCH
5 November 1940

Dear Mr. McCulloch,

Sorry I couldn't send this last week. "It turned out as I knew it would be"; the thing, suddenly released from compression within thirty minutes, shot out like a joyful jack-in-the-box, and had to be captured and brought back. So I spent an angry week-end trying to resqueeze it into its box. It's still about a page and a half longer (by count of words) than the second "St. Paul" play; but there are not so many shipwrecks and effects to allow for. But I took the opportunity of the extra 15 minutes to enliven things with a bit of crowdage and shoutery by introducing the famous episode of the Golden Eagle. This seemed good to me, as counteracting the necessarily rather pious and domestic effect of the Bethlehem scene. (I hate coping with this baby stuff – thank Heaven, one can only be young once, whoever one is!) It also gives Herod a good kick-off for his fury in the matter of the Massacre of the Innocents. It's important that this shouldn't be looked on as a mere piece of meaningless savagery. It was a perfectly reasonable political step, if you once allow that the good of the State is more important than the rights of the individual. The thing one wants to put up against the idea of the Kingdom of Heaven is the idea of the political kingdom, not the caprice of one wicked man. And finally, it gives Herod a final flare-up in his best manner – he handled that business rather well – and, as you will perceive, I have a weakness for the brilliant old ruffian. To the actor, of course, he is money for jam. I don't think any-one could go wrong in playing Herod, though I do rather see Cecil Trouncer in it, if he's available. I hope the allusions to his past – the Mariamne stuff and the political pretensions of the Hasmonaeans – [are] not too obscure. After all, children who have done any English history must have some acquaintance with the idea of the pretenders to the throne, and the claims of rival houses.

At this point, I have been depressed by a letter from Dr. Welch, saying that the "St. Paul" plays appeal "rather to adolescents and adults" than to children, and wistfully hoping that my plays will be understandable to youngsters "from 8 or 9 upwards". I feel that 45 minutes of a religious play, *every word* of which is to be understood of the eight-year-old, would be intolerably tedious to the twelve-year-olds. Besides, children differ so much. My own fancy, at that tender age, was for good, rumbling phrases, whether they meant anything or not. I should have liked the Kings' astro-logical speeches, and the mysterious prophecies about the Victor-victim, and the three parallel dreams. Nor should I have minded a little pleasing melancholy – in fact, in my youth I rather wallowed in gloom, and liked to have the myrrh along with the gold. It's the grown-ups who demand this everlasting brightness. But you will judge. My practice, when con-fronted with possible opposition from the religious authorities, is, first to satisfy the producer and enlist his support; then to sit back and watch while he fights it out on my behalf. This is called strategy.

By the way: I have two "things" about broadcast plays, both of which add greatly to my own troubles. One is, that I have a rooted conviction that all plays, even when broadcast, should explain themselves within their own dialogue. I don't like to hear the Narrator expounding the situation. This may be a prejudice inherited from stage practice. But the thing irritates me – just as I am irritated by those complicated ballets, where an acre of small print on the programme is required to inform you that when the Huntsman leaps in and executes three chassées and a pirouette, he is really telling the Princess that he is the disguised rightful heir who was ousted by the wicked step-mother and left in the wood to be eaten by a bear, but for the intervention of a kindly charcoal-burner. I feel that if that information is so necessary to the understanding of the action, it ought to be conveyed *in* the action. Consequently, I have cut down the part of the Narrator to four brief Bible texts. The first three merely indicate the scene-changes; the fourth summarily concludes the story, and spares us a second domestic scene, and another angelic intrusion. One really cannot have two warning dreams in one episode. The choice was between cutting the Kings' dreams and reducing Herod's second scene to an outline, so as to give a scene to the Flight into Egypt, on the one hand, and doing as I have done – elaborating Herod and the Kings and cutting the Flight. I chose to do it this way, (a) because Herod is good acting stuff and (b) because there wasn't very much that Mary and Joseph could say or do in the Flight scene, except be a couple of ordinary parents in a fright – and I don't think one should bring Mary in unless one has something really important for her to say and do. By the way, you will notice that I have put into the Kings' salutation a suggestion of the "Hail Mary", but only the bit that will please the Catholics without offending the Protestants. (Let no one try to stampede us into accepting that the phrase "Mother of God" is Papist! It is not Latin, but Greek, and the people who object to it are Nestorian heretics,[1] which is a very shocking thing to be!)

But I am wandering. The second "thing" I have about any series of plays, broadcast or otherwise, is that each should be, as far as possible, a complete and self-explanatory play in itself, with a beginning, a middle and an end of its own, and not just a slice out of a long narrative. This, again, is part of my prejudice against the Narrator, doing his bit of synopsis at the beginning: "Well, children, last week we saw how," etc. This is going to make things awkward in the middle of the series, because it means constructing each play at the same time as a self-contained unit and also as a structural unit within the series. It means some careful "planting" and also that each plant should have its own root and leaves. But if it can be done, I think it is worth while, because it makes everything much easier for the listener who has happened to miss an instalment here and there. I don't know whether I shall be able to manage it. Of course,

---

1 Those who adhere to the heresy of Nestorius (5th-century Patriarch of Constantinople) who attributed distinct divine and human attributes to Christ.

I may not have to! You and/or the other authorities may not care for the
first play, and then I shan't have to do the rest.

Having now read the "St. Paul" plays, I'm sorry I didn't hear them. I
think it is exceptionally awkward material – a continual succession of
shipwrecks and sermons – very gallantly handled. His dialogue is always
excellent. I feel my usual irritation with the narrator, jerking us back to the
question of what we know, or do not know about the subject. An author
has no business to button-hole the audience to explain the defects in his
knowledge – it makes him into a school-teacher at once. And I do feel –
as I nearly always feel with Christian plays and films – that it suffers from
a certain lack of theological guts. After all, it wasn't a new idea that there
was only one God (the Jews had had that, and got into trouble with the
State before), and it wasn't the idea that we should all be nice and kind all
round (the Greeks had had that) that gave the thing its terrific dynamism.
It was the sense that something which was the power of life itself had
gone through the world like a thunderbolt and split time into two halves.
I don't say that is quite the way to convey it to the children, but it's the
feeling one wants to convey somehow. And you don't quite get it by making the characters say: "There's something funny about you blokes", at
every turn. And I do wish Paul didn't address everybody as "Friend", like
a Communist writing to his comrades!

However, I've no business to criticise other people's plays, since mine
will probably be no good at all. And I shall certainly be told that I have
put in too much theology, too much obscure and mystical theology, too
much offensive and Catholic theology, and far too little "simple Gospel"
and plain, practical morality.

I've added a few notes on the characters. They must be real people –
except the Kings, who are rather fairy sort of people. I think that is right.
Tradition has bound the fairy-tale atmosphere upon them, and they come
and go in a perfectly unexplained, magical way. By comparison, the
Shepherds and their angel-vision are as plain as pie-crust. But what does
come clearly out in the Gospel story, if one reads it carefully, is that they
quite obviously thought they were bringing their message to Herod's own
household. Else why should they ask him to show them "him that is born
king of the Jews"? It was the natural assumption to make. And hence the
elaborate gifts of gold and myrrh and incense – the usual sort of present
from one kingly court to another. The upshot of the thing must have surprised them – though I haven't stressed this, since surprise is apt to sound
comic. Actually, I don't suppose Herod showed them how greatly "troubled" he was; the interview with the priests probably took place in private;
but that would have been too undramatic. Also, it's interesting that "all
the people was troubled with" Herod. That supports the idea that the
Kings made no secret of their (as they supposed) welcome mission; and

that it was taken up by the people, and by Herod, as an exciting rumour about the possible new Messiah. And that would excite Jerusalem at that moment, when Herod was dying, when a religious revolt was already seething among the Pharisees, and when there were at least three claimants to the crown. (Almost Herod's last act was to execute the wretched Antipater.)

In the hope that you may find the play workable, I will proceed to the next. I'm alarmed by the sweat this one has taken, and feel that time is short. The next one ought, logically, to cope with the Temptation in the Wilderness (since that was the moment when the idea of the wrong sort of kingdom was definitely faced and rejected). That means coping with the DEVIL – always an embarrassing character to make credible.

I hope you like the general title of the plays. It is an old fairy-tale title, and tells the story in six words.[2]

Hitler seems to keep fussing in and out today. One of these days our local siren will wear its whistle out. I hope Bristol hasn't been too much bothered lately. If things go well, and you do the plays, I should like very much to attend a rehearsal or two. The job is that with trains as they are it's a sort of pilgrimage to get anywhere these days.

The local warden has just come in to say that there is a time-bomb across the street, which "looks as though it might go off any minute". He adds that "the police and the military are surrounding it" – as though it were a truculent parachutist. It's a mild one, I gather – about 250 lb. But I had better retire from the window[3] and put the MS of the play in the air-raid shelter.

Yours very sincerely,
    [Dorothy L. Sayers]

---

2 The title, "The Man Born to be King", was also used by William Morris for one of his poetical legends. (See *The Earthly Paradise*. D. L. S. read this at school.)
3 Her desk was in the window of her library on the first floor, overlooking Newland Street.

24 Newland Street
Witham
Essex

TO MARJORIE BARBER
11 November 1940

Dearest Bar,

So glad the jersey fits all right. Muriel's has turned out quite satisfactory too, I think – I don't like her round neck quite as well as your square one, but she chose that and it seems to suit her all right. I thought, what with the weather and the war, we might as well have the wool, in case Christmas never comes. Though here I am again encouraged by Winston, who seems to think 1942 and even 1943 may arrive in due course.

I expect M. has told you that she arrived back here to find a truly homelike atmosphere. About one hour before she came, the cook came up and announced that Mrs. Pork-Butcher just opposite had been out in her garden and found a hole in the ground. Mr. P-B went to inspect it, and said: "Ho! I shall report that to the police". So the police came and looked at it and said, "Ho! We shall report that to the military". So the military came and looked at it and said: "Ho! that is a 250 lb. time-bomb". Having looked at it, and spoken thus, they went away. So the police said to the Pork-Butcher, "Would you rather evacuate your house and shop?" And the P-B said to the police: "Will I hell? Balls to you". So the local plumber-and-decorator came to tell us all about it, and the cook told me, adding that the bomb "looked as though it would go off any minute", but that no doubt it would be a harmless neighbour, since the military and the police were "surrounding it" – as if it were a truculent parachutist. The plumber-and-decorator then went and had a drink with Mac, who came in to tea later, with the information that the bomb had grown to 500 lb. We were much interested, and predicted that by the morning it would have increased to a land-mine. But evidently the swelling was not what we supposed; for the following evening my secretary came in and announced that the creature had apparently kittened in the night, as (according to the latest reports) there were now three or four of it; moreover, a quite separate one had turned up in the field behind her garden. That night, about 11.55, a heavy explosion was heard, followed by several more. Some of us thought the whole litter must have exploded simultaneously, but I thought not, and said it was a stick of bombs dropped at Braintree. Later, someone told us that a stick of bombs had fallen at Coggeshall; and my answer was adjudged correct, till our evacuee came in and said that somebody had told him that our bomb had gone off the night before at 11.30. This was as confusing as a detective story, because, owing to the conflict of evidence about the time, the bomb could prove an alibi, and the time that we heard the explosions could be proved by me, because I had the wire-less on, waiting for the midnight news. Also (circumstantial evidence) the Pork-Butcher still had his shutters up – a measure adopted as an anti-time-bomb precaution, and we supposed that if it had gone off just behind his premises, the shutters would by now be either taken down or blown out. Finally, the cook thrust her head into the sitting-room to announce (from the P-B's own mouth) that the Bomb Had Not Gone Off Yet. So we suppose it is still there. So is the Pork-Butcher's. And so is the New Post-Office next door to the Pork-Butcher's. And some of us think that the bomb must have been rendered fairly harmless, since the Government has only just finished the Post-Office at vast expense and wouldn't want it blown up. But Mac says, No – it is built with public money, and they wouldn't care whether it was blown up or not. Anyway, it is a very ugly building and much higher than our house. So if the Bomb goes off, the Post-Office will probably shield us from the blast, but come and die heroically on our roof. So we hope it will not go off; but, this being the country, nobody bothers at all one way or the other....

    Best love,
      Yours ever,
        D. L. S.

Muriel's best love – She says she knows she has something to say to you, but can't think what it is.

On 5 November 1940 D. L. S. sent off the first of her plays to Derek McCulloch. He acknowledged it but said he had not yet been able to read it. Only one copy had been sent, for fear lest others might be destroyed in an air-raid. He reported that "my staff tore it from me to read in relays, but judging from their excited remarks the general opinion seems to be 'favourable', as publishers with their extreme caution are fond of saying".

Everything seemed promising and D. L. S. began work on the second play. Derek McCulloch was obliged to go to Glasgow for a few days. In his absence, the Assistant Director, Miss May E. Jenkin, wrote to D. L. S. about the play. She began by saying: "We have now all read it and let me say at once that we are quite delighted with it. It seems to us admirably dramatic, and both profound and beau-tiful." She went on to say, however, that certain speeches would be over the heads of children and that in some places the idiom was too modern: "We wonder if you will allow us discreetly to edit? If you would prefer to make these small alterations yourself, I will send you the play back, but we are anxious not to delay having the copies duplicated and posts are so slow at the moment. We would, of course, get your O.K. for every change before the broadcast."

D. L.S., who had herself expressed to Derek McCulloch some doubt as to whether she was writing above the heads of children, reacted irascibly, evidently because she sensed that her work was now being judged by a committee.[1]

[24 Newland Street
Witham
Essex]

TO MAY E. JENKIN

22 November 1940

Dear Miss Jenkin,

Thank you for your letter. I am glad you like "Kings in Judaea". I shall now proceed to be autocratic – as anyone has a right to be, who is doing a hundred pounds' worth of work for twelve guineas.

I don't think you need trouble yourselves too much about certain passages being "over the heads of the audience". They will be over the heads of the adults, and the adults will write and complain. Pay no attention. You are supposed to be playing to children – the only audience, perhaps, in the country whose minds are still open and sensitive to the spell of poetic speech. The two passages you mention are those which I had already dealt with in my letter to Mr. McCulloch; because I knew that they would present a difficulty to adults – though not to children – and that your first impulse would be to cut them.

But you are not children. The thing they react to and remember is not logical argument, but mystery and the queer beauty of melodious words. To you and me, for instance, the poetry of de la Mare[2] is both obscure and fragile, because it evades all attempts at interpretation and breaks when forced into an intellectual pigeon-hole. But that does not worry children. Nor do children feel any particular religious awe at the Sermon on the Mount; what fascinates them is the mysterious Trisagion of A & M 160,[3] and the beasts and the wheels of Ezekiel. I don't suppose it would occur to you to put on a reading of the Athanasian Creed as an attraction

---

1 Cf. her comment concerning Thomas Lovell Beddoes' willingness to conform to the criticism of friends: "It is true that the majority of these drastic reconstructions were never carried out; but what writer whose trinity was strongly co-ordinated would even dream of revising his work *to conform with the majority report of a committee*?" [Italics added.] *The Mind of the Maker* (Methuen, 1941), p. 130.

2 Walter de la Mare (1873–1956).

3 Trisagion: a hymn beginning with a threefold invocation of God as holy. The hymn referred to is that by Bishop R. Heber, beginning "Holy, Holy, Holy! Lord God Almighty!", no. 160 in *Hymns Ancient and Modern*.

for the Children's Hour; yet I know of a small boy of seven who urgently demanded this of his mother as a special birthday treat. It is the language that stirs and excites: "Not three incomprehensibles and three uncreated; but one uncreated and one incomprehensible."

As regards Melchior's astrological speech: they will like the sound of the planetary names and the unusual words. The grand noise will convey its message without any need for understanding. (Read Greening Lamborn's[4] account of the effect on a class of elementary school-children of Homer in the original Greek.) It is true that the children may not grasp the implications of the "imperial star" and the "constellation of the Virgin" – does that matter? If they hear and remember the words, one day they may suddenly light upon the meaning. Though, actually, some of the older ones may be a good deal better up in astrology than the rest of us, since the poor little wretches have to do Chaucer's *Prologue* with notes, as a set book for Matric.,[5] besides coping with Spenser and God knows what. But the important thing is the magical sound of the words, not what their brains make of it.

The same thing goes for the "Mortal-Immortal". I will swear that no child has ever heard unmoved, "[So] when this corruptible shall have put on incorruption, and this mortal shall have put on immortality".[6] What does he know of corruption? Nothing. But it is moving to him precisely because his mind and ear are not corrupted like those of people who read the penny papers.

I knew how you would react to those passages; it is my business to know. It is also my business to know how my real audience will react; and yours to trust me to know it.

Nothing will induce me to let you put in explanations and bright bits of information at the beginning. If you do it here, you will want to do it at every change of scene. If you think the references to the Kings' visit do not set the scene enough, you must add a line in the text:

4 Edmund Arnold Greening Lamborn (1877–1950), Headmaster of the East Oxford School, author of articles on education and other subjects. The reference is to *The Rudiments of Criticism* by E. A. Greening Lamborn (Oxford Clarendon 1916, 2nd edition 1925), p. 20: "I lately heard a 'Greats' man read a passage of Homer to some boys of twelve who knew no language other than their own; they listened breathlessly and then told him that there had been a challenge, a fight and a song of triumph – which was really the 'substance' of the passage. He then read some lines of Vergil and they said 'it was a cavalry charge'; 'passer mortuus est' [the sparrow has died] of Catullus and they suggested that 'someone was speaking of a dead child'".

5 Matriculation, the examination which corresponded to the General Certificate of Secondary Education.

6 1 Corinthians, chapter 1, verse 54.

Ephraim: You have all the luck . . . . (querulously):
   They oughtn't to allow these disturbances
   right under the Palace windows . . . .
   Rumours? Rumours? What about it?

Joseph's idiom: This is entirely a matter for the actor; that is why I never give more than the very slightest hint of dialect. Let the actor settle his own accent and turn of speech, according to the particular dialect he can do. If he decides on a touch of Yorkshire, for instance, he will not say "it do be", but use some other form. When he has settled this, then, if he finds that "conduct you to your tent" is too formal for the speech he is using, he can say "see you to your tent", or "bring 'ee to your tent", according to the speech he is using. This is a matter for rehearsal, and you must learn to consult the actor. Since most of Joseph's speeches, after the beginning, consist of quotations from the Old Testament, these must obviously be dealt with by accent, and not by dialect phrasing.

Modern Idiom: Nonsense. The whole thing is packed with modern idiom. Why not? "I deeply distrust his intentions" is, as a matter of fact, far more formal than everyday modern speech. "Do as you like" – well, there is the choice of "Do as you choose", which is a jingle, and "Do as you will", which is good Wardour-Street,[7] but gives you two "will's" in one sentence. "Like" is right.[8] As for Proclus, he is as modern, prosaic, and matter-of-fact a person as you could find in a month of Sundays. That is what he is there for. He speaks like a soldier of any time and place, and the more modern he can be, the better. Why should an Army Captain talk Wardour-Street? Do you suppose they had no blunt speech or slang in ancient Rome or Palestine? The common Roman referred to his pal's face as "testa" – "your mug" – exactly like the common Englishman. If I wrote that, would you complain of my "modern idiom"?

Actors: For goodness' sake, handle Billy Williams[9] tactfully. He will expect me to ask him to play Herod. He could play a Herod – and I once started to write a Herod play for him – but that was a different Herod, more lyrical and less political. Try not to let him know that I asked for Trouncer, or he will be hurt in his feelings.

   It takes two months, generally speaking, to write a play of this kind. So I can hardly promise to produce them at the rate of one a fortnight, though I will try to get ahead as quickly as possible, so as to have something in hand.

---

7 Pseudo-archaic diction, from the name of a street in London where imitation antique furniture was sold.
8 In the printed version, D. L. S. had accepted "Do as you will" (Gollancz, 1943, p. 61).
9 Harcourt Williams.

I was asked for twelve plays. That was your arrangement. But if there is any doubt about it, you had better let me know. And quickly. I cannot possibly select incidents and arrange their place in the series, unless I know for certain how long the series is to be, and what proportion each is to bear to the whole.

Yours sincerely,

[Dorothy L. Sayers]

[24 Newland Street
Witham
Essex]

LADY BOILEAU[1]

22 November 1940

Dear Lady Boileau,

Thank you very much for your letter. I am so glad you liked "Creed or Chaos?". I do this kind of thing mostly to order and if anyone demands something on the Incarnation, no doubt I shall deal specifically with that subject some time – though in fact, anything one does on these lines is naturally based on a doctrine of Incarnation. The impression I get – I don't know whether you will agree with me – is that the average Englishman has no idea whatever what is really meant by the term, so that a great deal of Christian doctrine is completely incomprehensible to him. The fulminations of one Minister of Religion who announced that I had shocked all thoughtful Christians by the suggestion that God Almighty was crucified, suggest that some of our Pastors and Ministers know as little as their congregations. I meant to tell this gentleman that he apparently believed either that Christ was not God (in which case he was an Arian heretic) or that His divinity was withdrawn from him before the Crucifixion (in which case he was a Manichean[2] heretic). But it was too much trouble.

It is very sad about Helen.[3] I agree entirely with you that I have never met anybody who equalled her in vivid personality and in the intense interest she brought into her contacts with people and things. I don't really quite know just what was the matter, but immediately after her operation, I gathered that things had not gone well and that they had found something more extensive than they expected, so that from the

1 An administrator in the Voluntary Unit Training Centre, Women's Transport Service.
2 Relating to the heresy of Manichaeus (3rd century), who held that Satan was co-eternal with God.
3 Helen Simpson.

beginning I rather feared the worst. Of course, one could not get anything out of Browne[4] – in any case, one does not like to try and pump people too much. I am afraid I don't know where she was buried; of course I
wrote to Browne at the time but equally of course, he has not written –
she died down in the country and under present circumstances I should
think it likely she was buried there.

　　With again many thanks,
　　　　Yours very sincerely,
　　　　　　[Dorothy L. Sayers]

4 Her husband, Denis Browne.

[24 Newland Street
Witham
Essex]

TO MARGERY VOSPER[1]

27 November 1940

Dear Margery,

　　I have been having the usual struggle with the play at the B.B.C. What
happens is that the Producer goes away and a yammering kind of letter is
sent me by some female he has left in charge who thinks it her duty to tell
me how to write English and how to write for the stage! I have been firm
about this but I expect we shall have ructions, especially as I wrote rather
a stiff letter pointing out that they were buying about £100's worth of
work for twelve guineas – and intimating that they had to put up with
what they got!

　　Meanwhile it is only proper that you should know what they have got
and enclosed is a copy. They seem to have more or less accepted it, their
objections being mostly the fiddling and unnecessary kinds. . . .

　　With all the best,
　　　　Yours sincerely,
　　　　　　[D. L. S.]

1 Her dramatic agent.

Derek McCulloch, returning "somewhat travel-battered" after a 19-hour railway journey from Fife to Bristol, found D. L. S.' reply to May Jenkin. He supported all his assistant's comments and urged D. L. S. to come and visit them in Bristol: "You do not know us, but we flatter ourselves that by meeting each other we might soon sweep away all obstacles".

D. L. S. replied:

[24 Newland Street
Witham
Essex]

TO DEREK MCCULLOCH
28 November 1940

Dear Mr. McCulloch,

Oh, no, you don't, my poppet! You won't get me to do three days of exhausting travel to Bristol in order to argue about my plays with a committee. What goes into the play, and the language in which it is written is the author's business. If the Management don't like it, they reject the play, and there is an end of the contract.

If travelling is at all possible, I am ready to meet the Producer and the Actors *in rehearsal*. Then, if there is any line or speech which, *in rehearsal*, I can hear to be wrong, or ineffective, or impossible to speak aloud, I will alter it, if I think the objection to it justified. (But if the actor is merely being tiresome, I say, "No, darling, Mother knows best", and he has to get on with it.) And if the actor puts the accent in the wrong place (as from time to time he inevitably does) I assist him to get it right. And if neither actor nor producer is sure which way a thing is meant to be said, I explain as placidly as possible. And if either of them makes a good suggestion, I listen to it, and adopt it if possible. Anything that has to do with Production I am always prepared to modify – as in the matter of Joseph's dialect, or the extra lines required to set the scene.

But the business of getting my ideas across, and the writing of the English language, is the affair of the playwright; I will give you my reasons for what I do, but if you do not accept them, I can only say, "Take it or leave it". After all, if I am asked by the B.B.C. to do a play for you, it is because they think I can supply a quality of some kind which they cannot get from their staff. That is why outside writers of standing are asked to do things. This always involves the risk that the outside writer may do something which is different from the routine thing which the staff is accustomed to do – and *this difference is the thing for which the outside writer is engaged and paid*. If the writer's authority is not to be absolute in his own sphere, there is no sense in approaching him; he is approached because of his authority, and for no other reason.

You are the producer. Where production is concerned, I will respect your authority. But this is not a matter of production. It falls within the sphere of my authority, and you must respect mine.

You see, it is not merely a question of what children will, or will not, understand. This ground of defence is cut away by the attempt to tell me what sort of English idiom I should, or should not, use. You are, I know, bound to back up your colleagues and subordinates; but you must allow me to tell you that this kind of thing, phrased as it is phrased in Miss Jenkin's letter, is a blazing impertinence. If I am asked to write a play for you, it is because I have the reputation of being able to write. Do you think I should have that reputation if I allowed my style to be dictated to me by little bodies of unliterary critics?

I must also make plain to you that I am concerned with you as a producer for my play. In that capacity, you are not called upon to mirror other aspects of your work at the B.B.C.; you are called upon to mirror *me*. If you prefer to act as the director of a committee of management, well and good; but in that case, you cannot also exercise the functions of a producer. You can reject the play, in which case the matter is closed; or you can accept it, in which case you must offer me another producer with whom I can deal on the usual terms, which are perfectly well understood among all people with proper theatrical experience. I am sorry to speak so bluntly; but I am a professional playwright,[1] and I must deal with professional people who understand where their appropriate spheres of action begin and end.

I am writing to Dr. Welch to make the position clear to him; and shall suspend all work on the succeeding plays until the matter has been put on a more satisfactory footing.

Yours sincerely,

[Dorothy L. Sayers]

---

1 She had by then written five plays: *Busman's Honeymoon*, *The Zeal of Thy House*, *Love All*, *He That Should Come*, and *The Devil to Pay*, all of which had been performed. "Kings in Judaea" was the sixth.

[24 Newland Street
Witham
Essex]

TO DR JAMES WELCH

28 November 1940

Dear Dr. Welch,

I am sorry to say I have reached a sort of impasse with Mr. McCulloch. His first letters were sensible and friendly, and proper as from a producer to a playwright.

Unfortunately, while he was away, an excessively tactless letter from a Miss Jenkin obliged me to insist on the author's right to be sole judge of matter and style where his expert work was concerned. Mr. McCulloch (who is, as I quite understand, bound to back up his subordinate) now seems to have stepped out of the part of a producer into that of a Director, and to think it is part of his business to teach me how to write.

This will not do. He can, as a Director, reject the play. Or he can, as producer, undertake to interpret the play. But he cannot do both. Two objections which had legitimately to do with production, I have already dealt with, so as to meet his views. The other questions, which have nothing to do with production, are a matter for my judgement. These I have said I will not alter, and I have given reasons. This is as far as I am prepared to go. I am not prepared to accept the judgement of a committee upon my English style; though I am always ready to alter in rehearsal any phrase which presents difficulty to the actor.

The details of this controversy are not your affair, and I need not bother you with them. But the point is this: if the B.B.C. calls in an outside writer of standing to write its plays, it is because that writer has a quality, and an authority, which does not belong to the hack writers on the permanent staff. It must therefore take the risk of getting something different from the routine work of the department; in fact, *this difference is the very thing it has engaged and paid for.* That being so, it must trust its outside expert to know his own job.

Also, having called in a professional playwright, it must give him a professional producer who knows where a producer's job begins and ends. The producer's job is to deal with the play in rehearsal, and not to act as the Management. In his own sphere the producer is God – but he is not God in the author's sphere. The author is God there; and the producer's business is to produce the play.

No professional producer of standing has any doubt about where the dividing line comes. I have never yet had the slightest difficulty with a competent professional producer, nor he with me. But the thing that makes work impossible is this trail of amateurishness over the B.B.C.

departments, which results in interference by everybody in everybody else's job; and that I cannot put up with.

I knew at the beginning that this kind of trouble was likely to arise. That was why I made strong representations about getting Val Gielgud, who is a professional, and *does* know his job. I have never had any kind of impertinence or stupidity from him, nor (I think he would tell you) he from me. Although he is a writer himself, he never thought of informing me how I might improve my style; probably, being a writer,[1] he knew better. He would, of course, make suggestions in rehearsal, but always in connection with the acting, and in a proper manner, and I was always ready to listen and adopt them. But then, he knows his theatre inside-out, and is not an amateur.[2]

Theatre, you see, is theatre. It is because these little committees of the Children's Hour have no experience of the theatre that they never succeed in producing theatre, but only school lessons in dialogue. And I cannot do with it. Get me Val, and I will go to Bristol or Manchester or anywhere and work twenty hours a day, with the actors. But I must have a producer who is a professional producer and nothing else, and who can talk the language of the theatre.

If there is any more nonsense, there is an end of the plays and the contract. I have stopped work on the series, and shall do no more till this business is put on a proper professional footing.

I am sorry for all this, which is in no way your fault. You see now why I am disliked at the B.B.C., and why Gielgud enjoys (or so I am told) an extraordinary reputation as a Sayers-tamer! He knows his job; that is the secret of that, as of many other remarkable reputations.

Yours very sincerely,

[Dorothy L. Sayers]

---

1 Val Gielgud wrote novels and plays, as well as an autobiography, *Years of the Locust* (London, Nicholson and Watson, 1947).

2 Val Gielgud had a comparable respect for D. L. S. In *Years of the Locust*, p. 178, he wrote: "Miss Sayers is professional of the professionals. She can tolerate anything but the shoddy or the slapdash. Of all the authors I have known she has the clearest, and the most justifiable, view of the proper respective spheres of author and producer, and of their respective limitations. She is authoritative, brisk, and positive".

[24 Newland Street
Witham
Essex]

TO NANCY PEARN

28 November 1940

Dear Bun...

I am in a state of complete fury, with which you will sympathize. The Children's [Hour] plays I was doing for the B.B.C. have got held up owing to the usual violent struggle between myself and that body. As you know, the Director of Religion asked for the plays to be done in the Children's Hour and asked me about a Producer. I said the only Producer – and indeed the only person at the B.B.C. – for whom I would give a groat – was Val Gielgud. Val, however, being at Manchester, they offered me instead Derek McCulloch, who is one of the Directors of the Children's Hour. So far so good, and he and I exchanged very amicable letters about the play. Then he goes away on business and in bursts a female with a patronising and impertinent letter criticising my matter and begging me to improve my English style in places where "we" (whoever we are) felt it to be inadequate. I replied firmly to this gorgon that matter and style were my business, that I knew as well as "we" what children would be able to understand, though I should be willing to meet them on any point connected with the production, which in fact, I did.

Now comes a letter from Mr. McCulloch, backing up his subordinate and having turned from Producer into a kind of Committee of Management! I replied to him that he cannot be both and must be one or the other; but that if he is going to be a producer he must accept my authority for everything which does not concern production. At the same time I wrote a ferocious letter to the poor religious bloke¹ telling him what has happened to his play and saying that no professional writer of standing can get on with the B.B.C., just because of this frightful trail of the amateur smeared over all their departments!

So you see we are having a lovely row. Next time you see Val, if he comes to London, tell him that he is still the only person at the B.B.C. who can tame the tigress Sayers and I have told Dr. Welch that if I could have Val I would readily go and be bombed at Bristol or Manchester and work twenty hours a day with the actors, but that I will not be come over by amateurs in the Books for the Bairns department.

I know this will please you since you were instrumental in handing me

1 i.e. Dr James Welch.

over to Val and were pleased with the results.

God blast these twirps!

Yours affectionately,

[D. L. S.]

Dr Welch wrote, expressing dismay:

When [Derek McCulloch] wrote to you as producer, you and he seemed to understand each other, and everything seemed to augur well for a happy and successful production. My own suggestion is that we should ignore the comments made on the play as a work of art, that you and McCulloch should pick up where you were before Miss Jenkin's letter, and that McCulloch should make such comments as he wishes – including those made by Miss Jenkin – during the production itself.

[24 Newland Street
Witham
Essex]

TO DR JAMES WELCH

30 November 1940

Dear Dr. Welch,

Thank you so much for your kind letter. I am sorry it did not reach me yesterday, before I wrote to you and to Mr. McCulloch, as it would have enabled me to take up a less autocratic position. In any case, I am very grateful to you for supporting me in the attempt to put over to the children a mystical approach to Christianity by means of poetic language, and also for the tacit confidence you place in my work by the assumption that, having called on a writer to do something, you will leave him to have a shot at it in his own way. These are, of course, the two points in dispute.

I must say that, in the beginning of our correspondence, Mr. McCulloch seemed quite ready to go the whole way with me as regards the former point, quoting the expression: "Preach to the Sixth Form, and let the others pick up what they can". So much so, that I said to him – rather as a joke – that if you complained that I was writing over the heads of the eight-year-olds I should rely on him to fight my battle with your department! The next thing was the letter from Miss Jenkin, written as from a committee of the Children's Hour, requiring me to make six alterations. Two of these concerned precisely the "mystical" passages, on the grounds that they could tell me what would appeal to their audience. I replied that I must be the judge of my approach to the audience, and gave good reason for thinking that children were not incapable of appreciating strange and beautiful words, even if they could not take the whole thing in with their intelligence. Two of the others informed me that "we" the committee did not approve of the "modern idiom" that I was using in places. I replied that it was not their business to criticise my idiom – as indeed it is not, since if I have any reputation as a writer, it is for my ability to handle idiom. (Incidentally, it is by the use of modern idiom that I have from time to time been able to galvanise the public into the realization that events in the Bible took place in times very like our own, and were concerned with real people.) If, in rehearsal, I hear that something I have written doesn't sound right, it is my duty and pleasure to alter it; but I really cannot allow that I am to write to the instructions of a B.B.C. committee. If they want that sort of thing, they must get plays written by their own staff, and not by writers of standing in letters and the theatre. The other two alterations demanded concerned production; this was legitimate (though they should have been requested by the producer and not by the department). I replied by at once making one of the alterations – though on my own lines and not in the way they suggested; and by explaining that the other would have to be settled in the course of rehearsal, for reasons which I gave; viz: that this was a matter which primarily concerned the actor.

Mr. McCulloch then wrote, supporting Miss Jenkin, and asking me to come down to Bristol immediately in order that they might persuade me that the Children's Hour Department was a faithful mirror of its audience. I did not argue about this, but made it clear that, if he was going to produce this play, his business would be to mirror me, and not anything else; and that it was impossible for me to treat him at the same time as my producer and as the head of a department that undertook to teach me how to write. I also said bluntly that I considered Miss Jenkin's letter an impertinence.

The actual passages at issue may appear trivial; but I think you will understand that it would be quite impossible for me to write a series of plays, especially on so difficult and dangerous a subject, if my matter and style had to conform to the practice of a departmental committee. If any body of persons entrusts work to an outside expert of standing, it is because precisely, they look to him to supply something outside their normal practice. In a case like this, there are three authorities to which an author must be ready to submit: (a) that of the Church, if it can allege and substantiate that the matter complained of is heretical or blasphemous; (b) that of the State, if it can show that the matter is likely to lead to open schism, a breach of the peace, or the disturbance of international relations (e.g. anything likely to involve a Governmental department such as the B.B.C. in difficulties with the Catholics, the Jews, the Mohammedans, or what not); (c) the producer, if he can show that the lines and effects cannot be managed by the actors and effects department, or cannot be done in the time allotted, and so forth. But this is for the producer only, in his capacity as producer, and not for a department; and it must be conveyed personally, in connection with the production, and not as the ukase[1] of an editorial committee.

I am not at all unreasonable about alterations. I have rewritten almost an entire act at the request of a very young actor, doing his first production; but on that occasion the approach was very different. The issue was one of sheer dramatic construction, not of ideas or language; it was proved to me in rehearsal that I had made a mistake; it was done in collaboration with the actors, who felt the weakness in their parts; and I made the alteration along my own lines when I had seen for myself what was wrong. But I was not required to submit my judgment.

This kind of thing is the usual theatrical practice; and it is my experience that where the author knows his job, and the producer knows his job, and each will trust the other to know his job, all differences can be amicably settled. If anybody says, "The B.B.C. is not the theatre", the answer is that, if they call in professional playwrights, then it is the theatre, and they must supply a professional theatrical production. Radio technique is not quite like that of the theatre; but there was here no question of radio technique, but only of style and subject-matter.

As I said before, I am extremely sorry that this should have happened; and I think – though of course I do not know – that it is largely the result of applying Civil Service methods to the Arts; the same thing, in fact, which wrecked the propaganda side of the Ministry of Information. This happens when a department requires the outside authority to conform to its routine practice, and when it is thought necessary that every tactless error made by a subordinate must be backed up by the head of the department in order to secure solidarity. What happens, of course, is that the outsider, having nothing to lose and no axe to grind, walks out, leaving the department to reflect that it is useless to present ultimatums (ultimata?) unless one carries the guns!

The brutal fact is this: that I consented to do these plays, representing about 100 pounds' worth of my work apiece, for a derisory sum, merely because I so much liked the idea that I felt it would be a pleasure to do them. But if I cannot do them in my own way, it will no longer be a pleasure; and I may say that, even if the pay were adequate, I should still refuse to do them except along the lines which I feel to be artistically right. There is no money in the world that I would accept at the cost of

---

1 Arbitrary order (from Russian: imperial command).

surrendering my right of artistic judgment to the dictation of a committee – this is why dictators have to put artists in concentration camps.

The worst of the trouble is that, whatever happens now, I shall be faced, in Mr. McCulloch, with a sulky producer, which is the most desperate thing that can happen to a playwright. Here, again, I am all right; I withdraw the play, break the contract, and proceed with the arrears of my other work. But you will have lost your series of plays, and it seems rather hard lines. That is why I am bothering you with two long letters, in the hope that you may be able to exert some pressure somewhere or other. I am sorry I cannot send you copies of all the correspondence; I have sent it to my agent. However, I have no doubt you can get it from the Children's Hour people. You will see that everything was as harmonious as possible up to the moment of Miss Jenkin's interference. My reply to her was not conciliatory, I admit; but I knew that I had come to the point where to cede an inch was to cede the whole territory.

I apologise for adding my bombardment to that of Hitler; I'm afraid you have been having a stiff time lately.

Yours very sincerely,

[Dorothy L. Sayers]

Of course, all this is hanging up production. I doubt whether, under the best of circumstances, I should have been able to get the plays done at the rate of one production a fortnight. The first request was, I think, for twelve plays. Then they asked me how many I wanted to do. Now you suggest six. If I am to go on, I must know, because each play has to be written with reference to its place in the whole series. You couldn't plan a series of sermons unless you knew whether your doctrine was to be cramped into a Lenten mission or spaced over the whole year!

[24 Newland Street
Witham
Essex]

TO NANCY PEARN

2 December 1940

Dear Bun...

You will be entertained to hear that the B.B.C. have surrendered foot, horse and artillery! Dr. Welch rang up this afternoon saying he thought the best way would be to cancel the original arrangements for production and hand the whole thing over to Mr. Val Gielgud. I said with mild surprise that I had understood Mr. Val Gielgud was not procurable. He replied that in case of dire necessity heaven and earth would be moved to get hold of Mr. Gielgud and induce him to take over. I said that in these circumstances all would no doubt be well. So there you are, you see. In the meantime, production has been postponed, which is a great blessing, since as I gently pointed out to them, the writing of a play, if you write it properly, takes about two months and not two weeks as they seem to imagine. . . .

24 Newland Street
Witham
Essex

TO HER SON
5 December 1940

Dear John,

No, I don't think so – I really don't know, but I fancy the conference is by invitation – bishops and parsons and people with official interests.[1]

You needn't think it odd that you should only hear of my professional activities in the papers. Nobody ever does otherwise. Why should they? It isn't a personal matter. In fact, if anybody tries to make it so, I am quite unscrupulous in my efforts to choke them off! The last thing I should ever do is to send tickets or invitations to relations and friends....

I can't altogether explain my violent dislike of personal interest, except that I connect it with the atmosphere of solicitude which surrounded me in childhood and from which I have been trying to rid myself ever since. So much so that I can't be civil if I am told that I [am] missed when I am away or welcomed when I return, or that I ought to take care of my life because it is precious to other people. I should very much dislike being bombed, but there's no reason why I shouldn't be; I am no more important than anybody else. Solicitude only adds to the victim's discomfort by embarrassing them with a sensation of guilt.

I have always been sorry that I ever used my own name for my books or allowed my personality to become known at all, or ever appeared on a public platform. The fool newspaper public starts pushing one's self into one's work and exploiting interest in one's personality, which is intolerable. It can't be helped now, but it's a pity. The grass should grow over the

---

1 John Anthony, then at school at Malvern College, had asked if he might attend the Malvern Conference at which his mother was invited to speak on 8 January. He had read in the newspaper that she would be speaking. The Conference was held at the College during vacation.

living as well as over the dead, and there should be no memorial except the work. I have just had to write a "character sketch" of a dead friend[2] – a job that I hated and that one ought not to have to do. At least there are no lies in it, as there are in all the other obituary notices – the most silly and nauseating lie being the assertion that she and I were close friends at Oxford, where we never met.[3] Why should I be dragged into it? You may well ask. Because the blasted journalists thought that, since they knew nothing about her work, they could make their columns more spicy by connecting her with a "well-known personality". It makes me sick. I have killed the lie, anyhow – which is the only excuse for the article.

Let be, let be. Go on being interested in public affairs. That is needed. We have bottled up our lives into our own ties and our own emotions and let the *res publica*[4] go from bad to worse. There is no love for the thing – only a general solicitude of a vague kind for nice people, and an indefinite general kindness that doesn't like to think of anybody having to suffer. The best possible recipe for producing the greatest suffering for the greatest number.

Yes – I suppose we shall have to deal with exams and things some time. But God knows there's no money for anything these days. I am not making it as I did. The detective market – thank Heaven – has fallen off; I say, thank Heaven, because it was getting bad for people; encouraging them in the delusion that there was a nice, complete, simple, one-and-one-only solution to everything. There isn't. There is a solution to murder mysteries only because the murder is made to be solved.

I doubt, in any case, whether I shall be more than the one night at Malvern.

Yours affectionately,
     D. L. S.

2 Helen Simpson. D. L. S.' "sketch" was published in *The Fortnightly*, January 1941.
3 D. L. S. wrote: "I first met Helen de Guerry Simpson about ten years ago, when she was elected to membership of the Detection Club" and went on to express exasperation at the determination of journalists to maintain that they had been closely associated at Oxford.
4 Latin: public affairs.

On 4 December Dr Welch wrote to D. L. S. referring to a telephone conversation they had had. It had proved impossible after all to engage Val Gielgud as a producer of the plays. Dr Welch hoped that despite her misgivings D. L. S. would accept Derek McCulloch as a producer. He said:

Two hours after we had spoken, we had a hideous five hours of horror in Bristol, and what happened during those hours has rather upset one's scale of values.... All that seems supremely important at the moment is that we should broadcast to the children of the nation as perfect a picture of Our Lord as possible through the medium of your plays, in the belief that at least one or two children, and possibly hundreds, will get a picture of Our Lord from our broadcast of your plays which may be decisive for them in determining their attitude to Christ and the Church.

D. L. S. replied:

> [24 Newland Street
> Witham
> Essex]

TO DR JAMES WELCH
7 December 1940

Dear Dr. Welch,

Many thanks for your letter. I was rather afraid you would find it difficult to get hold of Val Gielgud.

Of course I shall be delighted to meet Mr. McCulloch, if he can possibly get to London. (That would mean only one day's travelling for me instead of three or four, which at the moment I simply can't afford time for.) I greatly appreciate the generous attitude he has taken; and, as I said to you at the time, I never felt there ought to have been any real difficulty so far as he was concerned. My feeling was that he was backing up a colleague in an ill-judged action, according to the departmental code. And I didn't say I wouldn't have him as a producer – only that he must decide to be either a producer or a department, but not both.

I am quite prepared to believe that Miss Jenkin has a great experience in the Children's Hour; but when you entrusted the job to me, you were taking the adventurous step of cutting out the juvenile experts, and trying a new experiment – that of giving the children "professional theatre". I think we must stick to the terms of that experiment, and deal with the thing on "professional theatre" lines. "If we fail, we fail", but we must try it out properly and not mess about with it.

I do sometimes wish that the experts would have a little more *respect* for their infant material. You remember Niebuhr: "Every child is a born theologian, which may be one reason why moderns regard theologians as obscurantists". Young children continually ask questions to which there is no answer possible except a mystical answer. I believe one should respect them enough to give them the true answer and not withhold it until they can understand it with the reason; because, by that time, the reason is already so corrupted as to refuse anything outside its own scope.

I really did take some pains to estimate in my own mind what weight of the mystical the uncorrupt mind might be expected to carry. I think it is greater than is generally supposed, and I am sure one must not depend too much on the criticisms of parents and teachers, or even on the expressed opinion of the children. I know I should have never dared to confess to any of my grown-ups the over-mastering fascination exercised on me by the Athanasian Creed. They were kind, but not so exceptionally sympathetic as the mother of the seven-year-old I mentioned to Miss Jenkin, and I felt instinctively that they would be surprised and amused, and say, "Surely you can't understand that", and tell each other about it as a quaint thing I had said. So I hugged it as a secret delight.

Children hate being told they can't understand. There was quite a   little row at Canterbury when some well-meaning person said the school-children oughtn't to have been taken to see Charles Williams' play, *Cranmer of Canterbury*. The children were bitterly offended, and wrote a letter, insisting that they had understood it perfectly! It is an excessively difficult play, but I am prepared to believe that, though they can't have understood it with their heads, they got more out of its rhythms than the average adult. Charles Williams seems to be a sort of test case. Educated audiences find his *Seed of Adam* almost incomprehensible; but Fr. MacLaughlin saw it played to a totally uneducated rural audience, who not only heard it with rapture, but were able to explain quite clearly and sensibly what it was all about. The same sort of thing happened when some people took their little R.C. servant to see T. S. Eliot's *Family Reunion*. They asked her if she understood the end of it – which was what all the reviewers and liberal rationalists found so baffling and repulsive. "Oh, yes," she said; "he was going out into the wilderness to make his soul, and then he would come back and do good." That, no doubt, was the effect of always having been given the mystical interpretation of life; it was taken as perfectly natural.

I am certain that it is desperately important to get the mystical and poetic approach to life accepted naturally at an early age or when the mind is uncorrupted by rationalisation – children and charwomen are the only audience to whom these things appeal directly; the adult and the educated can only make the difficult and perilous approach of the "twice-born", and may never get there. Even if they do, it is easier for them if they have had it once at first hand.

Now, if anybody had said that the *political* part of "Kings in Judaea" was rather hard going for children, I think he would have had a case. But I want to try it on them, because that side of it may catch and interest the older ones, who have already got beyond the direct appeal of rhythm and mystery, and are ready to use their reason about a human and historical situation. They must all hear a lot about international questions these days; and one mustn't forget that weekly attendance at the cinema had made them far more sophisticated than we ever were at their age. Incidentally, it is interesting that a friend of mine, teaching in an evacuated school, finds that, now that the children can no longer indulge in the accustomed cinema-crawl, they are far more interested and delighted by poetry than they were before. Which means, I suppose, that the age of sophistication has been set back.

Of course, one has got to remember that, with plays, it's impossible for the whole audience to get the full value out of every word. If, out of 800 people who find the show good entertainment, 8 are so thoroughly stirred that the thing becomes an experience in their lives, the playwright has done more than he has any right to expect. But he may hope that perhaps another 80 or so may carry away something – a word, a line, a situation, a picture – that may remain in the memory and later on come to mean something, when experience is ready to interpret it. I sometimes think that the B.B.C. is too much inclined to attempt the impossible task of pleasing everybody and offending nobody, and so producing that harmless mediocrity that vaguely insults everybody and stimulates nobody. You can't really follow the line: "It would be a pity if some children didn't understand"; you can only say, "If one child fully understands, then praise God for a miracle". The highest common factor of human intelligence is not so very high, and if a thing is fully understood by everybody, it is seldom worth understanding. But everybody may grasp bits here and there, and that's worth it. My guess is that the young children will like the mysterious bits, while the grown-ups will like the Little Zillah and the baby-talk – which I only hope to God will not alienate the children!

Anyway, let's try. I'm frightfully sorry all this has set us back, but by all means let us pretend that Miss Jenkin never happened, and return to the starting-point. When the next plays come along, I will send a copy direct to you (I should have done so before, but I gathered you had handed the whole thing over). Then, if you have any blasphemy, heresy or schism to complain of, we will get it mended, and the script can go to Mr. McCulloch as producer, without any committees, for his technical criticism about production. To that I'm always ready to listen. Honestly, I'm not out to be obstructive. What happened was that Mr. McCulloch and I got put into a false position, and it seemed necessary to do something to force the issue. This, in the theatre, is the process known as "Throwing a fit" – after which everybody bursts into tears and kisses everybody, and they all behave like lambs. Such behaviour is not usual, of course, in Government departments. A pity, I sometimes think. I should love to see a good theatrical fit thrown in the M.O.I.,[1] for example.

It's distressing that all this should have boiled up just when Hitler was making all other considerations seem so petty. But things do happen like that. He dropped a beautiful stick of incendiaries across Witham on Wednesday night, and I prepared to make a dash to safety, clutching a ms. on the Creative Mind under one arm, and John the Baptist (half-finished) under the other. Fortunately, the A.F.S.[2] got the things put out before the heavy stuff could follow them up.

Yours very sincerely,

[Dorothy L. Sayers]

1 Ministry of Information.
2 Auxiliary Fire Service.

Thus all seemed well and D. L. S. continued work on her second play. Unfortunately, Miss Jenkin, who had read the correspondence which had passed between D. L. S., Dr Welch and Derek McCulloch, felt moved to defend herself against charges of "impertinence, tactlessness and literary ignorance" which D. L. S. had made against her. She also made it clear that in the absence of Derek McCulloch it would be her responsibility to take over the production of the plays. And she concluded: "We cannot delegate to any author, however distinguished, the right to say what shall or shall not be broadcast in a Children's Hour play".

Two days before Christmas D. L. S. replied:

[24 Newland Street
Witham
Essex]

TO MAY E. JENKIN
23 December 1940

Dear Miss Jenkin,

THE MAN BORN TO BE KING

Under the circumstances you outline, I have no option but to cancel the contract. Kindly return all scripts of "Kings in Judaea" immediately. My agents will communicate with you.

Yours faithfully,

[Dorothy L. Sayers]

[24 Newland Street
Witham
Essex]

TO DR JAMES WELCH
23 December 1940

Dear Dr. Welch,

I am very sorry indeed to disturb your holiday with unpleasant news, but I think I had better let you know before you hear it from other quarters that I have been obliged to cancel the contract for the plays. Just after I had written to you I received a most unfortunate letter from Miss Jenkin which really left me no option. I am distressed about this. I hoped we were getting everything nicely smoothed out but her letter makes it clear we were back exactly where we were before your diplomatic intervention. I also gathered from her that in case anything happened to Mr. McCulloch she would expect to produce the plays herself and this, of course, I could not permit, nor if anything happened to me would my literary Executor[1] permit it.

The position is an awkward one since it was primarily yourself who commissioned the plays. If the Children's Hour Department insists on full control of what is broadcast during their periods, no doubt they are within their rights, but I am also within my rights in refusing to work under those conditions.

I need not say how very much I regret all this. Possibly at some future time you may be able to make another arrangement more satisfactory to all parties.

Yours very sincerely,
    [Dorothy L. Sayers]

1   Muriel St Clare Byrne.

The mind of a maker

crocroco

*D. L. S.' letter of 23 December 1940 had left the door open. Dr Welch replied:
"The position is now very difficult and will take a little time to straighten out."
The difficulty was that responsibility for the Children's Hour period on Sundays
was shared between Dr Welch and Derek McCulloch. "But much more",
Dr Welch stressed, "it belongs to the listening children of the country. I cannot
accept the cancellation of these plays, which means the denial to the children of
an entirely fresh portrayal of the life and teaching of Our Lord."*

D. L. S.' reply shows that she was determined to strengthen her position:

[24 Newland Street
Witham
Essex]

TO DR JAMES WELCH
2 January 1941

Dear Dr. Welch,

I do not greatly care about arguing business contracts on a religious
basis; it is difficult to avoid the appearance of making unwarranted claims
for one's self. But you have appealed over the head of Caesar, and I will
take you to the higher court if you insist.

When you say that a play by D. L. S. on this subject would be "a land-
mark in the history of religious education", I am not clear whether you
mean that my work would have a certain value, or that my name would
have a publicity appeal. If the latter, I can only express the opinion that
the Kingdom of God can probably scrape along without that particular
form of advertising, and echo your words, that it does not matter by

whom the plays are written or produced. So far as I am concerned, it can remain anonymous.

But if you are referring to the worth of the work itself, then I am bound to tell you this: that the writer's duty to God is his duty to the work, and that he may not submit to any dictate of authority which he does not sincerely believe to be to the good of the work. He may not do it for money, or for reputation, or for edification, or for peace's sake, or because bombs may fall on him or other people, or for any consideration whatever. Above all, he may not listen to the specious temptation which suggests that God finds his work so indispensable that He would rather have it falsified than not have it at all. The writer is about his Father's business, and it does not matter who is inconvenienced or how much he has to hate his father and mother. To be false to his work is to be false to the truth: "All the truth of the craftsman is in his craft."[1]

That other dramatists have re-written their work on request is irrelevant. I do not know their motives. They may have sincerely agreed that the change was for the better; they may have felt no particular sense of duty to their work; they may have been so anxious to get on the air that they were prepared to betray their truth; the work may have been of a kind that expected no high standard; they may have been so poor that even the B.B.C. pittance was a necessity for them. I am not their judge. But there is no law of God or man that can be invoked to make a writer tamper with his conscience.

To do Caesar justice, the general law of contract is devised to safeguard the writer's integrity as far as possible. The B.B.C. (for some reason) refuses to give proper contracts. I think, however, my agents made it clear that I was prepared to work on the usual terms, viz:

1. The author to approve the producer and cast.
2. Nothing in the text of the play to be cut or
   altered without the author's consent, such consent
   not to be unreasonably withheld.

As regards (2), I was (not so much asked as) instructed to make a number of alterations. Certain of these I refused to make – not, I think, unreasonably, since I advanced reasons which you admitted to be plausible.

In such a case, the management have only two alternatives: (a) to accept my decision; (b) to reject the play. They cannot compel me to alter. Owing, however, to the fact that in the Children's Hour Department the management is combined with the production, they tried to enforce

---

1 The words of the Prior in *The Zeal of thy House*, Scene 3.

alterations in matter and style on the pretence that these concerned the production. This was an unprofessional proceeding, and I said so plainly.

I was, however, prepared to go on with the job. Miss Jenkin's letter made this impossible. It is not correct to call this document "a purely personal affair", since it stated unequivocally that the management proposed to override both clauses (1) and (2) of the contract terms, by claiming the sole right to decide what portions of my text should or should not be broadcast, and by forcing upon me, under certain circumstances, a producer not approved by me. This left me no course open but to break off relations.

Contractual obligations hold good for all plays. There is also a recognized difference between work that is submitted by a writer on his own initiative and work that is commissioned. In the first case, the writer works at his own risk, and may expect to have it accepted upon conditions. But commissioned work is ordered at the risk of the management, which expects either to take what it gets or to refuse the work as it stands. This principle is accepted by all responsible professional bodies, and also by all responsible amateur bodies, such, for example, as the Friends of Canterbury Cathedral.

You say that my reaction was fierce and rude – but how is one to deal with a body that does not understand the terms of a professional engagement? You ask, why should I or anybody object to comment? – but the "comment" took the form of an instruction to alter, and in that form was an impertinence. I beg you not to use such expressions as "Dorothy Sayers is Dorothy Sayers" – I am not asking that rules should be broken in my favour; I am requiring that the common decencies of contract should be respected.

The notorious difficulty that professional people find in dealing with the B.B.C. is that it is usually quite impossible to discover who the contracting parties are. A piece of work is ordered by one department (e.g. yours), paid for by another department, and put on the air by a third; while the producer is not simply a producer, but also the head of an education committee and an unspecified fraction of the management. Under ordinary professional conditions, in a theatre, you would order the work, approve it or not, and, having approved, engage a producer to produce it, and you would be the party responsible, and to whom the other parties were responsible. As it is, I am not the only person to whom B.B.C. work is a sheer nightmare, because of the amateurishness, the confusion, and the preposterous overlapping of control. "Long experience in B.B.C. production" is not a professional qualification, because the B.B.C. (except on the engineering side) is not a professionally-run body, and has no professional standing.

Last night's deplorable exhibition[2] was typical. To summon "experts"

in science and philosophy and subject them to a sort of penny-paper quiz
on sailors' trousers and the miscellaneous information one can get from a
Handy Guide to Knowledge is bad. To call on them to deal with profound
and intricate conundrums in physics under a three-minute time-limit is
worse. To snigger archly about "the feminine line on the fourth dimension", and follow this with a put-up piece of futility designed to provoke
laughter is worse still. To pretend that this is done, "not as a 'stunt' programme but a serious attempt to provide useful information" is the worst
insult of all. It's not even amusing – unrehearsed, stifled in private giggles,
it stutters and drags on to no result, cheap, slip-shod, amateur, degrading,
and contemptible. This is the official B.B.C. attitude to art, science, philosophy and learning. Do you wonder that Mgr. Knox,[3] attacking the specious and the shoddy in the name of the only wise God, called his book
"Broadcast Minds"?[4] Do you wonder that those who have a respect for
their calling are sometimes reluctant to associate themselves with the
B.B.C.? Joad[5] and Huxley[6] lend themselves to these things. True. But
would Eddington[7] or Whitehead?[8] The stigma that rests upon the place is
that it is the spiritual home of the not-quite-first-rate – the artist, the
scientist, the philosopher with one ear turned from the work to catch the
crackling of thorns under the pot.[9] This is not an outburst of personal
spite: what I am saying is said by everybody; by everybody who has
reverence for the mind.

You have appealed to God, and to God you shall go. When the B.B.C.
treat art and learning like this, they crucify the Logos afresh and put Him
to an open shame.

2 A popular quiz programme known as the Brains Trust; cf. her letter to the Archbishop of
   York, 24 November 1941.
3 Monsignor Ronald Knox (1888–1957), author of detective fiction and literary comment.
4 Published in 1932.
5 C. E. M. Joad (1891–1953), professor of philosophy and prolific author; best known to the
   general public as a member of the Brains Trust. Asa Briggs, in *The B.B.C.: The First Fifty Years*
   (O.U.P., 1985, p. 200, note 1) reports that Dr Welch detested the way "Joad trots out stock
   answers to profound questions".
6 Sir Julian Huxley (1887–1975), biologist and writer.
7 Sir Arthur Eddington (1882–1944), British astronomer. His best known writings are *The Nature
   of the Physical World* (1928) and *The Philosophy of Science* (1939). See D. L. S.'s "Dante's Cosmos"
   a dialogue between Dante and Eddington, a paper given at the Royal Institution, 23
   February 1951, published in *Further Papers on Dante*, Methuen, 1957, pp. 78–101, in which
   Eddington reads to Dante from *The Nature of the Physical World*.
8 Alfred North Whitehead (1861–1947), philosopher and mathematician. He collaborated with
   Bertrand Russell in writing *Principia Mathematica* (1910–1913), a fundamental study of the
   structure of mathematical and logical thought.
9 "As the crackling of thorns under a pot, so is the laughter of a fool" (Proverbs, 6).

I am sorry to speak so strongly; last night's performance was more than usually sickening. My husband, who is no great lover of learning, was quite revolted.

To return to the plays. We will not argue about denial and sacrifice; one may sacrifice one's self, but not the work. If I am to go on, I must ask that there shall be one management, one producer who is not a secondary management, and one responsible contracting party, who understands the nature of contractual obligation. This ought not to be impossible.

Yours sincerely,
[Dorothy L. Sayers]

24 Newland Street
Witham
Essex

TO HER SON
2 January [1941]¹

Dear John,

Thank you very much indeed for your charming present. I'm afraid I firmly cut Christmas out this year – partly with being rolled under with business and my secretary away, and having to type all my own mss. Curiously enough, the book² I was just finishing deals to some extent with the point you raise about the connection between the personality and the work.

As regards statesmen, whose life is part of their public work, it is very difficult for me to speak. But as regards artists of any kind the position is this: that all the self which they are able to communicate to the world is in their work, and is manifest in its best form in the work. To expect to get more out of direct contact with the man than one gets from his work is pretty well bound to lead to disappointment – the work is his means of expression, and is his genuine self. What is left over is the discarded stuff, or the lumber-room of raw material, so to speak, out of which the next work is going to be made. People are always imagining that if they get hold of the writer himself and so to speak shake him long and hard enough, something exciting and illuminating will drop out of him. But it

---

1 The date in the original is 1940, but the contents of the letter show that 1941 was intended.
2 i.e. *The Mind of the Maker*, on which she was working during the autumn of 1940. It was published in July 1941.

doesn't. What's due to come out has come out in the only form in which it ever can come out. All one gets by shaking is the odd paper-clips and crum[p]led carbons from his waste-paper basket. If you notice, the first thing that usually crops up out of people's biographies is the nonsense things about them; so that the general effect made is that the man wasn't so very remarkable after all. Biographies are, of course, bound to be written – though in decency I think it is better to wait till the subject has been dead some time. But consider the number of writers (for example) of whose lives we know practically nothing – Homer and Shakespeare – or men like Newton, who seems to have had next to no private life – their work is none the less powerful. Indeed, it is more powerful. Nor do I think Byron's work (to take a classical instance in the other direction) has benefited by the colossal réclame of his personality. During the uproar, it was boosted miles above its proper value, to be sure; now it suffers unduly from the weight of that preposterous legend lying upon it. What we make is more important than what we are – particularly if "making" is our profession.

It is curious how little people are capable of grasping this. I've had secretaries of societies actually say (when I asked them what sort of speech, on what sort of subject their audience wanted to listen to), "Oh, I don't think they'll mind what you talk about – they just want to *see you*". The queer thing is that this is really intended for a compliment. The person, they think, must be more valuable to himself and to them than the thing, than the work. And the more one writes books to tell them that this isn't so, the more they refuse to believe it.

Now look – here I am trying to say all this personally and rather badly at the end of a day's slogging. But I've said it – said it once and for all as well as I know how to say it -

> Let me lie deep in hell,
> Death gnaw upon me, purge my bones with fire,
> But let my work, all that was good in me,
> All that was God, stand up and live and grow.
> The work is sound, Lord God, no rottenness there –
> Only in me...[3]

and all the rest of that speech. That, you see, is the ultimate truth of the matter so far as I can tell anybody about it....That is it – the truth about the artist – and that, in fact, is what the whole play is. "All the truth of the craftsman is in his craft." [4]...

---

3 From a speech by William of Sens, *The Zeal of Thy House*, scene 4.
4 See letter to James Welch, 2 January 1941, note 1.

You are bothered about education. So, in a sense am I – my trouble is that I don't really agree with any of my wise contemporaries. I find it difficult to say that I gained very much from it myself, and I cherish a heretical notion that it can do little for one except (a) to implant a desire for knowledge and (b) to give one a rough machinery for finding out for one's self the things one wants to know. I learned little at home – except, indeed, how to speak French; nothing at school – except, indeed, how to pass examinations; and at Oxford the only things I think I can say I was taught were the rudiments of Old French Grammar (which you wouldn't think very useful) and a general attitude to knowledge which I can only call a respect for intellectual integrity. And between you and me, I doubt greatly whether a liberal education can impart much more than those two things: a reverence for the working mind, and a knowledge of method, applied to some subject, no matter what. But if I said this in public, all the advanced people would be shocked to the marrow.

Again, I am not at all convinced about this business of teaching people about contemporary events. If it is so taught as to rest on no basis of history, it is shallow and dangerous…and the trouble is that to understand the past we need not only knowledge, but maturity. That is the paradox about "the future being with the young"; by the time they are ready to deal with the future they are no longer young. The "directed education" of Nazi Youth is absolutely dependent on their being kept from any knowledge of the "real past". But if one has learnt at all about the past, then presently the pressure of contemporary events will bring up the memory of what went before, and one can say, "Now I see what that meant".

Where I am at odds with the pundits, you see, is in thinking that it is not so much the young who need education as the mature. Always supposing, of course, they have not become too ankylosed to learn anything. That, youth should be taught – that there is no such thing as "completing one's education", and that the mind is an instrument which needs constant use and reverent treatment.

I must stop this now – I haven't really got it properly sorted out. But when it's ready for presentation to the world I suppose I shall write it down, and everybody will be furious.

I enclose cheque for birthday and for a sort of Christmas–New Year present: £5 for you and £5 for Aunt Ivy.

With much love,

D. L. S.

Early in January Dr Welch had the misfortune to slip on an icy pavement and break his collar-bone. This helped to soften D. L. S.'s attitude and she replied as follows to his conciliatory letter.

[24 Newland Street
Witham
Essex]

TO DR JAMES WELCH
11 January 1941

Dear Dr. Welch,

Thank you very much for your kind and sympathetic letter. I am greatly relieved to hear about your collar-bone since the rumour was going about at Malvern[1] that you had been put out of action by a bomb. I have no doubt that the correct version of the story was announced from the platform, but that was what it had turned into after passing through the bad acoustics of the hall and the imagination of the hearers. I was filled with that mixture of remorse and grievance which fills the person who has written an indignant letter, only to find that the recipient has been put in a position where it is cruel to jump on him. The fact that the indignation was righteous does not remove the sense of guilt; but one feels that destiny has taken an unfair advantage of one. I am, of course, very sorry about the collar-bone, quâ collar-bone; but if it has had the effect of getting you away for a bit from Hitler and the B.B.C. it may be what the authors of *1066 and All That*[2] call "a Good Thing".

As regards the immediate practical steps. My agent has written a formal protest to the department with which the contract was made, and calling for the return of the scripts. I have held up this letter, and she is now sending it in a revised form, still insisting on the contractual obligation and all the rest of it, but saying she understands that the matter is being reconsidered, and leaving the door open to further negotiation.

I should be quite ready to accept either of the alternatives you propose, with a strong preference for (2).[3] I feel that under (1), even if we could get Gielgud to consent, we might come up against the same problem of divided control, whereas he would be supreme in his own Drama Department. If (2) were adopted, I should still write the plays with the children in mind;

1 The Malvern Conference, presided over by Archbishop Temple, was called to consider what role the Church should play in social reconstruction after the war. D. L. S. opened the second session on 8 January with a paper entitled "The Church's Responsibility".

2 An amusing parody of the teaching of history by W. C. Sellar and R. J. Yeatman (Methuen, 1930). It was adapted for the stage, with words by Reginald Arkell and music by Alfred Reynolds. A London West-End success, the show is still performed.

3 i.e. of removing the plays from Children's Hour.

The Rev. Dr. James Welch

I should not, that is, put in anything smart or sophisticated or involved or "unsuitable" – such, for example, as the discussion on Greek philosophy in *He That Should Come*, or, in the same play, the "Greek Gentleman's" sneering wisecrack about the paternity of Christ. It is that sort of thing, not the mystical, which seems to me to be outside the scope of a child's mind.

As regards the "professional" side of the thing: Yes, Adrian Boult[4] is all right, bless his heart. But he didn't get his professional standing from the B.B.C. – he brought it with him, from the "real" musical world, from Hugh Allen[5], and the Royal College and the great professional orchestras. In fact, if my memory doesn't deceive me, the B.B.C. Symphony Orchestra began with the subsidising or incorporation of one of the great orchestras – was it the London Symphony? – and inherited that outside tradition.[6] Val Gielgud, too, is "real", just because he is a Gielgud and a Terry;[7] he came to the thing steeped in the tradition of "real" theatre. "Theatre" is, so to speak, just the professional word for what one means by the living tradition of drama; there isn't, as Miss Jenkin suggests, one thing called "theatre" and another thing called "radio drama". There are various kinds of *media* for drama – seen-and-spoken, which is the ordinary stage-play; seen-and-sung, which is opera; seen-and-not-heard, which is mime; heard-and-not-seen, which is radio-drama; but they are all "theatre", only with different techniques appropriate to their media. And the first thing the professional wants to know about any play is, "Is it theatre?" – meaning, "Is it a right thing for actors to present in any dramatic medium?" And the second is, "Is it technically right for this medium?" – meaning, "is it suitably constructed for interpretation by the stage, or by unseen voices, or by silent players, or what not?" The professional producer is known by the fact that he puts these things first, leaving it to the author to decide what kind of "message" he wants to put over, but dealing very firmly with him in the matter of the play's truth to its chosen medium.

Look, I think I can convey this sort of professional single-mindedness best by the concrete example. The Children's Hour people wrote remarks like, "Your play is beautiful, dramatic, moving, scintillating" and so forth,

---

4 Sir Adrian Boult (1889–1983), conductor.
5 Sir Hugh Percy Allen (1869–1946), conductor and musical administrator. He was conductor of the Oxford Bach Choir, of which D. L. S. was a member. In 1918 he was appointed Director of the Royal College of Music.
6 The London Symphony Orchestra was founded in 1904, the B.B.C. Orchestra in 1930.
7 His mother was Kate Terry Lewis (1844–1924).

"but we think there might be one or two children who mightn't understand some of its beauties, so please remove those beauties". Val never said a word about the beauties when we first met, but plunged into certain technical points about casting and production. After a bit, I said (timidly, because I knew I was new to the medium) "Do you think it will do, then?" He said, "Oh, yes; we're going to have some fun with this", adding, "I don't know what the audience will think of it, but it's the kind of thing I can enjoy doing". He hadn't got one eye on flattering the author and the other on placating the critics – he was only concerned with the play[8] and production. He did remove one set of speeches, which were rather "difficult", but using the technical arguments that they overweighted the play and that they would cause it to over-run the time-limit. I thought he was mistaken, but didn't feel sure enough to insist. If they do it again, I shall hope to persuade him to give those speeches a trial – since, as it turned out, my estimate of the timing was correct. But his objections were made on technical grounds, so I had to respect them. Of course, on other occasions I have let producers make cuts that I knew to be wrong, knowing that we had three weeks of rehearsal, during which the actors would infallibly discover the wrongness for themselves – which they duly did. But in radio work, one hasn't the time for that kind of game. But in all these cases, if I had absolutely insisted, the producers would either have given way or refused to produce – as they have a perfect right to do.

It's difficult to convey just that difference in attitude which either gives or destroys confidence in a person's professional competence, though one can feel it in the first word they say, so to speak. It has something to do with the thing I have called the "autonomy of technique" – a mutual assumption that each bloke knows his own job, and knows where it begins and ends; and it has a great deal to do with singlemindedness about the thing-in-itself – the autonomy of the work within its own sphere. The practical hitch is that the "professional" people talk a different language from the others – or rather, use a different category of thought, so that even if both use the same words they don't mean the same thing by them. It's like when one says: "The Incarnation means nothing unless one insists on the real humanity of Christ"; and the other person replies: "Oh, I do agree with you – if only we had the loving spirit of Jesus we shouldn't need all this theology". And you realise that it's all quite hopeless, because they don't understand what the word "humanity" means, and that when they think they are agreeing they haven't even begun to see what the question is.

As regards the B.B.C. in general, I should very much like to discuss this

8 i.e. *He That Should Come.*

some time, because it's bothering me quite a lot. What you say about the mixture of Civil Service and commercial Fleet Street is exactly what one feels about it. I shouldn't have said it was an "official" attitude, because, as you say, there is no real attitude – only a taking-over of second-hand and second-rate standards. But the peculiar position of the B.B.C. gives these a sort of official stamp and sanction in the eyes of the common man. It's not only that the Civil Service mentality prevents the saying of anything that could conceivably give offence to anybody – there are arguments for that, within reason. But it also prevents the saying of anything that could conceivably be unintelligible to the lowest mentality. You must not only refrain from using, say, a theological term that can't be understood by a simple person interested in theology; you must refrain from using any theological term that can't be understood by a stupid person who is not interested in theology, so that the fairly intelligent person who is interested in theology never gets catered for at all. Then you get this awful business of "attractive presentation", like the Howard Thomas "Any Questions?", intended to lure and trap and titillate people into thinking that learning is a kind of smart little parlour game. The net result is that the one great lesson is never learnt – the necessity of reverence for all wisdom and of humility in face of the facts.

I don't know what one can do with it. When – in peacetime, I mean – they first started broadcasting alternative programmes, I hoped they meant to make them really different in quality – a sort of junior and advanced grade, so to speak; but it all withered away into nothing. But I believe this would be the right thing to do. A "popular" programme, much what it is now, though perhaps so directed as to encourage people to look for something more satisfying; and a "specialised" programme, in which the performers and speakers could treat their work seriously, addressing only those who were genuinely interested in the subject and already knew something about it. In this programme one would aim for at least the standards of the University Extension Lecture, and pay no attention to criticisms from "Man in the Street" and "Suburban Housewife" and the log-rollers of the penny-press – except to tell them that if they wanted popular chat they could get it on the popular wavelength. One would then hope for serious reviewing from the respectable dailies and weeklies and from the professional men interested in the subject. Similarly, if people said that "Mourning Becomes Electra"[9] was too "heavy" for the tired stockbroker, one would reply firmly that it wasn't meant for him, and that he should leave that wave-length severely alone as he already leaves the bookshelves of the British Museum, and then it

9 A play by Eugene O'Neill (1888–1953), a re-working of Aeschylus' *Oresteia* in the context of the American Civil War.

wouldn't hurt him. The same with music. But one would have to be absolutely firm and consistent about this policy, and never mix the wavelengths. It is disconcerting for the stockbroker to find Einstein on Relativity intruding on Musical Comedy and Beethoven bursting in on Vic Oliver.[10] I know the theory is that the stockbroker, having accidentally found himself switching in to Beethoven may become so absorbed that he remains to be educated – but in practice he merely switches off again with a loud snort of fury. Whereas, I daresay, if you urged him to avoid wave-length 349 like the plague, he would tune in to it out of sheer curiosity. Of course, one would have to explain *exactly* what one meant to do, and *stick to it*. It's the wavering from one policy to another that does the damage.

What makes one weep is that the B.B.C. has such a grand opportunity for doing the good, uncommercial stuff, because it is state-supported. It could do the sort of thing one always wants from a National Theatre, but which the commercial theatre can't do for lack of security. Boult has grasped the possibilities of this on the musical side; and with a wavelength of his own to play with could do still more, without bothering about the people who tot up the number of hours given to "classical" music in the general programme, as compared with the hours consecrated to jazz and Variety. I'm not at all sure that the B.B.C. couldn't, on these lines, actually run a National Theatre, as it now runs the Queen's Hall concerts.[11] I mean, if the State could be persuaded to take the theatre seriously enough to finance the overheads, the State-Theatre-and-B.B.C. body could run its permanent stock company, giving public performances in the theatre (with occasional broadcasts from the theatre) and also running the radio drama with the same company, thus making full use of the actors' time and getting good value out of them. The actors to be, of course, on regular salaries under a three years' contract. As things are, the B.B.C. grossly over-pays its actors, as the actors are the first to acknowledge. Their attitude is: "Of course, the B.B.C. is money for jam – otherwise one wouldn't do it, because one can't take it seriously. But you don't have to work – only read things through after a few sketchy rehearsals and draw your money. But any of us would far rather do something worth doing, if only we didn't need the pennies so badly." What's more, they would cheerfully work harder for less pay, if the pay was regular and the work interesting – but they demand, and get, the high fees for B.B.C. work, because they despise it so that they wouldn't touch it for less. The

10 Vic Oliver (1898–1964), film and stage entertainer, who married Sarah, daughter of Sir Winston Churchill.
11 Conducted by Sir Henry Wood (1869–1944). The Queen's Hall, in Langham Place, London, was destroyed by bombs in May 1941. The famous Promenade Concerts which took place there were later continued in the Royal Albert Hall.

authors, on the other hand, are so grossly underpaid that the serious ones can't be bothered to do things for the B.B.C. unless they get the free hand which makes the thing worth while to them as artists.

Forgive my rambling on – giving you something to read in bed, as you might say – but the possibilities are all there, and so big that it seems a pity they should go to waste in this ramshackle way. Government Boards have an absolute genius for elaborately wrong organization – I don't know how they do it. Their institutions are a perfect example of the materialist's universe, formed by the random tumbling about of atoms according to the Principle of Least Action. They seem to have no Directed Purposes at all. There's a terrific appearance of Activity – again like the materialist's universe – the atoms rush round and collide madly and never have any time to spare; but where they are going they never think of asking. They make me feel like Lady Macbeth: "Infirm of purpose – give *me* the daggers!"[12] An old army man[13] said to me sourly the other day that he attributed Wavell's[14] success in Libya to the fact that he was a very long way from Whitehall, and that instructions might easily fail, in some unaccountable way, to reach him. The B.B.C. is less fortunately placed.

Well, anyway, we'll try to get a new start on this show. I've asked my agent, this time, to get the form of contract so definite in black and white that nobody can misunderstand it. It's characteristic that there is no real awareness in the B.B.C. mind that forms of contract exist, apart from the little thing they send out when one is going to speak one's bit – nothing, I mean, that governs them when they are commissioning the actual work, but we'll have it clear this time that you are the person who has to approve the play, and that I and the producer have our usual theatrical rights, and that no third party can put spanners into the works. With Gielgud, of course, I know there would be no misunderstanding on the principle of the thing, and if we disagreed we could do it in a nice, gritty, technical way, with enjoyment and mutual respect.

By the way, though I didn't bother to go into this with Miss Jenkin, I have taken some pains, though she might not think it, to ascertain what "the" elementary-school-child[15] of eleven may be expected to understand. As it happens, we have an evacuee elementary [-school] teacher in the house, and I consulted him on the subject. He said there was nothing in the play that his kids wouldn't be able to understand on their heads, even if it was only read aloud to them – and that the mystical bits would be no

12 Lady Macbeth's words to her husband, Act II, scene 2.

13 Possibly D. L. S.' husband, Major Atherton Fleming, who had served in World War I.

14 Field-Marshal Lord Wavell (1883–1950), British army officer, and leading figure in World War II. He defeated the Italians in E. Africa and liberated Ethiopia.

15 The elementary school, now termed primary, provides teaching for children from 5 to 11 years of age.

more difficult for them than for the average adult. He added that, in his experience, there were only two things one could be sure the average small boy would enjoy – one was mystery and the other was cruelty – a grim thought, but I know what he means. I also consulted a friend[16] who is English mistress in a big girls' school[17] – and *her* opinion was that you couldn't pontificate about "the" school-child at all, but she was sure that many of the children would really feel the questions Balthazar asks about the riddle of fear and poverty and all that, because of the war, and bombing, and one thing and another. I don't believe there's no such a person[18] as "the" school-child, and I don't think one should talk about "the" elementary-school-child as if he was something odd and inferior; I wouldn't expect him to understand Noel Coward, because Coward's plays deal only with a very restricted range of human experience. But what is meant by this unchristian distinction between the elementary and the secondary in the sphere of religious apprehension?

I hope both you and the Director of Programmes[19] will soon have recovered. The sooner the B.B.C. is removed from Bristol the better. And Manchester. What you want is a quiet place in the country, with an underground cable!

Yours, etc.,

[Dorothy L. Sayers]

16 Marjorie Barber.
17 South Hampstead High School.
18 Echoing the double negative in the phrase, "I don't believe there's no sich person", in which Betsey Prig casts doubt on the existence of Sarah Gamp's mythical friend in Dickens' *Martin Chuzzlewit*, chapter 49.
19 Mr B. E. Nicolls, who had been injured in an air-raid.

[24 Newland Street
Witham
Essex]

TO F. BLIGH BOND[1]

17 January 1941

Dear Mr. Bligh Bond,

Thank you very much for your letter. If the News Agency that reported the Malvern Conference had reported honestly what my speech was about you would have seen that it was directly centred about the whole

1 Yet another voice from the past. F. Bligh Bond, F.R.I.B.A. (1864–1945). See *The Letters of Dorothy L. Sayers: 1899–1936*, letters dated 11 July and 2 August 1917.

question of intellectual integrity. It is, however, practically impossible to get reporters to pay any attention to any matter to which they cannot attach some kind of sensational interest.[2] I believe that all the speeches made at the Conference will be published in full before long and if you get hold of the volume you will find that I did not neglect the important point you raise.

It was very nice to hear from you again after all this long time. Have you had any further communications from the other side of the "Gate of Remembrance"?[3]

With kindest regards and all good wishes,

    Yours sincerely,

      [Dorothy L. Sayers]

2 See her article "How Free is the Press?", *Unpopular Opinions*, Gollancz, 1946, pp. 129–130.
3 A reference to Mr Bligh Bond's interest in psychical research.

                      [24 Newland Street
                      Witham
                      Essex]

TO THE REV. ERIC FENN
The B.B.C.
Bristol
21 January 1941

Dear Mr. Fenn,

Many thanks for your letter. I will do my best to get out a synopsis,[1] provided you clearly understand that this is a kind of thing I do very badly and that I seldom stick to the synopsis! Will you ask the contract people to remember to get in touch not with me but with my agents, Miss Nancy Pearn, Messrs. Pearn, Pollinger and Higham, 39/40 Bedford Street, Strand, W.C.1. I say this every time and every time they write to me.

May I take this opportunity of passing on to you an interesting criticism made by an outsider to a friend of mine. This woman complains that the brand of Religion emanating from the B.B.C. is much more theist than Christian. She says it is all concerned with God the Father and not with God the Son, and that God the Father is presented too much in the aspect

1 Of a talk entitled "The Religions Behind the Nations". See letter to Val Gielgud, 24 February 1941, note 1.

of a divine dictator managing things from above. I was interested in this, because, as you may remember, I ventured to mumble the same sort of criticism to Canon Cockin when we were discussing that other series of Broadcast talks. As it comes from a quite independent source you may feel that there is possibly something in the criticism. My own feeling is – as I have mentioned before on various occasions – that we are still fighting the Arian heresy[2] and that we are inclined to divide the Substance rather in the manner of Dr. Pearks (if that is his name), (I mean John Hadam, who rose up so passionately on the first evening of the Conference), and leave people with the impression that there is somebody called God and a subsequent, inferior, but more sympathetic person called the Son of God, who had nothing to do with creating the world, and whose part in running it is rather that of a foreman of the works sadly put upon by the management. Possibly this has something to do with the "neutrality" and confusion of "Religions behind the Nations".[3]

Yours very sincerely,

[Dorothy L. Sayers]

3 See letter to Father Kelly, 4 October 1937, note 2.
4 See letter to Val Gielgud, 24 February 1941, note 1.

[24 Newland Street
Witham
Essex]

TO EDWARD HULTON[1]

28 January 1941

Dear Mr. Hulton,

Thank you for your letter and prospectus of the 1941 Committee. I am, of course, always interested in any effort towards reconstruction, and there are some details in your scheme to which I should, naturally, assent. But I could not ally myself with it, because I know it to be based upon the wrong assumptions – upon ideas which are not merely false, but already dead and discredited.

Here are all the nineteenth-century liberal fallacies that led the world into its present confusion – the "progressive" fallacy; the Utopian fallacy; above all, the economic fallacy; the schemes for the secure, prosperous,

1 (Sir) Edward Hulton (1906–1988), founder of Hulton Press, proprietor of *Picture Post*, author of *The New Age*, 1943.

insured life, and the extension to the whole people of the delusions that have rotted the middle classes.

Economic socialism is not the revolt against capitalism; it is the final form which capitalism takes in the desperate effort to stave off collapse. We must not go on thinking in terms of the last generation but one; we shall have to be far more drastic than that.

That is why I am very dubious of attempts to "define our aims" – because any such definition is liable to be couched in outmoded frames of thought, by men who do not grasp how far the real leaders of thought have moved on. I won't ask you to grapple with Reinhold Niebuhr and the great Christian thinkers, who got there before the secular socialists started. The others are catching up; Peter Drucker[1] has issued his warning on the negative side; and Lewis Mumford, in his *Faith for Living*,[2] published today by Secker, sees clearly the way things are going.

Also, as a purely practical point, I think that if we start now to put out a lot of ideological propaganda, it will be automatically discredited as propaganda. Propaganda, like every other vice or virtue, destroys itself by its own inward corruption; and the public hawking of rival New Jerusalems has pretty well reached the point of dissolution.

I won't go further into all this now. Perhaps some day we may get an opportunity to discuss the matter.

Yours very truly,

[D. L. S.]

---

1 Author of *The End of Economic Man*, recommended in *Begin Here*, under "Some Books to Read", where it is described by D. L. S. as "the most interesting and original book I have read recently. It deals with the failure of the economic state to provide man with a satisfactory and reasonable world to live in. Incidentally, it offers a really intelligible explanation of that very puzzling thing, the working of totalitarian economics".

2 Lewis Mumford (1895–1990)

By February 1941 Dr James Welch had succeeded in freeing the plays on the life of Christ from the control of the Children's Hour Department and Val Gielgud had agreed to produce them. Though they were to be broadcast on an adult network, the listening time would be suitable for children and it was understood that D. L. S. would bear them in mind. It is apparent from her letters and also from the first few plays that she continued to do so.

[24 Newland Street
Witham
Essex]

TO VAL GIELGUD

24 February 1941

Dear Val,

If I hadn't been so stupefied with flu, I'd have written before to say Thank God you'd consented to produce the Life of Christ plays I'm trying to write for Dr. Welch. (It did occur to me that I'd look an awful ass if you walked out and refused to have anything to do with them or me, after the way I'd been roaring that over *He That Should Come* everybody had behaved like perfect gents, and never anything in the nature of words passed between us – handing myself out certificates of good conduct in your name, so to speak! I'm sure the Bristol people think I'm possessed of a devil, but honestly I began by being as good as gold; only somehow we didn't seem to be talking the same language. And then God got sort of dragged into it, which is always so tiresome; it's easier if one just treats plays as plays and contracts as contracts and leaves God to run His own end of the show.)

Look, which days are you likely to be in Town? I was so sorry I couldn't come up last week, but I was still all wobbly and peculiar. But I should like to have a talk about this show, because it bristles with difficulties – more than any of them realise. I mean, it's difficult if one is trying to make the thing theatre, and not just scripture lessons in dialogue. That's why I thank God you're going to do it, because then it will be produced as plays; I heard a bit of a Children's Hour thing about Absalom the other day which sounded as if everybody was in the pulpit (miaou! miaou!). Have they shown you the script of the first play, or given you any idea about the rest of the series? I did write several explanatory letters to Derek McCulloch about it, but it would be easier to go into it by word of mouth. I've got to be in London on the 5th. to do a bit of religious twaddle on the air,[1] and I shall be passing through again on the following Monday. Or I could run up practically any day you were going to be there, if you would send me a line. I've only done the one play[2] so far, having become rather discouraged; but I will now begin to encourage myself again.

---

1 "The Religions Behind the Nations", a talk delivered at 7.40 p.m., 5 March. It was later included in *The Church Looks Ahead: Broadcast Talks* (Faber and Faber, November 1941), with a preface by E. L. Mascall. The other talks were by J. H. Oldham, Maurice B. Reckitt, Philip Mairet, M. C. D'Arcy, V. A. Demant and T. S. Eliot.
2 "Kings in Judaea".

How is everybody? Please give my love to Billy Williams[3] and all the other of my friends in your company. And all the best to yourself, and don't let a bomb get between you and the production, or I shall become finally discouraged and abandon the position.

By the way, I never did that detective thing I promised you, did I?[4] I didn't forget it, but I didn't seem able to get hold of an idea in that line. It may come yet, if you still want that kind of thing.

Yours ever,

[D.L.S.]

3 The actor Harcourt Williams.
4 See letter to Val Gielgud, 13 February 1940 and note 2.

> [24 Newland Street
> Witham
> Essex]

TO THE BISHOP OF SHREWSBURY[1]

3 March 1941

My dear Lord Bishop,

Thank you very much for your letter. I don't know whether I am at all the right sort of person to talk to a Moral Welfare Association. I am not at all good at talking to people about morals, but perhaps I could embroider the theme that morals are not entirely confined to the question of getting drunk and who goes to bed with who.[2] May the 15th is I am afraid quite impossible, but there is a chance I could manage May the 1st. I cannot tell just at this moment because I shall have to see whether I could fit this in with another engagement, the details of which are not yet fixed.

So may I leave it open for the moment and write to you as soon as I hear.

Yours sincerely,

[Dorothy L. Sayers]

1 The Rt Rev. Eric Knightley Chetwode Hamilton.
2 Compare her four lines of verse: "As years come in and years go out\ I totter towards the tomb,\ Still caring less and less about\Who goes to bed with whom." (See Barbara Reynolds, *Dorothy L. Sayers: Her Life and Soul*, p. 363.)

[24 Newland Street
Witham
Essex]

TO VAL GIELGUD

3 March 1941

Dear Val,

Your letter just received. Oh, thank you, Mister Copperfield, for that remark! It is so true! Oh, I am so much obliged to you for this confidence! Oh, it's such a relief, you can't think, to know that you understand our situation, and are certain (as you wouldn't wish to make unpleasantness in the family) not to go against me![1]

Quite providentially, a speech I was supposed to be making at Brighton on the 14th. has been transferred to another date,[2] so I will come up to Town and lunch with you with joy and alacrity. There are going to be lots of snags in this thing – in particular, the invention of ordinary, human, connecting dialogue for Christ. It's all right making up conversation for the disciples and people, but it's difficult doing it for Him; and if one doesn't, we are going to get just the effect one wants to avoid – namely, a perfectly stiff, cardboard character, different from, and unapproachable by, common humanity, doing nothing but preach sermons. He must be allowed to say at least things like, "Good morning", and "Please", and "Thank you", whether they are in the Bible or not. Also, it's going to be a job to make each play a more or less complete bit of theatre in itself. If you look at the New Testament, it's full of disconnected episodes – often quite good theatre in themselves (e.g. the raising of Lazarus or the little gem of domestic drama about the blind man at the Pool of Siloam) but not tying up together. Except, of course, the Nativity Story and the Passion.

It's not made easier by the fact that I still don't really know how many plays they want. They began by saying twelve, which would cover the ground pretty well. Then Dr. Welch startled me by saying they would want "six at least". I pointed out that in that case we should either have to give up the Ministry altogether, or deal very summarily with the Passion. He then said we had better compromise on "about ten". It doesn't seem to occur to people that one writes each play of a series with a view to its relation to the whole series.

The general theme of the series is to be the Kingdom. That seemed a suitable line to take on the thing just at this moment, when everybody is bothered about what sort of government the world should have. That

1 Echoes of Uriah Heep, in Charles Dickens' *David Copperfield*.
2 See letter to the Editor, *The Sower*, 21 April 1941, note 1.

means that we have got to get in certain things, whatever happens. We must, for instance, have the Temptation, in which Christ is faced with the choice between a kingdom of this world and a Kingdom of God in this world. This, I am sorry to say, involves us with the Devil – always an awkward character to make plausible. Also, it means we must get in one or two of the Parables of the Kingdom, which necessitates a certain amount of preachment. Further, we can't focus on the Kingdom and leave out the Entry into Jerusalem, which is the sort of queer ironic counterpart to the Temptation – the moment when it looked as though the kingdom of this world might be grasped after all. So at present we seem to have the following fixed points:

> Nativity Play – kingdom of Herod, and the sort of fairy-
>   tale kings of Orient.
> Temptation – worked in with John the Baptist as fore-
>   runner of the Kingdom, and the Baptism of Christ.
> Jerusalem – Entry into, with other episodes.
> Last Supper – including the arrest at Gethsemane.
> Trial Scene – Caiaphas, Herod, Pilate, with record of
>   crowing cock for Peter.
> Crucifixion – where the conflict between realism and
>   suitability for children is going to become acute.
> Resurrection – ending, I think, with that amazingly
>   atmospheric appearance at the Sea of Tiberias
>   (last chapter of St. John).

There, whatever Dr. Welch says, I propose to stop, and not go into what became of the Disciples and the Church afterwards. I know what we are leaving out, the Ascension and Pentecost. But I don't really see how anybody is to go up into Heaven by wireless. I could do it in a film, or even at Drury Lane; but in my opinion – my 'umble but fixed, opinion – the thing that speech-without-sight is least capable of conveying is physical movement of an abrupt and unlikely kind, and I fear the general effect would be that of the ascent of Montgolfier's balloon[3] amid the running commentary of a bunch of sight-seers. Nor do I feel that the "speaking with tongues" would sound like anything but a cross between a row at the League of Nations and the Zoo at feeding time.

Even as it stands, that gives us seven plays; and, if ten is the maximum,[4] the whole Ministry between the Temptation and the Last Supper will

3 In 1783 Jacques Etienne and Joseph Montgolfier, brothers, who were paper manufacturers, filled a large bag with smoke from a straw fire and saw it rise to a great height. Others soon made use of the principle but the earliest experimental flights, first with animals and later with humans, were made with Montgolfier hot-air balloons.
4 There were ultimately twelve.

have to go into three plays. That would be all right, only there is a certain difficulty about getting the characters properly set and prepared for the final catastrophe. Judas is the real difficulty. Nothing in the New Testament gives one any real idea of what that unhappy man was driving at. He just comes on with his mind all made up to be villainous. I've got a rather subtle idea about him, but whether it can be made intelligible in the time at our disposal I don't know. He's got somehow to be the *Corruptio optimi pessima*[5] – the man with the greatest possibilities for good, and the very worst possibilities of corruption. If he hadn't had good possibilities, why was he ever called as one of the Twelve? I mean, it's got to sound plausible if one isn't to make Christ look either a fool or something worse. And there's not much time in which to depict the gradual deterioration of Judas. And I won't have those awful explanatory bits by the announcer, saying "We do not know what motives led Judas to – "or, "But, alas! there was among the little band of the Disciples one who –" because it's that kind of thing that jerks one out of the theatre into the schoolroom. All this is my trouble and not yours, of course, but it may influence us if we want to make a combined stand about the number of plays, or anything like that.

I'm glad you like "Kings in Judaea". I think we ought to have some fun with the Herod scenes. (Billy Williams[6] will want to play Herod, because I once light-heartedly said I would write him a Herod play some day, but I don't think this Herod is his meat; I rather had Cecil Trouncer[7] in mind – he can do a good line in threatening sarcasm – only we mustn't tell Billy I asked for somebody else.) Proclus the Centurion will turn up again in later plays – as the chap who said "Surely this was [the] Son of God"[8] at the Crucifixion; and perhaps as the one whose servant was healed – you know, he said he knew all about being under authority – that one.[9] Mary is the world's worst snag; she has to be at the Crucifixion; she has no lines given to her on that occasion; and she only turns up in between at Cana in Galilee – which would make a charming scene if only we had time for it.[10] We shall want a good Peter and a good John (the Beloved Disciple, I mean); and a good bluff Thomas Didymus.[11] We can work Thomas into some of the earlier scenes, being literal-minded and stupid, and asking to have things explained.

---

5 Latin: the corruption of the best [is] the worst corruption.
6 Harcourt Williams.
7 See letter to *The New Statesman*, 17 February 1937 and note 5.
8 Mark, 15, 39: "And when the centurion, which stood over against him, saw that he so cried out, and gave up the ghost, he said, Truly this man was the Son of God."
9 Luke, chapter 7, verses 2–9.
10 Time was made for it. See the third play, "A Certain Nobleman".
11 Thomas the Twin, known also as Doubting Thomas.

We are going to be badly off for female relief – nothing but male voices. I wish most of Christ's female friends had been rather more respectable; but we must get in Mary Magdalen, however delicately we skimble over her profession. She really is fearfully important, because of the Resurrection; so I shall try to do the Lazarus-story and the household at Bethany, and if possible the precious ointment episode. (I don't care if the critics have said that Mary Magdalen and Mary of Bethany were different people – Church tradition has always made them the same, and [we] can't have all these hopelessly disconnected characters.)

I'm going to try and do as little as possible with effects and noises off. Du Garde Peach's plays on St. Paul are a perfect orgy of shipwrecks and camel-drivers. Some crowds we must be bothered with, I'm afraid, because "the multitudes" are always being mentioned. The two really important ones will be the ones shouting "Hosanna" in the Jerusalem scene and the Jews crying "Crucify Him!" in the Trial scene. Then there's the students in the first play, and a crowd of people being baptised in the second play and of course there will have to be some crowds to be preached at and to be astonished at miracles and things. That just can't be helped. Will it do if I keep to about the same number of speaking parts I've got in "Kings in Judaea" for each play? It's difficult to keep the numbers down when one is encumbered with all those disciples and Pharisees and so on. But all the decor shall be kept as simple as I can.

Dr. Welch has just written to say he will be in Town on Wednesday, Thursday, and Friday of next week. We had better have a talk with him, hadn't we? He really has been very nice and helpful and very patient with my screams of rage. But I should like to have a go at the problems with you in private so that we can deal with the technicalities unhampered. Shall I just refer him to you for the actual time of meeting? I can get to Town by about mid-day, if Hitler doesn't choose Thursday night to blow up the line, and can be at your disposal as and when you choose.

Don't bother to answer all this; I've just put it down to give you a line on the way I'm trying to work it out.

Yours ever,

[D. L. S.]

[24 Newland Street
Witham
Essex]

TO LADY FLORENCE CECIL

12 March 1941

Dear Lady Florence,

Thank you so much for your letter. It is very kind of you to enquire after a new novel, but at the beginning of the war I rather rashly made a vow to write no more detective stories until the Armistice. It is true that I am pretty busy on other things, but also it has been borne in upon me that people are getting rather too much of the detective story attitude to life – a sort of assumption that there is a nice, neat solution for every imaginable problem. I am now spending my time telling people that real difficulties, such as sin, death and the night-bomber, can't be "solved" like crosswords!

I have just finished a curious sort of book about the creative mind called *The Mind of the Maker*,[1] which Methuen will be publishing shortly. It is about the way the artist's mind works all mixed up with the doctrine of the Trinity. I can't imagine what the parsons will make of it, or the artists; however, it has been very entertaining to write.

With all good wishes,
    Yours sincerely,
        [Dorothy L. Sayers]

---

1 It was published on 10 July 1941.

In March Eric Fenn again invited D. L. S. to contribute to a series of broadcast talks on the Christian faith. The subject of the talks, intended for the Forces Programme, was the Nicene Creed. He asked D. L. S. to provide six, each to last ten minutes, on the theme, the Son of God. D. L. S. preferred the title "God the Son". Delivered on 8, 15, 22, 29 of June and 6, 13 July, they were: "Lord and God", "Lord of all Worlds", "The Man of Men", "The Death of God", "The World's Desire", "The Touchstone of History".

[24 Newland Street
Witham
Essex]

TO THE REV. ERIC FENN

20 March 1941

Dear Mr. Fenn,

I am sorry to have kept God the Son waiting all this time. I think I could manage to do it on the dates you mention, if, as you kindly suggest, some of the talks could be recorded.[1]

I have roughed out a possible line to take on most of the points, though I think I am going to have trouble with the clauses about Judgment. There are already such a lot of people who write passionate and slightly potty letters about the Second Coming, that I tremble at the thought of my correspondence. Still I fear that we cannot remove a clause from the Creed for my convenience.

My last talk[2] seems to have produced a more than usually fruity crop of candidates for the loony bin! There are two good souls who want to have the talk to read. I gather this series is not being printed in *The Listener* – or is it?[3]

Yours very sincerely,
[D. L. S.]

1 Only the first was given live.
2 "The Religions Behind the Nations", delivered on 5 March. See letter to Val Gielgud, 24 February 1941, note 1.
3 These talks were not published.

[24 Newland Street
Witham
Essex]

TO THE REV. ERIC FENN

26 March 1941

Dear Mr. Fenn,

I am sending you the rough draft of the first two talks on God the Son. I have tried to keep them at about the same intellectual level as the talks on the Christ of the Creeds and the Sacrament of Matter,[1] which you liked. It is difficult to hit upon the exact right level for the Forces, since

1 See letter to Eric Fenn, 11 June 1940.

everybody seems to be in the Forces nowadays, including those who know everything about everything and those who know nothing about anything. Also I did not realise before what a shocking lot of purely technical theological terms the Nicene Creed bristles with. Can you tell me whether the bloke who is following with God the Father, is going to be so obliging as to deal at all with the Trinitarian formula? Or is he just going to talk about the Fatherhood of a loving Creator and leave me to introduce the subject of the three Persons with no previous preparation? Similarly, is he going to tackle the meaning of the word "Heaven" which always requires a little cautionary definition, lest anybody should suppose us to mean by it a palace above the clouds!

I realise, of course, the special awkwardness of any wireless series, namely, that you cannot ever take it for granted that one single person who is listening to talk number three, has listened to both, or either, of talks one and two, or that he will then go on to listen to talks number four and five. Bearing this in mind I have tried in the second talk to bring in again the definitions of technical terms proposed in the first talk, so as to make each talk, as far as possible, complete in itself. I only hope that talk six will not be so taken up with recapitulations of previous talks as to have no room left in it for the subject matter!

Will you let me know if you think these suggestions are along the right lines. I have written them to a ten minute length, although in your letter you said that we might be able to get fifteen minutes. I only hope they are not too "packed". The Creed itself is packed as much as an egg with meat, and it's rather a job to unpack it, when you have to try to explain everything in everyday language. The extraordinary difficulty of explaining what is meant by the word "Person", without giving the impression that God the Father has arms and legs and a beard, may have caused me to veer dangerously towards the Scylla of Sabellianism,[2] but that is probably a lesser danger in these days than the Charybdis[3] of Arianism.[4]

Yours very sincerely,

[Dorothy L. Sayers]

2 See letter to Father Herbert Kelly, 4 October 1937, note 4.
3 Scylla and Charybdis are a rock and a whirlpool between Sicily and Italy, used as a metaphor signifying two dangers. To avoid one is to fall into the other.
4 See letter to Father Herbert Kelly, 4 October 1937, note 3.

Eric Fenn sent her a 7-page, 1500-word commentary, proposing, in particular, that she should begin "straight off with a question: Has it ever struck you how very oddly the Creed starts off its second main division?"...against which D. L. S. scribbled in the margin: "Children's Hour touch!" She replied as follows:

> [24 Newland Street
> Witham
> Essex]

TO THE REV. ERIC FENN

4 April 1941

Dear Mr. Fenn,

Many thanks for returning the scripts and for your careful and valuable criticism and suggestions....

I will go over my stuff again in the light of what you say. One thing, however, I'm afraid I shall be a little disappointing and tiresome about. I'm *not good* at the direct personal appeal – "Has it ever struck you – ?" "How about your own children?" "I want you to think about –" It always makes me embarrassed, and I can feel my voice getting that awful, wheedling, children's-hour intonation – very bright and encouraging, like somebody trying to screw rational answers out of an idiot school. Flat statement and argument is my natural line, and I shall make a ghastly mess of the other if I try it. For the other points:

(1) I gather from Mr. Williams[1] that Neville Talbot[2] is only doing the preliminary talks on why we believe or want to believe; "the particular bee at present buzzing in his bonnet is the idea that credal statements are cold and clammy unless you first get fired by the red-hot experiences and agonising questions which they are the answer to". So I expect he will cope only too earnestly with the question about why the Church believes. After the sort of opening he will produce, it may be rather a good thing to have a sober statement of what she actually *does* believe! The thing that horrifies me is that anybody should harbour such ignorant repulsive fantasies as, e.g. Ivor Brown,[3] whose latest outburst in *The Literary Guide* has been thoughtfully forwarded to me – no doubt as a rebuke to my article on "Forgiveness"[4] in *The Fortnightly*. It shows pretty clearly that the expression "God the Son" is one he has never

---

1 The Rev. J. G. Williams, assistant to the Religious Director, B.B.C., from 1946.

2 The Roman Catholic Bishop of Nottingham.

3 Ivor Brown (1891–1974), leader-writer for the *Manchester Guardian* and dramatic critic on the *Saturday Review*.

4 "Forgiveness and the Enemy", published in *The Fortnightly*, New Series, vol. 149, no. 892.,

separated from the historic Jesus. He is, of course, an old-fashioned and ignorant "rationalist" of *The Freethinker* type, brought up on Robert Blatchford;[5] but his ideas are the ideas which his generation has handed down to the younger generations as being the Creed of Christendom.

(2) The theology of "The Father" is, apparently, being handled by Fr. John Murray. Being a Jesuit, he will probably give a proper dogmatic basis from which to work, and erect the scaffolding for the Trinitarian formula. All the better.

(3) Opening sentences of each talk – It's difficult to begin brightly in the middle of the subject, when one remembers that half one's audience will not have heard the previous talks. If the "Summary" of where we get to and what we are talking about could be transferred to the Announcer's introductory remarks, it might help.

(4) "Father and Son" – I'm frankly a little afraid of stressing the "one of the family" idea too much, because of the Ivor Brown kind of misconception. (I have just written an entire book[6] on Trinitarian analogy – of which a whole chapter is devoted to clearing up errors about analogy and metaphor!) What I feel is that if one gives them the metaphor of a "family likeness", one is going to establish the concept of two personalities – whereas the point towards which I am getting is rather two persons with one personality. (Yes – I know you are thinking – "Sabellianism"![7])

(5) I will put this more clearly, and again explain that this expression is not concerned with the human Jesus. I can, I think, do it in a sentence – I can't add very much anywhere, because of the time-limit, even allowing for my galloping rate of speech, which so confuses the official B.B.C. mind.

(6) The same applies to Nicaea. I like your phrase – "people fought about this word"; though I expect we shall only be told that this just shows how Christianity leads to riots, persecutions, wars and the Spanish Inquisition! I don't mind that – except that it adds a good deal to one's correspondence. Actually, that particular talk is the shorter of the two, so I might be able to squeeze in my favourite bit of rhetoric about the power of words, and the Power of "the Word".

You know, there is scarcely a word or phrase in the Creeds that doesn't bristle with technicalities when one comes to examine it. An hour's care-

---

5 Robert Blatchford (1851–1943), author of *God and my Neighbour* (1903), a rationalist credo. He was the editor of *The Clarion*, a Labour journal. G. K. Chesterton crossed swords with him in an essay contained in *The Doubts of Democracy*.

6 i.e. *The Mind of the Maker*.

7 See letter to Father Herbert Kelly, 4 October 1937, note 3.

ful instruction on every clause might succeed in clearing away some of the
more rooted misconceptions about these things.

I heartily approve your suggested instruction-classes for the B.B.C.
Controllers. May I attend them and watch Duff Cooper's[8] reactions?

I have always thought it unfair to put "Lift Up Your Hearts"[9] just before
the eight o'clock news, so that one can't escape it – like the vicar waylay-
ing the congregation at the church-door. But now that Derek McCulloch
has started in on the six o'clock, I am foaming at the mouth, and the blasphemy in my household would shock Satan himself. I won't be prayed at
over and round like this; it's slimy, that's what it [is]....

8 Alfred Duff Cooper, 1st Viscount Norwich (1890–1954), was Minister of Information from
   1940 to 1941.
9 Title of a daily brief religious talk, which preceded the 8 a.m. news, later replaced by
   "Thought for the Day" or "Prayer for the Day".

[24 Newland Street
Witham
Essex]

TO THE REV. V. A. DEMANT[1]

4 April 1941

Dear Father Demant,

I am afraid I have had to refuse Canon Baines. I have had to do so
much talking and lecturing lately, what with H.M.'s Forces and various
well-meaning societies and assorted Bishops, that I am getting seriously
behind with work and must refuse everything during the summer months.
I have undertaken to do a series of plays on the life of Christ for the
B.B.C. They hung fire during the winter on account of a ferocious
quarrel between myself and the Children's Hour Department. After
an unchristian display of temper and pride on my part,[2] I succeeded
in getting the production of the plays transferred to Val Gielgud. Having
got my way about this I must now really do the plays and do them
properly....

1 Vigo Auguste Demant (1893–1983), an Anglican priest, associated with the Christendom
   Group. (See letter to Maurice B. Reckitt, 8 May 1941, note 1.) "Of all the able men and
   women...associated with the Christendom Group none was at any time more admired and
   trusted than Demant." (John S. Peart-Binns, *Maurice B. Reckitt: A Life*, Bowerdean and
   Pickering, p. 77.)
2 A nice touch of self-assessment! Cf. her letter to C. S. Lewis, 13 May 1943.

[24 Newland Street
Witham
Essex]

TO THE REV. V. A. DEMANT

10 April 1941

Dear Father Demant,
    How very good of you to write so large a letter with your own hand especially right in the middle of your busiest weeks! I am most grateful – and should have hastened to thank you earlier, but that when your letter arrived I was just starting off to address R.A.F.'s and W.A.A.F.'s at Mildenhall.
    I am extremely glad you like the book,[1] and very much relieved, because I feel sure you would have detected anything unsound or over-strained or fundamentally insincere about it. From the writer's end I think it is all right, but it is fatally easy, when drawing analogies, to be run away with by the intellectual elegance of one's own conceits and make the thing too neat to be convincing.
    You feel this is the way theology should be written – and that is particularly gratifying, because my literary friends don't look upon it as theology at all, but as an experiment in literary criticism. This encourages me to hope that I've so far succeeded as to get theology and letters where I want them – as two expressions of a single experience. The other books in the Series[2] won't at all take that line – it isn't a specifically Christian or religious series, and the writer of the book on medicine[3] is rather anti-religious than otherwise – but I hope all the writers will take what I rather vaguely feel to be the Christian attitude to their work, viz: that it is or ought to be the outward and visible sign of a creative reality. (This is a sort of Christian "attack by infiltration" – one must learn from the enemy.)
    I'm beginning more and more to think that this business about Vocation in Work is absolutely fundamental to any proper handling of the "economic situation". I have been hammering at it now, in a rather groping sort of way, since the War started, and I think I had better go on hammering. I've tapped at the W.E.A.[4] and thumped deafeningly at Brighton[5] (on Point 9 of the Archbishop's Manifesto[6]), and I have written this book, and now I am chiselling away at the troops; also I shall hammer at the

---

1 i.e. *The Mind of the Maker*. D. L. S. had sent Father Demant the typescript.
2 i.e. "Bridgeheads".
3 Denis Browne, the husband of Helen Simpson. His book was never written.
4 Workers' Educational Association.
5 See letter to Editor of *The Sower*, 21 April 1941, note.
6 Issued by Dr William Temple, Archbishop of York, after the Malvern Conference held in January 1941.

Sword of the Spirit meeting on May 11th, and at a Welfare Workers'
meeting in Leeds. It seems to be a thing I can make a shot at saying something about, so unless I am silenced by bombs, or by being carried away
to the asylum labouring under the impression that I am a woodpecker, I
shall hammer unceasingly. I am persistently knocking away at Tom
Heron[7], in the hope that I shall be able to knock a book out of him for the
Series; because he does understand what it's all about – as very few
employers of labour do; and if he can't write the thing himself, he can
give us the stuff, both from the men's point of view and his own.

One is hampered by the abominable phrase "vocational education",
which usually means the very opposite of what it says. It shows how far
we have lost the very idea of "vocation" in work, that we give the name
to a training which is chiefly designed to train people for employment. We
ought to recognise the profound gulf between the work to which we are
"called" and the work we are forced into as a means of livelihood.

I'm rather at a loss, too, about the "theological criterion". Basically, I
see perfectly that an Incarnate Creator is the fundamental sanction for
looking on all man's work in a sacramental light – the manifestation of his
divine creativeness in matter. And that this is all tied up somehow with a
proper reverence for man and matter, and is opposed to the exploitation
of the soil and of men's labour. But apart from that, which is somehow
implicit in the dogma, I can't find much explicit theological doctrine
about it. I recognise the ruthless imperative vocation in the visit to the
Temple and in the injunctions to hate father and mother and let the dead
bury their dead, but it's all somehow taken for granted. Is it that it was
only in these latter days that the inalienable divine right of man's calling
came even to be questioned? What workers say, when faced with the difficulty, is that "human needs" come before the "worth of the work"; and
it is difficult to persuade them that one of the first human needs is, precisely, the conviction of a purpose in the work they are doing.

I am persuaded that no economic schemes for giving workers more
wages and more leisure will do any real good if their sense of their own
purpose is so corrupted that they can neither get satisfaction from their
work nor employ their leisure in creation. And what is the use of preaching sexual morality to people whose lives are so deadened and embittered
that a dreary promiscuity offers them their only chance of even a

---

7 Thomas Milner Heron (1890–1983), a socialist-minded entrepreneur of Leeds who tried to
   improve conditions of employment in the clothing industry. He was also committed to the
   National Guilds League. He began a book for "Bridgeheads" but did not complete it. (Cf.
   letter to the conveners of the Theological Literature Association, 28 November 1941.) He had
   previously written a pamphlet, *Christian Vocation in Industry and Marketing*, 1926.

semblance of purpose and pursuit? Look at Charles Morgan,[8] fumbling away about single-mindedness in *The Flashing Stream*. If his male and female mathematicians had been really single-minded about their practical mathematics, they wouldn't waste three acts arguing about the ethics of going to bed, and whether or not they should humiliate themselves to a Government department as the price of getting on with the job. They'd have cheerfully allowed the War Office to think anything it chose, so long as the work was done, and they'd have been too busy to bother with the bedchamber crisis. The old, hackneyed stuff about "la femme jalouse de l'oeuvre" was much closer to reality: it is the person who hasn't got a real job to do who sticks the personal feelings and the human needs like so many spanners into the world's work.

We haven't begun to tackle the "woman-question" either. It's no good trying to bring the men back – or forward – to a sense of the sacredness of work if the women are left as an exploiting class to suck the heart out of them and demand that they should make money for money's sake. After the war there's going to be another drive by the Trade Unions to push the women out of "the men's jobs" and back into "the home" in the name of economics. But the women's jobs have in the meantime been collared by the men – they've disappeared from the home into the breweries and bakeries and jam-factories and distilleries and spinning-mills and power-looms;[9] there's nothing left in the home for the women to be vocational about, except one baby instead of nine and the job of "keeping" her man by exploiting his labour, and taking out her share of the loot in lip-stick and emotional crises.

It seems to me that the "planners" are getting further and further away from these root realities in their post-war schemes. It's only the Churches who appear to have the first glimmerings of a notion what the real question is. They must have got the idea from somewhere, so I conclude it is at least implicit, if not explicit, in their theology. But it seems to have to [be] looked for and shaken into view, and never to have been put into a handy formula.

Whatever "vocation" is, it is imperative. But I think it is often obeyed quite intuitively and without conscious tenacity. It works by a series of instinctive but peremptory rejections. Sometimes it is only in looking back that one sees quite a track of purpose made by one's self across time.

8 Charles Morgan (1894–1958), novelist and playwright, drama critic of *The Times* from 1926 to 1939 and contributor to *The Times Literary Supplement* under the pseudonym of "Menander". *The Flashing Stream* (1938) is a play.

9 Cf. "Are Women Human?", an address given to a Women's Society in 1938, published in *Unpopular Opinions* (Gollancz, 1946, pp. 106–116); see particularly pp. 109–110. See also "The Human-not Quite Human", first published in *Christendom: A Journal of Christian Sociology*, vol. XI, no. 43, September 1941, pp. 156-162, later republished in *Unpopular Opinions*, pp. 116–122.

While one was going along, one seemed to be darting about in aimless zig-zags, but seen in retrospect the track runs like the path in the *Pilgrim's Progress*, "straight as a rule can make it",[10] never deviating, and with no fundamental error anywhere in its course, whatever nasty messes there may be to right and left of it. Some of the messes turn out to be the peremptory rejections – which links up with your quotations from Denis Saurat.[11] I must get that book; it sounds as if it made sense.

Artists, who are emotionally sensitive to pain and suffering, are the last people who ought to have any intellectual difficulty with it, because their whole life and work consists in making sense of it. They do experience the difficulty, but that is largely because they are not consciously aware of their own creative processes. They make vocal the outcry of the bewildered common man, but in their hearts they know otherwise; – and in their actions they display the same ruthless purpose which they protest against when they see it in the universe; or, if they do not, they are false to their calling.

There is something in this which religion should be able to see and interpret for the common man; but some necessary link of understanding has been lost.

I seem to be spawning a whole shoal of half-warmed fishes[12], with which I ought not to bother you.

In the meantime, thank you again very much, and not least for your kind assurance of practical support. If, when the book appears, you could see your way to

(a) reviewing it anywhere in the theological and\or religious press (they are not quite the same thing) or steering it into the hands of a reviewer who will see what it's meant to be about;
(b) defending it against the assault of the Philistines in any correspondence that may arise;

I shall be deeply grateful.

    With all good wishes,

        yours very sincerely,

            [Dorothy L. Sayers]

---

10 *The Pilgrim's Progress*, First Part, Good Will to Christian: "Look before thee; dost thou see this narrow way? That is the way thou must go...it is as straight as a rule can make it."

11 Denis Saurat (1890–1958), professor of French, London University. The book mentioned may be *Regeneration*, 1940, or *Watch Over Africa*, 1941.

12 An echo of the phrase attributed to the celebrated Dr Spooner: "a half-warmed fish", by which he meant "a half-formed wish".

[24 Newland Street
Witham
Essex]

TO THE EDITOR
The Sower[1]
21 April 1941

Dear Sir,

CHRIST CARPENTER

I am greatly obliged to you for sending me the April number of *The Sower*, with its reference to my suggestion (made in an address at Brighton)[2] that a church might at some time be dedicated to "Christ Carpenter".

I particularly welcome the emphasis you lay upon "the kind of work which is not just 'a job' . . . but is indistinguishable from play, an end in itself, like the Holy Mass". This sentence, in fact, summarises the argument of my address, which was directed to show that the "economic" concept of work adopted alike by the representatives of Capital and Labour was corrupt, unchristian, and contrary to the true needs and nature of Man. The Divine joy in creation, which Man should inherit in virtue of his participation in the image of the Godhead, has been largely destroyed, persisting today almost alone among artists, skilled craftsmen, and members of the learned professions; and it is this loss of "the sense of a Divine vocation" in "Man's daily work" which lies at the root of our social and economic corruptions. In a letter to *The Catholic Herald* (18 April) I have briefly stated the theological grounds for my attitude; I am also taking the liberty of sending you a copy of the address itself, in the hope that you may find time to glance at it.

I am most anxious that nothing said by me should be supposed to commit me (still less, by implication, the Church of England) to the kind of political significance which has so unfortunately become attached to the word "Worker". In particular, the attempt to draw a distinction between manual and mental labour is disastrous, and calculated to make the reintegration of Man and Society impossible. As for its theological corollaries – the horrid suggestion that the Divine Person of Christ should be used

---

1 No periodical of this name has been traced. It may have been a church magazine. The address of the editor was 763 Coventry Road, Birmingham.

2 Entitled "Work and Vocation", given at the Dome, Brighton, 8 March 1941; reprinted in part as "Vocation in Work" in *A Christian Basis for the Post-War World* (Student Christian Movement Press, May 1942) and as "A Plea for Vocation in Work" in *Bulletins from Britain* (New York, 103, 19 August 1942, pp. 7–10). Later entitled "Why Work?", it was included in *Creed or Chaos?*, Methuen 1947, pp. 47–64.

as a kind of emblem in a class warfare, or should be so sub-divided as to
effect a virtual opposition between the Galilean Workman and the Eternal
Logos – I can only call them so blasphemous and so heretical as to shock
any Christian conscience. Any devotion to "Christ Worker" which starts
from a limited political and economic concept of Work is unsound. A true
devotion must find its theological basis in that Divine Energy "by Whom
all things were made", Who knows no necessity to work except His own
delight in creation, and after Whose image and likeness Man's proper
nature is made.

    Yours faithfully,
        [Dorothy L. Sayers]

                    24 Newland Street
                    Witham
                    Essex

TO HER SON

7 May 1941

Dear John,

    I have been galloping round the country addressing meetings, carrying
your letter with me in the hope of getting it answered, but I never seemed
to get a moment for thinking in.

    I'm glad you find the book[1] interesting. I think your first difficulty is due
to your having extended the analogy beyond its terms of reference. It
applies to "the mind of the artist engaged in an act of creation", and (for
the purposes of the book) is restricted to that and nothing else – i.e., it
doesn't set out to deal at all with the personality of the artist.

    It could, of course, be used so as to apply to that. In that case "the
Father" would be what one might call the "timeless self", comprising the
whole of the man's existence, "the end in the beginning" – the permanent
or eternal selfhood so to speak. "The Son" would be the whole of the self
as expressed in action (thought, word, deed, etc.) including the manifestation in space and time, from beginning to end. (This is all we ever see or
know directly of the personality – "the Father can only be known by the
Son".) "The Ghost" would be the man's self-awareness and other men's
awareness of him, including the power of his personality exercised in history. So that there is no "trinity behind the personality" – the trinity is the
personality.

    I didn't use this particular image because it is more involved and diffi-

---

1 *The Mind of the Maker.* It is evident that she sent him the typescript or a proof copy since the
book was not published until July of that year.

cult than the more restricted image. Also, when it came to including the creative work of the personality, one would have to define and display it in so many different and vague senses; the ordinary man's personality is a rather feeble "image of the Creator", whereas that of the-artist-creating, though more restricted, is more definite and satisfactory.

Rather similarly, the difficulty about God. It's not quite enough, theologically, to say that God "*has* will" – He *is* will, just as He *is* beauty, goodness, justice and so forth. The theologian's phrase is that "God *is* all that He *has*". It is true that God's will always issues in creation – He *is* creativeness. That is what is meant when people say that "God's creation is necessary to Him" – so it is: though not necessarily this or any particular creation. Thus one may take "the Resurrection of the Body" in the widest possible sense – not applying it merely to the power of the creature to remake its own form, but to the continual power and will of the Son to create, and manifest Himself in Form. I thought of writing a chapter on this, but the book was too long already. This is God's experience: but the Father cannot experience evil; the Son experiences it – or the results of it – in His manifestation by continually transforming it into good.

I hope this makes things a little clearer. Of course one can't limit God's Trinity to this one creation; why should one? Even the human creator isn't limited to a single work – not even to a single work at a time, though he doesn't enjoy God's infinite freedom in this respect. Since, however, we have no knowledge or experience of any creation but this one, we cannot very usefully argue about others.

I have been trying to drive the thing about "the integrity of the work" into the heads of the multitude – all very difficult. They always want the economic system altered before they begin to think what they want it altered to or for, and consequently, they end with exactly the same economic tyranny, rather differently administered. Except, of course, the pure mystagogues, who assume that as soon as control of the means of production passes into the hands of the workers, the whole of society will automatically become, not only selfless and virtuous but endowed with intellectual discrimination and impeccable artistic taste. This seems a large assumption! What they expect is the automatic emergence of Sinless Man – which, as certain of their own psychologists have said, is, to say the least of it, unlikely.

Hope you will have a good term,[2] and harvest like anything when the time comes along –

Much love,

D. L. S.

---

2 John Anthony was still at Malvern College, aged 17.

[24 Newland Street
Witham
Essex]

8 May 1941

Dear Mr. Reckitt,

Thank you very much for your letter and for the enclosure from Philip Mairet[2]. What he says is very valuable; in particular I welcome the realism that suggests we may be in for a "war period". Have you noticed the curious way in which we have come to talk about peace as a "normal" condition – not in the same sense in which we speak of "normal eyesight" (a standard generally desirable but seldom met with, by which we measure our individual defects) or as we might speak of Christ as "the norm of humanity", but as though it were a *usual* condition, into which we may expect the world to relax automatically when some exceptional pressure is removed? Historically, such a condition of world-wide peace has, I suppose, never been experienced; but because we are determined to look on war as an exception to the common run of things, we adjust ourselves badly to war conditions. Admittedly, this is a very large, alarming and unpleasant war, and it's difficult to "be ordinary" when one's liable to have bombs dropped on one at any moment, – nor, of course, do we want "Business As Usual"; but I can't help thinking that if we had faced the prospect of war as one of the things that do happen, instead of assuring each other that it was "unthinkable", we should have been more on the spot to prevent it from coming or to grapple with it when it came. When one looks at the flimsy houses and the glass palaces that we built in the inter-War years, it seems as though our whole way of life had been deliberately out of touch with a reality that included the likelihood of aerial bombardment. But if one says that to people, they reply that to take precautions against war is to accept and acquiesce in the idea of war, and so encourage it – though I notice they don't think that the putting of locks on the doors and safes in banks is a wicked acquiescence in the idea of burglary. I believe at the back of their minds they are superstitious about it – like the man who refuses to make his will because he doesn't like thinking about death, and feels he may bring it on by taking notice of it. But there it is; to be as realistic as the people who peppered the country with border keeps is to "admit that war is normal". It seems to me just as nor-

---

1   See letter to him, dated 21 February 1940, note.
2   Philip Mairet (1886–1975), to whom T. S. Eliot dedicated *Notes Towards a Definition of Culture*. The editor of *The New English Weekly* from 1934 to 1949, he was one of the contributors to *The Church Looks Ahead*. (See letter to Val Gielgud, 24 February 1941, note 1.)

mal as any other sin and wickedness. What's the good of saying "we ought to have progressed beyond the ideas of the Middle Ages" when, as a matter of brutal fact, we have not done any such thing so far as war is concerned. Progress (if there is such a thing) doesn't come all of a piece and all along the line – it happens in bursts, and sometimes we go back and have to start again. We wash more than the seventeenth century, but less than ancient Rome; we are kinder to some animals than we used to be, and the manners of village children have improved; but Spaniards are cruel to mules and Germans to Jews, and England is the only country that needs a N.S.P.C.C.[3] – so where are you?...

Goodness knows if we shall be able to do anything with the G.C.W.[4] The trouble is that we include a number of pious scribblers, but not nearly enough real writers. But we shall see. It's helpful to know that the N.E.W.[5] can offer us a platform – I only hope the paper shortage won't drive us all out of business!

Talking of writers, in an article the other day in *World Review*[6] I expressed the opinion that the leading Christian thinkers were writing about world-events with a depth and insight which left the secular builders of the New Jerusalem standing. (Not that that's saying a great deal, for the Utopians' combination of shallowness with wishful thinking doesn't take much beating.) Now comes John Gloag,[7] with the sneering question: "Leading Christian thinkers? Who are they?" I must give him an answer, and there are a number of names I'd like to mention. But, for confirmation and my better instruction, who should you say were the people who really had the surest grasp of fundamentals in "this present crisis"? The real high-level of Christian thinking? I'd like to hand him a list of about a dozen – including Romans and foreigners, on whom I'm rather weak. Actually, I'm weak on the subject altogether; I only know that when, in

3 National Society for the Prevention of Cruelty to Children.
4 Guild of Catholic Writers, affiliated to the Church Social Action Group (of which the Rev. Patrick McLaughlin, later associated with the Society of St Anne, Soho, was appointed Secretary). See also letter to Patrick McLaughlin, 28 August 1940.
5 *The New English Weekly.*
6 "The Church in the New Age", *World Review*, March 1941, pp. 11–15. It is preceded by the following introduction by the editor, Edward Hulton: "An uncompromising statement on the Church's function in the community by a distinguished laywoman who is more widely known as the creator of Lord Peter Wimsey. Her outspoken utterances on the Church's attitude towards morality at a recent ecclesiastical conference [Malvern] led to bitter newspaper controversy." In her article D. L. S. makes many of the same points as in her paper for Malvern.
7 In *World Review*, May 1941, under "Correspondence Cross-Section", p. 78, John Gloag (1896–1981), novelist and author of works on architecture and design, wrote: "I have read with interest and perplexity the article by Dorothy Sayers. In the one paragraph in which she is specific, she mentions 'the best Christian thinkers' and states that they are 'writing and speaking of world events with an insight and profundity'. Who are they?"

my desultory reading, I get hold of a Christian commentator – whether it's Maritain[8] or Demant[9] or Niebuhr[10] or Berdyaev[11] or yourself – he seems to be a damn sight closer to reality than the Human-Perfectibilitarians or the Scientific-Progressives or the people who invoke the Great God Economic-Planning, and the Sinless Proletariat.[12]

Meanwhile, in my efforts to carry out Philip Mairet's ideas about war literature, I have produced a curious book called *The Mind of the Maker* – a sort of exercise in Applied Theology. Demant thinks well of it, so I hope there's something in it. I'll see that the N.E.W. gets a review copy and will hope, as they say, for "favourable consideration". I shall certainly read your autobiography.[13]

Fr. McLaughlin is away at the moment. I shall tackle him about the G.C.W. as soon as he returns. I'm glad you approve our sub-committee – it seemed the only idea which held out a reasonable hope of getting anything done.

I heard you had been ill. I hope you are better now. I was sorry not to meet you at Malvern – but you had, on the whole, a happy escape.

Yours sincerely,

[Dorothy L. Sayers]

P.S. I return Mairet's letter.

---

8 Jacques Maritain (1882–1973), French philosopher, who opposed Bergson; author of *Humanisme Intégral* (1936), tr. M. R. A. Adamson, *True Humanism* (1938), *De la philosophie chrétienne* (1933), *Science et la sagesse* (1935).
9 See letter to V. A. Demant, 4 April 1941, note 1.
10 Ronald (Reinhold) Niebuhr (1892–1971), American theologian. His *Beyond Tragedy* was published in 1937.
11 Nicholas Berdyaev (1874–1948), Russian philosopher, who championed a return to religious values. Author of *The Meaning of History* (tr. G. Reavey, 1936); *Solitude and Society* (tr. idem, 1938).
12 Having received suggestions from M. B. Reckitt, D. L. S. wrote the letter which follows.
13 *As It Happened: An Autobiography*, Dent, 1941.

[24 Newland Street
Witham
Essex]

[TO THE EDITOR OF WORLD REVIEW]
No date[1]

Mr John Gloag asks for the names of some leaders of Christian thought who interpret world events with depth and insight. Here are a few: Jacques Maritain, Nicolas Berdyaev, V. A. Demant, Reinhold Niebuhr, William Temple, Christopher Dawson,[2] E. L. Watkin,[3] Charles Williams, T. S. Eliot, and that dynamic, if less strictly intellectual personality, Karl Barth. Perhaps these will do to begin with. If he desires to pursue his studies further, I shall be happy to present him with a further selection.

Dorothy L. Sayers

1 Published in *World Review*, July 1941, under "Correspondence Cross-Section", p. 78. The same issue published her article, "How Free is the Press?", pp. 19–24, later published in *Unpopular Opinions*.
2 See p. 334, note 18.
3 Ernest Lucas Watkin (1876–1951).

[24 Newland street
Witham
Essex]

TO THE RT REV. NEVILLE TALBOT
Bishop of Nottingham
12 May 1941

My Dear Lord Bishop,
Thank you very much indeed for your letter. I am struggling with the six talks on God the Son and am appalled by discovering how much technical knowledge of theological terms is required before the average uninstructed Christian – much more Heathen – can begin to understand what the Creed is supposed to be about. I am particularly embarrassed while dealing with the clauses about the Incarnation, by the fact that "for us men and for our salvation" demands a preliminary instruction on the nature of man and the nature of sin, which I can't possibly squeeze into a ten minute talk, which has to deal at the same time with "coming down from Heaven" the "Virgin Birth" and the perfect Manhood. The people who made the Creed were not faced with the preconceptions of the

modern man, to whom the whole concept of sin is unfamiliar and unconvincing; they could rely on people taking it for granted that whatever man
was he wasn't what he should be. I am relying on your opening talks to
hammer the idea of sinfulness into the listener's head – this is where it
properly belongs.[1] I shall have to say something about it I suppose, bearing in mind that one cannot count upon one's hearers having followed the
whole series of talks, but I shall only touch on the subject lightly.

As soon as I have got this talk done I will try and let you have a copy. I
am taking the line that my business is to explain as well as I can what the
clauses of the Creed actually mean, rather than to exhort people to belief.
I don't see how they can believe in a thing which is so much unintelligible
abracadabra to them. This seems to me the justification for a strong
emphasis upon "doctrine". After all, if people are to be exhorted to hold
the Catholic Faith, it is what G. K. Chesterton calls "an intellectual convenience"[2] for them to know what the Catholic Faith is....

---

1 The Bishop replied that he had only "rather incidentally" referred to sin.
2 A phrase used by G. K. Chesterton towards the beginning of the final chapter of *Orthodoxy*.

24 Newland Street
Witham
Essex

TO MAURICE B. RECKITT

14 May 1941

Dear Mr Reckitt,

Very many thanks for your prompt and helpful reply. I am delighted
that my remarks about the abnormality of peace started a fruitful train of
thought....

I have sent Mr John Gloag a short list of names, telling him that if he
wants to read further, I can xxxxxx

(Drat this typewriter! It is of German origin and I think it is suffering
from hallucinations, like Rudolf Hess.)[1]

...that I can oblige him with plenty more. I put in Temple and Dawson,
but I have disqualified Middleton Murry and I'll tell you for why.[2] He is
exactly the sort of writer whom the scornful critic might expect one to
quote as an example of Christian thought, and would take the greatest
possible joy in tearing to pieces. Murry is an extremely able man, and the

---

1 Rudolf Hess, Hitler's Deputy from 1933. He had flown to Scotland on May 10/11.
2 Cf. her letter to Father Kelly, 24 May 1938.

very last person to hide his light under a bushel. He has cashed in on the death of his wife[2], and on the death of D. H. Lawrence, and when it comes to the death of God or of Society, he will be there. And, you know, he is worse than erratic. He is inaccurate and question-begging. I don't mind his not believing in "the physical resurrection" – but why should he say that "St Paul (who, judged by the standards of history, is the chief witness) in no way distinguishes the appearances of the risen Lord to himself on the road to Damascus from the earlier appearances to the disciples"?[3] St Paul never pretended to be a witness of the Forty Days, and the evidence for the appearance on the road to Damascus depends on St Luke, whose Gospel is also the evidence for the "physical" appearance at Jerusalem, with the broiled fish and the honeycomb. This is no way to treat ones authorities. The point might be argued, but not in that way. Am I being a cat about Murry? Maybe; but the half-dead scholar rises up in me and protests against the combination of so effective an emotion with so slap-dash a critical judgment. His own world of Letters accepts him only with cautious reservations – and while I admit his originality and "drive", he offers far too easy a target for attack.

Williams and Eliot are much sounder; Williams is really an original interpreter of theology, I think; it is true that people who don't find him illuminating find him wholly unintelligible, but it is good for men like Gloag to tackle the unintelligible.

Of the others, I have put in Watkin and also Barth,[4] whom I have read. I find his style unendurable, but his influence is undoubted. He is a Calvinist, and accuses me of being a Pelagian[5] – but what is a little total depravity between friends?...

"Christendom" shall certainly have the "curious book".[6] It isn't a Gollancz publication, but the first of a series which is being edited for Methuen by M.St Clare Byrne and myself; I enclose a preliminary blurb.

With many thanks,

Yours sincerely,

Dorothy L. Sayers

2 Katherine Mansfield.

3 Cf. his book, *Life of Jesus*, 1926.

4 Karl Barth (1886–1968), Swiss theologian. He corresponded with D. L. S. and translated her two articles, "The Greatest Drama Ever Staged" and "The Triumph of Easter". He wrote: "I have read her detective stories with quite special interest and amazement" (quoted by Eberhard Busch, *Karl Barth*, SCM Press, 1975).

5 Relating to the heresy of Pelagius, a British monk of the 4th and 5th centuries, who held that good works were sufficient as a means of salvation.

6 i.e. *The Mind of the Maker*. It was reviewed by V. A. Demant in the March number, 1942.

[24 Newland Street
Witham
Essex]

TO THE REV. J. G. WILLIAMS
19 May 1941

Dear Mr. Williams,

I am reduced to complete pulp by Bishop Talbot, who says that in FOUR talks devoted to *Why* we want a God to believe in, it has not occurred to him to explain what is meant by the word "Sin"!!!! You wouldn't think anybody *could* overlook that theological trifle, would you? Consequently, I have had to squash Sin into two minutes filched from the Incarnation – since I have now ceased to put my trust in Jesuits or in any child of man – and am left to contemplate your letter with a gleam of wildness in my eye....

My talks, I find, fall naturally into three sections; Lord, Jesus, and Christ. But since you must have a separate title for each, here they are:

1. Lord and God.
2. Lord of all Worlds.
3. The Man of Men.
4. The Death of God.
5. The World's Desire.
6. The Touchstone of History.

I will send the text of the first four (I hope) this week.

I have firmly assumed that I shall be able to deliver about six pages in ten minutes – as Mr. Fenn knows, my natural pace is pretty quick, and efforts to alter it produce confusion! Tell Mr. Fenn I have decided to do the preliminary summaries myself in the text of the talk. This, I am afraid, rules out his desire of a "smash-hit" first sentence, but will save time, as I shall get over the ground quicker than the Announcer. *Don't* let the Announcer have a lot of verbiage on his own account! Let him just say, "Our [fourth] talk on the Creed is called 'The Death of God'. Here is Miss Dorothy L. Sayers" – and it's done. (But let him not say: "The World's Desire – Miss Sayers", which would be indelicate, as well as untrue.)

N.B. The people who thought of this way of spending a pleasant Sunday should be boiled – rather slowly – in oil.

Yours savagely,
[Dorothy L. Sayers]

[24 Newland Street
Witham
Essex]

TO BROTHER GEORGE EVERY[1]

21 May 1941

Dear Brother Every,
  Public Enemy No. 1 – if you must use these expressions – is a flabby
and sentimental theology which necessarily produces flabby and
sentimental religious art. The first business of Church officials and
churchmen is, I think, to look to their own mote and preach and teach
better theology. But the point which they do not recognise is this; that for
any work of art to be acceptable to God it must first be right with itself.
That is to say, the artist must serve God in the technique of his craft; for
example, a good religious play must first and foremost be a good play
before it can begin to be good religion. Similarly, actors for religious films
and plays should be chosen for their good acting and not chosen for their
Christian sentiment or moral worth regardless of whether they are good
actors or not.[2] (A notorious case to the contrary is the religious film
society which chose its photographers for their piety, with the result that
a great number of the films were quite blasphemously incompetent.) The
practice, very common among pious officials of asking writers to produce
stories and plays to illustrate certain doctrine or church activities, shows
how curiously little these good people as a class understand the way in
which the mind of the writer works. The result in practice is that instead
of the doctrines springing naturally out of the action of the narrative, the
action and characters are distorted for the sake of the doctrine with disastrous results.
  This is what I mean when I ask that the Church should use a decent
humility before the artist, whose calling is as direct as that of the priest,
and whose business it is to serve God in his own technique and not in
somebody else's. Matters are only made worse when Sunday Observance
Societies and other groups talk wildly about modern tendencies in art
and so bring the Church into contempt, not only for bigotry but also for
ignorance.
  I quite agree that a great deal of ecclesiastical bric-à-brac needs purg-
ing. It is, as you say, so difficult to choose the really sound authorities to
pronounce on the artistic merit of hymns and so forth. I believe that here

1 Of the House of the Sacred Mission, Kelham, Nottinghamshire.
2 Cf. D. L. S.' article "Why Work?", first given under the title "Work and Vocation" at
   Brighton in March 1941. Published in *Creed or Chaos?* (Methuen, 1947), pp. 47–64; see especially pp. 60–61. (For further details see letter to the Editor, *The Sower*, 21 April 1941, note 2.)

again the soundest method is to purge at once the works which express a sickly brand of religious sentiment. They are pretty certain to be bad on all counts; it is very noticeable how well the great mediaeval hymns stand up to the test of time and the test of translation, on account of the soundness of the theology which inspired them. But I think they should be purged definitely on theological grounds, if the work is being done by Ecclesiastics as such, since here they are on their own ground and are not going outside their terms of reference. The whole question is extraordinarily complicated because of the gulf that has grown up between art on the one hand and on the other hand both the Church and secular society, so that the artists tend to be out of touch with the common man, while the latter, whether Christian or not, has only a very fumbling critical judgment to rely on.

Yours sincerely,

[Dorothy L. Sayers]

> [24 Newland Street
> Witham
> Essex]

TO BASIL BLACKWELL[1]

30 May 1941

Dear Basil,

Here are the two Wimsey items I talked to you about. Of the Wimsey Papers[2] there ought to be about 150 copies already printed which are available. We had intended to keep these for private sale to people who might be interested, but we never tried to "stimulate a public demand" for them, and when Miss Simpson died her Executors handed the whole lot over to me. She was part author of the jest and responsible for some of the best passages. I am sure that there would be no objection at all on her husband's part, as there is certainly none on mine, to the books being printed in America, always with the stipulation that copyright must be safeguarded; this, of course, applies also to the sale in America of the copies printed in England. The copyright had better be vested in my name.

---

1 The Oxford bookseller and publisher, later Sir Basil Blackwell, for whom D. L. S. worked from 1917 to 1919. See *The Letters of Dorothy L. Sayers: 1899–1936*, letter to Muriel Jaeger, 8 March 1917, pp. 128–129.

2 *Papers Relating to the Family of Wimsey edited by Matthew Wimsey*, privately printed for the Family (Humphrey Milford, 1936).

Of the little pamphlet on Lord Mortimer Wimsey[3] I have also a certain stock by me – about fifty I should think, but I should not want to part with them all. As you will see, the whole point of this one was that it should appear to be an early nineteenth century print. Graham Pollard, who wrote that book on *The Forged Victorian Pamphlets*,[4] supervised the format for me, and I think has made a fairly good job of it, down to the wholly fictitious and misleading imprint.[5]

If you think that there is anything to be done with these two little works, go ahead. I don't know how far the Americans are likely to understand or appreciate the solemn jest of the pastiche. Some simple-minded friends of mine became quite disturbed in their minds about these delusive booklets, which they received, without comment, as Christmas presents, and before thanking me for them, hastily rang up a mutual friend to enquire "whether there really was a Wimsey family". It would be great fun to take in the American continent! – but I will leave the matter of presentation to you if you should decide to do anything about it.

Yours ever,

[D. L. S.]

P.S. The binding of the *Wimsey Papers* which were printed for sale is slightly different from this, and not quite so good.[6]

---

3 *An Account of Lord Mortimer Wimsey, The Hermit of the Wash*, privately printed by Humphrey Milford, November and December 1937.
4 *An Enquiry into the Nature of Certain Nineteenth-century Pamphlets*, by J. Carter and G. Pollard, 1934.
5 The imprint reads: BRISTOL:\ Printed by M. BRYAN, Corn-street.\ 1816.
6 The colour blue is lighter.

24 Newland Street
Witham
Essex

TO MAURICE B. RECKITT
"Date as Postmark"
[? June 1941]

Dear Mr Reckitt,

You should be receiving from Methuen, at the same time as this, a review copy of my "curious book" about the Trinity: *The Mind of the Maker*. As you will see, it is the first volume of a series called Bridge-heads, edited by M. St Clare Byrne and myself, of which the general idea is to deal with this business of "Creativeness" – both in theory and in practice. The object of this particular book is to start us off on the right lines by trying to examine, in the light of theology as interpreted by the writer's experience, what "Creativeness" is, and how it works, because the word is rapidly becoming one of those catch-phrases which people use without always understanding them very well.

I hope you will like it. Fr Demant says, "Whatever priests may say, I think that is the way theology should be written. It is the way it was written in the formative periods of the Church" – so I feel a little encouraged, because I think he'd have cracked down upon it if it was fundamentally unsound or insincere, don't you?

A copy is also being sent to the *New English Weekly*,[1] as you requested.

Yours sincerely,
Dorothy L. Sayers

1   This journal, edited by Philip Mairet, ceased to exist in 1949, when it became incorporated in *New Age*.

[24 Newland Street
Witham
Essex]

THE SISTER SUPERIOR[1]
The Hostel of God[2]
Lindfield
Haywards Heath
25 June 1941

Dear Madam,

It is a delicate and difficult matter to argue with pacifists, as with any people who have erected a single point of morals into an absolute.

The consensus of opinion in the Early Church is perhaps not quite as unanimous as your correspondent suggests; (it is handily summarised in A. C. F. Beales' "Penguin" *The Catholic Church and International Order* – Chapters five and six).[3] I think the sneer at the expense of the Church for changing the emphasis of her teaching after Constantine is scarcely justified. It was not until then that the Christians became responsible for the actual maintenance of world-order, and were forced to realise what a

1   Sister Magdalen (Ada Elizabeth Robson), 1896–1977.
2   Founded at Clapham in the 19th century for the chronic and dying sick, evacuated to Lindfield, West Sussex in August 1939.
3   Published April 1941.

policy of complete "pacifism" involved *in practice*. This was a necessary consequence of the transference of power into Christian hands; and however much one may regret the anomalies produced by the interlocking of spiritual and temporal power, it is useless to talk as though temporal power were not an important *fact*.[2] At all points we are brought up against the paradox so bitingly stated by Reinhold Niebuhr: "Goodness armed with power is corrupted; pure love, without power, is destroyed." (*Beyond Tragedy*: p. 185).[3]

But apart from the historical question, the difficulty which (as it seems to me) the pacifists fail to face is the inherent corruption of all human virtues by original sin, which produces impurities when any one of them is erected into an absolute. (The "absolutism" attached to the command about turning the other cheek is very marked – it is seldom, for instance, that anybody insists that when a decision at law is given against a litigant, he should pay double the penalty imposed; though that might be equally well deduced from Matt.V, 40.[4]) If everybody lived in a state of perfect grace, moral codes would no longer be necessary, and the virtues, being perfect, would not contradict one another. But when men fall from grace they are brought under the operation of the law. And the moral virtues, being "of the nature of sin", do contradict one another, so that any "absolutism" in them falls under the condemnation of the law. (See the very interesting passage in C. S. Lewis's *Problem of Pain*, p. 70 and note; Christian Challenge Series.)

The human virtues are not single-minded (see Lewis again, p. 63). In their best expressions they are corrupt; and in the pacifist position there is usually mingled, along with a great deal of genuine love of God and mankind, a number of other factors: personal fear, inertia, unwillingness to sacrifice private interest, and, more subtle and important, a certain refusal of responsibility, and a severing of the self from the universal guilt and its consequences. And there is also that secret accidie[5] which produces a pacifism "founded, not on the doctrine that other people's lives are sacred, but on the belief that nothing is worth fighting for" (Michael Roberts, *The Recovery of the West*, p. 48; Faber).

I feel that there is a kind of clue to all this in the much-disputed passage about the purse and scrip and sword in Luke XXII, 36.[6] When the Perfect Innocence is bodily present, no money, no worldly provision, no sword; but now "the things concerning Me draw to an end", and the

---

2 Cf. her Introduction to *The Emperor Constantine*.
3 See letter to Maurice B. Reckitt, 8 May 1941, note 10.
4 And if any man will sue thee at the law, and take away thy coat, let him have thy cloak also.
5 Sloth, torpor, one of the Seven Deadly Sins.
6 Then said he unto them, But now, he that hath a purse, let him take it, and likewise his scrip: and he that hath no sword, let him sell his garment, and buy one.

world's weapons will have to be used, with all they imply. It is as though only the Perfect Innocence can afford to ignore those implications, because He alone is completely single-hearted, and can practise a virtue which is altogether free from inward corruption.

I have always thought it curious that the last few generations should have so placidly recited, and approved, and taught to their children, that staggering passage in Tennyson's "Morte d'Arthur":

> And God fulfils Himself in many ways,
> Lest one good custom should corrupt the world[7]

without seeing how trenchantly it went to the very root of the moral paradox.

The history of the past twenty years shows nothing more clearly than the havoc that can be wrought by more or less well-disposed people concentrating on Peace (negatively conceived as the mere avoidance of War), and the appalling corruptions that grow up through an absolutist concentration on this isolated virtue within the sphere of legality. The refusal to admit that a technical "peace" was to the advantage of vested interests, the total neglect of the natural virtues of justice, and fortitude, and the quite extraordinary falsehood which refused to recognise the fact of temporal power (e.g. in the naive assertion, in the face of all experience, that "public opinion" must be a sufficient restraint upon the unruly wills and affections of sinful men) are evidence of the corruption produced by "one good custom".

War is, I think, not so much a sin in itself as a natural judgement upon sin – the bodily incarnation of a spiritual dialectic that has not found its synthesis; and the attempt to repudiate the judgement in this lower court is apt to be less a refusal of sin than an endeavour to side-step the consequences. But the whole question is very difficult, and any attempt to deal with it gives one the appearance of seeking to "justify the unjustifiable by specious argument and the slinging of isolated texts".

Yours very truly,
[Dorothy L. Sayers]

---

7 Words of the dying Arthur from the barge: "The old order changeth, yielding place to new…"

[24 Newland Street
Witham
Essex]

TO BROTHER GEORGE EVERY

25 June 1941

Dear Brother Every,

Art is long and life is fleeting, and I can't answer your letter properly. But there are one or two points I must pick up, because the whole subject is too important and fascinating to be left alone –

1. About Mr. Micawber. I'm never happy about E. M. Forster's treatment of the novel.[1] It is an outstanding example of the thing I was getting at under "Gnosticism" ("Docetism"[2] might have been more exact, but the word means nothing to the average layman). Both his novel writing and his criticism suffer from the fact that he is antagonistic to the medium he is working in. "A third man says in a sort of drooping regretful voice, 'Yes – oh dear yes – the novel tells a story'. . . the third man is myself. Yes – oh dear yes – the novel tells a story. *That is the fundamental aspect without which it could not exist.* That is the highest factor common to all novels, and *I wish that it was not so*, that it could be something different – melody, or perception of the truth, *not this low atavistic form*". (My italics). This contempt of and hatred for the "fundamental aspect" of what he is dealing with is a thing that paralyzes both creation and creative criticism, and is the source of all that is weak in his novels and untrustworthy in his criticism; because he persistently judges the thing by a standard which doesn't truly belong to it. And, approaching his judgments with the profound caution which this central anomaly engenders, I'm inclined to think that his distinction between "round" and "flat" characters may be a bit too sharply drawn. Even he has to allow for characters like Lady Bertram,[3] who bulge up out of flatness into roundness when the story (the *story*) requires it. And the mere fact that Mr. Micawber's end is felt to be incongruous suggests that he isn't as consistently flat as (according to the theory) he should be. The spasmodic rotundities of Dickens's characters are frequently ill-managed. Hence, e.g. the peculiar effect of indecency produced by the marriage of Mercy Pecksniff to Jonas Chuzzlewit. The assemblage of grotesques is suddenly brought into contact with bodily fact by the "serious" treatment of the married Mercy, and it all becomes curiously unpleasant. The end of Micawber would be in place in a book which nowhere touched

---

1 E. M. Forster (1879–1970), novelist. His critical work, *Aspects of the Novel*, was published in 1936.
2 A heretical view that Christ's body was a phantom.
3 A character in Jane Austen's *Mansfield Park*.

actuality; but *David Copperfield* is not pure fairy-tale; therefore the "miraculous" ending is out of key.

(By the way, I have used fictitious *characters* as the chief illustration for "the free will of the creature";[4] but I shouldn't necessarily confine myself to the characters. It's only that, with them, it is easier to make the analogy plain to people. It's hard to make them understand the free will of a *phrase* or a literary form, for instance: e.g. the work that insists on being a play and not a short story; but the principle is the same.)

2. Realism. Going on from this, I want to ask you to consider whether it is quite sound to talk about "realism" and "representationalism" as though these were synonymous with the "unforgivable sin". I haven't worked this out: but I rather fancy there is, again, both a time-element and a theological element in it. Do we perhaps stagger from a sort of Arian Humanism to a kind of Docetism about the universe, and is "representational" and "non-representational" Art a reflection of this dialectic? There seem to be periods when the human spirit feels itself to be "right with" the bodily form of the universe, and expresses it in a satisfying manner. Then we get the artist "pour qui le monde visible existe", delighting in, and expressing himself through the visible form. These are, I think, periods, not of decadence but of eager youth – G. K. C. says somewhere that it is the quite young child who can be excited by the "realistic" story. Then there comes a period when the spirit is no longer genuinely at ease in the outward form, and the Art becomes false, because it is still expressing an easiness and harmony which are no longer there: it is used sentimentally, as a "consolation" and pretence; and the "new" art comes along, which expresses, not the harmony but the dislocation between spirit and form. But this, too, has its time of decay, when the pattern of disunion in its theme becomes false, and one gets a stereotyped and consciously "archaic" art, contradicting the "new" sense of expression and harmony that by that time will be coming along. And then one has the divorce between life and art – a sort of schizophrenia – and perhaps a disjunction into hieratic and popular art. . . . I haven't started to examine this; but I notice a sentence in Michael Roberts' *Recovery of the West* (of which Faber has just sent an advance copy) which looks as though he felt rather the same about it. "The world of imagination and the world of material reality had fallen apart, *and the one could no longer be imaged through the other.*" (My italics again) "Reality" – that which corresponds to the thought? . . . My feeling is that there is nothing in itself wicked or inartistic about realism as such – only when it persists as a dead thing after the correspondence to the inner reality has ceased to be true.

---

4 D. L. S. is referring to *The Mind of the Maker*, chapter 5.

3. *Devil to Pay*. I don't want to bother with an apologia for my own work. But one thing seems important. The "conjuring-tricks" are there, of course, in the first place, because they are in the story (the story again!) and I was trying to interpret that story within its own convention. But the whole point is that the Devil is, precisely, the vendor of cheap (or, if you like, expensive) conjuring-tricks and magical utopias – his chief business today is the offering of short cuts to perfection, without responsibility and in defiance of the universal nature of things. Irresponsible power, producing effects without cause or consequence, is the very definition of magic. The thing is set out in the Pope's speech, where he says that it does indeed seem so much better and easier to:

> Lean through the cloud, lift the right arm of power
> And with a sudden lightning smite the world perfect.
> Yet this was not God's way, etc.[5]

And the whole conclusion of [Scene] Four is that there is no short cut, and no way out, except by destroying your humanity. So that Faustus cannot regain his soul except by willingly accepting all the pains of evil which he had tried to short-circuit. Every trick that seems to eliminate evil, merely produces the inevitable evil in a new form, so that, do as man may, and twist as he will, he must "go though the hoop" one way or the other at last. Helen (for Faustus) is the perpetual hankering to go behind evil to simple innocence – what Charles Williams calls the attempt to "recover the single and simple knowledge of good by tearing up the aprons". Christ is the passage to the good through the evil, so that in His presence Satan the enemy appears paradoxically as, willy-nilly, God's ally:

> The love of God urges my feet towards hell,
> The devil that seeks to have me thrusts me back
> Into God's arms.[6]

The terrifying thing about the play was the number of people who thought it so much nicer "to be a dear little doggie than a responsible human being". "De te fabula"[7] is all one can say to them. But I admit that Alistair Bannerman never succeeded in "getting across" the ghastly animal disintegration of the Young Faustus – the irresponsible enjoyment of bloodshed, the loss of all human standards and ideals ("Value? what does that mean? Helen was a troublesome baggage"[8]), and the whimpering,

---

5   *The Devil to Pay* (Gollancz, 1939, scene 2, p. 54).
6   op. cit., pp. 105–106.
7   Latin: it speaks of thee.
8   The words of Faustus, scene 3, p. 78.

unreasoning, animal terror. It's all in the script; but it wasn't, unfortunately, in the actor.

Yours very sincerely,
[Dorothy L. Sayers]

[24 Newland Street
Witham
Essex]

TO THE EDITOR OF THE DAILY TELEGRAPH
7 July 1941

Dear Sir,

WODEHOUSE BROADCASTS[1]

In the discussion about Mr. P. G. Wodehouse's unhappy broadcasts, there is one point of which we ought, I think, to remind ourselves.

At the time of the Battle of France, when he fell into enemy hands, English people had scarcely begun to realise the military and political importance of the German propaganda weapon. Since then, we have learnt much: we know something of why and how France fell; we have seen disintegration at work in the Balkans; we have watched the slow recovery of American opinion from the influence of the Nazi hypnotic.

But how much of all this can possibly be known or appreciated from inside a German Concentration Camp – or even from the Adlon Hotel? Theoretically, no doubt, every patriotic person should be prepared to resist enemy pressure to the point of martyrdom; but it must be far more difficult to bear such heroic witness when its urgent necessity is not, and cannot be, understood.

Yours faithfully,
[Dorothy L. Sayers]

1 When the Germans occupied France in the summer of 1940, P. G. Wodehouse (1881–1975), the creator of Bertie Wooster and Jeeves, who was living in his villa in Le Touquet, was taken into captivity. He was at first placed under house arrest and later interned. On 25 June 1941 news came that he had been released from internment and was living in the Adlon Hotel in Berlin. On the next day it was made known that he had agreed to do a series of broadcasts over the German radio. The first, on 26 June, took the form of an interview with Harry Flannery of the Columbia Broadcasting System. It was assumed in Britain that Wodehouse was "giving comfort to the enemy", a treasonable offence. Feelings ran high although nobody in Britain then knew what he had said.

24 Newland Street
Witham
Essex

TO MAURICE B. RECKITT

12 July 1941

Dear Mr. Reckitt,

I ought to have written before to thank you for sending me your autobiography[1], which I have read with so much interest and pleasure. There
are a lot of things in it that make me want to start discussions – if only
one had time for everything! Your kindly reference to me[2] makes me wonder how it was that I got through so much of my life without ever bothering about public affairs and "the structure of society", and all that. It
wasn't that my contemporaries didn't take an interest – they did. I suppose I was just lazy and deeply prejudiced by a Tory Church of England
upbringing. And completely self-centred.

But I fancy there may have been something else. I can only express it
by saying that there was something about the socialist doctrine of the
period that affected me vaguely like a bad smell. A faint indication of
something not quite right somewhere. Unless I am merely rationalizing
my dislike to the threat to my own privilege, I believe I can now put a
name to the thing – namely, that what was sought was often rather a shift
of power than a new understanding of power, and that both parties were
really working inside the same area of infection – the area where the concept of employment is substituted for the concept of work.

I gather from your book that you too have had your uneasy moments.
I wonder whether the years one wastes in not taking part in movements
are entirely locust-eaten, or whether, provided one has been doing an
honest job of work in the meantime, one gains any compensatory perspective through not having had one's young passions enlisted on one side
or the other.

Which brings me to the other thing I wanted to write to you about.
Women. I don't feel that any of your contributors has quite got on to the
mark in the June *Christendom*.[3] I was never a "feminist" – I didn't have to

---

1 See letter to Maurice B. Reckitt, 8 May 1941, note 13.
2 The reference is: "Such writers as T. S. Eliot, Middleton Murry, Charles Williams, and
   Dorothy Sayers are listened to because to prophecy they add, in their different manners, the
   compulsive power of art, and an insight which only the artist can have" (p. 279). To be listed with Middleton Murry cannot have pleased her very much (cf. her letter to Father Herbert
   Kelly, 24 May 1938), but she was no doubt gratified to be in the rest of the company.
3 *Christendom: A Journal of Christian Sociology*, a quarterly edited by Maurice B. Reckitt, Ruth
   Kenyon, V. A. Demant and P. E. T. Widdrington. The June issue of 1941 (volume 11, No. 42,
   pp. 104–109) contained a symposium entitled "The Emancipated Woman Comes of Age".
   The authors were W. G. Peck, Rosalinde Wilton and J. V. L. Casserley.

be – so I'm rather in the same semi-detached position as I am about everything else. What I feel that few people ever grasp properly – certainly not the Church – is that the question of equality turns on the fact that Man is always dealt with as both Homo and Vir, but Woman only as Femina and never Homo.[4] Take two points – one trifling, the other important.

Trousers are always made a point at issue. The fact is that, for Homo, the garment is warm, convenient and decent. But in Western countries (though not in China or Mohammedan countries) Vir has staked out a claim to it, and has invested it and the skirt with a sexual significance, for physiological reasons which are a little too plain for Puritans to admit. (Note: that the objection is always to closed knickers and trousers; never to open drawers, which are the foundation of a very different kind of music-hall joke.) It is this obscure resentment that complicates the simple "Homo" issue of whether warmth, safety, and freedom of movement are desirable qualities in a garment for any creature with two legs. Naturally, the trouser is also taken up into the whole "Femina" business of attraction, since Vir demands that Femina should be Femina all the time, whether she is engaged in what I may call Homo activities or not. But all discussion is vitiated, because the "Homo" part of the question is always left outside the argument.

Again, industrialization is blamed for "herding women into factories", and people argue naively that women "don't really like it". But the real question is whether Homo likes it, or ought to like it. What is the good of saying solemnly that we ought to decide which jobs women definitely ought not to do, and keep them to those they are fitted for, unless we start by admitting that most of the distinctively women's jobs have already been taken from them by men, when they were taken out of the home and transferred to the factory? Of course the women of the Middle Ages had effective power in the home, because the home was the centre of many industries – spinning, weaving, baking, brewing, distilling, perfumery, preserving, pickling – in which the mistress of the house worked with her own staff. But the control and direction – all the intelligent part of those industries – have gone to the male heads of industry, and the women have been left, not with their "proper" work, but with employment in those occupations, which is quite a different thing.

There has never been any question but that the women of the poor should take their share in the work of the world. The objection to

---

4 The Latin word *homo* means man in the sense of a human being; *vir* means man in the sense of a male human being; *femina* means woman. (The prefix *homo-*, as in "homosexual", is derived from Greek and means "same", "identical".)

woman's labour did not begin with a feeling that women should not do harvest work, or strip withies or plant potatoes. It began when the pluto-cratic and aristocratic notion that the keeping of an idle female was a symbol of social superiority spread to the commercial middle-classes. "My wife doesn't need to soil her hands with work." Therefore she must be confined more and more to a home from which all intelligent work was being steadily removed. It is simply idle to argue about the thing if half the relevant facts are ignored.

Homo – I have seen it solemnly stated in a paper that the seats on the near side of a bus are always filled before those on the off side, because, "men find them more comfortable, on account of the camber of the road, and women like them because they can see more easily into the shop-windows". As though the camber of the road did not affect male and female bodies equally. Men, you see, are given a Homo reason, and women a Femina reason, because they are not really human.

I do not think I have ever heard a sermon about Martha and Mary which did not somewhere hasten to remind us that, although, of course, Mary's was the better part, the work of the Marthas is necessary too – just by way of softening down the story. Because, after all, Martha's was a fem-inine job, whereas Mary was just behaving like any other disciple, male or female – and that is a hard pill to swallow.

Another point, which few people examine for its bearing on the subject, is the enormous hypertrophy of the idea of romantic love, which, from the late Middle Ages on, has distorted the earlier conception of the rela-tions of the sexes, and has produced – or at least exaggerated – the ten-dency to deny to the woman the common human needs and feelings. And, by the way, all that stuff about the husband's rights in marriage! What is poor dear Casserley[5] thinking of? As though the insatiable appetite of wives were not one of the oldest vulgar jokes in the world – quite as old as mothers-in-law, and much older than kippers!

From all of which you will gather that I find your contributors too, too genteel and ostrich-like for words. As for the "work" problem, you will notice that where the new equality in jobs has been working long enough, the difficulties have practically vanished. There is no movement in the theatre for the men to get back the playing of the female parts, taken from them in the seventeenth century; nor, in the literary world, does the

5 J. V. Langmead Casserley (1909–1978), author of *The Christian in Philosophy* (Faber and Faber). D. L . S. quotes from his book, *The Fate of Modern Culture* in *The Mind of the Maker*, Methuen, p. 7, note 1. He also contributed a volume to the "Signposts" series, *Providence and History*, 1941, No. 11. In the Symposium, Casserley had said: "The earlier convention conceded to the hus-band marital rights over his wife....The new convention has in effect transferred the sexual initiative to the wife, a transfer plainly at war with the physical facts."

woman writer encounter any real prejudice, other than a vague jealousy among some middle-aged males. That's why I said I had no need to be a feminist. But fifty years ago, there was still a real discrimination. And if you ask, Are women any happier for the opportunity to work freely at a job, I say, Yes – so long as they do not have to do it under conditions which would harass any human being. It is quite true that the majority of the ordinary vocationless woman would be glad if she didn't have to work for her living; but would you swear that the average vocationless man wouldn't jolly well like to "get away from work" if he thought he could? At any rate he would say so – Homo, male or female, always says so. But if a man says so it's human nature; if a woman says so, it's female nature, don't you see.

If the Church wants people to accept the idea that there is neither male nor female, bond nor free, she must really begin by allowing that women have, as the foundation of their special female nature, a share in common human nature – that they can plainly need warmth and convenience in their clothing, comfort in the bus, and an opportunity for intelligence in their work, quite apart from any peculiar "feminine angle" on the matter. One of the best things the war has done is to cause women to be killed as well as men – that at any rate is a human occupation which cannot be denied. And there will not be the same proportion of "surplus women" after this show to embitter relations and confuse statistics.

You may notice that I have not used the words "their rights". I don't believe much in "rights". I can see only common human needs; and I think that if the whole question has become bitter it is largely because of the indecent position produced by the commercial cult of the idle woman, and the removal of the creative occupations from the home. Any attempt to cope with the post-war economic situation must take these things into account.

In theory, I believe the Russians have got hold of the right end of the stick about this, though I don't know how it works there in practice, and I don't like their totalitarian organization anyhow. In this country, it looks as though the balance of intelligent work for all was being stabilised in – of all unexpected quarters – the Services, especially the Air Force. These girls who do the radio work have to be pretty well as intelligent as the pilots, and are often in nearly as much danger. But they are not doing that work in order to "ape the men", or to qualify themselves to be more bed-worthy, or in order to have a nice hobby, but because the work has to be done and done properly, otherwise we are all in the soup. To have work to do, and know that his work is wanted, is the basic human need – I don't care whether it's of man or woman. But we treat the woman as we treat the fighting man –

It's ape and slut and job-snatcher and "Polly, you're a liar",
But it's "Thank-you, Mary Atkins," when the guns begin to fire.[6]

Join up – your country needs you – but don't suppose that any of the jobs we train you for are going to be permanent. And, in the meantime, after eight hours a day being a bus-conductor, you can surely find time to clean the flat, cook the dinner, and make yourself attractive to your young man – because that's a woman's job. You can only be counted as a human being in an emergency, and in addition to being a full-time female.

I know the whole thing bristles with difficulties, like every other economic "problem"; but it can't be solved by leaving out all the common human factors.[7]

I wanted my friend Miss Byrne[8], who feels strongly about the business, to do you an article; but I don't know whether she will be able to manage it. If not, and you feel that some of these points are worth putting, shall I try to tidy them up into some kind of an article or letter?[9] Indeed and indeed, the Church must pull her socks up and introduce a spot of reality into this controversy, for if she will not allow the equal possession of a common human nature, who will?

Forgive all this splurge and emphasis, but the democratic new order is heading for another nasty cropper over the woman question if it doesn't look out.

    With again thanks and appreciation of the book,
       Yours sincerely,
          [Dorothy L. Sayers]

6 Adaptation of lines by Rudyard Kipling: "Oh, it's 'Tommy this an' Tommy that, an' Tommy, go away;'\ But it's 'Thank you, Mister Atkins' when the band begins to play." *Tommy.*

7 In a draft for a curriculum vitae, undated but drawn up in 1928, D. L. S. set down her views on Women and Marriage: "Consider that chief difficulties in most cases are economic. Extremely keen that all women, married or not, should be able to make money for themselves and take their share in the upkeep of the house. Consider that it will soon be thought as degrading to be 'kept' by a husband as 'kept' in any other way. Would welcome legislation to abolish husband's liability for wife's income-tax, personal debts and other unfair distinctions." (The MS is in the possession of the Marion E. Wade Center, Wheaton College, Illinois.)

8 Muriel St Clare Byrne did contribute to the following issue (Volume 11, No. 44, December 1941, pp. 234–247), entitled "'Emancipated' Woman and Vocation. Female or Human?", an incisive, cogent and factual article, to which J. V. L. Casserley replied briefly (Vol. 12, No. 45, March 1942, pp. 39–40). The same number contained an article by Mary Ryan, "Woman and Catholic Teaching", pp. 41–43.

9 The letter was "tidied up " into the article "The-Human-Not-Quite-Human", first published in *Christendom: A Journal of Christian Sociology*, vol. xi, no. 43, September 1941, pp. 156–162. It was later included in *Unpopular Opinions* (Gollancz, 1946), pp. 116–122. See also her article "Are Women Human?", included in the same volume, pp. 106–115, first given as a paper to a Women's Society in 1938.

Public indignation about the broadcasts by P. G. Wodehouse continued. In response the Minister of Information, Duff Cooper, directed that a statement should be made by the B.B.C. This responsibility was entrusted to William Connor on the staff of the Daily Mirror, *whose pen name was "Cassandra". Under this alias, on 15 July, he broadcast a talk which gave great offence to D. L. S. and to others.*[1] *See also her letter to* The Daily Telegraph, *7 July 1941.*

[24 Newland Street
Witham
Essex]

TO SIR STEPHEN TALLENTS
Director of Talks
Broadcasting House
London W.1

15 July 1941

My dear Sir Stephen,

In writing to you, I am probably addressing my protest to the wrong person – indeed, I hope I am. When I was at Broadcasting House last month, you received me kindly, and I should like to think you were in no way responsible for tonight's deplorable broadcast, and that you perhaps deprecate it as much as I do, and as many others must.

In view of the controversy that has arisen, I can understand that it may have been necessary to make some kind of public allusion to the unhappy affair of P. G. Wodehouse if only to dispel the notion that a popular and wealthy man would receive preferential treatment from authority. But was it necessary that this painful task should be entrusted to a speaker of whom I will say only that he faithfully serves and represents the journal whose name was advertised in the broadcast?

Was it necessary that the attack should be made with such vulgarity, that it should be directed against professional reputation as well as against personal character, that it should be such as to inflict the greatest possible pain upon any friends or relatives who might have had the misfortune to hear it, and that it should be embellished with a nauseating Scriptural parallel which, in the context, in that manner, and from that speaker, was as shocking as a blasphemy?

That the lightmindedness which we admired, and the money with

---

1 Four years later George Orwell wrote an article "In Defence of P. G. Wodehouse". First published in *The Windmill* in 1945, it was reprinted in *Critical Essays*, Secker and Warburg, 1946, pp. 156–169.

which we rewarded it, could lead a man to commit treason, whose penalty is death, is a fact grim enough to need little embroidery. And even the most sober statement should have been made only by someone whose standing and reputation set him above even the suspicion of envy, malice, or self-advertisement. If no man of unquestionable integrity could be found to undertake this hangman's office, that might have raised a doubt whether the thing should be done at all. However weighty the reasons of State which prompted it, it would have been better left undone than done like this. It was done without dignity, done without decency, and probably so done as to defeat its own object; since nothing so moves men to the condonation of crime as the spectacle of a vindictive judge, whose relish in pronouncing sentence seems sharpened by personal spite.

I have never heard anything like this from the B.B.C. before; I hope I never shall again. It was as ugly a thing as ever was made in Germany.

Yours faithfully,

[Dorothy L. Sayers]

Sir Stephen Tallents replied on 17 July stating officially that the broadcast was given under the direction of the Ministry of Information, but in his own handwriting he added the following note:

Since we have taken tea together I do not hesitate to add privately that this script was strongly objected to by all concerned at the B.B.C. The Minister ordered it, notwithstanding, to be broadcast. Your letter puts admirably, if all too temperately, what I felt about it. I should add only the point that it seemed to me contrary to the English tradition to abuse or condemn a man who could in no real sense answer. A disgusting business.

In the meantime D. L. S. had written also to the Public Relations Officer of the B.B.C.

[24 Newland Street
Witham
Essex]

16 July 1941

Sir,

Mr. P. G. Wodehouse

I do not know Mr. Wodehouse. I deplore that he should have become the tool of enemy propaganda, and I believe that his conduct should be the subject of enquiry by a legal tribunal when he is in a position to explain and, if possible, defend it.

Nevertheless, I feel that "Cassandra's" broadcast offends both justice and decency.

It appears to me to be a violation of the principles of justice that a man who cannot at present reply, and who may in the future have to appear before a judicial body, should in the meantime be attacked by an anonymous speaker, and that the B.B.C. should cooperate to give such an attack the widest possible publicity.

Furthermore, the terms of the broadcast must have struck many listeners as being in the worst possible taste. A compound of sneers and sanctimony, it descended almost to the Nazis' own level, and left a sense of shame that public opinion should be so vulgarly misrepresented.

If in the national interest it is thought advisable to express condemnation of the actions of one of our countrymen in enemy hands, let it be done as forcefully as necessary but with dignity by some responsible (and not anonymous) speaker.

I do not flatter myself that this letter from an obscure citizen will carry any special weight, but you will doubtless receive many others in similar strain, and I write in the hope that their cumulative effect may assist you to assess national opinion.

Yours faithfully,
[Dorothy L. Sayers]

[24 Newland Street
Witham
Essex]

TO THE REV. J. G. WILLIAMS

17 July 1941

Dear Mr. Williams,

Thank you so much for your letter. I enjoyed doing the talks and am very glad you were pleased with them. I expect they were rather stiff going for the majority, but my own feeling is that it may be quite as well to let people exercise their brains a bit; so many of them have the idea that the "simple gospel" is something that anybody can understand and put into practice without having to think twice about it.

I had a number of letters informing me that it was not possible for God to die and a number, of course, of the usual objectors furnished with texts to prove that Christ was not God. Also the usual collection of tracts and lunatics. I don't think any letters came from the Forces, but then I don't think the Forces have very much time to write letters. *The Resurrection* produced two protests – one accusing me of gross materialism and the other of being a Christian Scientist; so I think I must have about hit the happy medium.

What I have received is a number of thoughtful and appreciative letters asking whether my talks were going to be printed as they would like to study them. I have replied to this that it depends on what happens to the Series as a whole.[1] Do you think it likely that anything could be done about this? And would they make a really coherent exposition of the creed if they were all published together? I have a feeling that my line of exposition was probably a good deal more rigid and dogmatic than any of the others and that the Series might be too much of a patchwork to make a study-book.

I spent Tuesday night up to one in the morning writing a solemn protest against that atrocious broadcast about P. G. Wodehouse. Did you ever hear anything more indecent? No doubt something had to be said about him, but why they should have chosen the most notorious contributor of the most notorious trash paper to deliver a talk, so vulgar and so envenomed by spite, passes my comprehension. We were all flabbergasted. One usually accuses the B.B.C. of too much public-school gentility, but this came straight out of the gutter. As for the nauseating scriptural parallel, it turned my stomach. I hope that some of you people in the Religious Department have had something to say about it.

Yours very sincerely,
[Dorothy L. Sayers]

1 The talks on the Nicene Creed were not published.

24 Newland Street
Witham
Essex

TO MAURICE B. RECKITT

22 July 1941

Dear Mr Reckitt,

I find that Miss Byrne is doing her article after all. I must not, therefore, take her place – particularly as the remarks which I quoted to Fr McLaughlin, and which caused him to suggest the writing of an article for *Christendom*, were her remarks in the first place.

However, since you seem to think you would like to have something from me on the subject, I am elaborating some of the more frivolous and plain-spoken portions of my letter to you and finishing up the "Martha-and-Mary" passage, so as to produce a more or less coherent piece of rhetoric, which, if you have the space and inclination, could appear in addition to Miss Byrne's article, or in a subsequent number. I have left it to her to deal with the more practical aspects of the subject, on which she is far better qualified, both by training and experience, to speak than I am.

I do feel very strongly that this whole question is one with which the Church ought to deal, and deal honestly. Her past record is bad, and is responsible for a very great amount of anti-clerical feeling among educated and intelligent people, both men and women. The signs of the times suggest that after the War the issue will become an acute one, violently disputed; and unless the Church will face the fundamental issue, she will only make a surface contribution to the question, and bring herself into still further disrepute. I use that word quite advisedly.

If you think my article unsuited for the chaste pages of *Christendom*, I will take it away and place it elsewhere. But I would rather it appeared in a specifically Christian organ than that it should arrive, as it were, from outside, and be hailed as "another attack upon the Church". Attacks upon the church are, I think, better delivered from inside, for obvious reasons.

Oh, no! don't imagine that in my careless youth I really saw that Socialism was Capitalism turned inside out! I only, as I said, was faintly aware of a bad smell. Or rather, I was like a cousin[1] of mine, who took an odd, instinctive dislike to her bedroom in a particular house. She said she never felt comfortable in it, and suffered from peculiarly vivid and disagreeable nightmares. Eventually (upon some occasion or other) a technical expert arrived upon the premises, whereupon: "DRAINS!" said he in a voice of authority; and revealed an escape of odourless sewer-gas directly below her bedroom window. She accepted this explanation as intellectually satisfactory; and it proved, in fact, to be correct. In much the same way, I accept the "economic heresy" as the *fons et origo*[2] of my early instinctive dislike. But I could not have discovered it for myself.

G. K. Chesterton was a grand person – quite extraordinarily sound and shrewd about most things. Again and again I discover how right he was about literature and theology. But he seems never to have grasped that there was more than one kind of woman in the world: at any rate, there is only one kind of woman in his novels. But that is a common weakness among male writers – the correlative of the weakness of the female writer for whom every man is Edward Fairfax Rochester.[3] These are the dream-

---

1 Margaret Leigh, who was her contemporary at Somerville.
2 Latin: fount and origin.
3 The character in Charlotte Brontë's *Jane Eyre*.

men and the dream-women, begotten by Fantasy upon Desire, and tell us more about the limitations of their creators than they do about the sexes they are supposed to typify.

I gather, by the way, that Mrs Cecil Chesterton[4] has not dealt too kindly with Gilbert K. and Frances.[5] This seems a pity, especially as both are dead, and so recently. "The sweet war-man is dead and rotten; sweet chucks, beat not the bones of the buried".[6] I don't mind what hard blows are dealt to those who can hit back, but this working-off of old scores when there is no possibility of self-defence is indecent. I was glad that so many reviewers objected to it. I ought not to comment, not having yet read the book; but one passage that I did read quoted seemed to be quite indefensible....

4 Ada, the widow of G. K. Chesterton's brother, author of *The Chestertons*, London, Chapman and Hall, 1941.
5 The wife of G. K. Chesterton.
6 *Love's Labour's Lost*, Act V, scene 2.

[24 Newland Street
Witham
Essex]

TO F. H. JAEGAR[1]

23 July 1941

Dear Mr. Jaegar,

I quite recognise the importance of religious feeling, but I am quite sure that to concentrate on this, to the exclusion of the rational side of Christian philosophy, is a very great mistake. That is exactly what we have been doing of recent years, with the result that, so far as European society is concerned, the strong intellectual skeleton of Christian dogma has collapsed, bringing Christian ethics down with it. People of intelligence have drifted into the agnostic camp, and the world has become persuaded that it is impossible for any person with brains to be a Christian.

If the arousing of strong mystical emotion is a guarantee of true religion, then the Nazi religion of blood and soil is as good as any; nor is there any criterion by which we can condemn it. It represents, in fact, the direct appeal to the "unconscious" – a region which is packed with "original sin" and offers no very reliable guide to conduct.

As regards my broadcast talks, you will perhaps remember that I was

1 Identity unknown.

not asked to talk in a general way about "religion", but specifically to explain what the Church meant by certain clauses in a particular document: the Creed. This document does not purport to deal with feelings but with fact and doctrine. Perhaps you did not follow the whole series, and were therefore not aware of its general purpose?

Yours faithfully,

    [Dorothy L. Sayers]

                               [24 Newland Street
                               Witham
                               Essex]

TO DR JAMES WELCH

1 August 1941

Dear Dr. Welch,

I expect you will think I have been a long time about sending the next play[1] for you to see. I have, as you know, been very busy, partly through wrestling with Mr. Fenn's programme on the Creed, and partly with getting out a new book.[2] However, I have at last contrived to finish the play about John the Baptist, and I hope that I shall now be able to get along faster.

I am sending you the play, together with a copy of my letter to Mr. Gielgud which I have sent him along with the script. There are a couple of paragraphs in the letter in which I have explained my handling of the material. I have taken the line that nobody, not even Jesus, must be allowed to "talk Bible". I expect we shall get a good many complaints that I have not preserved the beauty and eloquence of the authorized version, and that Jesus has been made to say things which don't appear in the sacred original. It seems to me frightfully important that the thing should be made to appear as real as possible, and above all, that Jesus should be presented as a human being and not like a sort of symbolic figure doing nothing but preach in eloquent periods, with all the people round him talking in everyday style. We must avoid, I think, a Docetist[3] Christ, whatever happens – even at the risk of a little loss of formal dignity. I hope very much you will agree about this. I cannot forget the remark of one of my secretaries (which I believe I have quoted to you before) when she typed my other play, *He That Should Come*. She said, "I never realized before that Mary and Joseph, and all those, were real people."

1   "The King's Herald", the second play.
2   *The Mind of the Maker*, which had just been published.
3   See letter to S. Dark, 6 April 1938, note 4.

As I said to Mr. Gielgud, the material for this play was extremely difficult to bring into dramatic form, and I have had to take slight liberties with the text, such as telescoping the two occasions on which John Baptist pointed out Jesus to the multitudes and the disciples, and also making his arrest follow immediately upon the "bridegroom" speech. This is just for dramatic concentration, and, as you will see, I have followed the suggestion that James and John, as well as Andrew, were John Baptist's disciples, and Judas also. This enables me to get the characters firmly planted at the start and makes it unnecessary to invent anonymous disciples of John Baptist, who would be of no importance for the succeeding plays.

I hope you won't mind these tamperings with the text – if that is the right word for them.

I am thankful to hear from Mr. Gielgud that production is postponed until December;[4] that will enable me to make a better job of the thing. I have talked over general questions of production with him, and I feel pretty sure that he will be able to find us the right sort of actors, so far as war conditions allow. I know he will do a sensitive and reverent production, and I will promise you not to start any more rows!!

I hope all is well with you at Bristol. Thank Heaven and the Russians[5] for a period of rest from bombing and late nights.

With kind remembrances to Mr. Fenn and Mr. Williams,

    Yours very sincerely,

      [Dorothy L. Sayers]

P.S. I don't know that the small children will make very much of this play, the subject is not very suitable for them, but I have tried to do what I can to engage their attention by putting in the scene with the children at the beginning.

---

4 The first play, "Kings in Judaea", was broadcast on 21 December 1941.
5 Hitler had invaded Russia.

24 Newland Street
Witham
Essex

TO MAURICE B. RECKITT

11 August 1941

Dear Mr Reckitt,
Proof herewith.[1] You will see that I have obstinately refused to be brow-beaten by the printer!...

Yes, indeed; the predatory American female is precisely the logical and inevitable outcome of the "functional" attiutude to female nature – the exploited has become an exploiter of a very ruthless and disgusting type. Claire Boothe's play, *The Women*,[2] is its most bitter commentary, and the savage joy with which it was received on both sides of the Atlantic was revealing. I imagine that Miss Byrne will have something to say about it. But nothing else can possibly come of a society where the keeping of idle women is prized as a badge of wealth and success. It is revenge – a kind of wild justice.
                    Yours very sincerely,
                        Dorothy L. Sayers

1 Of her article, "The Human-not-quite-Human".
2 Claire Boothe (1903–1987), the wife of Henry Luce, and United States Ambassador to Italy, was the author of the play *The Women* (1936).

24 Newland Street
Witham
Essex

TO IVY SHRIMPTON

19 August 1941

Dearest Ivy,
I seem to have got rather mixed up about what's paid for and what isn't, however, some money has just come in, so I enclose cheque £20 – will you let me know how far this goes. I seem to have spent most of my time lately trying to find servants and to catch up with jobs that ought to have been done weeks ago. Otherwise, things go much as usual, except that there is a perpetual noise of our bombers going to Germany instead of Hitler's bombers going to London! This way is pleasanter. Not that we

ever got many bombs, but one dislikes the feeling that other people are getting them. However, one good thing about living in East Anglia is that people imagine we live in perpetual showers of bombs, and therefore evacuate themselves into other places, to the confusion of the rationing arrangements and the congestion of the traffic. Now the jugginses are all rushing back to London, and I suppose when the winter uproar begins again they will all rush out again. I was sorry to hear about your Aunt Marie. One or two of my friends have been bombed out too, but so far, touch wood, none of them have been killed. Well, that's war — and better on the whole than the last war, when the young men went and left the old people and the women feeling ashamed to be safe. Anyway, let's hope the Russians give Hitler plenty to think about for a bit.

Best love,
D. L. S.

[24 Newland Street
Witham
Essex]

MR. J. WILSHIN[1]
21 August 1941

Dear Mr. Wilshin,

Many thanks for your interesting letter. I entirely agree with you about the need for a change of outlook and I do understand how you, and people like yourself feel about it. The trouble is, as you will realise, that changes of outlook come slowly, and have to seep down, as it were, "from the top." I mean that the really big and profound thinkers have to do their thinking first, and then the new ideas spread slowly, through people like me, who try to understand them and explain them to the fairly well-educated, and so on, down to the simple and popular sort of books, till at last they get "into the papers." By the time they get there, the big thinkers have got a bit further on, and so it continues, with the mass of the nation always trailing a bit behind.

It has been the fashion lately to pretend that the big thinkers — the real trained minds — don't count, and that the ordinary man can get all the guidance he needs from cheap journalism and "practical men". But that isn't really true. The outlook that we have been suffering from lately — the idea that nothing matters except to "get on" and that whatever pays is right — can be traced back to the materialist philosophers of the

---

1 Identity unknown.

eighteenth and nineteenth centuries. It did its harm very slowly, though it was tremendously helped on by the "industrial revolution", and (as I tried to show in *Begin Here*) by the new kinds of sociology and psychology, based on the scientific discoveries of the machine age and the age of evolution. Now, the tip-top scientists are not nearly so sure of themselves as they were. But the new ideas are very difficult, and we can't expect them to be put into popular language all at once. And meanwhile, the people who have absorbed the nineteenth-century ideas are finding out that they don't work, and are discouraged, because they don't know of anything to put in their place. But they are still steeped in those ideas, which have become so much a part of their outlook that they hardly realize how much they are taking them for granted. The idea, for instance, that the value of all work is to be measured in money – profits and wages and expenditure. People denounce capitalism – but they do really still admire wealth and idleness, and go to see films about idle rich people in America, and wish they could live like that. And they do still in their hearts despise people who think or teach, and call them "stuffy highbrows", and look down on imagination as "not practical", at the very same time that they are complaining of "unimaginative" statesmen and lack of "vision" in public affairs.

I don't think the working people present nearly such a difficult problem as the middle classes. They live much closer to hard facts, and I always find an audience of working men very keen and interested in problems which need a bit of thinking-out. The really difficult people are those who have enjoyed a little bit of social security, without ever really needing to think and without ever really needing to struggle with life. My real job is, I think, to try and get hold of them – the people in the villas, the young people in the universities, the people who can get hold of books if they really want to and have enough education to try their teeth on something that isn't quite written in words of one syllable. Because those people are very much bewildered, and very unhappy, and there are a great many of them. One can't talk to everybody in the same book, but by tackling the people nearest to one's self one may get a little bit done.

It is, of course, quite true that ideas can't be violently imposed on people. In my novels – especially the last two or three[2] – I have tried to "infiltrate" a few general ideas, especially about the value of work and the absolute necessity for "intellectual integrity". But, as you understand so clearly, this kind of thing has to be done very carefully and must arise naturally out of the story. A story that has great gobbets of philosophy dumped into it very readily becomes unreadable. So, since the war started, I've been going at the thing rather more directly – an article here, a

2 *The Nine Tailors, Gaudy Night,* and *Busman's Honeymoon.*

speech there, a pamphlet or two, and a good bit of correspondence with readers who seemed interested. But there are so many wrong ideas that need up-rooting that it is very slow work.

However, you may be assured that the thinkers "at the top" are really getting hold of the right end of the stick and – if things go reasonably well – you will presently see the new out-look beginning to make its appearance. The great thing is that there are so many people who are really anxious to think matters out afresh. The war – especially the things that led up to the war – have given everybody a nasty jolt, and made them much readier than they would have been otherwise to admit that something has gone wrong with our sense of values, both in Europe and America.

I don't know that I can help you, personally, very much – indeed, you seem to have arrived at the right place already – but if there is any particular problem you want to examine I might be able to suggest books and so on. I'm sure that the best way to tackle the whole thing is for anybody who does come across a book, or article, or statement which seems helpful, to draw his friends' attention to it and discuss it with them. Like that, the ideas get spread about, and people come to realise that these matters are being thought about and that the ideas are really in the air. Then comes the next step – acting upon them, even if it's only in a small way, such as taking a paper a little less squalid than the *Daily Mirror*, or interesting one's self in what the Borough Council is doing, or listening-in to something a trifle more "highbrow" than hot jazz, or admiring a film for good dialogue and good photography, rather than for the dresses worn by the star and the amount spent on production. It's just in those small ways that one does gradually learn to acquire a new attitude to the really important matters; and they are ways that everybody can learn and that cost nobody anything. But so often people get disheartened because the difficulties look so big, and they feel that nothing can be done, except by huge national efforts and the expenditure of a lot of public money – with, as you say, the countenance and approval of Lord So-and-so and the influential Mrs. Thingummy-jig.

I'm afraid these suggestions sound very dull and trivial; but, as I said, if there is any line of inquiry you want to follow up, let me know, and I will be of help if I can.

Yours very truly,
    [Dorothy L. Sayers]

[24 Newland Street
Witham
Essex]

TO THE REV. T. WIGLEY[1]

1 September 1941

Dear Sir,

With much of what you say I agree: in particular that a great many religious difficulties arise out of entirely misconceived and mistaken notions of what Christian doctrine actually is. But it seems to me that it is impracticable to confine ourselves to "modern words and expressions" in dealing with theology, and that for two reasons:

1. The mere fact that we have to deal with the Bible obliges us to make use of the theological ideas and expressions in which it abounds, and which naturally reflect the current philosophies of the times at which its various books were written. Many, indeed, of the most crude and erroneous ideas about doctrine (especially as regards redemption) are directly derived from the reading of the Bible without sufficient knowledge of its theological and historical background.

2. The older theological words and expressions formed a real technical vocabulary, and it is at least possible to discover and say what they meant to the theologians who used them. But modern words and expressions change their connotation so rapidly, and are used so loosely by scientists and other amateur philosophers that they are at the very least as misleading as the old technical vocabulary and much more vague. From the purely practical point of view, there is an advantage in keeping the old words as the basis of a theological vocabulary, while explaining and interpreting them as far as possible so as to convey their meaning to the modern mind.

If we do not do this, we tend, I think, to get precisely the situation that has arisen: the general assumption that the language of the Bible is completely irrelevant to the present "world-view", and a breach of continuity with the past which is fatal to any historical religion. And there is always the danger of allowing people to suppose that our modern times are so wholly unlike any other times that the fundamental facts about man's nature have wholly changed with changing circumstances. I doubt whether, for example, we gain anything by abolishing the words "original sin" and substituting evolutionary terms about the "ape and tiger", or psycho-analytical terms about schizophrenia and the sub-conscious – though we may use these latter terms to illustrate some of the implications of "original sin". The newer words are much more limited in scope than

---

1 Identity unknown.

the old and are even more readily superseded by fresh theories; and further, they have the disadvantage of appearing to explain – or explain away – phenomena in terms of some particular branch of science, whereas "original sin", being a purely theological term, belongs properly to its own science and commits one to no passing scientific fashion. There are a number of new theological expressions – but these are, for the most part, quite as difficult for the common man as the older ones. D. Huizinga in *In the Shadow of Tomorrow*[2] issues a significant warning against the extremely ephemeral nature of modern scientific concepts; Eddington, failing to come to grips with the necessarily analogical nature of all language, seems to suggest in desperation that we should abandon language and think only in mathematical formulae and ejaculations; Michael Roberts in *The Modern Mind*[3] traces the changes in the use and meaning of certain words in a way that shows how necessary it is to keep in mind the actual meaning of any word at the time when it was used when the document in question was written. He points out, for example, that the word "reason", which at one time was held to include the whole intelligence together with the creative imagination, and was thus a fairly adequate translation of λογος, became restricted in the mouths of the eighteenth-century scientists to mean only the logical faculty. Consequently, all arguments about "the Divine Reason" are apt to end in misunderstanding. The original word λογος, however, does not provoke these confusions, provided its technical meaning is explained to the student. There is, in fact, no modern word that precisely corresponds to λογος – because recent methods of thought have tended to split up that general concept into a number of more limited concepts – word, reason, energy, intellect, imagination, and so forth. It is quite likely that this tendency to over-analysis will correct itself. In the meantime, it is of some assistance to know that St. Thomas Aquinas had already detected the tendency and made it plain that, theologically, the *ratio scientiae* could not be considered synonymous with the *ratio sapientiae*.[4]

I am quite of your mind about the teaching put forward in many churches; but I should not have said that this erred very much nowadays on the side of being too theological. My own complaint would be that it is apt to take the theology far too much for granted, and, instead of explaining and interpreting that, to offer either a set of ethical exhortations which are pointless apart from the theology on which they are based,

2 D. Huizinga (1872–1945), Dutch historian and essayist, author of *The Waning of the Middle Ages* (tr. F. Hopman, 1924) and *Homo Ludens* (1938). *In the Shadow of Tomorrow: a Diagnosis of the Spiritual Distemper of our Time* was published in 1936. D. L. S. quotes from this work three times in *The Mind of the Maker* (Methuen, p.18, note 1; pp. 32–33; p. 35).

3 Published in 1937. Michael Roberts was a schoolmaster and a poet.

4 Latin: *ratio scientiae*, the order of knowledge; *ratio sapientiae*, the order of understanding.

or else a good deal of talk about religious *experience* which means nothing to the hearer who has not shared that experience, and is seldom directly communicable.

You may be interested in a letter I have had from a master in a public school,[5] who is, as he says, in a position to "know what the young men want". He writes, "Christian principles without Christian dogma leaves most of them stone cold. But they'll take dogma with both hands and ask for more." The impression I get, for what it is worth, is that the modernist position belongs, like so many things calling themselves modern, to the last century, and that the younger people are looking for something that can be called dateless; and in their search they seem to be making the double swing back to Aquinas and Augustine – since tomorrow always seems to have to build itself on the day before yesterday; it never builds on yesterday – perhaps the greatest mistake of the "evolutionist" in applying their biological analogy in the spiritual field was to suppose that it did.

Thank you very much for your letter, and for the things you so kindly say about my books. I hope you will forgive me for appearing contentious – but the matter seems to me of too much urgent importance not to be discussed as frankly as possible.

Yours faithfully,
    [Dorothy L. Sayers]

5 Eton College; see following letter.

[24 Newland Street
Witham
Essex]

TO J. D. UPCOTT[1]
Keate House
Eton College
Windsor
1 September 1941

Dear Mr. Upcott,
    Thank you so much for your extremely interesting letter. I'm extremely glad to know what you tell me about "what the young men want". As you say, you are there, and you know. I can only guess – and though it's a

1 John Dalgairns Upcott taught classics and history at Eton from 1919 to 1945. He died in 1962.

novelist's business to guess, and guess right (since one's livelihood depends on guessing right) one is always liable to be shouted down by the people who clamour incessantly that young people don't want any of this nasty dogma. I have a shrewd suspicion that most of the anti-dogmatics are elderly people, who were brought up in the old-fashioned "Liberal" tradition and are quite out of touch with the young; but they don't always produce their birth-certificates to back up their views, so it's hard to be sure.

But, looking round at the world as it is, it seems to me (I speak as a fool) that youth is all out for dogma, and that if boys and girls grow up imagining that Christianity has no dogma to give them, they'll give themselves over to political dogma or economic dogma in its crudest and most intransigent form. And whether they end by accepting the Christian philosophy or not, it seems only right and reasonable that they should at least be told that there is one, of a quite coherent and really relevant kind, and what it is. Otherwise, as Michael Roberts says in *The Recovery of the West*,[2] they find themselves comparing their adult knowledge and science and politics with the simple notions of Christianity they acquired at their mothers' knees, and naturally conclude that the Christian religion is only fit to be put away with the other childish things.

I'm very glad your 16-year-olds enjoyed *The Devil to Pay*.[3] The imminence of the war, and other things, spoilt its reception in Town; also, I think it was, in a way, about a year too early for most people's mood. None of the critics and few of the public grasped the meaning of the Helen episode and the devastating relapse into irresponsibility. It was a little terrifying to find out how many of the audience thought it was so much nicer for Faustus to be a "dear little doggie" than to pay the price of his human dignity. *De te fabula*[4] was the only possible comment. Today, they might make more of it – especially the younger ones, who do seem to be grasping the idea of responsibility. At least, I hope so. But I'm rather afraid of all these "leaders" who seem to be heading towards the planned state and the planned citizen. Perhaps I have been reading too much Hermann Rauschning;[5] but I do seem to detect in nearly all the plans for a New Order the doctrinaire passion for over-simplification which refuses to take

---

2 See letter to the Rev. T. Wigley, 1 September 1941, note 3. *The Recovery of the West* was published in 1941.

3 There is no record of a performance of the play at Eton. Mr Upcott may have arranged a dramatized reading of it as part of "private business".

4 Latin: it speaks of thee.

5 Hermann Rauschning, an East Prussian military aristocrat who joined the Nazi movement in its early days. Later disillusioned, he wrote two books in which he exposed its essential nihilism: *Germany's Revolution of Destruction*, tr. 1939 (which D. L. S. recommended under "Books to Read" in *Begin Here*) and *Hitler Speaks*, tr. 1939.

account of the complexity of human nature or of the paradox that causes all human absolutes to issue in their own opposites. People proclaim peace, justice, liberty, democracy – as though by saying the word they could impose the thing – never mind what we mean by peace, liberty, justice and democracy. Never mind theology – all we have to do is to practise the ethics of the Sermon on the Mount; that's all we have to do; nothing, obviously, could be more simple and easy.

The other day, a well-known Socialist said to Maurice Reckitt that she now realised how much their youthful efforts had been nullified by "failure to face two problems: the problem of Evil and the problem of Power". And the other day I tried on a bright youngish Socialist Reinhold Niebuhr's statement: "Goodness, armed with power, is corrupted; and pure love without power is destroyed."[6] He found it terrifying (so it is), and indicated that he didn't want to believe it was true. Perhaps the young wouldn't mind so much leaving "security" behind them, and setting out, "A fire on the one hand and a deep water on the other", if people would only tell them that that is what is called for. I don't know. But it seems to be a fact that you can't get anybody to do anything worth a damn by telling them that everything's all right and the Golden Age just on the other side of the mirror; they just turn into dear little doggies and innocently let hell loose everywhere.

By the way, all the conjurations in *Devil to Pay* are quite authentic – guaranteed to produce results. I can't definitely say we conjured up anything worse than ourselves, either in Canterbury or London; but the production was attended by a series of extraordinary difficulties and catastrophes in both places. I hope no peculiar effects were observable at Eton!

With again many thanks,
    Yours sincerely,
        [Dorothy L. Sayers]

6 See letter to the Sister Superior, 25 June 1941.

[24 Newland Street
Witham
Essex]

TO DR JAMES WELCH
17 September 1941

Dear Dr. Welch,

I didn't acknowledge your former letter, because I gathered that a second was to follow it. I will now make haste to acknowledge them both, before dashing off to Hayward's Heath to address some people there about Christian New Orders and things.[1]

I'm so glad you all found "The King's Herald" *interesting as a play* – because when writing for production that is the first and greatest commandment on which hang all the Law and the Prophets. I'm quite prepared to find that a few people may be startled or shocked – I don't mind if you don't. The proportion of shocked people in my fan-mail for *He That Should Come* was exactly one in eleven, which isn't too bad, I think, since the angry people are usually much more ready to write letters than the contented people.

What you say about the theophany[2] touches really the central point of all this – the central point, I mean, of what I've been trying to do in these Bible plays. My feeling is that one of the principal reasons why the Gospel story is apt to appear unreal and stained-glass-window-like is, oddly enough, the enormous importance we attach to all the incidents. For the Evangelists, and for us, looking at the whole story in the light of what we know, Jesus is the centre, not only of His own story, but of all history, and it is with great difficulty that we remember how differently He must have appeared to His own contemporaries. In so many religious plays and books He is shown surrounded by people who are, so to speak, self-consciously assisting at, or assisting in, the fulfilment of prophecies. But they weren't really like that – they said, "Is not this the carpenter?" – adding, indignantly, "But we know these people" – and as for new prophets, though no doubt they always caused an excitement, most of them would be nine-day-wonders, and not really so urgently absorbing as the price of oil and the iniquities of tax-gatherers. The thing that is so dramatic, and so convincingly "real" is that the course of the world's history was being violently changed, and that practically nobody took any notice. To *us* the baptism of Christ is the earth-shaking moment when the Son of Man realized fully that He was the Son of God; but [to] the

1 Talk given on 17 September at 8 p.m. at the Senior School in Hayward's Heath. It was the 4th and last in a series entitled "A Christian New Order". It was acclaimed as a "profound and brilliantly reasoned discourse" (*The Mid-Sussex Times*, 23 September 1941).
2 A revelation or manifestation of God, such as occurred at the baptism of Jesus.

bystanders (who apparently didn't see the vision) that baptism would be just one of many – and to my "Hannah" the exciting thing would be that this was, unexpectedly, "Mary's boy" – an old friend with news from home. (It seems pretty clear from Luke IV.16–30 that Jesus had never said or done anything remarkable in the 30 silent years – he doesn't seem even to have been looked upon as the local infant phenomenon, still less as the local miracle monger. The Nazarenes complained that they weren't getting any of the exciting "things" that had been done at Capernaum.) So Jesus undergoes a really terrific experience – and *we* feel as though the world ought to have stood respectfully still – but instead it comes chattering and clattering in on Him, occupied with its own affairs. I've tried to indicate that it is, after all, the perfectly balanced temperament that can control itself and deal graciously with the intrusive world – that it is *John* who is thrown off his balance and can't attend to anything, and Jesus who can find time and patience to attend to a gossipy middle-aged woman and a couple of children. Incidentally, I put in this bit, and the children generally, because it seemed to offer the possibility of something fairly simple for the younger listeners. All the rest of the John Baptist story is difficult stuff for children – repentance, and all that. ...

I struggled a good deal with "thus it becometh us to fulfil all righteousness" but could find nothing for it that children could make anything of. It implies so much that needs knowledge – theological and historical, and it is all mixed up with the difficult business of sinlessness, and the vicarious assumption of the sins of the world; so I thought it best on the whole to substitute a simple phrase that might convey something rather than keep a difficult phrase that couldn't convey anything much.[3]

John's stammer – This sort of thing always looks maddening in print, but I think it will be all right in production. I'll explain to Val that we don't want a real stammer, but only a little trick of stumbling, due to his tripping over his own eager tongue. They did a little play the other night, in which the actor who played Charles Lamb[4] had got just the right effect, and it was very attractive. For broadcasting, any trifling trick of speech is of enormous help to the listener, because it helps him in the immensely difficult job of distinguishing one male voice from the other. And there are so many male voices in the Gospel story; it's going to be hard work for the listeners however much help we give them. I'm sure you can trust Val to do that part of it all right.

Humour – dreadfully difficult – especially as the reported humour of

---

3 Matthew, chapter 4, verse 15, relating the baptism of Jesus: And Jesus answering said unto him, Suffer it to be so now: for thus it becometh us to fulfil all righteousness. Then he suffered him. In *The Man Born to be King*, "The King's Herald", scene 1, Jesus says: "Do as I ask you now, John. It's right to begin this way, like everybody else."

4 Charles Lamb (1775–1834), essayist and poet.

Christ tends to be of the ironical kind which appeals to the adult mind. I owe to R.A. Edwards,[5] by the way, the suggestion that the conjunction of Simon's name with Simon's face must have been entertainingly incongruous. We've got to depend a lot on the actors about all this.

By the way (à propos of the comforting assurance to Andrew that the bread came from the baker) – I *wish* one of the Evangelists had thought to tell us *what the disciples felt* about living with a person who could turn water into wine and multiply loaves and fishes. Miracles of healing are not really so disconcerting – but the first staggering realization that solid material things might slide away and turn into something else – what *did* they think about it? Supposing somebody said to *you*, "I was seriously tempted to turn stones into bread" – even if you didn't think he was mad or lying, and indeed *especially* if you didn't think he was mad or lying – would you feel comfortable? The Evangelists are so exasperatingly matter-of-fact about themselves. The only thing that really seems to have upset anybody was the miraculous draught of fishes. I suppose that really was the first miracle (though I haven't room for it) – but even so, fish in the proper place for fish – though in large numbers – isn't quite so disquieting as the other things....

Whip or goad[6] – I'm sure you are perfectly right about the goad. But how can one ask the "effects" people to make a noise like a goad? One's only got people's ears to appeal to, and a whip helps a lot to make the starting-up of the cart audible. If you think strict accuracy essential, we'll do without it. But actually I'm not trying very hard to be pedantically Oriental. I feel that the best way is to give a slight Oriental flavour here and there, but to combine this with as much familiar daily-life detail as possible. Like those Renaissance painters, who dress Christ and the disciples in "Bible" costume, and Herod's soldiers in vaguely classical armour, and surround them with men and women in more or less sixteenth-century costume with a dash of oriental trimmings here and there. That's why I made John Baptist talk of the "bride-groom's friend" as the "best man" – a person the children know all about, instead of trying to preserve all the detail of the Eastern ceremony. I'm doing the same with the Marriage at Cana – keeping all the necessary water-pots, wine-skins and what not, but letting a friend of the family propose the health of the young couple much as it might be done by Mr. Smith of Surbiton, and avoiding pedantic

---

5 R. A. Edwards, *The Upper Room* (London, Methuen, 1941).
6 Dr Welch had pointed out that oxen were urged on by a goad, not a whip. Cf. D. L. S.' reference to this, *The Man Born to be King*, Introduction (Gollancz, p. 26): "It is doubtless true, as somebody pointed out, that a yoke of oxen would be driven, not with a whip but with a goad; but the lash of a whip can be heard on the air, whereas it is useless to ask the studio-effects-man to stand by making a noise like an ox-goad."

exactitude of detail. It won't please the historical-costume experts, but it's so much easier to get life into the thing that way.

The next play[7] is done, and you shall have it as soon as it is typed. But I'm depressed and discouraged by hearing from Val that after the first two plays the programme people are cutting the time down from forty-five minutes to forty. It is simply *maddening* to have all these upsets and alterations. Five minutes means a difference of about 3 and a half pages, and that's a serious matter – because it's always the lively, atmospheric bits that have to be sacrificed. Can you *possibly* do anything about it? Surely, that one day in the week, some fragment of light music or something can be dispensed with? What bothers one is the uncertainty. One tries to plan the plays so that they will each bear a reasonable proportion to the thing as a whole – but what will have happened by the time we get to the Last Supper? Will that find itself suddenly curtailed to half-an-hour? They treat this play-writing game as though it were like reeling off a set of gramophone records. But honestly it's the most difficult and delicate job I've ever struck and at each fresh obstruction one's heart goes down with a bump, and one's enthusiasm and interest get sort of sucked out of one. I seem to be always complaining about something, don't I? I *know* there's a war on[8] – but why pick on Christ, if you take my meaning? Can't somebody else suffer, for a change?

I don't think my "creative genius" is likely to conflict – consciously, at any rate – with the narrative; though of course one's obliged to take a few liberties of compression, addition, and adjustment, to avoid having a mere succession of disconnected episodes. And sometimes one has to interpret explicitly what seem to be the implications, and one may easily go wrong. I find, as I had expected, that where St. John (or whoever it was) is giving an "eye-witness report" he is incomparable. All his characters are real people and all his conversations are lively and precise. He leaves out a lot of what had been written down already, and he often summarizes briefly the things he didn't see for himself; but whenever he goes into detail he knows where people were sitting, and what they said and the connection between one thing and the other – the perfect "source" for the playwright.

I'm not sure when next I shall be in Town. I'm dashing about the country rather a lot these next few months, but I'd very much like to see you, and I'll let you know next time I can manage to be up on a Tuesday or Wednesday.

Please remember me very kindly to Mr. Fenn and Mr. Williams.

Yours very sincerely,

[Dorothy L. Sayers]

7 "A Certain Nobleman".
8 Eching the current reply to any request: "I suppose you know there's a war on!"

[24 Newland Street
Witham
Essex]

TO THE REV. NEVILLE GORTON[1]

24 September 1941

Dear Mr. Gorton,

Many thanks for your letter and your two very interesting memoranda. I don't know that I can do anything very direct to help on the good work – frankly, this "religious" business is already taking up so much time and energy in the way of making speeches, writing letters, and attending conferences that I am seriously hampered in my proper job of writing books and prevented from earning my living. But I will bear your activities in mind when a proper context occurs for making use of them.

As to your main point: I am well aware of the astonishing lack of any good theological literature for the layman. I am continually being asked for "a book which will tell me what Christian dogma is" – and, surprisingly enough, when one thinks of the British Museum shelves bending under the weight of theological volumes, I am obliged to say that there is no such thing. Everything one can think of is either (1) devotional (2) apologetic or (3) liturgical-ecclesiastical; moreover, one cannot seem to get the whole doctrine in one book, but only separate works on Christology, or Creation-doctrine, or the Trinity, or Sacraments or what not. I keep on complaining about this.

I believe that Messrs. Methuen are seriously interested in doing something along the lines you indicate for the use of Upper Forms, and that R. A. Edwards[2] is a leading spirit in the venture. If you are not already in touch with him about it, it might be worth while to get on to him, or to Mr. E. V. Rieu[3] of Methuen's, who is dealing with the scheme. Of course, all publication is very difficult at the moment, owing to labour, paper, and pasteboard shortage.

As regards agreement about doctrine. I think it would be well if those who can agree on a basis should make a public statement[4] about it. I

---

1 Headmaster of Blundell's School, 1934–1943, later Bishop of Coventry.
2 See letter to James Welch, 17 September 1941, note 3.
3 Later editor of Penguin Classics.
4 D. L. S. discussed the matter more fully in her letter dated 28 November 1941, q.v. She had conceived the idea of a symposium, to be entitled "The Oecumenical Penguin", to which she was willing to contribute, though anonymously. (See Giles Watson, *Catholicism in Anglican Culture and Theology: Responses to Crisis in England: 1937–1949*, Ph.D. Thesis, Department of History, Australian National University, especially chapter 8, "The Oecumenical Penguin: Dorothy L. Sayers and the popularisation of Christian dogma".) The project failed to materialize.

mean, *about doctrine*, and not about "religion" or "Christian ethics". Judging by my own experience in the last year or so, the "Christian" laity (and indeed the clerisy also) are quite plainly and simply divided into two camps:

1. Those who believe that Jesus is fully God.
2. Those who do not, but hold Him to be a teacher
   of ethics, "divine" only in a Unitarian, Arian,
   or Adoptionist[5] sense.

Between these two groups it seems almost impossible to patch up any real common platform, since the surface agreement will crack the moment any pressure is applied. As one correspondent has put it, the word "Christian" with its "implied theology" is [not] really applicable to Group Two, who might better be called "Jesuists".

In my own popular talks and pamphlets I have settled down to a line which seems reasonably satisfactory in practice. I make no attempt to conciliate the "Jesuists", but stick to what may be roughly called an "oecumenical and Catholic" interpretation of the Creeds. That is, I try to offer a doctrine that would be acceptable to the three "Catholic" branches of the Church: Roman, Greek-Orthodox, and Anglican. Differences of doctrine between these bodies I try not to discuss at all, considering that if the average ignorant reader or listener can get as far as grasping the main outlines of Christian doctrine common to those three communions, he will then be in a position to hammer out the details for himself. In practice, as I say, this kind of thing appears to be well received, not only by the bodies in question, but also by a great number of people in the Free Churches.

As far as the intelligent but uninstructed laity are concerned, I find they complain of *vagueness* in all the manifestoes, schemes, syllabuses, and suggestions put forward about "religious education". A personal friend of my own,[6] who has had to do with school and university education all her life, said to me the other day (*à propos* of the recent correspondence in *The Times*): "What I want to know, and what nobody tells me, is this: *What* do you suggest that children should be taught? Is there any ascertainable set of Christian dogmas that they could be instructed in? Can you formulate anything definite beyond 'Bible history' and 'Christian morals'?" I replied in the sense of the preceding paragraph, saying that I proposed (or should propose if asked) that children should be taught (in addition, of course, to the actual New Testament text) the dogmas contained or implied in the Nicene Creed, and should be made to understand that this was, in fact,

---

5 Adoptionist: one of a sect who believe that Jesus Christ was the son of God by adoption only.
6 Possibly Marjorie Barber.

the corpus of Christian theology, so that when they became adult, they could accept or reject it, but not until they had learnt what it actually *was*. She replied that this proposal satisfied her perfectly; but added that, although brought up as a "Christian" she had never had the Creed expounded to her, did not know what its clauses implied, and had never heard from any pulpit a unified exposition of Christian doctrine as a coherent philosophy. She said further that the haphazard and unconvincing way in which Christianity was commonly set forth in pulpits seemed to her completely contemptible, and the sort of thing that would not be countenanced in any secular lecture-room.

She *may* be an exaggerated case; even so, it seems surprising and regrettable that a well-educated woman of forty-five, whose work has been chiefly concerned with English literature (so strongly influenced by Christian thought) should have grown up so wholly unaware of the Creeds, or of the general structure of Christian philosophy.

One great trouble, as you say, is the late-nineteenth-century-science outlook. I have come to the conclusion that the majority of people who are in a position to *influence* the organisation of "Christian education" are middle-aged or elderly people out of touch with youth. A master at one of our greatest public schools[7] writes to me of his young men: "Christian ethics without dogma leaves them, I am glad to say, stone-cold; but they will take dogma with both hands and ask for more". But the influential people who write to *The Times* are *still* saying, "Youth does not want dogma; it just wants the spirit of love". Which isn't true; and in any case, how the blazes do they propose to embody the spirit of love in a school syllabus? It is useless to go on saying that general uplift and nice religious feeling plus science will draw the world together in concord – we've tried that for a couple of centuries, and just look at the world!

I know next to nothing about the present position in State-aided schools, except that it seems to satisfy nobody. But it seems clear to me that, in schools generally speaking, there can be no intelligent teaching of Christian doctrine unless the subject is taken seriously and taught *either* by

(a) members of the school staff who are qualified both by professional training and personal conviction to teach it,

or

(b) by outside teachers (e.g. priests, ministers etc.) who are allowed to enter the school and freely teach the doctrine of their communion, and who are also professionally qualified to be teachers.

7 Eton College. See letter to J. D. Upcott, 1 September 1941.

At present we seem to have either teachers who know nothing about doctrine or dogmatists who know nothing about teaching – a state of things that would scarcely be permitted in any subject that was considered serious, such as trigonometry or woodwork.

As regards books, we are in much the same difficulty. The people who are up-to-date in their theology can't write English, and the people who can write English are either untheological or have only a sketchy impression of nineteenth-century liberal-humanist ethics mixed up with a lot of outmoded "higher criticism" – in fact their "outline" of Christian theology is like that of Mr. Mantalini's admirers: "The two countesses had no outlines at all, and the dowager's was a demmed outline".[8] Or as Fr. V. A. Demant[9] put it: "The people who can think can't write, and the people who can write can't think".

Anyway, I like your memoranda, which contain some good pungent paragraphs that I shall take every opportunity of thrusting under the noses of the clergy, and of anybody to whom I think they may do good.

Yours sincerely,

[Dorothy L. Sayers]

P.S. One small personal bleat: in official memoranda, will you favour my fancy for having my name given as it invariably appears on my title-pages and in official signatures – with the "L" in it? I have a "thing" about "Dorothy Sayers" and never use that form. I don't mind "Sayers" by itself!

8 Charles Dickens, *Life and Adventures of Nicholas Nickleby*, chapter 34: Mr Mantalini to Ralph
   Nickleby. Instead of "demmed", Dickens prints "demd".
9 See letter to the Rev. V. A. Demant, 4 April 1941, note.

[24 Newland Street
Witham
Essex]

TO THE REV. DR JAMES WELCH

24 September 1941

Dear Dr. Welch,

Here is the Third Play – "A Certain Nobleman".

As you will see, I have taken one or two liberties with the material, so as to tie the various episodes neatly together:

1. (Following the Archbishop of York)[1] I have supposed that Mary has something to do with the household arrangement at Cana, as this obviously makes her interference in the matter of the wine much more convincing, and also gives an opportunity for introducing her account of the Finding in the Temple, and for linking that first "rebuke" with the "Woman, what have I to do with thee?" in a reasonably intelligent manner (I have put a line or two about this in the "Note on the Characters").[2]

2. I have made the "certain nobleman" of Capernaum a guest at the wedding, implying that the Bride was a native of Capernaum and that the Bridegroom was fetching her from Capernaum to Cana. The "nobleman" would be invited as one of the Bride's party. This links up the two miracles of the wine and the healing to the same set of characters, and prevents an unnecessarily congested cast, besides explaining how the nobleman came to hear about the Cana affair. The two places are not far apart, so the thing appears quite plausible.

3. I have inserted a bit out of the Sermon on the Mount into Scene Two. You will realise that it won't be possible to put the *whole* sermon into one play; and I believe many commentators think that the "Sermon" is to some extent an artificial collection of scattered sayings. The exhortation to faith in God seems to fit in pretty well with the general atmosphere of this play; and the bit of wayside talk allows the Disciples to be kept before the mind of the listener, and to display themselves at one of those less-inspired moments which seem to have been very frequent with them. They too, in their way, like Mary, are coming up against the human and practical results of divine missions.

4. Similarly, I have inserted the Parable of the Virgins into the Wedding Feast. It was dramatically unconvincing for Jesus to sit though the party without uttering, except to perform a miracle; so I had to choose between letting Him give one of the recorded discourses or parables, and inventing conversation for Him. The former seemed the better way, and the Virgins fitted in reasonably well, and offered something that the servants could apply to the business of the wine. I see no reason to doubt that Jesus like other Oriental preachers (indeed, most preachers!) frequently repeat-

---

1 The Most Rev. and Rt Hon. Dr William Temple (1881–1944) was Archbishop of York from 1929 to 1942 and Archbishop of Canterbury from 1942 until his death. In his *Readings in St John's Gospel*, 1939, Dr Temple had said: "[Mary] was apparently in some position of responsibility [at the wedding], as her concern about the wine and her instructions to the servants show".

2 D. L. S. said: "[Mary's] attitude to Jesus and His to her are always the great stumbling-block of this scene. I have linked this up with the episode of the Finding of Christ in the Temple, so as to show the human mother faced with the reality of what her son's personality and vocation mean in practice". (*The Man Born to be King*, "A Certain Nobleman", Notes, The Characters, Gollancz, p. 92.)

ed the same parable. If he did, this would account for the Evangelists having been able to remember and record them, for the occasional variations
in what looks like the same story (e.g. the King's Marriage and the Great
Supper, or The Talents and the Pounds) and for the reappearance of the
same story in different contexts in different Gospels.

    5. You will notice that I have followed St. John for the date of the
Cleansing of the Temple, for reasons which seem good to the Archbishop
of York[3] and to me! St. John is the only Evangelist with a really careful
chronology, and he is so convincingly right about most practical details
that he may very well be right about this. Again, I have expanded the
speech of Jesus in the Temple, and for the same reason as at the Wedding.
When one has to rely only on the ear and not on the eye, it is not impressive for an important character to come on suddenly and say only one
sentence – it doesn't carry enough weight to "get over". I have therefore
made Him recite the passage from Malachi to which the remark about
"the house of prayer" seems to refer (see Hoskyns[4] in *The Fourth Gospel*)
and have put the remark itself into His conversation with "the Jews"; leaving it to Simon to make explicit the reference to "the zeal of Thy house"
which (says St. John) the Disciples "remembered" in this connection.

    I hope you will not object to these tamperings with the text.

    For the Temple Scene I have tried a technique of "running commen-
tary", with the actual scene faded into the narration. I hope this will work
all right. To set an entirely new scene for it would have been very elaborate, and also very jerky. Done this way, it is made part of the
"Nobleman" story instead of being disconnected – and it also helps the
nobleman to get an idea of the new Prophet's importance.

    Forgive my boring you with all these technical details and explanations.
I don't want you to think that I am carving the text about irresponsibly or
carelessly. Nearly always, these things come down to some question of
dramatic structure or "theatre" presentation – the difference between the
thing narrated and the thing shown. What I am trying to do is to make of
the series as a whole, and of each item in the series, something that shall
have the quality of a play, and not simply of a Scripture lesson illustrated
by snatches of dialogue. That is why I have reduced the interventions of
"The Evangelist" to the minimum (altering the Bible phrases here and
there to provide extra information), and have cut out altogether the
"B.B.C. Narrator" giving historical, geographical and moral instruction.
This way of doing it demands a bit more alertness from the listener, to
pick up the necessary data from the dialogue; but I think it is worth it,

3 *Readings in St John's Gospel*, vol. 1, p. 42: "St John is right about it."
4 Sir Edward Clement Hoskyns, Bart., author of *The Fourth Gospel* (1940).

because it makes the thing more like drama and less like something intended to improve the minds of the young.

I do hope the treatment of Mary will not violently offend either the "Mariolaters" or the circles in which "Christian hateth Mary whom God kissed in Galilee". The position adopted by the Romans and "spikes"[5] when they present a Mary so divine that she apparently knows more about the Incarnation than her Son seems oddly inconsistent with the fact that she only appears in the Gospels three times between Bethlehem and Calvary, and each time to suffer rebuke; on the other hand, a Mary so utterly unaware of her Son's true nature as she is represented (I understand) in that American play, *Family Portrait*,[6] is irreconcilable with the Annunciation and Magnificat stories, and deeply offensive to Catholic minds. I have tried to strike a reasonable mean on the "highest human" level. The superhuman Mary is painfully undramatic – being, in fact, completely static; no character in a play can be made effective unless it experiences something in the course of the action. I shall be interested to know how this part of the play strikes your committee of all denominations – or nearly all, for the See of Peter is not represented – perhaps fortunately!

With much gratitude for all your encouragement,

Yours sincerely,

[Dorothy L. Sayers]

---

5 Anglo-Catholic clergy.
6 *A Family Portrait*, by Lenore Coffee and William Joyce Cowen, a 3-act drama, published in 1939 in *The Best Plays of 1938–39*, edited by B. Mantle.

24 Newland Street
Witham
Essex

TO HER SON

1 October 1941

Dear John,

Thank you for several letters – also an elegant birthday sonnet, which I find with distress I omitted to acknowledge before.

I think it is an excellent idea that you should try for a job or something non-academic in January, if Mr. Cosgrove and Co. think you have come

to the end of your furrow at Malvern. (Some Freudian complex prompted me to write "Marlborough" – effect of reading Winston Churchill, no
doubt!)

The whole question of the University becomes extremely complicated
in war-time. When things are normal, there is always a difference of opinion whether it is best to know a little of the world before going up, or to
ease one's self into the world though the 'Varsity gates. In war-time this
becomes acute.

In peace-time I believe it is best on the whole to take the academic part
first and get it over; because the University is wider than the school, but
much narrower than the world – so that a schoolboy going up there finds
himself liberated, whereas, if he comes back into it from outside he is apt
to feel it all very cramped and unreal.

But during a war, the unreality of college life can't help striking anybody. Last war, of course, it was specially unsatisfactory, because all the
young men were called up, and there was nobody there but the halt, the
lame and the blind, and the conchies[1] and people with something funny
about them. This isn't so this time. On the other hand, one goes there,
and in spite of the incessant noise of 'planes and the awful crowding of
evacuees and Govt. depts. and so on, one really wonders whether the
Senior Common Rooms have grasped the facts of life at all. (Especially at
Oxford; Cambridge is better, having had a bomb or two.) The place is full
of ardent young theorists among the undergraduates – but whether they
wouldn't theorize more usefully with a little experience to help them I
rather doubt.

There is, however, one thing you will have to bear in mind: namely, that
having once escaped from academics you may not want to go back there
at all! One year in a job may make you feel you couldn't stand Oxford at
any price, and that the other undergraduates would by that time be too
young for you. If you do feel like that, it may not matter much. During
the next few years, academic degrees will be less than ever a passport to
jobs – unless they are degrees in maths. and science, which seem not to be
your line. The other important thing is going to be languages, and some
sort of knowledge of how the minds of foreigners work – a thing which
nobody ever learns in the universities. There's going to be a devil of a lot
of cleaning-up to be done in Europe, when all this is over.

It would be easier if one knew how long the War is likely to last. I think
it will probably go on for some time, though of course I may be quite
wrong. But Churchill seems to think so, and to be making his plans to that
end, and he's usually right. If Russia can stick it out this winter, she will

---

1 Conscientious objectors.

probably stick it out till we are ready for a big offensive – and that may not be very soon. Or, of course, Hitler may collect himself for a big offensive on us in the Spring – and if so, it will really have to be all hands to the pumps; in which case you would probably find the University quite intolerable.

If I were in your place, I think I should be looking for something in the way of the technical side of air warfare or radio – where the maths might be of use and one's colleagues fairly intelligent. They seem to want any number of young men for that part of the game, and I know they are an intelligent lot, because I've met them. Also, you would be in contact with the really intelligent British mechanic, who is a person worth knowing. And it would be something real.

Nobody loves the Universities more than I do – but a war-time Oxford isn't the real Oxford, and that's what's wrong with it. It's neither flesh, fowl, nor good red herring. I know, because I had a war year of it last time. It had neither its own virtues nor the virtues of the world.

So my own feeling on the whole is: leave school if you've done all you can do there, and for preference, take whatever chance the war offers, leaving Academia to look after itself. If the war is over in a year – but I don't think it will be. And indeed, I believe we may have to arrange our lives for the next fifty years or so on the basis that wars are normal and peace the abnormality, instead of the other way round. This shocks the 19th-century Liberal Humanist, who forgets that, until the end of the Victorian era, this was the ordinary way of looking at things. It's only the "gospel of human perfectibility" that has got us into the way of being perpetually "taken by surprise", like Mr. Chamberlain's government, at the appearance of human perversities which all Christendom had previously taken for granted.

My own opinion about the Universities is that people now go to them either too late (the Elizabethans got them over and done with by the time they were sixteen, and were then ready for their responsibilities) or too early. If they were made places for serious scholarship, and *nobody* went up till they were well over twenty, then the play-boys would be weeded out, and the genuine seekers after knowledge would be able to make the whole thing a much more mature and responsible business. But that's only my opinion; and if I had my way I'd sweep all the people who merely want to qualify for a job into the provincial universities (which work on a much more general, "school" sort of curriculum), abolish the pass men at Oxf. and Camb:, and use them for the people who really wanted *learning* – for whom they would then have ample room – and who could come up when they already knew something about life. However, nobody is likely to take my suggestion in good part!

Bridgeheads are struggling against (a) the difficulty of finding people who

will undertake to write books and *get them finished* (b) the difficulty of getting any book printed and bound in view of the paper shortage. But we
toddle along and hope for the best.
    Love,
        D. L. F.

[24 Newland Street
Witham
Essex]

TO V. A. DEMANT
2 October 1941

Dear Father Demant...
    As you were so kind about *The Mind of the Maker*, you will be pleased to
know that it is selling well and steadily, and that the publisher has not only
put the third edition[1] in hand, but with a quiet Victorian pertinacity is
actually setting the fourth in hand! The Romans seem to have taken a
great fancy to it – the *Universe* emitting the usual dark mumble about hoping to see me follow G. K. C. into the arms of Mother Church. I have no
doubt it is their job to say these things, but I do dislike being made to feel
like a rabbit exposed to the slow fascination of a waiting serpent.
    Yours very sincerely,
        [Dorothy L. Sayers]

1 Actually the third impression.

[24 Newland Street
Witham
Essex]

TO COUNT MICHAEL DE LA BEDOYERE[1]
The Catholic Herald
7 October 1941

My dear Count,
    I ought to have written to you long ago about *Christian Crisis*,[2] which you
were kind enough to send me. The fact is that, owing to a series of acci-

1 Count Michael de la Bedoyère (1900–1973), editor of *The Catholic Herald*. He questioned the
  morality of area bombing and the propriety of demanding unconditional surrender.
2 Published in 1941 by Burns, Oates and Washbourne.

dents, my reading of it was interrupted, and it got laid aside until, a short time ago, I was able to take it up again and re-read it properly.

I don't know how your critique of the Roman position has been received by those to whom it is more particularly addressed, but from my (that is, the Anglo-Catholic) point of view it is most valuable, both as a means of clearing one's mind and also as a means of dealing with outside criticism. Only the other day, when writing to Fr. D'Arcy,[3] I mentioned the very odd sort of difficulties which confront an Anglican free-lance, who is often found in the peculiar position of having to defend Rome with one hand and Canterbury with the other against attacks upon [what] I may perhaps without offence call the combined Catholic front. The enemy has a nasty way of trying to turn the doctrinal flank – not only with what Fr. D'Arcy calls "Pope Joan" arguments (including such hoary monsters as Maria Monk, the Spanish Inquisition, Pope Alexander Borgia, and the Winking Virgin of What d'ye call it, together with the most surprising versions – or perversions – of the cult of Our Lady, the operation of the sacraments, and the pronouncement *nulla salus extra ecclesiam*)[4] – all of which one knows more or less how to deal with – but also with more awkward criticisms about recent Vatican policy and the behaviour of the Catholic countries in the present crisis. The difficulty in coping with all these lies is knowing how much to say and how far to go. To say that all criticism is unfounded would be absurd; to "knock" Rome would be neither charitable nor politic; while to offer apologia, apology, or explanation for another communion along lines which its own members would dislike or repudiate would be a most unfortunate blunder. For this reason, if for no other, I personally welcome your book, which I shall take every opportunity of recommending to those who want to know the Church's own mind in the matter.

Quite apart from this, there are two points which I find particularly interesting and an encouragement towards getting something practical done.

The less important, I suppose, though the most personally urgent to me, is the passage on p. 163[5] which deals with the Catholic attitude to the

---

3 Father Martin Cyril D'Arcy, S.J. (1888–1976), Master of Campion Hall, Oxford, 1933–1945; author of *The Nature of Belief*, 1931.

4 Latin: no salvation outside the church.

5 The passage of special interest to her contained such statements as: "I have said that the lack of a unified Christian culture …is one of the chief defects of Catholic education….We have almost reached the stage in Catholic public opinion when nothing is regarded as Catholic unless a religious or pious or apologetic label can be attached to it. The Catholic scientist, working in his field of research, the Catholic novelist, engaged in the study of contemporary life as it is, the Catholic artist, following his natural inspiration, to none of these is the name of Catholic publicly given…" (See chapter 4, "Where British Catholics Fail".)

arts and sciences – and in fact the whole of that chapter. As you may have
gathered from *The Mind of the Maker* and also from *The Zeal of Thy House*,
I feel strongly and indeed violently about this. Neither in my own Church
nor in yours can I find any general understanding of the facts that the
Christian artist (or other "maker") must serve God *in his vocation*, which is
just as truly his vocation as though he were called to be a priest; that if his
work is not true to itself it cannot be true to God or anything else; and
that bad art is bad Christianity, however much it may be directed to
edification, or adorned with emasculated Christs, spineless virgins and
cotton-wool angels uttering pious sentimentalities; and further, that to
take novelists and playwrights away from doing good work in their own
line (whether secular or devotional in content) and collar them for the
purpose of preaching sermons or opening Church bazaars is a spoiling of
God's instrument and defeats its own aims in the end. It's no good asking
the artist how he knows that he is "called" to write novels rather than
address meetings, and flattering him by saying that he addresses meetings
so well and does such a lot of good. How does a chisel know that it isn't
"called" to be a screwdriver? – though you can, no doubt use it quite
effectively for that purpose – if you don't mind it's presently going bust!
What is so maddening is the bland refusal to allow that God can take any
interest in a secular job *as such* – as though He only sat up and took notice
if He heard His own name mentioned in it. That point of view would be
natural from a Genevan "utter-depravitist"[6], but from Catholics it's
preposterous. One result of all this is a total lack of any sort of Christian
critical standard in the arts: whereby the Church is made to look an
ignoramus, and a philistine, and a fool. No writer seems to have tackled
this subject seriously – except perhaps our Brother George Every of the
S.S.M.[7] in that C.N.L.[8] booklet – and he's got T. E. Hulme[9] on the brain,
I think, with his hatred of "realistic", or what Hulme calls "vital" art.
(This is the Puritan, Barthian, not to say Manichee, fear of the secular
again – a natural revolt from humanism, but surely quite unsacramental.)
Besides, Brother Every doesn't really know enough about the arts and
generalises quite wildly. I tell him that the business of the ecclesiastics is
to teach the artist an intellectual Catholic dogma, soak it well into him,
and then, when he's properly saturated, leave him to get on with his
job in his own way. (Unfortunately, George Every doesn't much like the
general theological tone of my work, and this rather cramps my style –

6 Reference to the Calvinist doctrine of "total depravity".
7 Society of the Sacred Mission (Kelham Hall, Nottinghamshire).
8 *Christian News-Letter.*
9 Thomas Edward Hulme (1883–1917), poet, essayist and writer on philosophical subjects. His
   works were edited by Herbert Read in two volumes: *Speculations* (1924) and *Notes on Language
   and Style* (1929). His theories of Imagism influenced poetry and the visual arts.

especially as I cannot by any means discover what his objection is.)
However, he has tried to do something about this business of the
Church and the Arts, which is greatly to his credit. I harangued the
Malvern Conference insistently on this point – of the artist's "autonomy
of technique" – the only result being that the Bishop of Chichester tod-
dled amiably onto the platform and said: "And I do agree with Miss
Sayers that the Church must manage to get hold of the Arts again". – Oh,
dear! The C. of E.[10] does suffer a great deal from her bishops.[11] Mercifully
we don't have to take them quite so seriously as you do; still, some of them
are a great and sore trial, however well-meaning.

The second point really is important. You say only too truly that it
is hopeless to base any action on the lowest common denominator of
agreement. But I am coming to think that a great deal might be done if
we could among us contrive to formulate a "Highest Common Factor of
Consent" about doctrine; and I believe that that factor would be higher
than is generally supposed.[11] One can't, of course, hope to include in the
"Church universal" the very numerous people who call themselves
Christians without believing that Christ was fully God. They are not
really "Christians" at all – a friend suggests that "Jesuists" would be a
better name for them. But, disregarding their protests, what I've usually
tried to put before the general public is the body of what I feel able to call
"Oecumenical Doctrine" – that is, the content of the Creeds, interpreted
in a way that would be acceptable to Roman, Anglican, and (so far as I
know anything about them) Greek-Orthodox Christians – leaving out
those points on which those bodies differ. This amounts, roughly
speaking, to the doctrines accepted and defined at the Four Great
Councils.[12] In practice, I find that this substantial body of doctrine also
commands the assent of a great number of Free Church theologians; and
I have been surprised to find, in reading Dr. J. S. Whale's book *Christian
Doctrine*,[13] how far a Congregational theologian is ready to go along

10 Church of England.
11 Cf. her letter dated 28 November 1941.
12 Nicaea (325), Constantinople (381), Ephesus (431) and Chalcedon (451). These were all oecumenical councils, accepted by both Eastern and Western Churches.
13 J. S. Whale, D.D., *Christian Doctrine: Eight Lectures Delivered in the University of Cambridge to
Undergraduates of all Faculties* (Cambridge University Press, 1941, 2nd edition 1956). It was
reviewed by D. L. S. in *The International Review of Missions*, in which she said: "Dr Whale's
book is extremely welcome, both as an assistance to those who need, for themselves or others, a comprehensive and coherent exposition of Christian doctrine that is at once brief, profound and adapted to the adult mind; and also as affording ocular proof of essential doctrinal agreement among the churches. Moreover, it is written in a vigorous and pithy style...Of
its trenchant and memorable phrases there is room to quote only two: 'Belief in God is an
absolute presupposition of all rational enquiry.' 'The obligation to be intelligent is always a
moral obligation'."

"oecumenical" lines. In places, of course, (especially as regards the Catholic-Apostolic Church, Sacraments, and the Four Last Things)[14] his exposition seems rather incomplete, but there is very little in it that anybody could actively object to.

It does seem to me that it ought to be possible for the Churches to say plainly: "These things, at any rate, we all believe"; and if the British public, and their children, could be made to understand *at least that much* of Christian dogma as a coherent theology, they would be very much better placed than they are now (a) to understand what it is all about and (b) to unite themselves intelligently to some communion or other. At present, a shocking number of them are completely ignorant that there is any rational Christian theology or philosophy, or that there is any substantial agreement whatever among Christian bodies – other than a vaguely humanist assent to the Sermon on the Mount, adorned with various horrifying scraps of mythology, ranging inconsistently from Baby-worship to savage blood-sacrifices.

I haven't got a pastoral mind or a passion to convert people; but I hate having my intellect outraged by imbecile ignorance and by the monstrous distortions of *fact* which the average heathen accepts as being "Christianity" (and from which he most naturally revolts). And it does seem to me that, in the present state of confusion, the mere assimilation of the *basic dogma* would offer sufficient exercise for the mental teeth and stomachs of people; and further, that it would be helpful if writers and speakers and broadcasters would concentrate on those facts, and if they were able to say: "It doesn't matter where you go – ask the Pope, ask the Patriarch, ask the Archbishop of Canterbury, ask the Moderator of the Free Church Council – they will all say the same thing about this bunch of dogma." (I admit the obvious diplomatic difficulty of extracting anything definite from Cosmo Cantuar,[15] or of coaxing the Pope and Patriarch onto one platform – but there! the Barren Leafy Tree's very reasonable excuse that "this was not the time for figs"[16] was held to be unacceptable, and there do seem to be moments when one must perform the impossible or perish!)

I don't know why I am badgering you about all this, or what I expect you to do about it; but reading your book and Dr. Whale's together, I am struck by the idea that in violently assaulting one another's positions we are half the time battering at open doors, to the extreme scandal of a cynical and astonished world. I entirely agree that it is all wrong to try and

14 Death, Judgment, Heaven and Hell.
15 William Cosmo Gordon Lang (1864–1945), Archbishop of Canterbury from 1928 to 1942.
16 Mark, chapter 11, verse 13. The wording in the Authorized Version is: "for it was not the time for figs".

compromise on dogma; but if we in fact agree about seven-tenths of the dogma, why the blazes shouldn't we say so? If you say that the infallibility of the Pope follows logically on the Incarnation and I say it doesn't, all right, that's an argument; but until you and I have together hammered the Incarnation into the head of the heathen, he's not in a position to appreciate what the argument is, still less to take sides about it; and he's much more likely to get properly hammered if we all concentrate on that job like navvies driving a pile and get him from all sides in rhythm, so to speak. At any rate, we're much more likely to get him that way than by a "lowest common denominator" of saying, in the liberal-humanist way, that at any rate all Christians agree that we should "believe in God and follow Christ in the spirit of love" – which means almost exactly nothing, but is what most of the people who write to *The Times* about religious education seem to think a suitable basis for instruction.

It seems to me, too, that a sort of "H.C.F. of Consent" might be produced with regard to "world-reconstruction on Christian lines" – this emerges from your page 19.[17] I mean that we might attempt to sort out and put down in a form generally accessible how much in Nationalism, Dawnism,[18] Socialism, Fascism, etc, is consistent with Christianity, and try to arrange it so as to make sense. You may say the Pope and people have done this already: no doubt they have but not quite in that form. It has usually been a sort of, "All these other things are wrong and you've got to get back to the Church, which says so-and-so" – which is O.K. from the negative side, but makes these people think their most passionate beliefs are unsympathetically received. Surely it would be possible to say somehow: "What's wrong with all these things is simply that they have been defined separately. But we agree with Fascists that it is right to acknowledge values which are not merely cash-values, and with the Nationalists that patriotism is a true value, and with the Socialists about the importance of the community, and with the 'Dawnists' about the importance of the individual man in his body-soul, and with the Fascists about the importance of people's secular jobs in the body politic, and even with the Capitalists that there is virtue in a reasonable measure of private property, and with the 'State-ists' that the secular power is to be respected – so that in a Christian society all those people would in fact discover their 'H.C.F. of consent'." If we could possibly make some statement of that kind, and *relate it to the H.C.F. of consent in dogma* at every point – wouldn't it bear some appearance of being rational and

17 In chapter 2, "Christianity and the Last War", referring to the failure of the settlement after World War I.
18 The belief that the use of reason would usher in the dawn of a new age. Widespread in the eighteenth century, it became associated ultimately with nationalism and dictatorship. See Bedoyère, *Christian Crisis*, chapters 4, 5 and 6.

attractive? And if all the Churches would so to speak, put their names to it, it would be rather impressive – also, we could say the same thing both at home and abroad, without having to scratch our heads each time to remember whether [those] in the Balkans were Orthodox or Uniates[19] or Lutherans, or disliked the Vatican or had never heard of the Archbishop of Canterbury, because the name of their own head bloke would be there to assure them that it was O.K. by him.

But I dare say I'm only twaddling; and the minute one tries to put anything down in black and white it always sounds exactly like what has already been done by somebody and fallen as flat as a pancake. All the same, I rather stick to that phrase, "The Highest Common Factor of Consent" as a sort of guiding principle, to suggest, not that we should jettison as much as possible in order to keep afloat, but earnestly see how much stuff we can possibly squeeze into the lifeboat in order that we may survive – because there's no point in just floating if we're all starved to death at the end of the voyage.

It's frightful of me to have gone on at such length. I hope you will forgive me, and put it down to my having liked your book very much. And let me take the opportunity of thanking you for your exceedingly kind reception of *The Mind of the Maker*. I am much relieved to find that the more "Catholic" the critic, the better he likes the book – "Catholic" including a bunch of Greek-Orthodox people, who seemed delighted to find that it had all been said by various Greek Fathers in the year dot. This is certainly a "H.C.F. of Consent", for I have never read a word of the Greek Fathers! The only people whom it seems to worry are the vague Protestants, (who are always given to mumbling about "danger" and "presumption", as though God might come to pieces if you pulled Him about to see what He was made of) and a few of the heathen, who think that God ought to know His place and keep Himself to Himself and not go poking His head into the kitchen.

Yours apologetically,
    [Dorothy L. Sayers]

---

19 Uniat(e), a Russian, Polish or other member of the part of the Greek Orthodox Church which, retaining its own liturgy, acknowledges the Pope's supremacy.

[24 Newland Street
Witham
Essex]

TO THE REV. GEOFFREY L. TREGLOWN

22 Milton Avenue,
Romford
9 October 1941

Dear Mr. Treglown,

As you will see by my address I live not very far from you, though there is the disadvantage that very few Witham trains ever seem to stop at Romford, and I have no car.

Just at present I am very full up with work and engagements, but possibly by April the pressure will have slackened. I don't think I could face preaching on Sunday evening, but I might manage the meeting on Monday afternoon, April 20th, if that would suit you as well. I will try not to be "tiresome and irrelevant"; I think that is perhaps a weakness of politicians rather than of women as such!

I am interested, as well as pleased, to learn that you find my theology sound, because as you probably know I am an Anglo-Catholic, and it is being borne in upon me that the theological differences between the various communions are much less acute than one might imagine, at any rate, as far as fundamentals are concerned. At present I am spending my time urging Christians of the leading denominations to pull their socks up and get out a statement on doctrine on which everybody, from the Pope to the Moderator of the Free Church Council, can agree to agree. It seems to me that this would have a good effect, besides saving lay people like me a good deal of unnecessary time and labour in telling the heathen what Christian doctrine is.

Yours sincerely,
[Dorothy L. Sayers]

24 Newland Street
Witham
Essex

16 October 1941

Dear Mr Eliot,

I was delighted to get your letter yesterday, making an offer for *Common or Garden Child.*[1] Miss Byrne is at Cambridge, but I rang her up last night, and she rejoiced greatly, expressing herself as very well content with the terms, very glad that you proposed to publish at a moderate price[2], and particularly pleased that Faber should be the publishers. However, she is writing to you herself today, so I will now get out from under your feet and leave her to treat with you directly.

I am personally very glad you like the work, because I like it myself very much, and I also know that it will be a great encouragement to her to have it taken. Also, I must again thank you for having been so kind when I accosted you, so to speak, on the tooth-snatcher's very doorstep.[3] I do hope that his odious ministrations have done all that was expected of him and that you are now really feeling a lot better. The world is quite tiresome enough, even if one is in the best of health and spirits. I really see no reason why the war should not go on for ever – at least, no cheerful reason. I suppose a complete Hitler victory might stop it, but I'm not even sure about that! Perhaps we should make up our minds to accept war as a natural state of things and adapt ourselves to it. Poets and story-tellers, facing a perpetual paper-shortage, will have to re-learn the art of recitation; and we must firmly refuse to be surprised at the phenomenon of sudden death, or the absence of bananas.[4] I am rather glad to be relieved of bananas – they taste of nail-polish, and I can't imagine why we ever spent money on them.

With all good wishes and most sincere thanks,
     yours very sincerely,
     Dorothy L. Sayers.

---

1 Muriel St Clare Byrne's memoir of her childhood was published in 1942.
2 Seven shillings and sixpence.
3 They appear to have met at the dentist's.
4 Cf. her poem, "Lord I thank thee…", first published in 1942: "I detest bananas,\ A smug fruit, designed to be eaten in railway carriages\ On Bank Holidays,\ With a complexion like yellow wax\ And a texture like new putty\ Flavoured with nail polish." (See *Poetry of Dorothy L. Sayers,* ed. Ralph E. Hone, ed.cit. 1996, pp. 123–128.)

[24 Newland Street
Witham
Essex]

TO THE REV. DOM. R. RUSSELL

Downside Abbey
28 October 1941

Dear Father Russell,

Mrs. Mitchell has kindly forwarded to me your most generous review
of *The Mind of the Maker*. I am very glad indeed that it has pleased you, as
well as other Catholic theologians, who have treated it in a very friendly
way. Anybody who rushes in on theological ground without any sort of
technical training naturally lays himself open to the severest criticism, and
ought to be only too grateful if the experts refrain from tearing him into
fragments and dancing derisively on the remains. But everybody has been
most indulgent. (Even the Protestants seem more apprehensive than
angry – but then they *will* treat God as an elderly invalid who might collapse from shock if suddenly intruded on by a common person bouncing
in suddenly.)

Perhaps I ought to say something about your censures. I entirely agree
that "Bigamy is a crime" – that is precisely what it is, for us – though not
for Abraham, Isaac and Jacob. *Luxuria* is on the other hand, always a sin
– though either may occur without the other. (Thus, bigamy committed
in ignorance is still a crime, and lust, though it leads to nothing illegal, is
still a sin.) But the point I was making was that the *criminality* of anything
depends upon the consent of opinion; its *sinfulness* is an entirely different
matter.

It should be fairly clear, I think, from the book as a whole that all three
persons of the Trinity are *essentially* concerned in creation. My emphasis
on the particular function of the Son is due to the fact that surprisingly
few people realise that the Son is supposed to have anything to do with *the*
Creation at all. The prevalent idea is that God the Father made the world
(with perhaps a little assistance from the Spirit of God, since He is
mentioned in Genesis as "brooding" over the business), but that the Son,
the Logos, the Energy, took no part in the job at all, and apparently took
no interest in it except to redeem it when it had gone wrong.... The
majority of Protestants are, in their hearts, Adoptionists[1], or Arians[2] at the
best, and the common-or-garden heathen has no more idea than the man
in the moon that the Son is supposed to have had any existence prior to
the appearance of Jesus on earth. Consequently, the very idea that *the same*

---

1 See letter to the Rev. Neville Gorton, 24 September 1941, note 5.
2 See letter to Father Herbert Kelly, 4 October 1937, note 2.

God who made the world also suffered in the world is to the ordinary man an entirely alien notion, and if you try to tell him that this is what is meant, he thinks you are making it up. No language, however strong, violent, or emphatic will expunge from the mind of the average anti-Christian the picture he has formed of Christian Soteriology,[3] viz: that Jehovah (the old man with the beard) made the world and made it so badly that it all went wrong and he wanted to burn it up in a rage; whereat the Son (who was younger and nicer, and not implicated in his Father's irresponsible experiment) said: "Oh, don't do that! if you must torment somebody, take it out [on] me." So Jehovah vented his sadistic appetite on a victim who had nothing to do with it all, and thereafter grudgingly allowed people to go to heaven if they provided themselves with a ticket of admission signed by the Son . . . . This grotesque mythology is not in the least exaggerated: *it is what they think we mean* – consequently the whole Incarnation doctrine is for them completely meaningless. I say, "the average anti-Christian"; I don't say "the average un-Christian". One man, for instance, wrote to me that the idea that the God who suffered and the God who created were the same God was to him a complete novelty, which if it were really what Christians believed, would clear up a whole area of what had been Stygian[4] obscurity. Might he say that God the Father suffered? I said that, strictly speaking, he might not – that was Patripassianism,[5] and would land him in difficulties later on; but that even Patripassianism was a distinct improvement on the barbaric superstitions which he had had presented to him as the Christian religion, and that he might certainly say that the Creator suffered . . . . I don't know what happened to him after this; he was a naval officer, and I am afraid he may have been a casualty, as he promised to keep in touch, but has not done so....

I didn't set out to "defend my thesis", but only to show that I had, at any rate, paid attention to those parts of your review which were less favourable. My original and chief intention was to thank you for having given my odd theological adventure so kind and serious an attention. In particular, too, for your resolute support in refusing to regard the book as a "personal angle on God". I am weary of this evil and adulterous generation, with its monstrous deification of insignificant personalities. If a thing is not true in itself, the fact that I say it will not make it any truer; nor is it any addition to God that a popular novelist should be so obliging as to approve of Him. Since the book deals with creative art, it is a rele-

---

3 The doctrine of salvation.

4 From the river Styx, one of the rivers of Hades in classical mythology, meaning dark, obscure.

5 See letter to Father Herbert Kelly, 4 October 1937, note 5

vant fact that I am a professional writer; it might also be relevant that I am a Master of Arts and former scholar of Oxford University – since this would tell the reader what standard of judgment to expect. But the publisher thought it would be unwise to mention this fact – the public might, I suppose, be alienated by any suggestion that the writer is educated or qualified for his job. "The name is enough" – and of that fact I am still scholar enough to be ashamed.

I am sorry to conclude on this gloomy note! But what fun it would be if all books were compelled by law to appear anonymously for the next twenty years or so! There would be such a bonfire of reputations.

Yours with much gratitude,

[Dorothy L. Sayers]

[24 Newland Street
Witham
Essex]

TO MURIEL ST CLARE BYRNE

16 November 1941

Dearest M...

The other day I went to speak to some soldiers about Detective Fiction, at a camp near Harwich. Driven there by a very nice girl who has to do with the Entertainments Committee. All very good going; but on the way back, the car conked out completely in a desert-looking place in the pitch dark. Garage turned out to be fortunately near. Garage man happily a pet – but, less fortunately, an enthusiast. He put the thing partially right (the girl so ignorant that she didn't even know a sparking-plug when she saw it: "are those the long things on wires?"). We started again, but were unhappily inspired to stop and ask the way, whereupon the engine conked out again in a place still more dark and deserted. Meanwhile, the enthusiast had had his doubts about us and pursued us in a car; which was nice of him. But such was his enthusiasm that he could not be persuaded to leave the ruddy car alone and run us home in his. He proceeded to take the engine to pieces by torchlight. This game went on till about 11.30 (nobody having had dinner). The car, having had its plugs changed and been given dope to clean its valves, grew more and more sulky and nervous. Then he proceeded to take down the carburettor, clean the jets, and hint darkly that the petrol was full of sand and paraffin. The car began to

show signs of collapse; and was stimulated by having the mag[neto] taken
to pieces and the points reset. Happily, this was too much for the poor
creature, who, having suffered many things of this particular physician,
gave a hollow groan and rendered up the ghost. So the enthusiast had to
drive us back after all; and it turned out he was the local comic man and
dance-band enthusiast, so all the way back he enlivened us with items
from his repertoire. I reached home at 12.40, very cold and empty. Mac
said I had been on the binge with the soldiers, and that I was drunk and
a liar. So I threw my boots at him and so to bed![1]

In the midst of all this agitation, I have finished the fifth play.[2] They are
coming out fairly well, but not one bit Children's-Hour. Judas is shaping
rather nicely, I think; and Matthew is a poppet. He is *so* common and so
sweet. Dr. Welch is deeply in love with Matthew. Eric Fenn apparently had
a qualm, because he didn't like to think that a gospel should be named
after a person so vulgar and illiterate, and began mumbling about the
"Fragment of Papias".[3] Dr. Welch, however, said strong-mindedly, "Never
mind that qualm, old boy! Matthew is a real live person". I said (over the
'phone to Welch) that I thought it was rather rubbish to say that a person
couldn't have a Gospel named after him on account of his commonness
– and that anyhow Matthew was a tax-collector, and they were the lowest
of the low – like rotten little Vichy officials putting the screw on their own
countrymen for the benefit of the Nazis – and one couldn't get over that,
could one? I think Val will like Matthew; he will be a nice change from
the dignified and refined stage-peasant who always haunts religious plays.[4]
Matthew comes into the fourth play mostly, but I've managed to squeeze
a little fun out of him in the fifth. He is a landsman (he would be, of
course) and doesn't at all like being in a storm on the Lake of Galilee, with
water sloshing into the boat and people walking on the water at him, poor
lamb! I am getting quite fond of the disciples. And, by the way, I have the
feeling of "guessing right" about Judas, because the things seem to be fitting in – you know how they do. The only thing that still bothers me is the
thirty pieces of silver. They bother everybody. But I daresay it will all
come out in the wash....

    Yours rather irritable but still going strong,
      With love,
        D. L. S.

1 An echo of the Diary of Samuel Pepys, who ended several of his entries: "I threw my boots
  at her [his wife] and so to bed".
2 "The Bread of Heaven".
3 Papias (c. 60–130), Bishop of Hierapolis, credited with fragments on the origin of the Gospel
  of St Matthew by Irenaeus and Eusebius.
4 The dialogue between Matthew and Philip in Scene 1 of the fourth play, "The Heirs to the
  Kingdom", was read aloud to journalists at the press conference on 10 December. Reported
  sensationally, it caused an uproar.

[24 Newland Street
Witham
Essex]

TO MAURICE B. RECKITT

19 November 1941

Dear Mr Reckitt,

Many thanks for your letter and for the proofs of Miss Byrne's article.[1]

The origin of the latter was really that I mentioned to Fr McLaughlin (on the way to Malvern) that Miss Byrne felt very strongly that unless, in the various plans for a Christian Social Order, the Church was ready to face the difficulty about the status of women, there would be no chance of any real improvement, since the continued existence of an exploited class exploiting the exploiters would hamper any efforts towards a stable economic situation. In consequence of this, Fr McLaughlin suggested that she should contibute something towards the forthcoming discussion in *Christendom*. Unhappily, when the first articles on the subject appeared, it was clear that, while Miss Kenyon had not, perhaps, precisely shirked the issue, she had so framed the question as to allow of its being shirked. Worse still, both Peck and Casserley – particularly the latter – had profited by this loophole to introduce both the revolting vulgarities and the factual inaccuracies that usually disfigure these discussions.

One really cannot allow such things to pass, lest one should seem to admit them by default.

There is, of course, every reason to distinguish what are, properly speaking, "feminine functions". The fundamental assumption, however, that has to be attacked is the unexamined dogma that this functionalism extends to the *whole of life*, and that they are the most important disjunction of human activities. For example: the domestic function of a cat, quâ cat, is to catch mice; the question whether a tom or a moggy should be employed for this purpose rests on no distinction of ability in that vocation, but on the individual preference for kittens or smells about the house. Indeed, this particular vocation can quite well be exercised by a neuter (a solution of the problem against which there is a prejudice in the case of humanity). The tom is not held to be "aping" the moggy or the moggy the tom, when either carries out the common feline function of hunting.

The thing that is intolerable is the assumption that woman's preoccupation with sex extends to all her activities, and that, when performing any common task (whether agreeable or disagreeable) which is not demonstrably determined by sex, she is "trying to beat the men at their own game". In actual practice, when the fitness of a woman for a partic-

1 See letter to Maurice B. Reckitt, 12 July 1941 and note 8.

ular job of work has been established for a long enough time, and when that job is a thing which the workers themselves take seriously, it is never judged by the sex of the worker, but by the standard of accomplishment. For instance, nobody, I am happy to say, has reviewed *The Mind of the Maker* as a "feminine angle on God": though if the book had been written 100 years ago, nothing but a male pseudonym would have saved it from such treatment.

The vote, as you say, was merely a symbol. Of itself it can do nothing while the minds of both men and women are clouded by the obsession of sexuality. The letter killeth; the spirit giveth life. But it is something to have even the letter of the law, since it provides a framework within which the spirit can work.

That women are not satisfied with their present "emancipation" [I] readily admit – how could they be, when the letter of it is continually traversed by a spirit which does all it can to make their status as uncomfortable as possible?

The present uproar about the calling-up of women is typical. When the war began, eager women were told to go away and play: the men must be absorbed first. Now, women are wanted: but they are not conscripted on a common human basis, with a promise of hard work and adequate pay. All they get is sloppy "appeals" and low wages....[2] Why should they be treated like that? I am not treated like that by my publishers, who take my work seriously. My sex does not exonerate me from necessary labours, nor does it debar me from proper remuneration; consequently, I do what has to be done and do it with reasonable readiness.

But do not tell me that things are not better today than they were. I remember my father's sisters, brought up without education or training, thrown, at my grandfather's death, into a world that had no use for them. One, by my father's charity, was trained as a nurse; one, by wangling, was received into the only sisterhood that would take her at her age – an ill-run community, but her only refuge; the third, the most attractive[3], lived peripatetically as a "companion" to various old cats, saving halfpence and cadging trifles, aimlessly doing what when done was of little value to God or man. From all such frustrate unhappiness, God keep us. Let us be able to write "hoc feci"[4] on our tombstones, even if all we have done is to clean the 29 floors of the International Stores.

Yours very sincerely,

[Dorothy L. Sayers]

2 She refers here to a letter in *The Times* of 17 November 1941, signed by Katharine Furse, who wrote: "...women have been called on mainly to fill gaps, but not to take a lead in responsibility"...

3 The sisters mentioned are Edith (1859–1917), a nurse: Anne (1858–1948), joined Community of St Katherine of Alexandria: Gertrude (1860–1931).

4 Latin: this I did.

[24 Newland Street
Witham
Essex]

TO THE ARCHBISHOP OF YORK[1]

24 November 1941

Your Grace,

I am afraid I had already written to Miss Carcaud to cry off the Brains Trust idea. I probably said I was very busy, which is quite true.

But also, I have to admit that I am not fearfully fond of Brains Trusts. The way in which the B.B.C. is running their show has made me shy off the thing. They seem to be giving people the idea that art and learning are a kind of parlour game, in which the fun is to shoot questions at well-known "authorities" on these subjects, in the hope of catching them out. The result is, especially in the lamentable case of Professor Joad,[2] that quick wits and superficiality ring the bell every time, whereas the sounder people, who never advance any statement without verifying their references, are put at a great disadvantage. This seems to me a pity, because people are already sufficiently inclined to despise facts and authority, and to prefer snap judgment[s] and personal opinions. I am a fairly good examination candidate myself, and this probably inclines me all the more to distrust this particular game, since I know, only too well, through having been constantly judged above my merits during my scholastic career, how unreliable a game it is.

Consequently, I really should very much prefer not to take part in a Brains Trust if you will not think me too tiresome, and obstructive – greatly as in some ways, I should enjoy the fun. I ought also to add that the plays I am doing for the B.B.C. are going to keep me pretty busy up to Easter, what with writing them and going up to London for rehearsals, and so forth; so that a good deal would depend on the proposed date, even if my constitutional shrinking from the game itself could be overcome.

Trusting that you will understand my reluctance,

Yours sincerely,

[Dorothy L. Sayers]

1 The Most Revd Dr William Temple.
2 See letter to Dr James Welch, 2 January 1941, note 5.

[24 Newland Street
Witham
Essex]

TO MISS AMY DAVIES[1]

26 November 1941

Dear Miss Davies,

It is curious and interesting that you should have been first "interested and thrilled" by *The Mind of the Maker* and afterwards startled by the unintelligibility of "The Greatest Drama Ever Staged", because that is rather like being charmed by the Differential Calculus and disconcerted by the Multiplication Table. Because the one, in each case, presupposes the other; and if the doctrine summarized in "The Greatest Drama Ever Staged" is not true, *The Mind of the Maker* is meaningless nonsense.

I'm afraid it would take too long to answer all your questions fully. But I may try to clear up a few misconceptions.

First of all, you seem surprised that "The Greatest Drama" should contain "all the old arguments". Actually, it contains no "arguments"; it is merely concerned to state, in the simplest possible language, what it is that the Church asserts about Christ. Naturally, the statements are the "old" statements. A primer of Arithmetic, whether written by some one as ancient as Euclid or as modern as Einstein, will still contain the same old stuff about the product of two plus two and the same uncompromising information as to how many beans make five. The Christian Creeds contain certain statements of what purport to be historical and philosophic fact, to which the whole apparatus of Christian ethic and principle form the superstructure. Without those facts, the whole structure collapses; and the first task of "clear thinking" is to realise that such is the case.

You are more confused, I think, than is really necessary about the doctrine of Christ's "double nature". His personality is, according to the Christian faith, the personality of God, expressed in human terms . . . . And, as far as that goes, of course Shakespeare was an "ordinary commonplace person" with genius. Did you think he was some kind of monster? The word "commonplace" of course begs the question, since, if you start by saying that a genius is something out-of-the-common, then "commonplace man of genius" is a contradiction in terms. But there is no sense whatever in which a genius does not share the common humanity of the ordinary commonplace person; indeed, in so far as he attempts to dissociate himself from common humanity, he is so much less the genius . . . . But the Divinity asserted of Jesus is the Divinity of His personality; His

---

1 Identity unknown.

body, mind, and emotions were fully human, and the Church has never thought otherwise. (The Nestorians, who thought He had two personalities, human and divine, were pronounced heretical — and that line of thought has always proved sterile and contradictory.)

As regards the miraculous — Jesus never said He was able to work miracles because He was God. He said over and over again that anybody could work miracles. The working of miracles is, or should be, a human power. But they can only be worked under certain conditions. The will has to be wholly submitted to God's control, for one thing. There must be a similar response in the wills of those receiving the miracle (a concentrated atmosphere of antagonism could prevent even Jesus from performing any miracles). And the miracles could not, or must not, be worked for selfish ends. If Jesus had multiplied food for himself, or if he had called in "legions of angels" to escape crucifixion, he would have been doing something contrary to his own nature. That is the meaning of that story about the Temptation. A power derived from complete selfishness literally cannot be used for selfish ends; because the egotism dries up the power at the source. It was literally true that "he saved others, himself he could not save".

What makes you assert that he was "apparently sexless"? This is a very wild statement, supported by no documentary evidence whatever. Of his thirty-three years of life, we know about only three. By that time we certainly find a person in whom the passion for the work that was to be done had swallowed up all other passions. But whether that state was arrived at without struggle we simply do not know at all. A single devotion will, in fact, destroy all lesser devotions; the single-hearted person has usually no attention to give to competing interests — but this has nothing to do with physical peculiarity but with dominant purpose. One thing at least is very remarkable: that Christ, alone of all religious teachers, made no difference between women and men, laid down no separate rules for female behaviour, was equally unselfconscious with both sexes, gave just the same serious attention to the questions and opinions of women as of men, never used female faults and failings to point any particular moral, and indeed, made sex no part whatever of his teaching, except to say, when challenged, that men were as much to blame as women for sexual sins, and that dirty thinking was just as bad as dirty living. He appears, in fact, to have been completely sane on the subject — a thing quite impossible to any abnormal person, and unusual in anybody. But he certainly did not give that exaggerated importance to sex which became fashionable among European romantics, who somehow got it into their heads that it was the be-all and end-all of existence. The Christian Church has admittedly been very much less sane than he was; but it had to cope with a bad Jewish and pagan tradition in the matter, which it has not yet got rid of. Here, by the way, Art and Christianity are at one; sex has inspired great works of art; but not the very greatest. The very greatest music and poetry and painting and architecture deal with things more important and fundamental.

Naturally, the whole stigma of crucifying God is in the fact that He came "incognito" – that is to say that, so far from "loving the highest when we see it", we do *not* see it, and merely hate it instinctively. Nor did He come with the "determination to be crucified"; but in the face of the fact that (as it very soon became obvious) men were determined to crucify Him. Every man crucifies God, and every man is crucified with God, wittingly or unwittingly. But crucifixion is redemptive only if it is accepted by the will. But the thing called "original sin" is precisely the direction of the human will towards itself instead of towards its own real nature – the inability to do the things one really *wants* to do, because of the determination to exercise a selfish choice which conflicts with one's real aims. (Psychologists know about this splitting of the will all right, though they don't always recognise that it is the same thing which the Church has known about for many centuries under a different name.)

Then you say "what is the crucifixion of one man – even if he were a God-man – compared with all the pain and agony of hundreds of men etc now?" – But that is the crucifixion, as St. Paul says. Every time it happens, the Son of Man is crucified afresh. The Crucifixion of God is an epitome of all history[2]....

I think you would find things clearer if you were to read a little real theology, because, if I may say so, you give me the impression of never having been grounded properly in the subject. I get the impression that you acquired a sort of "child's-eye" view of Christian doctrine in early youth, and have never done any stiff reading on the subject, so that you are now judging with an adult mind doctrines which have only been presented to you in very simplified form – rather as though you were to say that Shakespeare's profundity had been much over-rated, when actually you had never read the plays themselves, but only something called "Shakespeare for the Nursery". I say this, because you seem to have supposed that *The Mind of the Maker* was something different from "the same old arguments", whereas it is, in fact, just the same old arguments, founded on the same old dogmas. I think what you really want is to see how one gets, as it were, from the one to the other. Because, as I said before, *The Mind of the Maker* is pure nonsense if you regard it as a piece of original invention – or at least, if not absolute nonsense, it is quite irrational, because it corresponds to no historical reality.

2 Cf. her play *The Just Vengeance*.

I suggest that you might like J. S. Whale's book *Christian Doctrine*, just published by the Cambridge University Press, seven shillings and sixpence, which is a remarkably sound and "modern" statement of "the same old arguments". C. S. Lewis' *The Problem of Pain* might be useful, too, on the particular point bothering you.

Yours very truly,
[Dorothy L. Sayers]

[24 Newland Street
Witham
Essex]

TO THE REV. W. T. ROBINSON[1]
27 November 1941

Dear Mr. Robinson,

Thank you for your letter. I am very much honoured by your choice of *The Mind of the Maker* as a study book for your group.

I'm afraid I'm not very good at setting "examination-papers", especially on social subjects.

One question, however, I do feel ought to be discussed, and that is the whole question of "work", and the connection and contrast between "employment" and "vocation". I have dealt with this matter in one or two public speeches – not as yet available in print – and have outlined the question in the "Postscript" to *The Mind of the Maker*.[2]

In particular, there is the question of the *secular vocation*, and the mutual responsibility between it and the Church. The complaint of the secular vocational worker against the Church has been very ably voiced by Michael de la Bedoyère[3] in his book *Christian Crisis*... viz: the failure of the Church to respect the integrity of a secular vocation as such and to give it religious sanction. She thus contrives to separate man's activities into work done specifically "to serve God" ("religious" activities), and work done for other ends; ignoring the religious obligation of the worker to the work itself – i.e. the service of God in the service of the work. I'm not putting this very clearly. I mean, allowing that "who sweeps a room as to

---

1 Identity unknown.
2 Postscript: "The Worth of the Work" (Methuen, 1941, pp. 177–184). D. L. S. here says that what distinguishes the artist from someone who works to live is the desire to see the fulfilment of the work. "As the author of *Ecclesiasticus* says, he 'watches to finish the work'...that is, he sees the end-product of his toil exactly as the artist always sees it..." (p. 179). D. L. S. quotes *Ecclesiasticus* also in *The Zeal of Thy House*, where parts of Chapter 39, verses 27 to 34 are sung as an interlude after the first scene.
3 See letter to him, 7 October, note 1.

God's praise makes that and the action fine",[4] the primary act of "worship" involved is, not to sing hymns as you sweep, or to look on sweeping as a devotional act, but to sweep properly. In other words, unless the room is "made fine", the action will not be fine and will not be worship.

One aspect of this is the one I have touched on in the "Postscript" – the failure to demand that the work required of the citizen shall be "worth doing and well done". I need not say any more about this – except, perhaps, one thing, which you might think it worth while to discuss. I believe it is much more right to teach people to "serve the work" than to "serve the community". The latter phrase sounds more Christian and altruistic; but it leads to some very unfortunate results in practice:

1. It is apt to be interpreted as: "to satisfy public demand", and so lead to the production of things worthless and even harmful. If economics demands the mass-production of cheap trash, it is readily supposed that such production is justified, since it "satisfies public demand" for such things and also "creates employment" – a vicious circle.

2. If a worker thinks of himself as "serving the community", he will probably proceed to think that "the community" ought to serve him in return. The thing becomes reduced to an assertion of personal rights, on a system of "social contract" and barter and exchange. The corruption of egotism begins to work at once, and falsifies everything that is done. But to "serve the work" leaves less room for egotism; since the artefact has no obligation towards the artificer, but only the artificer to the artifact.

3. In practice; to make any work with one eye on the audience does, in fact, tend to damage the integrity of the work. That is why books and plays written to please a public are so brittle and bad. If the work is good, it will (eventually) please the public by its goodness; but you can't get that sort of goodness if you "take your eye off the ball". There is a sort of fundamental insincerity about work produced for anything but its own sake.

4 From the poem by George Herbert, set as a hymn by Sandys, beginning "Teach me, my God and King". The lines are misquoted; they should read: "Who sweeps a room, as for Thy laws \ Makes that and the action fine."

There is also the very important (as I think) matter of the specialization of labour. However satisfactory it may be economically, to keep one workman perpetually doing a single process, or to prevent a worker from transferring himself from one kind of work to another, the net result of this, in human terms, is that the worker gets no idea of the job as a whole, or of the connection between one kind of job and another, and is thus prevented from ever really "looking to the end of the work". (A W.E.A.[5] man told me the other day how dreadful it seemed to him that in the silk manufactory where he had worked most of his life, the girls on the looms never even saw the beautiful stuff they were producing. Another confirmed the delight and pride of some women employed on making naval equipment – I forget exactly what – on being taken to a war-ship and recognising their own work in the finished product, which they had never before seen.) Employers, of course, find it cheaper to run things on the one-man-one-process basis; but when, for the sake of speeding things up in war-time, or from a desire to give workers a more intelligent attitude to their work, they do try to shift workers about a bit, they complain that the Trade Unions are mulishly obstructive. This needs arguing out.

I think, too, one might discuss whether "the crushing burden of armaments" is really any more crushing than the burden of making and marketing unwanted goods for the sole purpose of keeping up production and forcing surplus exports on countries that don't want them, in order to keep world-markets going. (Peter Drucker's *End of Economic Man*[6] has something about this; also there's that alarming little book *Ouroboros* by Garet Garrett[7] in Kegan Paul's Today and Tomorrow Series – as cogent now as when it was written. Also V. A. Demant's essay in *Christian Polity*: "Nationalism and Internationalism"). – And query: Whether the war-time restrictions on consumption and compulsory saving etc, necessary for the production of armaments might not be borne with equal cheerfulness for the production of public works in peace-time, and if not, why not? And here again: if we were as much interested to produce the works of peace as the weapons of war, could we achieve some such end voluntarily, or *must* we be planned and compelled into it? (Note: that the production of weapons of war is *obliged*, to a great extent, to "serve the work", because nothing but good work will stand up to the strain of

5 Workers' Educational Association
6 Published in 1939. D. L. S. recommends it in *Begin Here*, under "Books to Read", p. 157.
7 *Ouroborus: or the Mechanical Extension of Mankind* by Garet Garrett was first published in 1926. D. L. S. read it then and it increased her uneasiness about the advertising profession. In 1944 she wrote a Foreword to another book by Garet Garrett, *A Time is Born* (Basil Blackwell, Oxford, 1945), expressing views she had been putting forward in her letters during the early 1940s.

battle. Is war-work, in that sense, more healthy than the merely commercial works of peace?)

Apart from all this, there is the relation of religion to the arts. They are now hopelessly at loggerheads. Artists, on the whole, get from the Church no strong backbone of religious faith to direct and inspire their work. They are brought up, of course, on the same doctrinal pabulum as the common man, which is mostly vague and sloppy. The Church, knowing and caring nothing about the integrity of art *per se*, keeps on making feeble efforts to drag the artist away from serving his *own* work, to serving official religion; or else falls back on bad and wishy-washy "religious art". (For note: if, e.g., a writer does happen to be writing books or plays with a strong Christian backbone, or is, on other evidence, known to be a Christian, the parson does not cooperate by urging people to read the books and see the plays, and so encourage the writer to go on producing them. No – he gets in the way of the writer's work by hauling him off to address meetings, open church bazaars, preach sermons, and talk to young people – work for which the writer may be quite unfitted and for which, if he is to remain an honest workman, he has neither time nor energy. And note further: that the writer, by undertaking work for which he has no genuine vocation, damages his own powers; but if he tells the parson this, the parson always replies: "Think of how much good you will do and how you will be serving the community". Which brings us back to the previous point about "serving the work" and "serving the community". All this happens because official religion does not take secular vocation seriously; it is a special instance of this general question.)

I'm afraid I have jotted all this down rather sketchily, but it may suggest some lines of argument.

I feel very strongly about all this question of work and vocation, because it seems to me that the whole thing has got topsy-turvy, and that the planners of New Orders are starting from the wrong end. They so seldom bother about what work is to be done, or *to what purpose*; and "the worker" is coming to mean less and less somebody whose life is bound up in his work, and more and more somebody who uses his enforced labour as a political weapon – in fact, an instrument of "power politics" in the most truculent sense of the words. And I don't like it. I don't like it at all.

Yours sincerely,

[Dorothy L. Sayers]

[24 Newland Street
Witham
Essex][1]

28 November 1941

I have started several times to write to you about the Theological Literature Association, and each time some other urgent matter has cropped up and interrupted me. It was not possible for me to attend the meeting in Oxford; but I hope things went well.

I am in entire agreement with you about the urgent need both for readable books which present Christian doctrine in a form that can be assimilated by adult pagans, and for books to instruct the ignorant, whether children or adults. Quite apart from anything else, the unhappy "Lay Apostolate" are at present in a most harassing position. The hungry sheep who (for various reasons) refuse the official pabulum, baa round them insistently, and are fed only with the greatest difficulty from very insufficient material by these amateur shepherds. And it's all very well for our bishops and pastors to encourage us with approving shouts – we still have to scratch for the stuff, cook it up and serve it out as best we can, to the peril of our souls and tempers, and at imminent risk of handing out a lot of poisonous weeds with it, in our haste and lack of preparation.

One of our biggest difficulties is this: that so extreme is the public's ignorance of what the accepted doctrine is, and so great its distrust of orthodoxy, that whenever we present it in assimilable form, we have to spend hours of time and pounds in postage-stamps explaining to correspondents that this is not a a new gospel of our own invention, and that it differs from the regulation diet in nothing but in being served up in plain English and without slop-sauce or sectarian skewers. If only, having, as it were, attracted the sheep to the church door, we could then hand them over, saying "Go in – you'll find all the stuff there". But they won't go in, and half the time the stuff isn't there, but something that looks quite different. So we find ourselves frantically trying to feed sheep with one hand and do our proper work with the other, to the neglect of both and the great scandal of everybody!

---

1 This letter is reproduced from a typed copy of the original. It has no salutation and it is not known to whom it was addressed. A copy was sent to Mrs Bell by D. L. S., enclosed in a letter dated 26 April 1942, thanking her for hospitality and saying she hoped the "memorandum" would amuse the Bishop. The copy in Lambeth Palace Library is headed "Letter from Miss Dorothy Sayers". This indicates that it was not typed by her secretary, who would not have omitted the "L". It may have originally been addressed to the convener of the Theological Literature Association, whose meeting in Oxford D. L. S. had been unable to attend.

Well, now, what do my sheep want? They keep on bawling for

(a) "A book which tells me all about Christian dogma." They want it written in reasonable English and not in technical theological jargon. They want it to be aware of the particular difficulties experienced by the adult 20th-century mind. And they don't want it "churchy", or polemical; and they don't want everything in it to be contradicted by the next book they read, which happens to be written by a member of a different communion.

The best I've found so far are J. S. Whale's *Christian Doctrine*[2] and Leslie Simmonds' *Framework of Faith*.[3] The former slips into anti-Roman polemic here and there, and the latter occasionally seems to leap a gap of argument without quite bridging it; but they both cover the ground and are up-to-date and reasonably aware of the common man's habits of thought. Bede Frost's *Who?*[4] is good for the purely theistic argument, but goes no further; and there are some goodish books on Christology, but what's wanted most is orderly presentation of the structure of Christianity *as a whole*. (N.B. Fr Simmonds' book was burnt alive in the London blitz, which has made it rather useless to recommend it; I don't know whether it is now available again. And Whale's book only came out this autumn – so that hasn't yet helped much. But these two books seem to me on the right lines.)

(b) "A book about the New Testament." People want to know the order in which the books of the N.T. were written, and what modern scholars think about their dates, authenticity, and so on. Most people still imagine that the "Higher Criticism" has more or less exploded half the Scriptures, and they don't know anything about the results of recent archaeological research or textual criticism. And it's no good giving them bibliographical treatises on the Synoptists, full of tables of comparison and hiccuping references to "Q" and "Proto-Matt" and "M" and "m" and "LM" scattered all over the shop, because they didn't read a Language School at Oxford and don't know what to make of all those games. The popular idea they have got of the results of biblical criticism is something like this:

"Everything in the N.T. was written centuries after it all happened, by people who pretended to be the disciples, but weren't really, and who misunderstood most of what they had been told and deliberately altered the rest.

"Mark wrote a simple human story without any theology in it.

"Criticism has proved that Matthew and Luke, where they are 'early',

2 See letter to Michael de la Bedoyère, 7 October 1941, note 12.
3 Leslie Frank Simmonds, *Framework of Faith* (Teaching of the Church Ser., 1), London 1939.
4 Bede Frost, *Who?: A Book About God*, London 1940.

are a bad rehash of Mark, with some tendentious theology put in; and where they are 'late' are liars.

"John was written at least several centuries after all the disciples were dead, by a Greek philosopher who invented a lot of things for Jesus to say, to link up with Plato, or something.

"Paul invented the Church, contrary to Christ's intention.

"Any 'early' document is 'purer' than any later document; if Paul's Epistles are really earlier than the Gospels it looks as though there was a screw loose somewhere – but there isn't a handy book which gives us the dates; and we know Paul must be wrong because that is a well-known fact, proved by Criticism.

"None of the historical dates and facts in the Gospels agree with contemporary history. There is some sort of muddle in Luke about the census, for instance.

"The Protestants say that the Church depends on the Scriptures; the Catholics say that the Scriptures depend on the Church. We think that the Scriptures were selected and made into the Bible by a committee of Fathers, but we don't know when, or why they selected those particular books. Nor do we know if there really were any other books to choose from, still less what they were like.

"Criticism has proved that the texts of all the books differ a great deal and are very unreliable. Most of the texts people argue about and use to prove theology are interpolations. Whenever we find a text that seems to prove Christianity, our agnostic friends tell us that one can't use it, because it is John, or Paul, or Matthew, or late, or an interpolation or only found in one manuscript; and Criticism has proved that everything that is any of these things must be wrong."

Going on from these two persistent bleats, I am inclined to demand further:

(c) A book that will give some coherent and intelligible account of how *doctrine* came to be formulated – at what dates, under what pressure from events and popular heresies, under what other circumstances, and by whom. Also, in what way these doctrines are implicit in the Scriptures and in the teaching of Christ and the experience of the early Church. (The general impression is that everybody was getting along nicely with the Simple Gospel, consisting chiefly of the Sermon on the Mount and Suffer-little-children, till a number of professional argufiers took it into their heads to have some theology, and so gave rise to heresies.)

(d) A Handbook to Heresies – *not* arranged under the names of the Heretics, but according to the subjects: Heresies about God, about Christ, about the Trinity, and so on, so that one can look them up quickly; with the dates and history of the people who started thinking that way, and why it was an unsatisfactory way to think; also, who refuted them, and

what Council condemned them. And also, the names of the gentlemen
who hash them up for public consumption today under the impression
that they are brilliant new contributions to contemporary thought. (I am
tired of being taunted with "neo-Orthodoxy"; I want, for a change, to see
a few "original and revolutionary thinkers" identified as neo-Manichees,
neo-Nestorians, neo-Sabellians, and so on.)

(e) A scholarly book along the lines of Cochrane's *Christianity and
Classical Culture*,[5] only not so bulky, difficult and expensive, showing how
the happy pagan thinkers got themselves into much the same sort of intellectual and religious muddle, and the same "flight from reason" as ourselves, through too much all-round tolerance and devotion to scientific
humanism; and how "Athanasian" orthodoxy didn't produce the Dark
Ages, but was the only thing stiff enough to get through them and come
out the other side. Also, that the apparent alteration of the Church's attitude to State affairs after Constantine (with the appearance of compromise, casuistry, legality, and all the rest of it) was not just naughtiness and
truckling to Caesar, but a consequence of the fact that she had, for the
first time to accept *responsibility* for what happened in the world and the
State, and was thus brought up against the "problem of power" in an
acute form.[6]

(f) A book about the technical terms used in Theology, most of which
are now meaningless to the common bloke, or else carry quite misleading
meanings: e.g. person, substance, being, sacrifice, reason (*ratio sapientiae*,
including what we know now as "imagination", not merely *ratio scientiae*[7]
– if you talk about the "Divine Reason" or the "Logos" people think you
mean inductive reasoning and logic), prophecy, sin, "begotten of the
Father" (always supposed to refer exclusively to the paternity of the
human Jesus), nature, worship, flesh, etc. etc. Anderson-Scott has done a
little pamphlet on these lines, called *Words* (S.C.M. sixpence), but it is limited to New Testament words and does not, I think, deal fully with the way
words change their meaning in course of time, or in passing from one
technical vocabulary to the other. (For instance, the gradual deterioration
of the word "reason" in passing from the Middle Ages, through the 18th
century, to the 20th-century scientific use, or the similar change in the
word "science" itself; or the difference in meaning between "energy" as
used in physics, in theology, and in common speech. Also, the book should
make it clear to people that Theology is a science, with technical terms of
its own, which its exponents have as much right to use as other scientists

5 C. H. Cochrane, *Christianity and Classical Culture: A Study of Thought and Action from Augustus to
   Augustine*, Oxford 1940.
6 Cf. her Introduction to *The Emperor Constantine*.
7 See letter to the Rev. T. Wigley, 1 September 1941, note 4.

have to use their technical terms; and that it is just as silly to argue about theology without bothering to learn its technical vocabulary as it would be to dispute physics with physicists under the impression that "force" means to them what it means to Hitler, or to try and disprove the proposition $(a + b)(a - b) = a^2 - b$ on the ground that, as a is a vowel and b is a consonant, you cannot subtract one from the other. (At least half the misunderstandings of the common man are due to the fact that he supposes theological terms to mean exactly what they mean in common speech, and that he thinks they have *no right to mean anything else*. And it's not much good to say to him, "Go away and learn the vocabulary", because he would immediately say, "All right, but where is it?")

You will notice that a number of these suggestions more or less coincide with those made by Cross, Manson, etc.[8]

I also heartily endorse the demand made by Symons for some sort of statement about oecumenical Christian *doctrine* (not "Christian principles") to be issued by leading theologians of all the great communions, both as a basis for school instruction, and also as a reply to the common allegation (see, e.g. Mozley in the October *Hibbert Journal*)[9] that it's no good the Churches demanding instruction in doctrine because they can't agree about what the doctrine is. But I have hopes that something may be about to materialize in this field, if all goes well with a plot that is a-hatching at the moment.[10]

Whale's protest against dogmatic theology is happily belied by his practice in his recent book on *Christian Doctrine*, which is almost classic in its dogmatic orthodoxy. In my experience (such as it is) the resentment and hostility of which he complains are aroused in their most violent form by any assertion that Jesus is fully God. It seems to me that on this point Christians would do well to stick to their guns and take whatever hostility is coming to them. The early Church that people are so fond of quoting doesn't seem to have shrunk from exciting hostility on this subject. If the battle of Nicaea has to be fought all over again, it might as well be fought now, without any further attempts at appeasement.

I agree with Prestige[11] *et al.* that some sort of guide to existing publications would be very helpful. It must be a *catalogue raisonnée*, with brief outline of content and treatment, and indication of the amount of "theological literacy" each book presupposes in the reader. The catalogue should also contain references to books like R. O. Kapp's *Science versus*

---

8 It is evident that a memorandum of the proceedings of the meeting of the Theological Literature Association had been sent to her.
9 Lieut.-Col. E. N. Mozley, D.S.O., "Religious Liberty and the B.B.C."
10 D. L. S. and Dr James Welch were planning a series of talks by representatives of the chief Christian denominations.
11 See letter to Maynard D. Follin, 23 July 1942, note 10.

Materialism,[12] which, while not specifically Christian or even Theist, aim at cutting away the ground from under the various pseudo-scientific antagonists within their own territory.

As regards books on Christian Social Order, it seems very necessary that something should be done about the matter of Work and Vocation, which has got into a most hideous muddle. It is not pleasant to see men's labour, which should be their life, reduced to being a mere aspect of power-politics. I [had] got T. M. Heron[13] to write a book about this for the Bridgeheads series; but unhappily, just as he was getting along beautifully, Lord Woolton[14] came and took him away, and God knows when he will be able to get finished. I believe Demant is also interested in this question. Along with it goes the question of the Church's attitude to secular vocation concerning which Michael de la Bedoyère has an impassioned chapter in Christian Crisis;[15] and the relations between the Church and the Arts, on which I touched at Malvern.[16] It's not a matter of the Church "getting hold of the Arts", as the Bishop of Chichester seems to imagine.[17] It's a matter of (a) presenting the artist with a brand of Christianity which can inform and inspire his secular work, and (b) recognising the autonomy of the artist's vocation as such. As it is, the greatest living creative force in the secular world is functioning right outside the pale of Christendom. Incidentally, this is why so many religious books are ill-written and incomprehensible to the ordinary man with no practice in, or reverence for, words, no vital power with words, and no sensitiveness for the associations which words arouse in the reader. (Ditto with Church painting and music.)

This letter is already more than sufficiently long, more than sufficiently belated, and much less than sufficiently helpful. But the whole thing gives me the feeling of struggling with an octopus in a jungle. Christopher Dawson[18] seems to feel quite hopeless about it – but I think he exaggerates!

Yours sincerely,
    [Dorothy L. Sayers]

12 Reginald Otto Kapp, *Science Versus Materialism*, London 1940.

13 See letter to V. A. Demant, 10 April 1941, note 7.

14 Woolton, 1st Earl of (1922–1969), Director-General of Equipment and Stores in Ministry of Supply (1939–1940), Minister of Food (1940–1943).

15 See letter to him dated 7 October 1941.

16 At the Conference held in January 1941.

17 See letter to Count de la Bedoyère, 7 October 1941.

18 Christopher Dawson (1889–1970), Roman Catholic author and lecturer. D. L. S. recommends his *Beyond Politics* under "Some Books to Read" in *Begin Here*.

On 10 December a press conference, organized by Dr Welch, was held at Berners Hotel, Berners Street, London. Dr Welch addressed the assembled reporters and D. L. S. read aloud a statement she had prepared about the plays, stressing the use of modern English and the impersonation of Christ by an actor. She was asked to read a few examples of the dialogue. One of the scenes she chose was the beginning of the fourth play, "The Heirs to the Kingdom", where Matthew reproaches Philip for having been cheated by a merchant. The journalists leapt on the informality of Matthew's speech.[1] The Daily Mail came out with the headline: "B.B.C. Life of Christ Play in U.S. Slang". Other papers reported sensationally on the use of modern English and the representation of Christ. There was a violent public reaction. The Lord's Day Observance Society and the Protestant Truth Society mounted a determined opposition. Petitions were sent to the Prime Minister and to the Archbishop of Canterbury. Questions were asked in the House of Commons. The desks of newspaper editors were deluged. Leaflets of protestation were handed out in public places.

1 Matthew: "Fact is, Philip my boy, you've been had for a sucker. Let him ring the changes on you proper. You ought to keep your eyes skinned, you did really. If I was to tell you the dodges these fellows have up their sleeves, you'd be surprised."

On 13 December Dr Welch wrote:

...It is outrageous that the cheap press should write of these plays as the *Daily Mail* has done...But I am entirely convinced that the conference was well worth holding, partly because we wanted to capture the attention of listeners who do not normally listen to religious broadcasts...but chiefly because I entirely support you in your determination to cast the whole play into modern language and to make the characters real....

D. L. S. replied:

[24 Newland Street
Witham
Essex]

TO DR JAMES WELCH
15 December 1941

Dear Dr. Welch,

The Man Born to be King

In case any difficulty is being caused by the attitude of the cheap Press and the Lord's Day Observance people, I think it may help to clarify your position if I make my own position clear.

Under the terms by which I am contracted to the BBC, I have the right to insist that the plays shall be performed as I have written them, subject only to your personal approval (which I have already received in writing) and the technical requirements of production. If there is to be any question of tinkering with the general presentment, or with isolated passages, in order to appease outside interests, I shall be regretfully obliged to withdraw the scripts, under the terms of the contract.

You will understand, I am sure, that I would not consent to complete the series, or permit any parts of it to be broadcast, under conditions which would interfere with the integrity of my work; since this would be fair neither to yourself nor to me, nor to the producer.

Yours very sincerely,

[Dorothy L. Sayers]

24 Newland Street
Witham
Essex

TO HER SON

18 December 1941

Dear John,

Best congratulations on your scholarship.[1] I thought you would pull it off all right. Well done.

Now, of course, all the arguments begin over again. Mr. Ridley[2] naturally thinks you would be better at College than doing war-work, and passionately rebuts the suggestion that Oxford is behaving in a remote and academic way. It's very difficult to tell how to act for the best. It depends a good deal on how long the war is going to last, and that's a thing nobody knows. I mean, if it's going on for another ten years or so, there will be plenty of time for doing Oxford first and the war later. If it only goes on for another two or three years, your generation will find itself in that rather awkward position of being at one and the same time "privileged" and out of touch, when it comes to tackling the problems of peace. I'm sure that we have got to avoid, this time, any sort of chasm between the "intellectuals" and the rest of the nation. Of course, the whole thing is really a hopeless dilemma. Last time, the best younger intelligences joined

---

1 John Anthony had just won a scholarship to Balliol College, Oxford. (Balliol was Lord Peter Wimsey's college.)

2 Roy Ridley was to be John Anthony's Tutor. He was the physical original of Lord Peter Wimsey. See Barbara Reynolds, *Dorothy L. Sayers: Her Life and Soul*, pp. 56–57. See also letter to Catherine Godfrey, 29 July 1913, pp. 79–80, and note 21; letter to Muriel St Clare Byrne, 6 March 1935, pp. 345–346, and note 2 (*The Letters of Dorothy L. Sayers: 1899–1936*).

up instantly, went to France and were killed; so that we were left with a remnant of C3[3] people and conchies,[4] who (being inflicted with an inferiority complex about the war) started a de-bunking campaign against all the "manly virtues" and landed us with a lot of difficulties. So that's an argument against war and for education. But this time, if we try to hold on to the younger intelligences, it may only mean that they will still be in the same position, but that there will be more of them – and they may also find that there is a certain class-prejudice against those whose educational facilities have given them shelter.

Anyhow, I quite agree with Ridley that it's a question of how you feel about it. If you like to go up straight away, take Oxford at a gallop, so to speak, and then carry on, it might after all be the best way. The loss of one term won't really matter much. You have brains enough to catch that up. What are you thinking of reading?[5]

If you think it over and tell me what you really judge would suit you best, I'll make whatever financial arrangements are necessary.

Love and again congratulations,

D. L. F.

3 A medical category which exempted men from being called up.
4 Conscientious objectors.
5 John Anthony read Modern Greats, i.e. Philosophy, Politics and Economics, known as P.P.E. He obtained a First-Class degree.

Despite the continuing uproar, rehearsals went ahead, not in Broadcasting House, where a suite of dramatic studios had been demolished in a raid, but in the tiny Grafton Theatre in Tottenham Court Road, from which all the plays were broadcast. The first play, "Kings in Judaea", went out on 21 December and D. L. S. wrote in gratitude and relief to Val Gielgud:

[24 Newland Street
Witham
Essex]

TO VAL GIELGUD
22 December 1941

Dear Val,

This is just to say, once more, thank you for giving "Kings in Judaea" such a grand cast and such a lovely show. Whatever happens, I do and shall always feel most tremendously grateful for the sympathy and enthusiasm you've put into it all, and I'm frightfully sorry that you should have had all this extra bother and fuss and worry about it, especially when you were so overworked and so tired. It really is a shame, and I feel it's all my fault. I *do* think you're a delightful person to work for – and if there's anything you want me to do for your shows I'll do it if I possibly can – always supposing that both our names aren't mud when the fighting is over; in which case, all we can do is to stick in the mud together and suffer for our convictions.

I came home to find my husband full of enthusiasm – and he is a person difficult to enthuse about serious shows. He thought it came over splendidly and was a fine show. So did my friend Miss Barber, who is staying with us – (she is writing you a little fan-letter on her own account; I think you probably met her once with me and Muriel Byrne).

There were one or two little points I forgot to say in the fuss and flutter yesterday – for instance, Laidman Browne[1] made such an excellent job of reading the Evangelist bits. That's not a showy job, but it's one that can do a lot of damage to the show if it's done wrong, and he got it dead right, without being either flat or unctuous. And I didn't have an opportunity to praise Val Dyall,[2] who was a perfect bit of casting for Melchior – or the chap who played Matthias[3] and had such a grand demagogue style of oratory. For some reason, actors often get that kind of thing unconvincing, but he was excellent. These little bits, quite apart from the work of the leading people, most of whom I did manage to thank. Oh! except "little Zillah" – I didn't see her, to speak to, but I did say to you how good I thought she was.[4] Nobody could want a show better cast or produced, and I feel you done me proud.

I hope you weren't too utterly exhausted. I nearly fell asleep in the train coming home, though I hadn't been doing any work at all, and it really was dreadful for you having to toil to Manchester. I hope your dinner tonight will be worth it!

Well, bless you and all the best – and as good a Christmas as any producer can possibly hope to spend on the panel!

Yours ever,

[D. L. S.]

D. L. S. wrote in similar terms of gratefulness to Dr Welch, who replied on 24 December:

You thank me! Oh no: *thank you*, for a play which brilliantly handled a complicated historical situation, for giving the actors something which really "got 'em" and for your lovely and reverent handling of the Nativity....

1 Laidman Browne (1896–1961). He is remembered in the roles of Caesar, William the Conqueror, Henry V, etc. in *1066 and All That*.
2 Valentine Dyall (1908–1985), son of the actors Franklin Dyall and Mary Merrall.
3 Abraham Sofaer (1896–1988), Burmese actor on British stage from 1921.
4 Maureen Glynne.

1942

A landmark in broadcasting

eɔeɔeɔ

The public uproar in protest against the broadcasting of the plays continued. Dr Welch now had the task of persuading the Central Religious Advisory Committee to allow the plays to continue. There was no time to call a meeting before the broadcast of the first play, but he sent copies of the second and third plays to all thirteen members, asking them to comment by post, telephone or telegram.

[24 Newland Street
Witham
Essex]

TO DR JAMES WELCH
6 January 1942

Dear Dr. Welch,

This is just to wish you good luck in your fight with the beasts. I'm rather past caring now what happens to the plays from a personal point of view. But if these wire-pulling, vociferous, and excessively ignorant sects manage to beat us *again*, there will be a loss of face which ecclesiastical and civil authority will hardly recover. Already the papers are sneering at the Laodicean¹ policy of the Churches; and if the Advisory Board, who originally sanctioned the thing, don't stand to their guns, they will look pretty feeble. "Wars are not won by evacuations"² – and though we can rely on you to make a Dunkirk of it, there will be a loss in armaments, baggage and fighting-power that will take some time to make up.

The fury of the iconoclasts is to be expected. What is depressing is the

---

1 Lukewarm, after the church of the Laodiceans. (Revelation, chapter 3, verses 14–16.)
2 Churchill, "Their finest hour".

attitude of the pious who dislike having the *actuality* of the Gospel forced upon their notice. "Kings in Judaea" is "so unlike the beautiful, simple Gospel" – so it is; because they have managed to forget the whole background of the Gospels. Herod is a child's ogre, Rome is a decorative frieze, the rough inn is an arbour in rustic trellis-work, the common people of Galilee are curates with Oxford accents, and the brutal Roman gallows a pattern stamped in gilt on the cover of a prayer-book. "The play", said one correspondent angrily, "seemed to bring God down to earth" – so, one would think, did Christmas – "instead of raising man to God"; and I suspect that this is the old Arian serpent raising its head to say again that salvation is of man – *Gloria in excelsis homini*, for man is the master of his fate and captain of his soul (always provided he speaks like a gentleman and doesn't use slang or go to the theatre).

Well, set up the labarum[3] in Langham Place,[4] and *in hoc signo vince!*[5]

Yours ever,

[Dorothy L. Sayers]

3 The Roman imperial standard with Christian symbols added.
4 Where Broadcasting House is situated.
5 Latin: in this sign conquer. The words shown in a vision to the Emperor Constantine before the Battle of the Milvian Bridge, A.D. 312, are usually quoted as "in hoc signo vinces", in this sign thou wilt conquer.

On 8 January Dr Welch wrote to report that at a meeting chaired by the Bishop of Winchester, Dr Cyril Garbett, only a few minor objections were raised to some of the wording of the second and third plays. And he said: "We stand where you and I have always wanted to stand."

[24 Newland Street
Witham
Essex]

TO C. ARMSTRONG GIBBS[1]

12 January 1942

Dear Mr. Armstrong Gibbs,

Thank you so much for your delightful letter. I am very glad indeed that you enjoyed *The Mind of the Maker* and it is particularly good to know that your experience as a musician bears out what I have tried to say about the mind of artists in general. It is always tempting to generalise from one's

1 Armstrong Gibbs (1889–1960), composer, student of Vaughan Williams and Sir Adrian Boult at the Royal College of Music.

own personal experience, and when one has done it, one is overtaken by qualms lest a painter, or a composer, should rise up and say that may be how the writer works, but that he does the thing quite differently.

It is most interesting that you have had the same sensation of things being "right" in a particular place, and have only afterwards discovered why. Another helpful and kind correspondent unearthed for me a letter of Mozart's, in which he said that while writing a composition he was able to "survey it at a glance, like a beautiful picture, . . . and I do not hear it in my imagination successively, as it must afterwards appear, but as it were all at once". Being myself only musical, and not a musician, I had no idea whether a musician could have such an experience, and was enchanted to discover that he actually could and sometimes did.

I am most grateful to you for having written, and I hope that your musical work in Westmorland will prosper, in spite of war difficulties, which must be very great.

With renewed thanks,
    Yours very sincerely,
        [Dorothy L. Sayers]

On 13 January Eric Fenn wrote:

I'm glad we seem to be getting to a thinning of the trees, even if we are not yet out of the wood. But it's been a trying time for you – probably more than for me, I imagine....When you move the settled stone of religious complacency such very odd creatures run out, don't they?...It must feel as if you'd had a severe illness....

Val Gielgud also wrote an encouraging letter, to which D. L. S. replied:

> [24 Newland Street
> Witham
> Essex]

TO VAL GIELGUD
13 January 1942

Dear Val...
    Bless you and thank you – yes. The first round is won, and let's hope they now keep quiet till next time.[1] Oh, gosh! I should like some peace

---

1 D. L. S. received abusive telephone calls, insulting letters, many of them anonymous, and was the subject of disparaging comment in the press, all before even one of the plays had been broadcast.

about this show! How right Christ was about bringing not peace but a sword. One has only to mention His name and everybody is up in arms. I wish it didn't make one so self-conscious about the job. I wish one didn't see Mr Kensit[2] lurking behind every page of the A.V.[3] I wish one hadn't to fight desperate rear-guard actions with the Press, trying to shut them up, and yet not to alienate them so hopelessly that they would start a fresh campaign of hate against the next play. When we go to heaven all I ask is that we shall be given some interesting job and allowed to get on with it. No management; no box-office; no dramatic critics; and an audience of cheerful angels who don't mind laughing....

I do think Dr Welch has fought a courageous and skilful fight. And the unanimity of the Committee was really rather a triumph....

I've had lots of praise for the performance of "Kings in Judaea", and reports of two sets of children of tender age who thoroughly enjoyed it – especially Baby Jesus' bib! I saw the Pilgrim Players act this scene on a small stage and in modern dress. It was quite alarmingly intimate and real. However, an old lady next to me wept buckets all through it, so it must be more or less all right....

I mustn't forget to congratulate you on your O.B.E. Just fancy your being decorated by His Majesty, when you are living in the Temple of Blasphemy[4], and working hand in glove with one who has (according to my kind correspondents) emulated Judas and committed the Unforgivable Sin! Anyhow, you deserve to be decorated –

"Take him and cut him out in little stars" [5]

and may you twinkle for ever.

Yours,

[D.L.S.]

---

2 The Secretary of the Protestant Truth Society.

3 The Authorized Version of the Bible.

4 Cf. Val Gielgud: "Every possible attempt was made by prejudice, by sensational paragraphs in the newspapers, even by advertisement, to damn the project in the eyes of the public. A headline went so far as to proclaim Broadcasting House 'A Temple of Blasphemy' ", *Years of the Locust*, Nicholson and Watson, 1947, p. 110.

5 *Romeo and Juliet*, Act III, scene 2, line 22.

[24 Newland Street
Wtham
Essex]

DR. JOHN SHIRLEY[1]
Trenarven House
St. Austell
Cornwall
16 January 1942

Dear Dr. Shirley,

I am so sorry but I find that what with one thing and another I simply cannot find time for a holiday in Cornwall this term. I should have greatly liked to come and see you all, but I have already a great many engagements, and now that it seems as though our radio plays on the life of Christ were really going through, I shall be kept hard at work with writing and rehearsing them. It is a great disappointment, but there it is, and I fear I shall be tied by the leg to London for some months to come.

I don't know whether you have followed all the details of our fight with the Lord's Day Observance Society, and the Protestant Truth Society! It was the kind of skirmish you would have enjoyed. All the same, we are rather horrified by the amount of fetish worship which it has revealed to us among the Christian people of this country. I never before really believed in the apocryphal gentleman who said, "never mind the 'ebrew and the Greek, give me the sacred English original" – but he exists in enormous numbers. The helpful people who have arisen to point out that the Greek of the Gospels is extremely colloquial will probably have administered a still further shock to the unfortunate gentleman's constitution. Rather fortunately, the protesters were so eager to attack (a) the B.B.C., (b) the Church of Rome, (c) the stage, (d) the enjoyment of anything whatever on a Sunday, that they have succeeded in thoroughly putting up the backs of a great number of people. There were thirteen men of different denominations on the Religious Advisory Committee, ranging from a Monsignor to an Ulster Protestant, and their vote was unanimous – a thing I should imagine that has not occurred in England since the Reformation!

With again the deepest regrets, and kind remembrances to you all,
    Yours very sincerely,
        [Dorothy L. Sayers]

---

1 Canon Shirley, Headmaster of King's School, Canterbury. The school had been evacuated to Cornwall. (Cf. letter to him, 6 July 1937.)

Witham

TO MARJORIE BARBER[1]
27 January 1942

Dearest Bar,

Thank you so much for your letter, my dear – I hoped you might find time to send a report[2] – not only because you know what one's driving at and can tell about the children, but also because you're one of the few people who remember that the p– b–[3] actors and producer have anything to do with the show. And bless me! how I missed you when I got back from Town, very much exhausted, on Sunday night! Mac was very sweet, and said he had liked it, and that we had "got a good Christ";[4] but what I wanted was the ever-open sympathetic ear into which I could pour remorseless details, as to one who had suffered play-production!

We had three days for the four rehearsals; I suppose waiting for an invasion would be really more nerve-racking, but this was quite a good preparation. The first read-through was all right – only enlivened by Christ being twenty minutes late, owing to another engagement. This (as the streets were slippery) gave us just nice time to wonder what would happen if he broke his leg, after all the fuss and kerfluffle about him. The actors seemed pleased with their stuff. It was evident that we'd have to do some pretty fierce cutting – however, I'd more or less allowed for that. The second day we rehearsed in a ghastly great studio miles away in Maida Vale – all warming up nicely; but this, of course, was the rehearsal in which Val took the show to pieces, and told John Baptist not to be too grandiloquent and Christ not to be too ecclesiastical. One knows what happens next. Unfortunately, other people didn't: so next day along comes Dr. Welch, as nervous as a cat, to hear J-B wavering and staggering between two different readings, and J-C gambolling through his part at a canter, and sounding exactly like everybody else, while the Crowd reacted by being as slow and fumbling as possible. So poor Dr. W. cheered us up with a few of those remarks which begin, "I'm rather disappointed . . . ." I assured him that nothing else was to be looked-for at the moment, that all would yet be well, but he found it hard to believe. However, he gave Val and me a superb lunch at the Dorchester, and we went to it again – making a final (in Val's words) "murderous" cut, which removed bodily the whole story of the birth of John-Baptist, and so cut out the last faint pretence that we were telling Bible-stories in the Children's Hour! (Poor

1 South Hampstead High School, where Marjorie Barber taught English, had been evacuated to Berkhamsted, Herts.
2 On the broadcast of the second play, "The King's Herald", on 25 January 1942.
3 poor bloody
4 The actor Robert Speaight (1904–1976).

Robert Speaight, later to play Christ

Dorothy L. Sayers, Robert Speaight and Val Gielgud rehearsing
The Man Born to be King

Derek McCulloch! Thank Heaven, he wasn't there, Val having got rid of
him with a firm hand.) Naturally, things now went more smoothly, J-B
and J-C having wobbled back to stability, and Dr. W. said he felt "much
better". He said, "The morning rehearsal did worry me." "Oh," said I, "I
knew it would be like that." "Did you?" said he, with a naive veneration
for Grandma's omniscience. "Yes", said I, "I know exactly what actors are
like at 10.30 a.m., after all their readings have been altered." – So he took
heart, and entered keenly into a conspiracy with "Effects" to provide God
with an extra allowance of thunder. After which we had tea; everybody
fighting against a vague sense that Bobby Speaight was about to undergo
a major operation.[5] Dr. Welch would insist on inquiring of him tenderly
whether he felt nervous – a suggestion which I thought inadvisable at that
late hour – Bobby put a bold face on it, and said he was firmly looking at
it as a job of professional work and trying not to think of anything else.
At 5.10 we all patted him on the back and took leave of him, with an
inward impression that we might never see him again. The actual perfor-

5 i.e. the experience of acting the part of Christ, a role no actor had performed in England
  since the time of Oliver Cromwell.

mance was – rather surprisingly and unusually – better than any of the rehearsals. I must say the cast behaved quite nobly; not one of them lost his head at any point. We were running fearfully close to time, especially as we had urged Bobby to let himself rip in the Temptation Scene and not let himself feel hurried; and by a miracle the three old funnies playing the Jews in the last little scene, stimulated by knowing that we had dropped forty seconds, and keeping their eyes on the clock, suddenly played their bit with galvanic briskness, and we ran out comfortably thirty seconds ahead of the time-pips. Poor Val was sweating like a pig....

The newspapers apparently decided that the thing didn't offer the vulgar sensations they had hoped for, since none of them seem to have said much about it, except *The Star*, which couldn't help itself, having delivered a slashing attack on the whole thing the previous Saturday. As you will see from the enclosed, the critic is a little hampered by the fact that he can't distinguish John Evangelist from John Baptist – and he also raises doubts in my mind whether in fact he knows much about the Gospels, since he shows no surprise at finding Judas in the company of John Baptist, or any of the other additions to the narrative....

Well, bless you, my dear! and thank you again and again –
    Yours ever,
      D. L. S....

                    [24 Newland Street
                    Witham
                    Essex]

TO VAL GIELGUD
8 February 1942

Dear Val,

This is just to say that, fluffs or no fluffs, my husband thought this the best show of the three,[1] and says he astonished himself by ending up very much moved – giving, indeed, a touching impersonation of the "gruff warrior with tears in his eyes", familiar to sentimental fiction! – a thing, according to him, which hasn't happened to him for years. He says that anything which moved *him* would move anybody! – Personally, I think gruff warriors tend to overestimate their own insensibility; still, there's no doubt about it, the thing did get across to him, especially the ending.

---

1 The third play, "A Certain Nobleman", broadcast on 8 February 1942.

Play Number Six is being typed, and you shall have it with the usual notes, etc. in the course of the next few days. After that, we shall find ourselves with:

7. Events centring about Raising of Lazarus
8. " " " Entry into Jerusalem
9. Last Supper and Gethsemane
10. Trial (with crowing cock for Peter, and suicide of Judas)
11. Crucifixion
12. Resurrection...

Oh, and by the way, I suppose we shall have to have some voices of dear little babes and sucklings to cry "Hosanna!" in Play Eight.

I'm bothered about Peter's cockcrow. One cock pooping off by itself may sound too "arranged" and slightly comic. Would it be possible to have a proper "cockcrow", starting with one cock in the far distance, and taken up and answered by adjacent poultry? That's the way it usually happens in actual fact. Other little troubles to come from Effects are the earthquake at the Crucifixion and Judas's thirty pieces of silver on the Temple floor, *and* the nasty crowd saying A-r-r-h! a-r-r-h! a-r-r-h! and, if possible, the breaking of the unleavened bread at the Passover!! It would be a thing like a Jewish motze – or a thin Captain biscuit – And it would be nice if we could hear Pilate washing his hands, provided we can distinguish it from a storm at sea!

Love and blessings,
[D. L. S.]

My old Cook thought it was lovely, and the voice of Mary was beautiful.

24 Newland Street
Witham
Essex

TO MURIEL ST. CLARE BYRNE

The Old Rectory
Fen Ditton,
Cambridge[1]
11 February 1942

Dear Muriel...
I saw Rieu[2] on Friday, and found him in the act of concocting the

---

1 Bedford College, London University, at which Muriel St Clare Byrne was teaching, had been evacuated to Cambridge.
2 Dr E. V. Rieu, Literary and Academic Adviser to Methuen, later Editor of Penguin Classics.

enclosed letter, which, having dealt with, I now pass on to you. I do wish that when these elderly gents get excited about religion it did not take them in these incalculable ways![3] I told him that whereas there might be no logical objection to what he proposes, and perhaps even no sound theological objection, I should as editor[4] oppose the starting of this particular hare, since it would arouse all the reviewers rushing away down a side-track. I also said that while there was, in fact, no insuperable difficulty to prevent women from preaching in Church (I had just arrived myself from delivering a sermon in St. Martin-in-the-Fields)[5] the priesthood of women was in some respects open to the same objection which I personally feel for seeing Elisabeth Bergner play *King David*.[6] He said he was deeply disappointed by my attitude....

   With love,
      Yours ever,
         Dorothy

3 Dr Rieu had raised the question of the ordination of women. He had said: "I now ask whether the one chance which the Church has to regain its leadership of mankind is not to use both sexes equally. Why, to take a little thing first, should not girls sing in choirs as well as boys? Would not a parish be run best by a man and his wife both in orders and both paid servants of the community? Why, to put it in a nutshell, should you not be Archbishop of Canterbury?" He said that he had talked the matter over with his wife, "an extremely intelligent lady who played a part in the suffragette movement years ago".
4 i.e. of "Bridgeheads".
5 But see her letter to G. C. Piper, dated 24 January 1939!
6 Elisabeth Bergner (1900–1986) played the title role in J. M. Barrie's *The Boy David* in 1936 at His Majesty's Theatre.

                              [24 Newland Street
                              Witham
                              Essex]

TO DR JAMES WELCH
16 February 1942

Dear Dr. Welch...
   The last batch of letters you sent on was a nice one. People seem to have more or less settled down to the thing. The C.E.N.[1] seems to be of the opinion that we removed vast excesses of slang in express deference to its wishes. I am going to be obstinate about St. Matthew. If we may only leave that "test-case" unaltered, people will have to believe that everything

1 *Church of England Newspaper.*

else has been played practically as written. *The Daily Express* had the nerve to ring up on Monday to ask me what cuts had been made in "A Certain Nobleman". Unhappily, I was in bed at the time with a slight cold, and my husband answered them. I hope he didn't say anything indiscreet. He says he was careful, and informed them (a) that he knew nothing about it, (b) that so far as he could gather such cuts as there were were made for time and (c) they weren't to quote him because it had nothing to do with him; but of course he may have said more than he should, because he was rather angry with them for ringing up at all. So far, I haven't seen anything in the *Express* about it, so I hope no harm was done.

I do think that when the plays are published you or somebody ought to write an introduction with an authoritative account of the stand made by the Churches' Committee.[2] I say, "or somebody", because I don't know how far your official position allows you to "reveal" (as the papers say) the inner history of the battle; but you are the obvious person, "having had perfect understanding of all things from the very first". It does seem to me extremely important that something should be said about it, because the popular idea is that the blessed laity are all for boldness of policy and a march forward in a spirit of Christian brotherly love, and are only impeded by the timidity and bickering of their ecclesiastical leaders; whereas in this business the Churchmen were united, bold and intelligent and the laity obscurantist and divided. (Not all the churchmen, of course, but the official spokesmen, of whom one might have expected the worst.) And the extraordinary discovery that the united voice of an undivided Church can silence ministries and parliaments ought to be an encouragement to somebody or other to do something or other when the time comes. So do think it over, won't you, so as to be prepared when the time comes.

Yours very sincerely,
[Dorothy L. Sayers]

---

2 Dr James Welch did write such an account in his "Foreword" to the published version of *The Man Born to be King*, Gollancz, 1943, pp. 9–16.

It was Dr Welch's responsibility to submit every play to the Central Religious Advisory Committee and to pass on their comments to D. L. S. For the most part the alterations they requested were minor ones, to which D. L. S. agreed. With regard to the fourth play, "The Heirs to the Kingdom", a difficulty arose. The Bishop of Winchester, Dr Cyril Garbett (soon to become Archbishop of York), who for twenty years had been Chairman of the Committee, objected to the informality of the dialogue. D. L. S. decided that the time had come to make a stand.

[24 Newland Street
Witham
Essex]

PRIVATE AND CONFIDENTIAL

TO DR JAMES WELCH
19 February 1942

Dear Dr. Welch...

Look here; I rather think the time has come when I must dig my toes in a little. Otherwise I see trouble ahead. I have accordingly written you a formal sort of letter about the alterations, which can be passed on, if you think well, to the Bishop.

You will see that I have not actually refused to do anything, or threatened to stop work, or to give interviews to the papers. Nor have I invoked the thing called "artistic integrity". But I have said rather plainly what I feel about these matters on doctrinal and other high-minded grounds, and indicated the position into which I have been pushed. I do not want to make a row; but to count upon my – and your – being ready to put up with anything for peace' sake is a genteel form of blackmail. The objections are of varying importance: the one about the Americanisms raises the most immediate danger; the one about "ducks and drakes" is the silliest; the one about the expressions used by the Caiaphas gang is going to land us in the most serious differences of opinion as time goes on. I cannot deal with the Bishop as I should deal with Miss Jenkin; and, after the uproar that has been made, you know quite well that I shall not make a to-do and call in the scripts. But I am frankly appalled at the idea of getting through the Trial and Crucifixion scenes with all the "bad people" having to be bottled down to expressions which could not possibly offend anybody. I will not allow the Roman soldiers to use barrack-room oaths, but they must behave like common soldiers hanging a common criminal, or where is the point of the story? The impenitent thief cannot curse and yell as you and I would if we were skewered up with nails to a post in the broiling sun, but he must not talk like a Sunday-school child. Nobody cares a dump nowadays that Christ was "scourged, railed upon, buffeted, mocked and crucified", because all those words have grown hypnotic with ecclesiastical use. But it does give people a slight shock to be shown that God was flogged, spat upon, called dirty names, slugged in the jaw, insulted with vulgar jokes, and spiked up on the gallows like an owl on a barn-door. That's the thing the priests and people did – has the Bishop forgotten it? It is an ugly, tear-stained, sweat-stained, blood-stained story, and the thing was done by callous, conceited and cruel people. Shocked? we damn well ought to be shocked. If nobody is going to be shocked we might as well not tell them about it.

It's very bad luck on you, and I *don't* want to make trouble. But I do want the Bishop to know what I feel about it – not from the "artistic" point of view, but from the point of view of *what we are trying to tell people.* The scandal of the Cross was a scandal – not a solemn bit of ritual symbolic of scandal. "The drunkards make songs upon me" – I daresay they did, and I don't suppose they were very pretty songs either, or in very good taste. I've made all the alterations required so far, but I'm now entering a formal protest, which I have tried to make a mild one, without threatenings and slaughters. But if the contemporary world is not much moved by the execution of God it is partly because pious phrases and reverent language have made it appear a more dignified crime than it was. It was a dirty piece of work, tell the Bishop.

Sympathetically yours,

[Dorothy L. Sayers]

[24 Newland Street
Witham
Essex]

TO FATHER TAYLOR[1]

after 8 March 1942

Dear Fr. Taylor,

Thank you for your delightful and encouraging letter. I'm absurdly pleased that you liked the Centurion's *batman.*[2] My Roman army man seemed to come much more alive when I had removed from him the faithful slave, or the hypothetical "son" (παις) beloved of biblical commentators and fixed him up with a batman. Also, I wanted the play to bring out as much as possible the blessing upon the "uncovenanted" people and relationships – on the one hand the born "heirs to the Kingdom", and the religious leaders, so disappointing, and the traitor joining himself even to the disciples; and on the other "those who come in from the east and from the west" – the heathen Roman, with his trade of warfare, and the relation of friendship between superior and inferior in a State machine.

Did you approve – or at any rate not dislike – the (so far as I know) quite unorthodox interpretation I put on the Centurion's "Lord, I am not worthy"? It has always seemed to me curiously unconvincing that a Roman

---

1 Identity unknown.
2 In the fourth play, "The Heirs to the Kingdom", broadcast on 8 March, D. L. S. interpreted the centurion's servant as his batman. (word denoting an officer's servant) See Luke, chapter 7, verses 1–10.

soldier, of all people, should be overcome all of a sudden with a terrific sense of personal sinfulness and abasement, such as one associates with quite advanced Christian penitents, at the mere sight of a Jewish prophet, however impressive in appearance. But I could very well understand his feeling that here was a "holy man" of a different race, and his personal saintliness – much as a British soldier of the nicest type, who had lived a long time in India, might show delicacy of feeling when approaching some venerable and holy Mahatma, and understand that he ought not to ask him to pollute himself by contact with dogs or cooked beef or other things offensive to his religion. The speech about being a man under authority doesn't seem to have any grovelling sense of inferiority about it – only a recognition of Christ's personal authority, and a nice appreciation of the general fitness of things.

You know, I think some of the "unreality" that clings about the Gospel story as we hear it in the ordinary way is due to the impression one gets that anybody who is said to have "believed" in Jesus was immediately inspired, as by a prophetic revelation, with a full comprehension of the Nicene Creed in detail. There must have been all sorts of different grades of "belief" – belief that this was the Messiah, implicit confidence in this remarkable person, acceptance of the teaching, a dim sense that here was a man with something unearthly about him – according to the religious and social background of the believer; the central and important thing common to them all being, I suppose, a generous and unshakable *trust*. We are so apt to read the story backwards, with our minds steeped in the Resurrection and the Hypostatic Union.[3] But to the people at the time, the whole thing must have seemed very queer and vague and puzzling. Obviously the disciples were all at sea to the very end – what, then, must have been the condition of mind of Roman soldiers, Syro-Phoenician women, wandering lepers, blind beggars, and "the multitudes"?

No – I don't suppose the objectors listen to the plays; or if they do, they are committing a grievous sin by their own standards. They object on principle. "Thou shalt not make graven images" – still less, therefore, allow a wicked actor to "masquerade" (their word) as Our Lord. And you must not allow Christ to speak any words, however harmless and suitable, that are not recorded and prescribed in King James's Bible, because there is a curse in Revelation against adding anything to "the Book". And "Thou shalt not take the name of the Lord thy God in vain"; and any sort of acting is worse than vain, it is the Scarlet Woman in her worst abandoned guise. Also, acting the Gospel is a thing only done by idolatrous Roman Catholics in the ages of superstition, or by nasty foreigners at

---

3 A theological term, meaning the union of the divine and human natures in the person of Christ.

Oberammergau; and the whole thing is Popery, and closely connected with the mummery of the Mass. Further, even if you do not take this extreme view of the damnable nature of the whole enterprise, the thing is irreverent. The characters in the Bible are *all sacred*, and one must not suppose that sacred personages ever used slang or made jokes. Not only Christ, but even His enemies are "Sacred", because they are in the Bible. One correspondent objected to Herod's saying to his court, "Keep your mouths shut," because he did not like to hear such vulgar expressions from anybody "*closely connected with Our Lord*". (Just like the old lady who rebuked the young man for saying "What the devil?" on the grounds that she could not bear to hear a Sacred Personage so lightly spoken of.) Here is another gem from a gentleman in the *Stoke Newington Observer:*

> The two following objectionable parts were noticed; one character says to another: 'do the dirty on you'; and the Centurion who was commended by the Jews, and had built them a synagogue, is made to refer to the building in a conversation, with a levitous (sic) and jocular air.

You see, you mustn't try to think what a Roman Centurion would be really like. He is a sacred Centurion, and the little sacred building is sacred to *him*, and his daily conversation is sacred – and so the whole notion that the Son of God came in the flesh to the roaring, jostling, chaffering, joking, quarrelling, fighting, guzzling, intriguing, lobbying, worldly, polemical, political, sophisticated, brutal, Latinised, Hellenised, confused, complicated, careless civilization of first-century Jewry is utterly dissipated and lost. Christ wasn't born into history – He was born into the Bible (Authorized Version) – a place where nobody makes love, or gets drunk, or cracks vulgar jokes, or talks slang, or cheats, or despises his neighbours, but only a few selected puppets make ritual gestures symbolical of the sins of humanity. No wonder the story makes so little impression on the common man. It seems to have taken place in a world quite different from our own, – a world full of reverent people waiting about in polite attitudes for the fulfilment of prophesies.

Forgive this outburst. Story-telling is my profession, and even if I believed *nothing*, it would offend me to the soul to see that tremendous story so marred and emasculated in the handling. It's not the fault of the Evangelists; they sketched in the characters with a firm hand; shake off the dusty phrases and there are the real people, recognizable and alive: Caiaphas (the smug beast), and Pilate "all tied up with red tape", and the Samaritan woman setting down her pitcher, and the Blind Man at Siloam with his salty peasant wit, or the wedding guests getting harmlessly "merry" with good wine, and the disciples over-working themselves to the edge of nervous break-down and being told to lay off and find a quiet spot and take it easy for a bit (a humane suggestion oddly disguised by the stately and involved "Come ye yourselves apart into a desert place", which sounds so ascetic and uncomfortable) – it's all *there*, but it's got silted up with rumbling phrases and heavy-handed veneration. "He was in the world and the world knew Him not" – that's the great ironic tragedy; it was this actual world, and they simply *did not know* what was happening.

I know a priest who had the extraordinary experience of having to tell the story of Jesus to an adult educated Englishwoman who had never heard it before. (She was a society sort of person, I gather, and it just hadn't come her way – though you would hardly believe that possible.) Apparently it staggered her completely, and she asked in astonishment, "But does everybody *know* about this?" (Nor, I am sorry to say, when she afterwards attended church, was she at all persuaded by the behaviour of the congregation that they knew about it, either.)

The answer seems to be that they don't know; what they know to the point of boredom is something quite different – something that never happened, something that never looks to them remotely like anything that actually *happened*. My job, as I see it, is to present the thing, as best I can, as something that really did happen, as actually and unmistakably as the Battle of Britain, and all mixed up, like other events, with eating and drinking, and party politics, and rates and taxes, and working and sleeping and gossiping and laughing and buying and selling and coping with life in general. I am most grateful to you for telling me so kindly that, with all their faults (which obviously must be legion) the plays do really come over with something of that effect.

It is a shame to inflict all this upon you. I must stop, and get on with the Raising of Lazarus. (What on *earth* did Lazarus's friends say to him at that incredible supper-party? Did he make them all feel desperately uncomfortable, or did they just ask inquisitively: "*Do* tell us! What does it feel like to be dead?" Or did they think it would be better taste, on the whole, not to refer to the incident? Or succeed in pushing the whole peculiar affair into the background of their minds and forgetting that it had ever really occurred?)

He told it not – or something sealed
The lips of that evangelist.[4]

(But if you are writing a play, you have to make the characters say *something* or other!)

Yours very sincerely,

[Dorothy L. Sayers]

---

4 Tennyson, *In Memoriam*, 31.

At the request of Dr Welch D. L. S. agreed to visit the Bishop of Winchester and discuss the vital point of not "watering down the crudity, indeed the truth, of the Prosecution, Trial and Crucifixion".

24 Newland Street
Witham
Essex

TO THE BISHOP OF WINCHESTER[1]

17 March 1942

My Lord,

Thank you for your letter and invitation. I will certainly come and see you if I possibly can, though at the moment it is difficult to make any arrangements, since I am practically without servants and am thus tied to the house. I hope, however, that this situation may have cleared up by the end of the month, and that I shall be able to get to Winchester on Monday, March 30th.

I will do my best to discuss the forthcoming plays – though I ought to make it clear that works of art do not thrive on discussion beforehand – they are apt to "go stale" on the writer. But the general consideration which I feel I ought to lay before your Lordship is the necessity of making the characters and behaviour of the persons who brought about the trial and crucifixion of Christ real to the listener, even at the cost of some slight shock to the pious. For the story is a shocking one, even by human standards; but because its brutality is disguised for the common man by stereotyped expressions which have lost their power to shock, he accepts with mild complacency facts which ought to startle and horrify him like a blow in the face. If we cannot give him that blow in the face, what are we there for? "Christ was mocked and railed upon, buffeted, scourged and crucified" – everybody knows it, and few people are really startled by it – it is part of a Good-Friday service. But the playwright can show them the facts: "Here was God delivered over to the mercy of men, and what did we do to Him? Listen and you shall hear. We insulted and made a joke of Him. We smacked Him in the face. We gave Him the cat. We dragged Him through the streets and had Him nailed up on the common gallows by soldiers who took it all as part of the day's work — and the crowds at the gallows' foot made fun of Him. We had God here, and we said He was a lunatic, we said He was a blasphemous fellow, we said He was a political traitor and a criminal – we hated Him on sight and we killed Him with every circumstance of injustice and brutality. Listen to the facts, not

1 The Rt Rev. Dr Cyril Garbett.

camouflaged by Elizabethan ecclesiastical language. If you are not shocked, you ought to be – for if that cannot shock you, nothing can."

My Lord, the people have forgotten so much. The thing has become to them like a tale that is told. They cannot believe it ever happened. They look at the atrocities of wicked men today, and wonder that God does not interfere. They forget that those same atrocities were once perpetrated upon God. Priests and elders and Roman dictators no longer seem to them to be "wicked men", as we understand wickedness, for the old familiar obsolete phrases have been sterilized by pious associations and hurt nobody any more. In trying to avoid the hurt, we draw a veil between man and his own sin, and in trying to avoid irreverence we protect the wicked from the world's judgment. But how can it honour God to make His enemies seem less cruel, less callous, less evil than they were?

The people are apathetic, because the story has become unreal, and the priests are in despair how to bring its reality home to them. If a blunt phrase or an ugly word can show the listener exactly what it was that man did to God, ought we to mind if he recoils in horror? And if we are blamed, shall we be the first or the greatest to be blamed for startling people with the truth?

I am, my Lord,
Yours sincerely,
Dorothy L. Sayers

I find that I have neglected to congratulate your Lordship upon your call to the See of York. And – which is the more discourteous – that I have also neglected to thank you for the support you have given to these plays of mine. Please accept the congratulations and the thanks, together with my apology.

Having won a scholarship to Balliol College, Oxford, John Anthony decided to put in some war service before going up. Accordingly he signed on with the Technical Branch of the Royal Air Force, where he remained for three years.

As from 24 Newland Street
Witham
Essex

TO HER SON
28 March 1942

Dear John,

Here's your cheque – with love – I think the only snag that could possibly occur about banking it is that sometimes banks aren't keen to open an account with so small a sum. But this will probably be quite all right if you can show that you are in employment and known to somebody – e.g. the head-bloke at the works or what not – somebody local, I mean. I *think* so – I remember starting my own account in Town with £100, on the strength of working at S. H. Benson's, who also bank at Lloyds.

I think you're quite right to have got more comfortable rooms. And I shouldn't consider a certain sensitiveness about clean tables to be a sign of decadence! There is no particular merit in dirt and disorder. I rather thought you would find the working population interesting at close quarters, but if the quarters are too close, too long at a time, the situation is apt to be trying. A different background and a different sense of humour *do* make a difference. The workers of this country are damned good stuff, take them all in all, though it is an error to suppose that, merely by being a worker, a man becomes endowed with infallible virtue and wisdom. That's not the case, though a great many Socialist Utopias are built on that curious assumption. The intelligent humanist is liable to make a major divinity of the proletariat – but they are merely human beings, with their own virtues and vices like other people. And, having discovered for yourself the deficiencies of a too-intellectual education, you will probably now discover those of a too exclusively technical education – one of which is to place the victim at the mercy of words and generalizations.

All is well at home, except for the difficulty of getting any sort of servants. We are in the middle of an upheaval of this kind – coinciding, of course, with the moment when I have to go and interview the Bishop of Winchester about "realism" in Biblical plays! But no doubt things will sort themselves out eventually.

Love and best wishes,
    D. L. S.

[24 Newland Street
Witham
Essex]

4 May 1942

Dear Miss Storm Jameson,

I have no biography! I was born, educated, and married as per *Who's Who*, and shall presumably die some day and depart from that volume into *Who Was Who*!

I am all agin the notion that the public should neglect one's work, such as it is, for one's incidental circumstances, such as they are. *A fortiori*, of course, such as they are not – I have just read in an American paper that "Mrs. Sayres-Fleming . . . plays poor contract bridge, is not quick at puzzles, even the crossword variety, and abhors solitaire." Every word of this is incorrect, and I can't think where they got it from. My name is not spelt like that, and we don't hyphen our maiden and married names in this country, I have never played contract bridge, even poorly, but I am fond of puzzles, a dab at crosswords, and a confirmed player of what right-minded people call "patience". *Home Chat* once announced that I was devoted to gardening; I cannot imagine a greater lie. If I had done anything really spectacular, such as being divorced ten times, or being nearly eaten by cannibals, or having been the first detective novelist to swim the Channel, I should doubtless be charmed to see these exploits figure in a biographical note; but from the humdrum triviality of my career I fear I cannot spin out any exciting story.

I do hope you are now really rested and are feeling better, and that your husband[2] also has recovered.

Kind regards,
Yours sincerely,
[Dorothy L. Sayers]

---

1 (Margaret) Storm Jameson (1891–1986), novelist and author of poetry, essays, criticism and biography.
2 The historian Guy Chapman.

[24 Newland Street
Witham
Essex]

TO DR JAMES WELCH
6 May 1942

Dear Dr. Welch,

I think you will be pleased and amused by the enclosed letter from my friend, Miss Barber, whom you met in the Studio two plays ago. She is English mistress in an evacuated school, and House-mistress of a small bunch of children in Berkhamsted. Most of her little bunch are Jewesses, but she has two or three small Gentiles, whom she faithfully collects on Sundays to listen to the shows.

> . . . I loved it,[1] and so did the children who had duly returned from their tennis. We were alone this time and sat quietly round the wireless – and it moved them to the deepest and most searching questions as to the necessity of the Cross and the origin of evil and what not. My young Edith – whom the others call our liquorice Allsorts, because she is a blend of Greek-Turk and Hungarian Jew, born in Rotterdam and brought up in Vienna – is nominally a Christian – and is rapidly becoming one under the influence of the plays and S. Mark with me on Thursday afternoons! She made a revealing remark, "I know He didn't stay dead because I've been reading on ahead". Which just shows the pagan world one lives in. They were particularly pleased with Mrs. Pilate and the carriage bit – which I thought awfully well done, but the high light for me was Bobby Speaight's reading of the Lord's Prayer – more beautiful than I've ever heard it . . . I was thrilled with Judas, surnamed Pétain.[2]

I don't think Miss Barber's little mongrel is alone in not knowing the end of the story! I keep on trying to tell parsons that half the youth of this country is pagan, but they won't believe me.

I am driving on with the eighth play[3] – of course it is packed much too tight; there seems to be a fearful lot of necessary incidents to be got in during that hectic week in Jerusalem, including "suffer little children", which under the circumstances we can scarcely omit. There is a very

---

1 The sixth play, "The Feast of Tabernacles", broadcast on 3 May 1942.
2 Marshal Henri Philippe Pétain (1856–1951), who signed an armistice with Hitler on 25 June 1940 and thereafter became head of the Vichy Government. His name became a by-word for treachery.
3 "Royal Progress".

vulgar heckling party about the lady who married the seven brothers, which would have been still more vulgar if I didn't have to remember the Children's Hour and the Archbishop elect.[4]

Yours ever,

[Dorothy L. Sayers]

4 Dr Cyril Garbett, about to be transferred from Winchester to York.

> [24 Newland Street
> Witham
> Essex]

MISS KATHLEEN M. PENN[1]

15 May 1942

Dear Miss Penn,

Thank you very much for your kind letter. I am so glad you and others were interested by the ideas I tried to throw out at Eastbourne.[2] I am afraid the great thing is not so much to do something energetic instantly – though, of course, it is all the better if one can – but to get such a change of attitude in one's own mind to some of those things, that when one is faced with a practical problem, one instinctively takes the right line of action about it. It is interesting for example, and useful, when examining schemes for post-war reconstruction, or reading books and articles, or newspaper correspondence, to see how far the writers are still clinging to false conceptions about work and money, etc – conceptions which they take so much for granted that they have never even begun to question them. I find myself that when one makes a habit of doing this, one really does begin to see how deep the trouble lies, and how important it is to tackle it from the very root. Naturally, all this kind of thing can be done extremely well in Study Groups. I often think it would be a good idea if these Groups were to take for their study, not merely the pronouncements of politicians and Archbishops, but now and again the correspondence columns of some paper like *The Daily Telegraph*, or even *Picture Post*, and examine the surprising assumptions that very often underlie the expressed opinions of the ordinary mind.

There are a good many people like your R.A.F. officer; one of their troubles is the rooted assumption that human nature ought to be steadily progressing towards a state of perfection, and that life is not worth living

1 Identity unknown; she lived in Eastbourne.
2 "Why Work?", given at Eastbourne 23 April 1942. Given previously at Brighton, in March 1941, it was later published in *Creed or Chaos?*, Methuen, 1947, pp. 47–64.

if this is not the case. This is not a Christian assumption – indeed the Christian assertion is quite different, namely that there is a snag in human nature, which causes it to always deviate from the normal, and that when its deviations become too great, it lands itself in an intolerable position and draws down upon itself the judgment of war, famine, or some other calamity. Consequently, the Christian life must always be a struggle, in which the grace of God so works as to redeem the evil by turning it into good; the supreme instance being, of course, the redemptive power wrought by the suffering of the supremely innocent God. However, this is theology and too complicated for discussion in a letter.

As for the subsidiary question about personal immortality, the great Russian writer, Berdyaev[3], has pointed out that many of the finest minds feel no relish for the idea. I think we have made it much more difficult for people by leading them to suppose that immortality has something to do with a prolonged existence in time; whereas time is something that ceases outside this universe, and has no connection whatever with eternity, or what the Church calls "life everlasting".

The answer to what your sergeant friend said is, I think, contained in what I said earlier, namely that if a moral revolution is not effected peaceably, then bloodshed will be the only way out of the intolerable situation, but bloodshed does not, in itself, produce a better world. The mistake we made after the last war was I think in supposing that we could abolish wars merely by disapproving of them, but nobody can abolish the consequences of sin and error, merely by cutting them in the street! As a matter of fact, for the last couple of hundred years we have been hoping to get rid of human selfishness by merely saying loudly, and repeatedly, that we don't believe there is any such thing, which is rather as though when an incendiary bomb fell on the house, we were to shut our eyes tightly, and say that we didn't believe in bombs. That wouldn't prevent the house from burning down.

With all good wishes,
    Yours sincerely,
        [Dorothy L. Sayers]

---

3 Nicolas Berdyaev (1874–1948), Russian philosopher. His two best-known works are *Freedom and the Spirit* (tr. O. F. Clarke), 1935 and *The Meaning of History* (tr. G. Reavey), 1936. D. L. S. considered this "one of the world's really great books" (See letter to L. T. Duff, 10 May 1943, list.)

[24 Newland Street
Witham
Essex]

TO VAL GIELGUD

[No date, but May 1942]

Dear Val,

As proof that I am doing *something*, and because it is urgent, I am sending you Mary Magdalen's song to be set. You remember where it comes
– the Soldiers will not let her and her party through to the foot of the
Cross unless she sings to them – "Give us one of the old songs, Mary!"[1]

The song is thus the, so to speak, "Tipperary" of the period, and must
be treated as such. That is to say, the solo portion is nostalgic and sentimental, and the chorus is nostalgic and noisy; and the whole thing has to
be such as one can march to. We want a simple ballad tune, without any
pedantry about Lydian modes or Oriental atmosphere.

I enclose, by way of guide, the "pattern tune" to which the song was
written. (I think all lyric-writers fit their lines to some such vamped-up
melody, composed of reminiscent bits and pieces.) The composer is not,
of course, asked to incorporate any of this hotch-potch, but there are one
or two points which it illustrates, desirable for the dramatic effect:

1. Note that the solo verse is to be sung by a trained singer – the Gracie
Fields[2] touch is what we want – and wants to be cooing and fluid, so as to
make tough legionaries burst into tears and ask to be taken home to Dixie.
The chorus is to be sung by the soldiers (with the singer, of course) and
should therefore be quite straightforward in style and rough in execution.
I take it that the thing will be recorded by a professional soloist – will the
composer and music department please take care that the pitch of the
song and the quality of the voice are such that we can readily believe that
Marjorie Mars[3] is the singer. (Unless she is the singer, in which case it
would be best if she could record it herself.)

2. I have given the whole song with its two verses complete; but in the
play, Mary breaks down at the third line of the second verse.
Consequently we want one thoroughly soppy phrase at that point, rising
to its highest point at the word "brooks" in the first verse ("lad" in the
second), and including one of those heartbreaking, not to say vulgar,
musical intervals which the crooner loves, and all chaste musicians
deplore.

3. There is no reason, I think, why the soldiers should not put some

1 In the 11th play, "King of Sorrows", scene 2, sequence 3, 'At the Foot of the Cross'.
2 (Dame) Gracie Fields (1898–1979), a popular singer.
3 Marjorie Mars (1903–1951), singer.

simple harmonies into the chorus – we may imagine them, if we like, to have as much musical capacity as, say, the average Welshman. But, whether or no, the words "Company, halt!" must be sung in unison, on a rising melody that mimics the word of command, and with a strong break after them.

I implore you, in the bowels of the Lord, not to destroy yourself with work before the next show!

Yours ever,

[D. L. S.]

I want a tune that is both obvious and haunting – the kind that when you first hear it you go away humming and can't get out of your head! And quite, quite, low-brow.[4]

4   For some unknown reason, the task was entrusted to Benjamin Britten, who disregarded her wishes and wrote something totally unsuitable, to her great disgust. He also composed the Soldiers' Song in Play 10. See her letter to Val Gielgud, 22 September 1942.

In June Dr Welch wrote to tell D. L. S. that the members of the Central Religious Advisory Committee had expressed delight with the plays: "They agreed that the Church would have to learn something about evangelism from your plays! Personally I believe that drama, and possibly feature programmes, provide the finest weapon for the Church to use today; the old-fashioned methods are done for and the spoken word is at a serious discount....We must make you a prophet to this generation and hand you the microphone to use as often as you feel able."

[24 Newland Street
Witham
Essex]

TO DR JAMES WELCH

9 June 1942

Dear James,[1]

I have unfortunately forgotten all the handsome Scriptural names I once invented for you! There is a certain ceremony about "James", unsuited, I feel, to your energetic character – though I notice a touch of the Old Boanerges vein when you sail into the L.D. Observers,[2] which links you fittingly with the Apostle your namesake....

Yes, do go on opening the letters, and make a note of anything significant. I am keeping most of them, in case they may come in useful when

1   They had now advanced to the use of Christian names.
2   Lord's Day Observance Society.

we write our prefaces to the published plays. I have unhappily destroyed some of the really potty and abusive ones, which might have adorned a page; but I daresay you can produce plenty of these from your own collection. This last little lot were all favourable, but not specially interesting – except that there was another person exercised in mind about the identification of Mary of Bethany with Mary Magdalen. I told him, more or less, that what was good enough for Augustine was good enough for us; having just learned from Fr. Biggart C.R.[3] that the theory is, in fact, Augustine's, though he didn't give me the reference. This confirms my general impression that if there is anything at all that was *not* dealt with by Augustine, it was dealt with by Aquinas, and that if one could give one's self up to read the whole of the works of these two saints one would never need to read anything else....

When we come to the denarius itself, I'm afraid verisimilitude must give way to dramatic necessity. We simply cannot hold up the action while the chap pops round the corner to borrow half-a-crown, leaving Jesus to entertain the audience with patter, like a conjurer waiting for his props.[4] We must just carry on and hope the purists won't notice. (There was once a purist who objected, in much the same way, about *Zeal of Thy House*, saying that the Prior ought not to have heard William of Sens' confession till he had said, "Excuse me a moment", and run off to the Cathedral to fetch his stole. I replied on that occasion that, quite apart from the tedium for the audience of waiting while his aged limbs carried him there and back, the delay would have caused the reluctant penitent to go off the boil, and that in dealing with a sinner as tough as William, the only way was to make a sharp and unceremonious grab at his soul the moment it poked its head out, without bothering to observe ecclesiastical Queensberry rules!)...

A correspondent begs me to go on and dramatise the Acts of the Apostles. After that, I suppose it will be the Early Fathers, the Schoolmen, the Reformers, and the Missionary Activities of the S.P.G.[5] Will no one deliver me from the body of this death?

Yours in the expectation of Judgement,

[Dorothy]

---

3 C.R. stands for the Community of the Resurrection, also known as the Mirfield Fathers, an Anglican religious community in Yorkshire.

4 The reference is to Matthew, chapter 22, verses 17–21: "Tell us therefore, What thinkest thou? Is it lawful to give tribute unto Caesar, or not?...[Jesus answers] Shew me the tribute money. And they brought unto him a penny." In the Vulgate these last words are, "At illi obtulerunt ei denarium", the implication being that the denarius had to be fetched from somewhere.

5 Society for the Propagation of the Gospel.

[24 Newland Street
Witham
Essex]

TO MAYNARD D. FOLLIN[1]

23 July 1942

Dear Sir,

Thank you for your letter, and for the elegant stamps adorning it, which my husband immediately seized upon with loud cries of delight.

As for the frivolity of my Trinitarian book[2] – never, I beg you, be led into imagining that the English take a thing less seriously because they handle it lightly. We may "take our pleasures sadly", but we make up for it by taking our real interests cheerfully. Misunderstanding of this simple fact is at the root of half the accusation of hypocrisy levelled against us by those more sober-minded nations who habitually express themselves in correct and appropriate attitudes. In *Strictly Personal*, Somerset Maugham[3] tells us that the French were affronted because the British troops marched to the strains of the "Lambeth Walk",[4] instead of to something dignified about death and glory. "These men", he told them, "will die for you; but they will do it with a joke – probably a bad one – on their lips." The French did not believe him; they are now experiencing the Germans, who do not joke on serious subjects.

From this national tendency to ill-timed hilarity the scientists are, perhaps, the most free – particularly, of course, sociologists and psychologists, who are strongly continentalised. But biologists also, in their degree, are earnest and sensitive, and the Mendelian limerick[5] distresses them. It is true that the colourful results alluded to would not appear till the second generation; it is also true, that, had the offspring in fact been only four in number, the colours would probably not have been distributed with so engaging a symmetry, though in a generation of four hundred the proportions would no doubt be approximately correct. In future editions I shall label the thing in large letters: THIS IS A JOKE – for it is just about as serious as that other famous limerick on the Trinity, which, though expressed in French is (as the rhyme shows) "British-made", and which British theologians relish:

---

1   A correspondent in Detroit, Michigan; identity unknown.
2   *The Mind of the Maker.*
3   Somerset Maugham (1874–1965), novelist, short-story writer and playwright. *Strictly Personal*, expressing his views on life and art, was published in 1942.
4   The best known tune of the popular show *Me and My Girl*, starring Lupino Lane.
5   Quoted in *The Mind of the Maker*, Methuen, p. 4, note 1: "There was a young lady named Starkie,\ Who had an affair with a darkie;\ The result of her sins\ Was quadruplets, not twins,\ One black and one white and two khaki."

Il était un jeune homme de Dijon
Qui aimait beaucoup la religion;
Il disait, "Ma foi!
J'adore tous les trois,
Et le Père et le Fils et le Pigeon".[6]

No – I shall not write a book about the Scriptural sanction for the doctrine of the Trinity. Why should I? The thing was hammered out six hundred hears ago at Nicaea, by men who were fifty times greater sticklers for Biblical authority than any one living today. It has since been dealt with by qualified theologians in scholarly works to which I could add nothing of weight. There is no point in doing badly what competent persons have already done well. And any discussion of the sort would have been quite out of place in *The Mind of the Maker*, which, as I hoped I had made clear in the introduction, is not a work of Christian apologetic, but an examination of that particular doctrine in its application to creative mind. The origin of the doctrine is outside my terms of reference; my only concern is to show how far it is true in a particular case. About that particular case I may claim to speak with some "authority" not because I was educated at Oxford, but because I am a writer – i.e. because I have direct experience of mind in the [act] of creation. My Oxford training is only some sort of guarantee that I know (or ought to know) the way to handle a subject – as, for example, that I should not step outside my terms of reference.

"Thus saith the Lord" is, therefore, not within my terms of reference at all. But since you demand Scriptural warrant for everything, where is your Scriptural authority for the Scriptures themselves? On what texts do you rely for the make-up of the Canon as we have it? Where, for example, does the Lord say that there are to be those four Gospels and no more? or that the *Revelation of Peter*[7] and *The Shepherd of Hermas*[8] are not authoritative – though the first was read in churches as early as the second century, and the second was included in the Codex Sinaiticus[9] as late as the fourth century? The doctrine of the Trinity was worked out and formulated in the Church – the same Church that is the authority for the Canon itself. If you want to see how, as a matter of historical fact, the

---

6 There was a young person of Dijon\, Who dearly revered his religion.\ He said. "As for me\ I adore them all three,\ the Father, the Son and the Pigeon".

7 *The Apocalypse of Peter,* dating from the early second century, accounted Scripture by Clement of Alexandria.

8 Hermas, accounted one of the Apostolic Fathers, was the author of *The Shepherd*, a text consisting of Visions, Mandates and Similitudes.

9 The manuscript of the Greek Bible, discovered in the monastery of St Catherine on Mount Sinai, now in the British Museum. It contains part of *The Shepherd* of Hermas.

Trinitarian formula was arrived at, read Prestige's *God in Patristic Thought*[10] (you will find it toughish). Or if you want to see how a contemporary Congregationalist arrives at it (by studying the Canon and using his brains) read J. S. Whale's *Christian Doctrine*[11] (which is easier going).

Finally, let me hasten to assure you that I do not belong to any "Anglican Group". I am a member of the Church of England, but owe no allegiance to any group, clique, caucus within the Anglican Communion.

Yours faithfully,

[Dorothy L. Sayers]

---

10 George Leonard Prestige, *God in Patristic Thought* (1936). He also wrote *Fathers and Heretics* (1940).
11 See letter to Michael de la Bedoyère, 7 October 1941, note 12.

[24 Newland Street
Witham
Essex]

TO MISS DOROTHY M. E. DAWSON[1]

5 August 1942

Dear Miss Dawson,

Thank you very much for your letter, I am glad you like my two books.

With regard to the general attitude of women, I agree with practically everything you say – except the suggestion that I should head a Women's Crusade! For one thing, I have no time to take on a new job of this kind; and for another, I am the wrong person to do it. I belong to a profession in which women suffer from no inferiority; and when that is the case, the best proof one can give of the equality of the sexes is to stay where one is and do one's work, taking that equality for granted. To get up on an openly feminist platform would be, in a sense, to admit inferiority and throw away all the advantage gained. I do occasionally draw attention to the fact that society in general and the Church in particular will have to cope with this particular aspect of social justice; but actually, my own work is my best argument, since it is quietly accepted, not as woman's work, but simply as work – which is the point to which our aims are directed. That is why I think it is a mistake to talk about "replacing" the masculine conception of this and that by a feminine one. That would be

---

1 Identity unknown.

mere aggression on the part of the female! What is wanted is a merely "human" approach to every question, with neither sex trying to force the other under any sort of domination.

Yours very truly,

[Dorothy L. Sayers]

> [24 Newland Street
> Witham
> Essex]

TO VAL GIELGUD

18 August 1942

Dear Val,

I had an awful sort of feeling that my reminder about the tune for the song in "Princes of This World"[1] hadn't registered! I hope I made myself clear to Miss Eaves (was it Miss Eaves?) on the phone; I want just a plain straightforward tune – nothing oriental or antiquarian – and rather jolly; and it must be sung rough, like soldiers singing in a canteen. It would, of course, be much best if sung "live" in the studio, so that it could be interrupted naturally by the arrival of the message from Pilate. But that I leave to you.

To my horror, your young lady was under the impression that "Lalage" was a kind of "tra-la-la". I shouted the correct pronunciation over the phone – but in case the composer should share the same delusion, would you see that it is made clear to him that it is a girl's name, and is accented on the ante-penultimate, as:

> There was a young lady called Lalage
> Who took her degree in metallurgy –
> She received her first-class
> With a forehead of brass –
> But only by way of analogy.

I have finished the Crucifixion – except in cutting and polishing. It is pretty brutal and full of bad language, but you can't expect crucified robbers to talk like a Sunday-school class. The Archbishop will probably fall dead and all the parents will complain. The children won't mind – they like blood and tortures and Miss Barber says that the vocabulary of her

1 The 10th play.

Hampstead youngsters among themselves is enough to startle anybody –
and the Elementaries are probably worse – but the adults always delude
themselves with visions of childish innocence and sweetness. Mr.
McCulloch will swoon away. Perhaps it is as well that the script will have
to be passed in a hurry!

Yours ever,

[D. L. S.]

[24 Newland Street
Witham
Essex]

TO VAL GIELGUD

22 September 1942

Dear Val,

I've just had a very nice letter from the poor dear Archbishop of York
(who, after all, has suffered many things) thanking me for writing the plays
and saying a lot of kind things about them. After apologising in the most
friendly way for having sometimes had to ask for alterations, he says: "I
should like to add how greatly moved I was at listening yesterday to the
Crucifixion play. I shall be very interested to see if I have any letters about
it".[1] So he *did* take the trouble to hear it after all, and if the performance
moved him, that is a big tribute to you and the company, because I
gather he didn't much like the script when he read it. (For which I didn't
altogether blame him.) Also, he seems prepared to stand the racket (if any)
like a man, bless his heart. So it looks as though all was well in that
quarter. He's not a bad old stick, really.

I was most awfully proud of the company – they worked like absolute
heros, and the crowd-work was just about as good as it could be. I'm
afraid I did land you an awful packet this time. But it's no good going on
apologising for that – I *always* do it! (They will write on your tombstone:
"Here lies a chaser who never refused a fence"!) I hope I said thank you
properly, but I was rather dazed, and when I got out and found a taxi, I
couldn't remember what road the house was in, and said Maida Vale
when I meant St. John's Wood. I don't know why I should have come over
so stupid – I hadn't been doing any of the work.

I am deprived this time of Miss Barber's comments, because she had to

---

1 The Archbishop added: "During the first months of your plays I had a stream of letters all
   on the critical side, most of them quite unreasonable and many very abusive, but these have
   almost entirely died away during these last months." (Letter dated 21 September 1942)

go and look after a sick friend and get her to hospital, and couldn't listen in. But her school-children listened, and reported that they had just sat together and cried all the time. I hope it doesn't haunt them, or anything! But they are fairly toughish youngsters, I gather. According to the news, Hitler has recently chosen to crucify fifty people in Jugo-Slavia, or at any rate string them up on stakes, which is much the same thing. So we haven't got very far in close on 2000 years. And it's just as well people should know that Christianity deals with that kind of thing, and not with merely deprecating the pleasanter sins and urging people to go to church. I mean, whether anybody believes in it or not, it's got to be reckoned as belonging to that kind of situation and not exclusively to Little Puddlecombe vestry-meeting.

Dr. Welch seems to think that our party will go through all right. I do hope we shall be able to get together as many of the scattered people as possible. There are so many of them I haven't thanked properly, and I want to most frightfully. I don't think I've ever had such a devoted and enthusiastic bunch of people to work with – not even in *Zeal*, and there they did at least get their names on the play-bills.[2] I've written a line to John Laurie[3], by the way, whom I somehow missed altogether on Sunday. I think I managed to say something to most of the others, either individually or collectively. I thought Hermione Gingold[4] did uncommonly well – though I'm still furious with the man[5] who wrote that silly tune – she got hold of the idea and played it with very real sincerity, I thought. And Jonathan Field's[6] was a lovely performance – I didn't want an inflection different....

Bless you, dear, and thank you again.

> Yours ever,
> [D. L. S.]

2 At the time of the broadcasts, all the actors were anonymous, except for Robert Speaight, who played the part of Christ. It was thought best to make his name known to put an end to inquisitive speculation. The casts are printed in full in the published version of the plays.

3 John Laurie (1897–1980) played the part of Gestas; he later played in *Dad's Army*.

4 Hermione Gingold (1897–1987) played the part of Mary Magdalen.

5 Benjamin Britten!

6 Jonathan Field (b. 1912), author, director, composer: played the part of Dysmas.

24 Newland Street
Witham,
Essex

TO MARJORIE BARBER
22 September 1942

Dearest Bar,

What a shame![1]   Never mind – we'll hope there will be a re-play one of these days. Anyhow, I greatly rejoice in the determined enthusiasm of Liquorice-All-Sorts and Co., and I'm glad they enjoyed it.

We had an awful time with rehearsals. Everything seemed to go wrong – it was one of those days. Claudia's Dream had been done badly (owing to my not being there to explain just what I wanted!) and the ASS[2] who set the song disregarded all my instructions, and not only set it in $3/4$ time instead of march time, but had the vile impertinence to alter my lines because they wouldn't fit his tune. I threw my one and only fit of temperament, and we sang the thing in march-time and restored the line, but it wasn't a good tune anyway! Half the principals seemed to be missing on Saturday, and on Sunday Val lost his tobacco pouch! And poor Hermione Gingold had great difficulty with Magdalen – but in the end she was quite good. And the play did run too long – so we had eventually to cut the second little scene with the Romans (the one about the Hippocratic death-countenance) but it didn't matter much, and as a matter of fact the man playing Glaucus was not very good, so in the end we were probably better without it. But it was a trying two days – oh, yes! and we had to modify one or two bits that the Archbishop jibbed at (I don't blame him) – altogether, everything was hot, agitated and under-rehearsed.

Having said all that, I will say that the company played up simply nobly. My God! I've never heard anything like the crowd.... They were in a crucifying mood, and upon my word, they frightened me. Yes, Bobbie[3] was grand – and I do wish you had heard John Laurie[4] as Gestas and Jonathan Field[5] as Dysmas. John Laurie was simply terrifying – I have never heard anything that sounded so like somebody being crucified, the passion he put into it scared the people on the floor stiff – they said it was quite frightening to play with him. And Jonathan Field got that difficult Dysmas

1 Marjorie Barber had missed hearing the eleventh play, "King of Sorrows",
   through having to take a friend to hospital.
2 Benjamin Britten!
3 Robert Speaight.
4 See letter to Val Gielgud, 22 September 1942, note 2.
5 See letter to Val Gielgud, 22 September 1942, note 5.

speech perfectly – I couldn't have asked for anything better. I was very glad I put in the Balthazar bit at the end; Robert Adams's[6] lovely rich voice seemed to bring it all back into the realm of the mystical and fold it up and put it to bed in the right spirit. We were unfortunate in not having our usual Proclus – he was doing some other show – but the man[7] who took his part made quite a nice job of it.

But I tell you again, the crowd-work was the best we have done, and it certainly was pretty brutal. We had an excellent "shrieking harridan", and the "Tyburn" stuff with Dysmas sounded more like Hogarth than I should have thought possible. Dr. Welch was quite shattered, poor dear! Said he hadn't ever realised that the Crucifixion would have sounded like that, even though, in a sense, he knew it must have. (I don't mean he wasn't pleased – he was; but the fact is, we all succeeded in shocking ourselves.)

Golly! it was a strain. Poor Val at the end looked as if he'd been put through a wringer. And I was so exhausted that instead of trotting round to see Muriel as I'd promised, or going back to Witham, I fell into a taxi and returned to Shippie (with whom I was staying) and flung myself on the sofa in a state of coma! (I had warned Mac that I wasn't returning, because I knew what it was going to be like.) All the actors were noble – there wasn't one fluff or a mistake from beginning to end.

Meanwhile, I see that the Germans have just crucified fifty people in Jugo-Slavia – at least, they hung them up on posts to die, which is the same thing in all essentials. So there you are.

The Archbishop, it seems, didn't agree with my Dysmas, but he was quite good and didn't interfere. Dr. Welch said, maliciously, he was glad we'd upset his ideas about his "Three-Hours' Devotion" sermons, that he'd been doing all his life! I said that if a man had been doing the Second Word in conventional lines all his life, he couldn't possibly be pleased to have a new notion thrust on him at this time of day, but that I'd never been able to accept the moral interpretation, and had got to the point where I'd had to say: "Lord, I can make neither head nor tail of this – if you want it done, you'd better let me know what happened": and that revelation had then come to me in my bath, and it seemed to me to be right, as also to you, when I communicated it to you in the grocer's shop....[8]

Well, dear, have a good term and come back at Christmas to pay us a

---

6 Robert Adams had played the part of Balthazar in *He That Should Come*. See letter to the Editor, *Glasgow Herald*, 2 January 1939.

7 Arnold Ridley (1896–1984), producer, actor and playwright; he later played in *Dad's Army*.

8 D. L. S. explains her interpretation of the words of Dysmas, the robber who says "Lord, remember me..." in her Notes on the play: "I have affronted all the preachers and commentators by making [these words] an act, not of faith, but of charity." (Gollancz, p. 290.)

nice long Eighteenth-Century visit.

I hope you'll like the Resurrection play. It's not as exciting as the others, but that isn't really my fault altogether. The thing ends on a quiet note, and I think that is really right. But NINE supernatural appearances are a bit stiff, dramatically speaking – all in forty-five minutes!

     Best love,
       Dorothy

                              24 Newland Street
                              Witham
                              Essex

TO HER SON

22 September 1942

Dear John...

Sorry you find life so boring. Wars are, unfortunately, won by the side that (other things, such as armaments, being equal) best knows how to stand boredom and inconvenience. That is the real secret of the thing called "morale". When one has seen two wars, one begins to know that. The English, on the whole, stand boredom and inconvenience rather well – always provided they are allowed to grumble when they feel like it. The great difficulty is to realise that by enduring boredom one is actually doing an important job of work. It is easier to feel that one's work is important when it involves excitement – that's why it's such a problem to keep the U.S.A. and Canadian troops in good spirits – they are not used to "standing and waiting", as we are.

By the way, I don't think I do take a gloomy view of the war. I am inclined to take a gloomy view of the peace, largely because so many people have got it into their heads that it will somehow or other usher in the millennium. It won't. Why should it? It will usher in a very hard, difficult, delicate, and strenuous period. It will require exactly the same qualities as the war, only more so. Which is all right if people make up their minds to it beforehand. But not if they are looking forward to a sort of Golden Age. There are too many people going about who think they can abolish human nature by disapproving of it, or passing Acts of Parliament about it. But they can't. I only hope that before the War ends, they will have grasped this fundamental truth. If not, we are in for a bad time. I do think they are a bit nearer grasping it than they were in 1918.

Meanwhile, I'm glad you're all set to make a job of this engineering business. It will be needed – the job, I mean. It's frightfully important not to look on war as a sort of interruption to the business of life. It's part of life, and the more one can take hold of it and do something with it the better.

I must now write letters to about twenty people, thanking them for the work they did in our last play. Bless their hearts, they did work, too! And of course my secretary is on holiday, so I shall have to toil through them with my own hand.

All the best,
Mother

I couldn't write before because I was up in Town, and didn't get your letter until last night.

[24 Newland Street
Witham
Essex]

TO DR JAMES WELCH

30 September 1942

Dear James,

I am sending along *The Man Born to be King* fan-mail for you to have a look at. I have destroyed some of the more abusive anonymous letters, including the postcard which began "You nasty old sour-puss" (I'm rather sorry I did that!), but I think most of the rest are here, with the possible exception of one or two letters from personal friends. I haven't made any effort to sort them, but I am sending two or three sheets, on which we collected a few of the more interesting testimonies, about the effect on children and on people who have found the plays more stimulating than the conventional presentations of the story. I hope you may find them of some use.

By the way, as you have made no objection to the use of Mary Cleophas[1] in the Emmaus story, I take it that it is o.k. by you and I shouldn't think the Archbishop would have any serious objection if you have none. How about that confounded sailing boat?[2] Will it do?

Yours ever,
[Dorothy]

---

1 In her Notes on the characters in play 12 D. L. S. says concerning Mary Cleophas: "The suggestion that she was the 'other disciple' in the Emmaus story comes from the Bishop of Ripon." (The Rt Rev. Geoffrey Charles Lester Lunt.) See published version of the plays, p. 320.

2 In play 12, "The King Comes to his Own", scene 3, 'The Sea of Galilee', the disciples, who are fishing, hear a voice from the shore telling them to cast the net on the right side of the boat. They tow in a full net.

Dr Welch replied on 14 October:

My nautical friend says that all the details about this sailing boat and the fishing are correct, except that he does not believe it would have been possible to tow ashore at the stern of the dinghy a catch of fish which it was impossible to haul on board the larger vessel. But I think we must blame the Gospel record and not D. L. S. for this!

The last play was broadcast on 18 October 1942. Mr B. E. Nicolls, Controller of Programmes, wrote as follows:

I feel I must seize the occasion of the final broadcast of your plays of the Life of Christ to write and make some attempt to express our gratitude to you for providing one of the great landmarks of broadcasting. I don't know about the ranks of Tuscany¹, as we have seen nothing and heard little of the protestants since the initial controversy, but I do know that everyone who has heard the plays has been genuinely convinced of their value from the religious point of view as well as of their place as a great broadcasting achievement. We all want to repeat the plays, and I very much hope that we shall be able to arrange to do so at satisfactory intervals somewhere between Christmas and Easter.

1 An echo of the lines from Macaulay's "Horatius", *Lays of Ancient Rome*, stanza 60: "And even the ranks of Tuscany\ Could scarce forbear to cheer."

D. L. S. replied:

> [24 Newland Street
> Witham
> Essex]

22 October 1942

Dear Mr Nicolls,

Thank you very much for your kind letter about *The Man Born to be King*. Let me hasten to say that I am deeply grateful to the B.B.C. for having entrusted me with this important and enthralling job of work. To do it was a delight as well as a great honour, and I am very glad to know that you were not dissatisfied with the work, and that it was well enough received by the listeners to justify this rather bold undertaking. And I am also full of gratitude for the encouragement and cooperation I received from the Corporation – from those "at the top" who sanctioned the production, as well as from the Religious and Dramatic Departments, with whom my relations were extraordinarily happy throughout.

The ranks of Tuscany, though perhaps forbearing to cheer, have mostly fallen silent. A few abusive letters still arrive, but the majority of them are anonymous – and one need not pay much attention to the opinion of anyone who hasn't the courage to put his name to it. One of these letters arrived yesterday – apparently from Jesus Christ in person; but since he, too, omitted his signature, preferring to address me through an anonymous "prophetess", I am inclined to believe that the communication cannot really have come from that exalted quarter – one in which courage, as a rule, was not lacking.

One thing that I thought very encouraging was that appreciative letters came from people of all ages and professions – septuagenarians and parents speaking for their young children, clergy of all denominations, school-teachers, and factory workers.

It is most good of you to send me such a generous gift of all the records. I shall prize them most deeply, as a memory of the happiest production with which I have ever been associated. You cannot think how I shall miss the broadcasts. And I do most tremendously appreciate the lavish generosity which gave us so free a hand as regards big casts and distinguished actors.

I do hope the repeat performance will go through all right.[2] I am continually getting letters asking for a replay at a more convenient hour for adults, and I judge that there is a good public for it. And I think the series will be more impressive when the plays are given at closer intervals, so as to produce a cumulative effect – though it is just as well that we had a four-weeks' interval between them in the first instance, otherwise we should have fallen dead with exhaustion!

Again thanking you very much,
   Yours sincerely,
     [Dorothy L. Sayers]

---

2 In 1943 a repeat, recorded performance of the original production was broadcast. The last five plays in a new production by Val Gielgud were re-broadcast during Passion Week in 1944, 1945 and 1946. In 1947 a totally new production, under Noel Iliff, was put in hand. A further production by Peter Watts was broadcast in 1951. This was followed by two more, in 1965 and 1975.

24 Newland Street
Witham
Essex

TO MARJORIE BARBER

26 October 1942

Dearest Bar,

Thank you so much for your letter. It is, as you say, "curious" to be done with *The Man Born to be King* – which has been a major, and increasing, preoccupation for exactly three years from the moment it was first suggested.[1] But there is a sense of triumph at having actually got through to the end without interruption, internal row, or major catastrophe! We had a small party after the last show, at which I made an incoherent speech of thanks and presented Val with a stop-watch. This seemed an appropriate gift, since we had not only lived in mortal terror of the stop-watch all the way through, but had actually undermined and ruined the constitution of one of these instruments in the process! (At any rate, it gave up the ghost during rehearsal of the trial-scene, and passed out quietly.) And one of Val's major causes of pride was that we had never, in fact, once over-run the time, despite many narrow squeaks. So he was pleased and Dr. Welch was pleased, and the company was pleased, and I was pleased, and an orgy of embraces was enjoyed by all.

I didn't think there was anything very much wrong with the production last time – it may have been the set. Most of the cast were the same – Hermione Gingold was playing Magdalen again (you didn't hear her in the Crucifixion), and there was a new Nicodemus – but I don't think we've *ever* had the same Nicodemus twice! – and a new Philip; on the other hand, we had our original James back. And Mabel Constanduros[2] was playing Mary Cleophas in place of Molly Rankin – but that wouldn't affect you, because you didn't hear the Crucifixion. All the other principals were the same – Jesus and John and Peter and Caiaphas and Matthew and Thomas and the Pilate family and Eunice, and, of course, the Evangelist. Did you recognise Henry Ainley as Gabriel?[3] He was perfectly sweet – very much the old actor, lion-like, courteous and full of airs and graces, and many compliments flowed elegantly. We apologised for offering him so small a part, saying that we should not have dreamed

---

1 Dr Welch first put the proposal to her on 5 February 1940. The time is therefore exactly 2 years and 8 months.

2 Mabel Constanduros (1880–1957), comedienne.

3 Henry Ainley (1879–1945). There is an error in the cast list as printed, the name of Henry Ainley being given as playing a Roman guard.

of doing so, had it been anything less than an Archangel; to which he replied, ("the affable Archangel") that the honour was his to be included in so beautiful and notable a production; and he clasped my hand in both of his, wishing me success in the traditional manner, and we all felt as though we had been laid away in lavender.

My Mrs. Rice (the daily woman) is intelligent. She told me that she and the children had listened to the plays and thought them beautiful. Her little girl (age not stated) had said at the Crucifixion: "Mummy, it's very cruel", and Mummy had said, "Well, you don't realize – that's how it was when they used to have public executions" – and off her own bat she made the connection with Tyburn and the way they did things in "those old days". She said she found the whole story "hard to believe" – for which I didn't blame her. She also said that she had never cared much for the New Testament – the Psalms and bits of the O.T. were so beautiful, weren't they, madam, but the N.T. was rather dull and dry. (I don't know if she used those words exactly, but I gathered she meant it was just straightforward narration of facts, without any purple passages of poetry.) But she liked the plays, which made it seem real and exciting. Also she said, "There was one thing I never liked about Him – He was meek; I don't like people to be meek – I always felt, couldn't He do something, stand up and fight for Himself? But the play (the Crucifixion) made me see that what He did was really braver, wasn't it?" Apparently Baruch and the "shrieking harridan" got home all right. I've always thought that "gentle Jesus meek and mild"[4] was a most disastrous hymn – one of the half-truths that are far more damaging than any open lie....

Mac is distressed and aggrieved. He hoped to get some things shown at an exhibition of the National Artists' something or other, and to be elected a member; but he and a lot of others were crowded out for lack of space on the walls. This has upset him quite a lot. He had done a big study of you – a variant of the one you had before – which he was very proud of. He was holding up sending it to you, in hopes that he could announce that it was being exhibited, and it was all a great disappointment. But I hope he has now sent, or is sending it.

My name is mud to-day. I had to speak yesterday at a W.E.A.[5] one-day school at Maldon, and was an hour late for dinner. I can't think how it happened, because the Chairman said: "Now, I faithfully promised to get Miss Sayers home by eight, so we must stop now". So we stopped almost immediately, and came home with very little delay. I think he must have mistaken the time on his watch and thought it was 7.20 when it was

---

4 See letter to Father Herbert Kelly, 19 October 1937, note 11.
5 Workers' Educational Association.

actually 8.20. If so, I must have been more interesting than I thought! However, Mac would listen to no explanations and punished himself by refusing to eat his dinner – a kind of behaviour which I think, and have always thought, quite silly. It was a good meeting, and the discussion was very lively; I rode all my old hobby-horses, and got in a good strong passage about the place of Women in the State, which was received with applause from the strong female contingent present.

Going back to the plays – one of the actors came up to me during rehearsal, just after we'd been doing the "my Lord and my God" bit,[6] and said, "That's the first time I've ever heard the Atonement explained – so as to mean anything, that is". Which shows the advantage of putting things in words of one syllable, without technical theological terms, and linking them up to the *action of the story*. I admit that it's not a complete explanation, but so long as one can persuade people that it has a meaning of some kind one does at least save the thing from appearing completely irrational. In the manner of my friend Mrs. Rice's grand mamma, who, apparently, always told the children that one must just accept these things and not ask questions about them. "Whatever you do, Mrs. Rice", said I, "never tell your children they mustn't ask questions." She assured me she would never dream of doing so. "Tell them," said I, "that you don't know, if you like, and that they must read books about it, or ask somebody who does know. But don't give them the idea that the whole thing will fall to pieces if one starts asking questions." The Church has suffered a good deal, I think, from the sinister figure of Mrs. Rice's grand mamma. I see her, deeply reverent in black bombazine, standing protectively between the pushing interviewer and the frail and aged figure of God in a bath-chair. "Now, don't you speak rough to Him – He's very old and shaky, and I wouldn't answer for the consequences."...

Last Tuesday was the foulest day I ever was out in. I was in Town, having addressed a bunch of clergy in the morning, and spent the afternoon and evening trudging about in a downpour. No taxis – buses crowded and anyhow not going to any of the places I wanted to visit – and one could scarcely even take refuge in a shop, because the streams of water that poured off one's hat and clothing were an absolute menace to the stock-in-trade. But I was determined to go to the theatre and went – the St. James – no bus goes nearer to it, of course, than Piccadilly! The wretched programme-girls and people had (so the woman in the cloak-room said) all come in soaked, with their shoes and stockings wringing wet and nothing to change into and nowhere to dry themselves. I blessed the chance that had made me put on hand-knitted woolly stockings, which

---

6 Play 12, "The King Comes to His Own", scene 2, sequence 4: the words of Doubting Thomas.

were certainly very hot (the day being muggy) but didn't let in a drop of water. But one couldn't wear a sopping coat in the theatre – still less, a drowned fur, which smelt like a wet dog and was acutely embarrassing all day – and there was a draught from the stage the like of which I have seldom encountered! However, I enjoyed the show – *The Duke in Darkness*[7] – good melodrama, with striking performances by Leslie Banks[8] and Michael Redgrave, and a lot of Renaissance colour. But an elderly man and woman next me were bored and resentful to the point of antagonism. They made me feel adolescent, as though I really ought to have grown out of my liking for the drama of cloak and sword. I think I'm really rather uncritical in the theatre, ready to take things at their face-value and be pleased with any story the author chooses to tell. Is it weakness of intellect, birdie, I cried?[9] – After which, I made my sodden way to the Moulin d'Or,[10] had two drinks, and a Hamburger Steak, and chummed up in George's sanctum with two bobbies. I'd seen them come in, and thought George must have been infringing the food laws; but it appeared that one of the diners had bought a farm somewhere, and was showing his friend a map of the place over dinner; whereupon a woman at the next table had taken it into her head that they were Fifth-columnists discussing war-maps and had rushed out and fetched the police. They were friendly cops, and rather apologised for having come to investigate the mare's nest, but it was their duty so to do. I replied that no doubt 999 of these scares were all nonsense to attract attention, but the thousandth time there might be something in it, and we might find a traitor clever enough to do the bluff of discussing his plans openly in a public restaurant. They said eagerly that that was just it, madam, and we became very chummy, and debated how many people could be conveniently knocked on the head or thrown off bridges in the black-out with complete impunity, and how greatly war-conditions must add to the work and worries of the police force. By this time, the police had had their drinks (at poor George's expense, I suppose) and I feared my last bus had gone. So I departed under police escort, hoping for a taxi. They said that, even if there was one, they were unfortunately not allowed to call taxis for the public. I replied that they need only pretend they had arrested me and were hauling me off to custody, and we made merry over this till, happily, the last bus arrived after all and

---

7 By Patrick Hamilton (1904–1962).

8 Leslie Banks (1890–1952).

9 A line from Ko-Ko's song in Gilbert and Sullivan's *The Mikado*, Act II.

10 A restaurant in Great Newport Street, where D. L. S. had an account and entertained her friends in London.

11 The Palm Sunday hymn beginning "Ride on! ride on in majesty", stanza 2, line 2: "In lowly pomp ride on to die". (Words by H. H. Milman.)

I was carried off, "in lowly pomp" as the hymn puts it." I almost think I shall be sorry when "war-conditions" are over: one gets so much simple fun.

Bless you, dearie, and all the best,
    Dorothy

I didn't know I'd written such a lot of twaddle. Sorry!

"We must make you a prophet to this generation and hand you the microphone to use as often as you feel able", Dr Welch had written. This the B.B.C. proceeded to do, to D. L. S.'s increasing dismay, as this letter shows.

                                    [24 Newland Street
                                    Witham
                                    Essex]

[14 December 1942]
TO THE REV. ERIC FENN

Dear Mr. Fenn,

I have just been passionately writing to Dr. Welch that I think it is rather a mistake for me to go on with this business of direct exhortation or instruction in the Christian faith. I am so obviously getting to be considered one of the old gang, whose voice can be heard bleating from every missionary platform; and when that happens the surprise value of the amateur theologian has pretty well disappeared and it is time to make way for the professionals. Also, the theme that "God is Agape"', is not really my line. Had you said Logos now!

Look! I shall be seeing Dr. Welch shortly after Christmas; may I talk it over with him before deciding? I think he understands my position, which I have already explained to him in another connection. After talking it over with him I may be able to see a little more clearly whether it would, or would not, be a good thing to take part in this particular series.

With kindest remembrances,
    Yours very sincerely,
        [Dorothy L. Sayers]

1 *Agape* is a theological term signifying God's love, as opposed to *eros*, earthly love.

1943

Responsibilities of fame

ઝ૭ઝ૭ઝ૭

Though reluctant to continue speaking in public about Christianity, D. L. S. never-theless responded generously to individuals who wrote to her in good faith. A great deal of her time and energy was spent in this way.

[24 Newland Street
Witham
Essex]

TO THE REV. G. E. WIGRAM[1]
14 January 1943

Sir,

Four hundred years ago the Church understood her proper relation to the artist and craftsman and their functions, and it was then true that the best architecture, music and plastic art were to be found in the churches.

Today it is not so. The Church of Christ has, generally speaking, lost the allegiance, both of the arts and the sciences. With comparatively few exceptions the men who are taken seriously by their own profession nei-ther work directly for the Church, nor derive inspiration from her Faith; and it is hardly too much to say that the name of Christianity has become identified with artistic frivolity and intellectual dishonesty.

The first Christian duty of a man, as man, is to serve God; his first duty, as a worker, is to serve his work, since this is the only means by which his work can be made to serve God.

---

1 The Rev. Gerrard Edmund Wigram, b. 1898; vicar of Leamington Hastings.

You will find the whole question of the *finis operis* and the *finis operantis*[2] fully discussed in *Art and Scholasticism* by Jacques Maritain[3] – one of the very few regular theologians to understand the theology of art and work.

By "the Church" I mean the whole body of those who profess the Christian faith, and by "the official church" I mean, more particularly, those priests and ministers whose official duty it is to represent her.

Yours faithfully,
[Dorothy L. Sayers]

2 Latin: aim or conclusion of the work, of the worker.
3 See letter to Maurice B. Reckitt, 8 May 1941, note 8. *Art and Scholasticism* was first published in French in 1920; English translation 1927.

[24 Newland Sstreet
Witham
Essex]
TO FLIGHT-LIEUTENANT BRYAN W. MONAHAN
R.A.A.F. Overseas H.Q.
15 January 1943

Dear Mr. Monahan,

Thank you for your very interesting letter. The distinction between "work" and "employment", and the still more vital distinction between creative work (man's divine occupation) and work for a living (the curse of Adam) are questions with which I dealt in another speech[1] – the one mentioned in a footnote to "Why Work?"- so I won't pursue that matter now, except to say that I quite agree that we have fallen into a verbal confusion, by using "work" and "employment" as though these were synonymous terms. In yet another speech (about to be published as a pamphlet by Methuen under the title "The Other Six Deadly Sins")[2] I have also tried to say something about wasteful production to provide "employment"; and perhaps you will forgive me if I refer you to this to save writing again (and probably worse) what I have already tried to write to the best of my ability.

1 "Work and Vocation", given at Brighton, 8 March 1941. Published in *A Christian Basis for the Post-War World*, ed. A. E. Baker, S.C.M. Press, May 1942.
2 Published on 11 March 1943.

The one point in your letter about which I should like to raise a query is the statement about the upper limit of production for the fruit of the earth. In a sense we do not know it – yet there are signs that there is a limit and that we are within measurable distance of reaching it. It may be true, for example, that the applications of coal to production have been touched upon: but there is a fixed quantity of coal in the earth and no more, and if we too brutally exploit the source of power we may find ourselves up against a limit of another kind. The same is true of oil – and, in a more alarming way, of the actual fruits of agriculture. If we make ourselves greedy and grasping tyrants of the earth – ravishing and not serving it – it takes its revenge in waste lands, barren soil, flood, drought and dearth. Every time we upset the balance of natural forces by over-cultivation, either of earth, animals or what-not, we seem to come up against some law which sends back to us in famine or disease the catastrophes we tried to avoid. And there seems to be also some compensatory law about the use of machines, by which, the more vigorously we endeavour to eliminate labour, the harder and more desperately we have to work to keep things going. R. K. Barlow's book, *The Discipline of Peace*[3] is an attempt to examine this state of things. We have got it into our heads that, as a speaker remarked to me the other day at a W.E.A.[4] meeting, "the earth is for us to *use*", but I think we shall be making a great mistake if we interpret this as meaning that it is there for us to exploit without reverence and without caution. That is to make nature, our fellow-creature, into our slave – and not much better, perhaps, than making slaves of our fellow-men.

Otherwise, as I say, I agree with you. Except that, provided the worker is engaged in his "own" or "proper" work, I don't see that it matters much whether the employer is public or private. At the moment, the public body of the State seems to be concerning itself almost exclusively with the idea of providing "employment" rather than "work" – and most of our public men are thoroughly confused in their minds between the two meanings of the word "work". The emphasis on providing paid employment is likely to end either in the establishment of a vast bureaucracy or a population engaged in preparing munitions of war, or both together, as in *The House That Hitler Built*[5] – not a very cheerful prospect!

Yours truly,

[Dorothy L. Sayers]

3 First published 1942; second edition 1971.
4 Workers' Educational Association
5 By Stephen H. Roberts, published 1937, second edition 1939.

[24 Newland Street
Witham
Essex]

TO DR. BRYAN W. MONAHAN

29 January 1943

Dear Dr. Monahan,

Let me say again that with your main contention I heartily agree. The root trouble is that we have come to assess everything in terms of profit and loss in a ledger, losing sight of the real values – even the actual concrete values of men and things, whenever they cannot be reduced to this simple and superficial method of accounting. We have almost lost respect either for men or objects, and therefore waste them regardless. There was an excellent article on the subject in a fairly recent number of *The Christian News-Letter*, showing clearly the effects of this subjugation to the "profit-rule", as distinct from the so-called "profit motive", which was the more striking because it was written by an industrial accountant, who might well be expected to over-estimate, rather than under-estimate, the importance of "book-keeping".

As to the morality or otherwise of having to "work for a living" I cannot argue. Generally speaking, I think the effect of being given a living without working for it is not too good, either for the man or for such work as he may do without having to live by it. Unless he is possessed by a real passion for his occupation, there is a tendency to amateurishness, whenever the product is not judged by the rule of thumb of the common market. But what is undoubtedly corrupt or wrong is the assessing of the value of work solely by the living it brings in. And one gets a number of old and vicious perversions. There is, for instance, the insistence by some Marxists that unless a worker gets back from the community the full value of the work he does, he is being somehow cheated – which is nonsense, because it leaves out all the incalculables, and reduces the "value" of the work again to something that can be written off in an account-book. And there is the dreadful situation that it has come to be considered a sort of social crime to do any work for nothing, however one may enjoy it, because it is taking somebody else's living away – an argument which was largely responsible, after the last war, for keeping men idle on the dole, rather than allowing their work to compete with the vested interests and those of the trade unions.

The suggestion that the work of the world could be done by each person about an hour a day has often been put forward, but seems to imply that machine work is all the work there is. How about farming? It will be a long time before, say, lambing ewes will fall in with the scheme – or take kindly to being attended by relays of workers doing an hour at a time.

How about sailors and fishermen? How many decent meals can be cooked in one hour? (unless you are going to eat exclusively out of tins, which would not suit me for one). How about the professions? Could a doctor, surgeon, actor, school-master, discharge his obligations so briskly? Or have you, too, insensibly fallen into the way of thinking that nothing is really "work" unless it comes off the assembly-band?

That, of course, might well come to pass in the establishment of a new and vast leisure aristocracy of factory hands, exercising by their numbers a strong tyranny over a new sort of "workers"; but what political and social results this would have, I cannot say.

As regards the "point of attack" – I think it is really necessary somehow to get people to see that an evil is an evil before they can direct their efforts to getting it put right. That work should be, in the words of a great Labour leader,[1] "the proper exercise of the creature", and that this is not the same thing as mere "paid employment" is a truth which, I am sure, one has somehow got to put across to people, whether they are all ready to receive that gospel or not.

Yours very truly,
    [Dorothy L. Sayers]

---

1 Possibly Keir Hardie.

                                    [24 Newland Street
                                    Witham
                                    Essex]

TO THE REV. CANON S. M. WINTER[1]

2 February 1943

Dear Sir,
    The trouble is not so much the official teaching of the Church as the practice and general attitude of mind of ecclesiastics and official Church bodies – which in turn influences the general attitude and practice of Christians as such. I said something on this subject at the Malvern Conference[2]... and there are also a number of passages in Michael de la Bedoyère's *Christian Crisis*[3]... which bear on the question – e.g. pp. 144, 147–8. (This book, of course, deals particularly with the Church of

---

1 The Rev. Stephen Miller Winter, Wargrave Vicarage, Berkshire, Honorary Canon of Christ Church Cathedral, Oxford.
2 See *Malvern 1941* (Longman).
3 See letter to him, 7 October 1941.

Rome, but *mutatis mutandis*[4] what he says holds good for the Churches
generally.)

Taking the thing in its widest aspect, there is, I feel (a) on the negative
side a great failure to envisage Christian Truth as the great co-ordinate of
all truth (whether in science, art, workmanship or anything else), with an
accompanying lack of respect for what is called "the autonomy of technique" in all departments of human activity. With this goes a tendency to
separate the ecclesiastical from the secular, and to consider that only to be
"Christian" art, science, work etc which is specifically directed to
Christian apologetic as an extrinsic end, rather than co-ordinated by
Truth-to-itself as a principle of inner unity. To exclude the latter from
"Christianity" amounts to a tacit denial that all truth is in Christ, so far as
it goes. (b) On the positive side, there is the direct encouragement by the
Church of much that is false to itself (as science, art, workmanship etc),
on the ground that it is morally edifying. This attitude, which is only the
(a) attitude turned inside-out, as it were, is largely responsible for the current impression that Christendom, as a body, is artistically imbecile and
intellectually corrupt – an impression which is naturally reflected upon
Christianity as a philosophy.

The chasm between the secular and religious vocations becomes, I
think, wider as one gets to the top (most chasms do). That is, the common
workman is rather more likely to be exhorted by the Church to use honesty in his work as a Christian duty than the more intellectual kind of
worker. The latter, indeed, frequently has to assert his technical integrity
in the face of Church opposition or indifference – which is the reason why
the Church has to a great extent lost the support and inspiration of the
intellectuals and the artists – the two most powerful movers of public
opinion. Some of these people are, no doubt, Christians – do the
Churches know how many, or which? Do they trouble to find out, unless
one of them, suddenly losing patience, bursts out into apologetic or into
a spontaneous confession of faith?

The thing which the Churches at present most lack in the work of making Christian truth widely understood, is a body of experts who are able
and willing to write *on their own technical subjects with Christian assumptions
behind them*; correspondingly, the strongest attack upon Christianity comes
precisely from the enormous output of technical literature which assumes
an anti-Christian philosophy. It cannot be an accident that the scales are
so heavily over-weighted; and the only conclusion one can draw is that
either the majority of technical thinkers [are not Christians], or if they
are, the Christian "explanation of the Universe" has not become so intimately a part of their minds as to impregnate and inform their secular

4 Latin: the necessary changes being made.

work, as, for example, materialist philosophies impregnate and inform the work of innumerable writers on bio-chemistry, philology, history, and economics, to mention a few subjects at random.

That the Church herself tacitly acquiesces, or is at any rate pretty well resigned to, this separation between her philosophy and the fruits of secular labour, is betrayed by her pathetic astonishment and gratification over any person with a reputation in secular affairs who will condescend to approve or patronise Christianity in public. "Here", she cries, waving flags, "is actually an intelligent person – an astronomer, novelist, diplomat, stockbroker, painter, somebody with a proper job – who nevertheless is a Christian, or almost a Christian, or at least not actively anti-religious; how unexpected and complimentary!" True, she does not always inquire very closely whether the worker in question is taken seriously by his professional colleagues; that is part of her failure to respect the integrity of the work. And it is also unfortunately true that, having discovered a Christian who is serving God in his proper job, her next step is to do all she can to distract and impede him in the exercise of that job by taking him away to address meetings, write apologetics, and generally exhaust himself in ecclesiastical work which is not his proper job, and which – if unduly persisted in – will end by unfitting him for the secular job to which he is called. (The opening chapter of Stephen Spender's *Life and the Poet* [5] is a strong warning against the results of serving propaganda aims outside, instead of through, one's vocation; and what he says about political is equally true of religious amateur activities.)

What is in question, you see, is not a revision of doctrine, but a metanoia[6] – a determination to recognise the Logos wherever He is found, week-days as well as Sundays; in the carpenter's shop as well as in the Temple; in the workman's truth as well as in the theologian's truth, to do so in practice, and not only in theory. It is difficult, because the Church has insensibly allowed herself to acquiesce in the materialist's mental habit of departmentalizing the truth; but her professional integrity is involved in the synthesizing [of] truths to make up the Truth....

Yours faithfully,

[Dorothy L. Sayers]

5 Sir Stephen Spender (1890–1995).
6 From the Greek, signifying a change of mind, repentance.

During the War many commodities were unobtainable, lemons among them. In
February 1943 Marjorie Barber happened to obtain one and sent it, as though it
were a precious jewel, to D. L. S.

24 Newland Street
Witham
Essex

TO MARJORIE BARBER
13 February 1943

Dearest Bar,
   Very many astonished thanks for the Museum Piece – so appropriately
packed in a jeweller's box – which arrived quite safely. Mac looked at it
with a stupefied gaze and asked, "What is it?" Our only difficulty now is
to decide how to dispose of it. Mac thinks it should be kept in a glass case,
and people be invited to see it at so much a head; I (being of low, common clay with a pragmatic sort of mind) suggested that we might now
have that curry which he formerly rejected on account of its "being no
good without a squeeze of lemon". He said it would be a pity to destroy
it; I said it would be a pity to let it dry up or grow green whiskers; he said
it would keep a long time yet. So we put it back in its wadding and laid it
carefully aside; and when he has forgotten about it I shall probably hike it
out on my own responsibility and serve it up with curry or fish or something. It is a very beautiful and encouraging lemon, anyway, and I thank
you again most heartily. Mrs. Rice was much impressed, and said: "Where
ever did she get that?"
   Much love and blessing,
      D. L. S.

Five days later an even more remarkable present arrived: 75 double-sided gramo-
phone records, being the recording of the entire performance of The Man Born
to be King.

[24 Newland Street
Witham
Essex]

TO MR B. E. NICOLLS
19 February 1943

Dear Mr. Nicolls,
   Thank you very much indeed for The Man Born to be King, who

arrived safely under special escort yesterday afternoon. This is indeed a magnificent present, and when I look at the tremendous number of records involved I am at a loss to thank the directors of the B.B.C. properly for their generosity. I am also a little staggered by finding that any work of mine could make so bulky and impressive an appearance! This is certainly the handsomest and most important looking of my published works. However, I certainly can't say "Alone I did it", and may I take this opportunity to renew my thanks to the B.B.C. in general, and to all the people in the Religious and Dramatic Departments, who, together with the engineers, carried this lengthy and exacting production through in spite of so many trials and difficulties.

I am so glad that you feel it to have been successful and worth the doing, and I can only repeat my very sincere thanks, and remain

Yours sincerely,

[Dorothy L. Sayers]

In March 1943 the recording of The Man Born to be King *was broadcast.[1] Someone who listened to part of the third play, "A Certain Nobleman", was a Mr L. T. Duff, who wrote angrily on 15 March:*

Dear Madam,

I heard part of your radio play last night, but eventually switched off in disgust that such drivel should be given over the air, and that a person of your standing should write it.

I can quite understand people of little education accepting and taking in such things as these, but you must have made research and enquiries into the actual so-called miracle and in view of your findings, I cannot understand why you should then write a play based on a pack of lies.

In point of fact the miracle never occurred and can be proved from many reasons. One being that it was physically impossible for Jesus to have been at the feast at all in view of the distance of a 100 miles or so that he was away a day or so earlier, and the time in which to travel.

A very good book to read is *The Life of Jesus Christ* by Hall Caine[2]. Especially read the part on which your play was based, and you will no doubt feel heartily ashamed of yourself for being a party to such deceit.

Yours faithfully,

L. T. Duff

---

1 See letter to B. E. Nicolls, 12 May 1943.
2 Sir (Thomas Henry) Hall Caine (1853–1931), novelist. He began work on a life of Christ in 1893, which was published after his death in 1938.

To this insulting letter D. L. S. took the trouble to reply:

[24 Newland Street
Witham
Essex]

L. T. DUFF, ESQ.

22 March 1943

Dear Sir,

I am sorry that you should have sustained such a shock. Is this really the first time you have realised that quite a large number of educated persons profess the Catholic Faith – even persons of (God save the mark!) "standing"?

But let me beg you not to agitate yourself too much. For a person of excitable disposition it is extremely wearing to live in a constant state of virtuous indignation. Forget that materialism is out of fashion, that the physicists are all going metaphysicist, and that psychologists have sapped the very foundations of rationalism. Console yourself with despising us – nothing is more soothing than to contemplate the folly and depravity of one's inferior.

Poor Hall Caine! That is a very pathetic book. The labour of a lifetime, hopelessly unscholarly, and published fifty years too late to flutter even the popular dove-cotes. Mercifully he did not live to learn that it was dead before it was born.

Yours faithfully,
[Dorothy L. Sayers]

24 Newland Street
Witham
Essex

TO MARJORIE BARBER

23 March 1943

Dearest Bar...

We have eaten the LEMON at last! I kept it in its box for a bit till it began to look a little wrinkled; then, acting on your advice, I put it into water till it plumped out again. Then, seeing that it was showing signs of growing whiskers, and happening to have received from "George" a consignment of appropriate offal – to wit, sweetbreads – I cast reverence to the winds, cut the precious creature open (it was in perfectly good condition), used half the juice for the sauce and served up the sweetbreads adorned with slices of lemon as per Mrs. Beeton. Mac looked at it and said in an awful and accusing voice: "You've CUT the LEMON!" I said, "Well, you never looked at it and it was beginning to grow whiskers, so I thought I might as well." So we ate it, and I used the peel to make barley-water, and I've still got a small piece left and shall eat it with a piece of fish for breakfast. So I think the lemon has done its duty nobly, and I thought humbly and gratefully of you, and of our Armies in Africa and of the Merchant Seamen and the Warships and all the other kind and coura-geous beings who had toiled to bring the lemon and the sweetbreads. "So that was all right, Best Beloved."[1]

By the way – we had another shock on the kitchen front! No sooner was the cook settled than my little Mrs Rice came in, almost weeping with rage and frustration, to say that her little boy had come out all over spots, and she thought he had measles. So she would be shut up in the house for about a fortnight, and she was so cross, because she liked coming here, and she liked doing her work, and now she'd hear nothing all day but "Mrs So-and-so's baby was due next week" (instead, I gathered, of my improving conversation). So I sympathised very much, said she musn't worry so far as we were concerned since Mrs Goodwin was now coming earlier; and Mrs Rice tied her little woolly cap viciously on her head and went wrathfully away. This was on Saturday. On Monday (being her wash-day) she doesn't come, but we had resigned ourselves to measles and thought to see her no more, anyhow, and I instructed Mrs Goodwin that instead of doing the brass and the silver and turning out her cupboards and the stinking little hole where the refrigerator lives, (on which she had set her heart) she would have to make beds and dust the sitting-rooms.

When lo and behold! this morning in walks Mrs Rice as bright as a but-ton. The measles had turned out to be only nettle-rash. To make up for this, however, the elder boy had had an abscess in his ear, the little girl had had a whitlow on her finger, and on Sunday night, just as Mr Rice was going off to work, the boiler burst. Mr Rice said, "I'm sorry for you, but I can't do nothing about it, I've got to go." So Mrs Rice and a neighbour drew off all the water and emptied the boiler, and next day "the men" came, and they were all over the house, and they found that a new elbow-joint was needed in the pipe, and they tried all round Witham to get a piece of pipe and there wasn't one to be had anywhere, and Mrs Rice said, "Can't you *mend* it?" and the man took it away and mended it and thought it was all right but when he brought it back it burst again and there was nothing for it *but* a new piece of pipe; so the men went away,

---

1 The catch-phrase "Oh Best Beloved" occurs in Rudyard Kipling's *Just So Stories*. The version "So that was all right, Best Beloved" occurs several times with minor variations in the story "The Beginning of the Armadilloes".

leaving it all anyhow, to try again to get a piece of pipe, and Mrs Rice's friend next door said the same thing had happened to *her* and *she* had waited 18 months for a piece of pipe and was still waiting. And "the man" said it was the fault of these Council Houses – he knowed when they put in that cheap piping there'd be trouble. So there Mrs Rice was – no water anywhere and they couldn't use that room, and how she'd manage she didn't know – "but anyway", said Mrs Rice, triumphantly, *I'm here*, and it's better than measles, isn't it?" – I think Mrs Rice is really one of the nicest people I know....

Well, bless you – looking forward to seeing you at Easter –

Best love,

D. L. S.

I forgot to ask what happened to Mrs Rice's wash-day. It can't have been very successful! If they can't get a pipe I shall have to suggest that she brings the family washing to our hot water for the next 18 months!

24 Newland Street
Witham
Essex

TO HER SON

28 March 1943

Dear John,

Herewith cheque – Hope you are getting on all right and overthrowing Hitler with what speed you may. Though if rumour is to be believed, that gentleman has already been dealt with on the *quem Deus vult perdere*[1] principle, and has gone rotten like a medlar, but not, perhaps, before he was ripe.

As for me, the state of affairs I outlined in my last letter went steadily from bad to worse, and left me virtually a prisoner in the house for six months. And if anybody wants to know what I have been doing – why, I have been dirtying saucepans and washing them up again – a process which leaves me with strong notions about the general futility of things. I don't really mind being unable to stir from my own doorstep, and I don't

1 Latin: Whom God wishes to destroy (He first makes mad). Joshua Barnes, in his edition of Euripides (Index Prior, under "Deus") quotes the saying as "Deus quos vult perdere, dementat prius", which he translates as "Whom God would destroy He first sends mad". It was rumoured at the time that Hitler had gone off his head.

really mind not being able to fool around the country delivering addresses; but when it comes to the point that one cannot get any work done at all, one foresees the moment when one will become a burden upon the rates. Eventually, therefore, I appealed to the Ministry of Labour, saying that either I must be able to earn my living or the State must make up its mind to support me. This startled them, and they allowed me the services of a woman in the evenings, as a result of which I escaped to London for the first time since I don't know when. I have also discovered that, having once lost the habit of work, it is very difficult to get into it again. The minute one settles down to anything and tries to think, one is shaken up, as out of sleep, by the thought that something is probably boiling over! So that all I have done since last October (except cooking, washing-up, mending and making) is to write a few letters to people, imploring them not to think or lead others to think that the "Post-War World" is going to be a time of peace, plenty, and expanding markets. It won't, you know. After the first few years of making good in the occupied countries (which will provide plenty of markets, always supposing nobody wants or expects payment for commodities supplied) the markets will shrink, as the result of having so many more fully-industrialised countries. I'm not sure, but I think we are going to see mass-production come full circle and destroy itself – not in my time (unless we have another war rather quickly) but probably in yours. This will be interesting. I can't imagine anything more interesting. But it will be extremely painful if we don't realise in time what's happening, and make preparation accordingly. I *think* (again) that, after the aristocracy of managers, the next thing will be an aristocracy of technicians. You will probably come in for that – after which, perhaps, we shall be ruled by the Land again, if we have not destroyed it first.

Damn! I must go and do lunch. *No* woman on Sundays!

Love,

D. L. S.

[24 Newland Street
Witham
Essex]

TO LADY FLORENCE CECIL

30 March 1943

Dear Lady Florence,

Thank you so much for your letter. I am afraid I don't think I could write a play about Martha and Mary. For one thing my own bias would be too much on the side of Mary to suit the Mothers' Union, though there is certainly scriptural warrant for this point of view! For another, I have got several heavy jobs of work on hand, and I couldn't possibly get down to it for a considerable time. Thirdly, of course, there is always the tiresome difficulty about money. One has to live unfortunately, and if one is relying exclusively on amateur fees for a specialised show of this kind it does take a frightful long time before the work pays for itself, unless one exacts the top scale of royalties, which is more than it would be reasonable to expect Women's Institutes to pay. Not that this last consideration would be of great importance if the subject was one that I passionately wanted to write about, but at the moment I don't feel drawn to it – indeed, I am rather anxious, just at present, to get off the religious onto the secular drama, because it is rather a bad thing to get into too much of a rut. I have now written fifteen religious plays, in almost unbroken succession if one counts the twelve parts of *The Man Born to be King* separately, which is fairly good going.

Perhaps later on if I feel an urge to do more religious drama[1] I might feel differently about Martha and Mary.

Yours very sincerely,
[Dorothy L. Sayers]

---

1 She did write two more religious dramas, *The Just Vengeance* (1946) and *The Emperor Constantine* (1951), but no drama about Martha and Mary.

On 30 March, L. T. Duff wrote again:

Dear Madam,
I was very pleased and also surprised to receive your letter. I actually did not think you would trouble to reply. I usually find that religious followers are quite content to sit smugly behind their Bible, and refuse to answer questions, or enter into any arguments about their religion...

I am sorry you think so poorly of Hall Caine's book. Perhaps if you read it, you would see what a poor house of cards your religion is....

There are many questions I would like to ask you, but I will content myself with two. Do you honestly believe that the miracle of the wine took place? And, if it is not too blasphemous, do you believe in the "Miraculous Conception", that Mary was a virgin?

That excitable person,
L. T. Duff

[24 Newland Street
Witham
Essex]

TO L. T. DUFF

2 April 1943

Dear Sir,

You complain that Christians do not usually reply to your attacks. Don't you think, perhaps, that they would do so more readily if you addressed them with rather more courtesy? In your first letter to me you accused me (a complete stranger who had offered you no personal provocation) of ignorance, of dishonesty, and also of illiteracy, since you seemed to take it for granted that I was entirely unacquainted with the literature of my subject. I should not dream of using such ill manners to anybody, no matter how wrong I thought him; and I may say that, had you expressed yourself with more civility I should have answered you less tartly. But can you be surprised if many people put the affront in the waste-paper basket, for fear of losing their temper?

You now suggest that I have criticised Hall Caine's book without having read it. You have no grounds whatever for jumping to that very insulting conclusion. Naturally I have read it; if I had not, I should have said so, and offered no opinion. It is the work of a man undertaking a highly-skilled technical job without the proper training or the proper critical apparatus. No serious student of the subject attaches any importance to it.

I think you are a little out of date in what you say about the present-day attitude to religion. What has become abundantly clear in the last twenty-five years or so is the complete collapse (both on scientific and philosophic grounds) of humanistic philosophy. In consequence, there is now a very vigorous revival of interest in dogmatic religion and Christian theology, especially among the younger people. This has not, so far, led to a great increase in regular church-going; but the demand for instruction has become so wide-spread and insistent that it is almost impossible to keep pace with it. At the same time, publishers are reporting that the demand for books about religion has enormously increased, in some quarters even over-topping the demand for fiction, which always used to head the list; and by "books about religion" I do not mean devotional works, but books which present Christian dogma as a rational explanation of the universe and a coherent philosophy of life. I mention these facts because, judging by your letter, you are a little out of touch with what is happening. Obviously, the truth and value of a theory does not depend on the number of people who are interested in it – otherwise you might compare the number of people who follow the predictions of astrologers in the daily press with those who attend lectures by Einstein, and conclude that astrology was more valuable and true than physics.

As regards your questions about miracles, I think the simplest way is to send you the text of a broadcast talk I gave some little time ago in a series on the Creeds.[1] The distinction which people used to draw between the so-called nature miracles and the miracles of healing seems by now to have lost its usefulness, since it depended upon a belief in the discontinuity of mind and matter for which modern physics appears to offer very little warrant.

Yours faithfully,
[Dorothy L. Sayers]

Do you ever read any really advanced and modern Christian apologetics? And if so, which?

---

1 Probably one of the talks she gave for Eric Fenn's series. See letter to him, 20 March 1941. If so, Mr Duff was privileged, for these talks were not published.

[24 Newland Street
Witham
Essex]

TO STEPHEN HOBHOUSE[1]

7 April 1943

Dear Mr. Hobhouse,

Thank you very much for sending me your pamphlet on "Retribution". Of all the ethical problems which Christians have to face, this is one of the most perplexing. Indeed, all the problems which involve an opposition between the Law and the Gospel are extremely difficult, in a world where the one is not yet established and the other (consequently) not abolished.

I note with interest, in this connection, your reaction to "The Man With No Face".[2] I may as well begin by saying that it is not the business of the story-teller to preach sermons or draw moral conclusions; his job is to depict men and events as they are, and it would be ridiculous to make

---

1 Identity unknown.
2 A short story by D. L. S., published with the title "The Unsolved Puzzle of the Man with No Face" in *Lord Peter Views the Body*, Gollancz, 1928. Adapted as a play, it was broadcast on radio on 3 April 1943, the first of a new series, "Saturday Night Theatre", with the title "The Man with No Face". This is the version which this correspondent heard.

Peter Wimsey (who is only the most conventional sort of Christian)[3] act otherwise than a man of his habit and training might be supposed to act.

What he does, in this case, is to inform the police of what he suspects and leave the matter in the hands of the law. The law is not convinced, and does nothing. What do you expect him to do? Pursue the guilty with a private vengeance and insist on the exaction of the full legal retribution? In that, I think, he would be justified only if he thought the man was likely to commit more murders. Utter moral sentiments expressive of reprobation? It is not in his character. With whatever sympathy for the man who gave way to a sudden and irresistible fury, he has done his plain duty to society, and society has refused to take action. Then he leaves it.

Did you want the man hanged?

Or merely that somebody should pronounce judgement on his actions? But Wimsey had already pronounced judgement, and that in the most emphatic manner possible – by offering him up to the retribution of the law. But accident intervenes to prevent the exaction of the penalty – accident, and a policeman's routine lack of imagination.

May I suggest that perhaps the act of revenge is becoming to you the one sin for which you can find neither mercy nor charity? This often happens when we have pondered a good deal about one particular sin – it seems to become THE sin, and the rules we apply to other sins do not apply to that. Thus people become intolerant of intolerance, cruel to the cruel, and revengeful against the avenger.

I only suggest this – but, as I said before, the business of a story-teller is to tell stories, not to devise moral fables. And the first thing he has to learn is that the heart of man is full of devious complexities, odd and frightening impulses, and curious contradictions.

Yours very truly,
[Dorothy L. Sayers]

3 Cf. *The Mind of the Maker*, Methuen, p. 105.

On 19 April Mr Duff replied:

Dear Miss Sayers...

I can see now, that my accusations were wrong, and I apologise, for there is no doubt that you have studied and read widely on the subject and honestly believe in what you say. But that you still do believe in all this – the miracles, virgin birth, etc – after your studying, is something that I cannot quite understand unless it is simply – faith....

I carefully read your broadcast talk. You state that Jesus was the "perfect man restored to his normal relations with nature". But I do not agree. One fact alone that stands out so plainly is that the Jesus you depict had no sex life. And that is certainly not normal to nature or to a perfect man....I am inclined to think however, that Jesus was nearer to a natural man than you think, and did have some sex life. But as he was not married, such a thing would be horrifying to you....

I have not read many modern Christian apologetics. I should be glad to know what you recommend.

Best wishes for Easter,
          yours faithfully,
              L. T. Duff

                                        [24 Newland Street
                                        Witham
                                        Essex]

TO L. T. DUFF

10 May 1943

Dear Mr Duff,

Many thanks for your letter. It was nice of you to apologise – most people don't. And I am sorry I should have troubled your quiet, though I cannot really take the blame for that. For I did not forcibly intrude into your room; you brought me there by the turn of a switch, and had you chosen to dismiss me by the same means I should have gone quietly. But no! you deliberately chose to sit there and be vexed, so that you might have the pleasure of cursing me afterwards. Let me hasten to say that I do not in the least mind people writing to argue or contradict; only it always makes for a better discussion if arguments are directed to the subject and not to the person.

I agree with you – and you will remember that I said so at the time – that the mere numbers of those who, at one moment or another, are "interested" in a subject are no proof either way of its truth or value. When things seem to be going nicely, man puts his trust in man; when they seem to be coming unstuck, man either yells to God for assistance or blames God for letting the mess occur – or both at once. Rather like the man who has "never had a day's illness" and "doesn't believe in doctors". That doesn't prevent him from sending for the doctor when he does fall ill (usually explaining at the same time that he has no use for physic and no intention of carrying out the medical man's instructions). It makes no difference to the value of medicine – except, of course, that lack of faith in the doctor may tend to impede the patient's recovery.

As regards faith, I may as well say at once that I, personally, have no great gift of faith. Even if I had a "blind" faith (that is, an irrational faith) it is not the kind of thing the Christian Church approves. Nor am I able to approach Christianity by the way of what is called "religious emotion". That is a perfectly possible, and indeed a usual way, of approach (though it has its dangers) but it doesn't happen to be mine. To me, Christian dogma seems to offer the only explanation of the universe that is intellectually satisfactory. My intellectual approach also has its dangers. Still, everybody has to approach a subject from some point of view or other, and that one happens to be mine. One act of faith must, indeed, be made before one can accept Christianity: one must be prepared to believe that the universe is rational, and that (consequently) human reason is valid so far as it goes. But that is an act of faith which we have to make in order to think about anything at all. If we say, "There is no truth to be apprehended", or "human reason is not an instrument for apprehending truth", then we must stop making any statement at all; for those statements in themselves are judgments of truth made by the reason, and if the judgments of reason are valueless, those judgments are valueless too. Accordingly, in the very centre of the Christian scheme of things we find the Divine Word (that is, the Eternal Reason, or Intellect, or Mind – which is what the Greek word Logos means) worshipped both as God and Man, as the sole way by which man can get in touch with the truth of things. Admittedly, we cannot prove that the universe is rational; for the only instrument by which we can prove anything is reason, and we have to assume the rationality of things before we can trust or use our reason. But every act and word of our daily life – not to mention all art and science – are based on that assumption; without that act of faith we could not live or act.

Why do you say that "religion should be understandable by the most uneducated and simple person"? You got that idea, I think, from Jesus of Nazareth. In one sense, of course, it is perfectly true: *religion* is as simple as falling in love with a girl. You can do that without any education, and if you are so happy as to be able to live quite simply by the rule of love, married life will present no difficulties in practice. But what you have been asking about is not religion but *theology*, which is the science of religion (or, more strictly, the science of the knowledge of God) – and, like all sciences, it requires some education and training. It bears much the same relation to "religion" as the biology and psychology of sex bear to the simple act of "falling in love". Besides, you know very well that just "living by the rule of love" is not so straightforward as all that. The simplicity of the heart sometimes fails us; when that happens, it is sometimes necessary to try and regain it by studying the science of the thing and so understanding with our heads what it is that the heart has been trying to do. By the way, you will notice that Jesus never said "unless you *remain* as little children you cannot enter the Kingdom of Heaven" but "unless you *become* as little children". It is not very easy, when one has grown up, to recapture with the adult mind the child's eager curiosity, freshness of mind and simplicity of approach. Indeed, it breaks everything up, and involves a complete remaking of the self. That, however, is a different matter. What you are concerned with is nothing to do with religion in that sense; you are using your brains to tackle the theology. Consequently, it is useless for me or for anybody else to say, "Never mind all these intellectual difficulties – just believe without reasoning." You have got to the point where you must understand the thing with your head, or not at all.

I won't stop now to go into the theology of what is meant by "perfect Man" – it would take up too much time, and you can read it better set out in books than I can explain it in a letter. But as regards the particular point you raise I will say two things. The first is that (taking the thing entirely on the human plane) the canalization of energy in a single tremendous task is frequently such as to preclude sexual and domestic preoccupations – nor has this concentration of energy ever been held as a sign of weakness, except in the present age, which gives to sex a supreme importance, such as in any other period of history would have seemed ridiculous. Secondly, in this or any age, what matters is not sexual "experience" but sexual normality. The remarkable thing about Jesus of Nazareth is that of all religious teachers He is perhaps the only one who is completely sane on this subject. There is nothing whatever in any act or word of His that suggests any peculiar mystery, danger, excitement, or oddity about women or sex; and in His dealings with women He was completely unselfconscious, treating them quite straightforwardly as human beings with minds and souls of their own. In fact, He walked straight through all the sex-taboos as though they did not exist. Neither the Jews and pagans before Him, nor the Christians and Mohammedans and neo-pagans since have ever achieved anything like His normality; only a few exceptionally well-balanced people here and there have ever got within miles of it.

Sin – well, sin (that is "original" sin, as distinct from acts of sin) is that inner division of the will which the psychologists know and recognise: the "will to destruction", as they call it, or sometimes the "will to death", fighting against the "will to life". It is what makes every human being false to his true self and corrupts all his virtues, so that they frustrate themselves and each other. For the last two hundred years or so we have been trying to persuade ourselves that there was no such thing as sinfulness – that there was nothing intrinsically unsatsfactory about man as such. But isn't there? I am sorry for the Humanists – they trusted in man so blindly, and now they are so bewildered by the present condition of the world. All this science and education and toleration of opinions, and enlightenment and so forth, issuing, not in peace and progress, but in frustration and reactionary violence. But it isn't surprising if one recognises that the inner division is still there, and that increased knowledge and science and power have only enlarged the scope and opportunity both for good and evil, not altered man's nature, which remains what it was – capable of choice because its will is free; capable of and indeed inclined to make, the wrong choice, because it centres itself on man and the relative rather than on God and the absolute.

However, I can't undertake to write you a whole book about sin! You ask for titles of some Christian apologetics. It is a little difficult, because there are so many of different kinds, and I don't really know where you want to start from. I mean, I don't know what your "cultural background" is, or what you do believe, if anything. I know you don't believe in sin or miracles, but that's about all I do know. I may recommend something that will merely put you off, because it starts from some position which you do not hold, or requires some training (e.g. in philosophy) which you don't happen to have, so that its vocabulary will be unintelligible or misleading. In any case, no book is going to persuade anybody of anything! The subject's too big, and no single book can cover it. The best way is to browse about among a number of books till one finds something that seems to make sense, and then to follow that up with more along the same lines. Only, don't start off with a set determination to find sense nowhere. After all, if some of the most astute and powerful intellects in the last nineteen centuries have found Christianity reasonable, it cannot be wholly nonsensical.

At any rate, I have made a list of books, some of which you may find interesting. And I do think that, if you are bent on attacking and denouncing Christianity whenever it makes a public appearance, it would be only fair and reasonable to study it a little first. Because it really isn't true that the anti-Christian case gets no chance of a hearing. Actually it is extremely vocal and the cause of "irreligion" is preached in season and out of season, and that with great venom and violence. Nineteen people out of twenty nowadays get their notion of Christianity (often very distorted and fantastic notions) not from any Christian literature but from the incidental attacks made on Christianity in works which purport to be about something else. H. G. Wells, for instance, talks a surprising lot of nonsense on the subject; so does Julian Huxley. Or you get a book like Stuart Chase's *Tyranny of Words* [1] which, pretending to be all about the art of thinking and speaking clearly, is really a vicious attack on all religion

---

1 *The Tyranny of Words* by Stuart Chase, Methuen, first printed in Great Britain in 1938.

and all philosophy (with the most dreadful tumbles into fallacy and illogicality by the way). In my lifetime I have seen Christianity driven out of politics, school and university, as in the previous three centuries it was gradually driven out of commerce and finance – all in the name of freedom and progress. And, after all, Britain is just one country in Europe. In Germany and all the occupied countries, as well as in Russia, Christianity is actively persecuted and rigorously put to silence. Here, in America, and in the Vatican City, it can still speak on the radio, but hardly anywhere else. So, taking it by and large, the balance is perhaps less heavily weighted to Christian advantage than you are inclined to think.

Finally – if you decide to read some Christian literature, give it your serious attention. Don't just explode into fury when you meet something that challenges your assumptions – that is behaving like the people who were outraged by Galileo and indignant over Darwin. Christianity does and will challenge almost every conviction you have. That is its business. So don't blame me – You have been warned!

Yours faithfully,

    [Dorothy L. Sayers]

There follows the list of books which accompanied the letter. Since she mentioned many of them frequently in her letters to other correspondents they must represent her own reading. Her comments, intended to be helpful to Mr Duff, also reveal her own opinion of the works. Three of them (John Macmurray's The Boundaries of Science, *V. A. Demant's* The Religious Prospect, *and Charles Williams'* He Came Down from Heaven) *are included in* Begin Here, Gollancz, *1940, under the heading "Some Books to Read", pp. 157–160.*

A. Books dealing with the nature and limitations of scientific method, etc.

J. Macmurray: The Boundaries of Science (Faber)
R.L.Kapp: Science versus Materialism (Methuen) (Written by an
    engineer – not particularly from the Christian point of view)
A.H.Whitehead: Science and the Modern World (Penguin) (Note
    especially the passage which stresses the dependence of scientific
    method on an act of faith in the rationality of the universe)

B. On philosophic method:

Michael Roberts: The Modern Mind (Faber) (This book deals with the
    historical development of methods of thinking from the late Middle
    Ages onwards. Contains valuable cautions about the way in which the

meaning of certain technical terms – e.g. "reason", "imagination", "science" – gets altered in common use as time goes on.)

C. Books about the failure of Humanism (the doctrine that Man is self-sufficient) and the present World-Situation generally:

J.V.L.Casserley: The Fate of Modern Culture (Dacre Press: Signposts series) "Signposts" are a series of little books on Theology, published at one shilling. They are all by Anglicans.
Michael Roberts: The Recovery of the West (Faber)
V.A.Demant: The Religious Prospect (Muller) (This is much the most profound and important book of the four. Unfortunately the author writes rather crabbed and involved English, so that it is by no means easy reading.)

All these books deal primarily with the negative side – i.e. the result of ignoring Christian philosophy and the failure of rival philosophies. The books which follow deal more positively with the Christian religion itself.

D. Books about the Existence and Nature of God.

C.S.Lewis: Broadcast Talks (Bles) (Lewis started out as an atheist, and can therefore tackle the whole subject from personal experience. He is extremely pungent and witty. Being a set of radio talks, the book is very simply written in a popular style, but it is not at all superficial.)
H.H.Farmer: Towards Belief in God (S.C.M.Press, 2 vols.) Written some years ago, but now rewritten and its treatment brought "up-to-date". It hasn't Lewis's sparkle and punch, but is quietly and soundly reasoned.
Charles Gore: Belief in God (Pelican) An old book, but still a very good one.

E. Books about what the Christian Faith actually is:

A lot of the people who attack Christianity have only very inadequate or inaccurate notions of what Christians do actually believe – often denouncing alleged "Christian doctrines" which Christians would be the first to repudiate as distortions and travesties.
J.S.Whale: Christian doctrine (C.U.P.)
Bede Frost: Who? (Mowbray) (The doctrine of the nature of God – i.e. not chiefly Christology. The method is what is called "scholastic", i.e. abstract and intellectual, in the manner of the mediaeval schoolmen, rather than inductive or empirical. The author is an Anglican.)
Leslie Simmonds: What Think Ye of Christ? (Bles) (A handy little statement of orthodox Christology – i.e. what the Church believes about the nature and person of Christ.)
Eric Mascall: Man: His Origin and Destiny (Signposts) (The Christian

doctrine of the nature of Man is probably the point at which it most conflicts with "modern" thought. There are not many good books about it, but this one will do as a start, and there are more in the next section that deal with it.)

D.L.Sayers: The Mind of the Maker (Methuen) (I've put this in here because some people say it has made the doctrine of the Trinity more comprehensible to them than the more regular theological treatises. It is really a book about the nature of creative mind, illustrating the Christian doctrine of God by analogy with the mind of the artist. It is a "freak" sort of book, and by rights I should have shoved it in at the end under "miscellaneous".)

F. Books about Evil, Sin and Redemption:

T.M.Parker: The Re-Creation of Man (Signposts)
C.S.Lewis: The Problem of Pain (Bles) (A brilliant book, that made a small sensation when it first appeared. If anybody was really troubled about human suffering and wanted to know something of Christianity as a living faith, I should be rather inclined to give him this book to start with.)
Charles Williams: He Came Down from Heaven (Heinemann) (It is rash of me to recommend this, because the treatment is mystical, and there-fore – according to temperament – people find it either intensely illuminating or completely incomprehensible. It's a case of like it or leave it.)

Miscellaneous:

C.H.Cochrane: Christianity and Classical Culture (O.U.P.) (A very brilliant book about the collapse of culture under the Roman Empire and the rise of Christian civilization through the storms of the Dark Ages. The parallel between Roman and present-day philosophies is very interesting and illuminating. But one needs to know something about Roman history and Greek philosophy, and even then it's not exactly light reading.)
N. Berdyaev: The Meaning of History (Bles) (This, I think, is one of the world's really great books, and very exciting – but again, it is not alto-gether easy reading. The author is Russian Orthodox and a mystic.)
L. de Grandmaison: Jesus Christ: His Person – His Message – His Credentials (Sheed and Ward, 3 vols.) (This vast work by a Roman Catholic theologian covers almost the whole ground of Biblical criti-cism, and I have heard of at least one person who was converted to Christianity on the strength of it. I don't know that I should expect it

to have such a drastic effect on most people. I put it forward here, chiefly as proof that Catholic theologians are not – as most people suppose – ignorant of, or loftily indifferent to, problems of textual criticism, comparative religion and all the rest of it.)

G.K.Chesterton: Orthodoxy (Sheed and Ward) The Everlasting Man (Hodder and Stoughton) (Some people are merely infuriated by Chesterton's "paradoxical" style. But for going down to the centre of things and hitting the nail plumb on the head, it's hard to beat him. But the average materialist, rationalist or atheist – who is usually very serious-minded – tends to dislike him, and fails to realise how genuinely serious he is, and how shrewd.)

This list, of course, leaves out all the great Christian classics – because I was confining myself to modern apologetics. But of course Christianity is a historical religion, with a tradition of nearly twenty centuries, and one can't really understand its history and development without a nodding acquaintance with Augustine, Aquinas, and so on, any more than one can follow the development of modern science without knowing something about Aristotle, Bacon and Newton, etc.

I haven't put in any devotional books, or books dealing with purely "personal" religion, or books with an emotional appeal. Nor have I included books which confine themselves to Christian conduct, ethics and sociology – I have tried to keep it doctrinal.

I haven't been able to find a book particularly devoted to the subject of miracles. Apparently this isn't a burning question at the moment as it was in the 19th century. This is probably because, on the one hand, the distinction between "mind" and "matter" has become so hazy since the new theories of physics, and partly because, if one once believes that Christ really was the Person he claimed to be, one can no longer see any real opposition between "nature" and "supernature". But I will mention one short book dealing with the evidence for the one miracle that is of central and supreme importance – the bodily Resurrection of Christ; and that is:

Frank Morrison: *Who Moved the Stone?* (Faber)

The interesting thing about this book is that the writer began with the *a priori* assumption that "miracles do not happen"; but *ended* by drawing a conclusion based on the actual documentary and historical *evidence*: a change of attitude and method which is rather unusual. The author is not a theologian but (I believe) a lawyer.[1]

---

1 He was a colleague of D. L. S. at Benson's. His real name was A. H. Ross.

Mr Duff took over a month to reply ("you gave me many things to think about"). He expressed himself amazed at the trouble she had taken. He could not undertake to read all the books she recommended but would choose a few and promised to approach them with an open mind. In his long letter he raised many points on which he disagreed with hers. She replied at once. See her letter dated 16 June 1943.

[24 Newland Street
Witham
Essex]

TO B. E. NICOLLS

12 May 1943

Dear Mr. Nicolls,

Thank you for your letter. I didn't think the recording of *The Man Born to be King* was at all bad, all things considered, and seeing the very considerable variations of volume the sound-track had to carry. But, of course, so far as I am concerned, nothing could be more agreeable than to do the show again "live", with the time-limit eased, the cuts restored, and the various slips and errors remedied. (Human nature being what it is, they will of course be replaced by new errors, but even here variety is pleasing.) All that sort of thing is a playwright's paradise – the blood, tears, toil and sweat[1] fall to the lot of the producer. If Mr. Gielgud is game, I shall be only too delighted.

I shall be seeing him in about ten days' time and will discuss the matter with him, including any changes in the cast that may seem desirable. In the meantime, judging from my correspondence, the re-play seems to have been well received. The opposition has more or less folded up, and criticisms have been almost entirely confined to questions of verbal detail. The most entertaining comment was that of a friend of my secretary's, who solemnly informed her that the second performance was far superior to the first, "because this time they had got hold of some people who knew how to act". My secretary assured her that it was the same people and the same performance – in fact, a recording. The friend pooh-poohed this, maintaining that it was "quite a different thing altogether". "But", said my secretary, frustrate with rage at an obstinacy so irrational, "I know it was a recording! Who should know, if I don't?" The friend, however, would not be persuaded, though one rose from the dead. Which just shows!

Yours sincerely,

[Dorothy L. Sayers]

---

1 Echo of "I have nothing to offer but blood, toil, tears and sweat", from a speech in the House of Commons by Winston Churchill on 13 May 1940 on the motion of confidence in the new government.

It is not known precisely when D. L. S. first wrote to C. S. Lewis or when they first met. From such evidence as exists, Walter Hooper has pieced together the following account.[1]

Dorothy L. Sayers was very impressed by *The Screwtape Letters*, and she had possibly singled out Letter XIX as containing much good sense about Love and Marriage... About the beginning of April 1942, Dorothy L. Sayers asked Lewis to write on this subject for her Bridgehead series. In his reply, which is undated, he said: "But why not write the book yourself?"...She would not give up and asked again for a book. He replied on 6 April 1942: "Come and lunch on 2 or 3 June – I've booked them both."

This may have been their first meeting.[2]

The earliest extant letter from D. L. S. to Lewis is the following. Intended for the "Lowest Official Circles", it accompanied an advance copy of The Man Born to be King *(published on 24 May 1943). Written in a spirit of wry self-mockery, it apes the style of* The Screwtape Letters. *An entertaining "behind the scenes" supplement to her correspondence with L. T. Duff, it belies the great trouble she was taking in her response to him.*

24 Newland Street
Witham
Essex

TO C. S. LEWIS
13 May 1943

Dear Mr. Lewis,
    Knowing that you have the entrée into the Lowest Official Circles, may I beg you to hand the enclosed volume[3] to the person whose name[4] appears on the fly-leaf.

1 C. S. Lewis: *A Companion and Guide*, Walter Hooper, Harper Collins, 1996, pp. 33–34.
2 C. S. Lewis did not contribute a book to "Bridgeheads" but, as Walter Hooper suggests (p. 34), "much of what Dorothy L. Sayers asked him to say probably went into the character of the unhappily married Jane Studdock in *That Hideous Strength*".
3 i.e. *The Man Born to be King*.
4 i.e. presumably Screwtape.

My Personal Attendant[5] desires that the following Memorandum may be forwarded to the same address:

Memo on Policy: Ref: 7734\rev[6]
In connection with the attached volume, I would draw your Sublimity's attention to a certain lack of Planning, which seems to permeate the whole policy of the Low Command, and threatens to disintegrate our entire war-time strategy,

I should begin by stating that I have always been a Liberal Regressive and convinced Deteriorationist. By this time, surely, the old-fashioned doctrine of Original Righteousness is completely discredited. I can, therefore, only attribute the anomalies which have come under my notice – not to anything inherently virtuous in the make-up of the Creation, but to some failure on our part; some lack of scientific method, perhaps, if it is not sheer slackness in certain departments.

So far as *my* department is concerned, I can assure your Sublimity that no fault can be found. The effect of writing these plays upon the character of my patient is wholly satisfactory. I have already had the honour to report intellectual and spiritual pride, vainglory, self-opinionated dogmatism, irreverence, blasphemous frivolity, frequentation of the company of theatricals, captiousness, impatience of correction, polemical fury, shortness of temper, neglect of domestic affairs, lack of charity, egotism, nostalgia for secular occupations, and a growing tendency to consider the Bible as Literature. You will remember that it was agreed that a work undertaken and carried out in that spirit could only do Harm in the best sense of the word, and that the original well-meant opposition was withdrawn, after strong representations from Below.

But I must point out that the success of the policy adopted is contingent upon proper collaboration among the departments. What is the use of my doing my duty if other Tempters merely sit on their tails in complacent inactivity? The capture of one fifth-rate soul (which was already thoroughly worm-eaten and shaky owing to my assiduous attention) scarcely compensates for the fact that numbers of stout young souls in brand-new condition are opening up negotiations with the Enemy and receiving reinforcements of faith. *We* knew, of course, that the author is

---

5 i.e. Sluckdrib. See the signature to the Memorandum.
6 This is a private joke going back to her childhood. The numbers 7734 turned upside down spell HELL. When she was 13, a young man named Cyril Hutchinson, who used to visit Bluntisham with his parents, told her it was the devil's telephone number. (See *Letters of Dorothy L. Sayers: 1899–1936,* letter to Ivy Shrimpton, 3 September 1907, p. 7.) It is touching to find her, a month from her 50th birthday, thinking back to her flirtation with Cyril Hutchinson at the age of 13.

as corrupt as a rotten cheese; why has no care been taken to see that this corruption (which must, surely, permeate the whole work) has its proper effect upon the listeners? We ought not to take the Enemy's word for it that a corrupt tree cannot bring forth good fruit. If He is telling the truth, this stuff ought to poison people. But the fools eat it and it does them good. Either the Enemy is really able to turn thorns into grapes and thistles into figs, or (as I prefer to believe) there is mismanagement somewhere.

A flagrant instance of the same kind of thing has just occurred here. A sound Atheist of the old-fashioned materialist kind wrote my patient a highly offensive letter about miracles, accusing her of ignorance and dishonesty in the vulgarest language. I persuaded her to answer it still more rudely and offensively. This should have inflamed the situation. Instead, the man seemed pleased to be taken notice of. His subsequent letters (though still discourteous and infidel) became more moderate in tone, and his latest effusion contained an apology and expressed readiness to read some Christian literature, if my patient would send him a list. This I could not prevent her from doing,[7] though I saw to it that her motive was mere pride and self-sufficiency, not in the least contaminated by "love" for the Atheist or interest in "saving" his moth-eaten soul. I hasten to say that I do not expect the books will have the slightest effect upon the creature. What is so sinister is his growing good-will (which is beginning to affect my patient), and the disgustingly false impression made in his mind by the correspondence. He actually *thanked* my patient for troubling to be insolent to him; he thinks *better* of Christians because she treated him like dirt and gave him a harsh answer. He does not *see* the despicable meanness of her motives, which is enough to make a cat sick.

My clerk Swilltosh (who is getting too big for his boots) has the impertinence to say I was trying to be too clever: I should have encouraged the patient's laziness so as make her drop the man's original letter into the waste-paper basket. I have pointed out to him that my first duty is to my own patient - why should I let her get off with one trivial act of sloth when I have the opportunity of raising a great weedy growth of pride, vainglory, wrath and hypocrisy on the opportunity provided? He maintains, further, that the mistake was to permit any activity at all, since all activity is borrowed from the Enemy and can be turned to His advantage. Surely this is heresy: otherwise Sloth would be the greatest of all the sins. Anyhow, I refuse to admit that the Enemy can, as He claims, turn Evil into Good. That is just one of His propaganda boasts. It doesn't make sense. If it did, what are we Devils *for*? I do not like to hear

---

7 See letter to L. T. Duff, 10 May 1943.

24. Newland St. _ Witham _ Essex

13. 5. 43

Dear Mr Lewis,

Knowing that you have the entrée into the Lowest Official Circles, may I beg you to hand the enclosed volume to the person whose name appears on the fly-leaf.

My Personal Attendant desires that the following Memorandum may be forwarded to the same address: —

Memo. on Policy: Ref: 7734/rev.

In connection with the attached volume, I would draw your Eminence's attention to a certain lack of Planning, which seems to permeate the whole policy of the Low Command, & threatens to disintegrate our entire war-time strategy.

The Devil's Telephone Number.

these opinions bandied about Down Below – a very nasty spirit of defeatism seems to be getting about among the younger fiends, which I can only attribute to Fifth-column activities.

So – as I said, the trouble is sheer lack of Planning and failure to cooperate. I have been informed that this wretched Atheist's Tempter has been complaining about the episode. I must enter a protest. It is all his fault. Why did he not get into touch with me at the time? Why did he not warn me that the fool was merely spoiling for a fight and asked nothing better than a slap in the face? Something has gone very wrong with our Intelligence. It's no good telling me that all our best Tempters have been called up for war-work; the defence of civil atheism is a reserved occupation. What is the use of winning victories in the exterior field of physical violence, if we are going to collapse on the Home Front? I beg that you will take this matter in hand immediately; otherwise I shall see to it that a question is asked in the Lower House. You may think the opinion of a mere Tempter in private practice of very little importance; if so, I can only say that the Civil Service Mentality should be left in the Human world, where it belongs: we have no use for it Down Here.

Yours, &c.

SLUCKDRIB

Thus from my Attendant. I confess it had not previously occurred to me that the corruption of all the vices by righteousness must cause as much theological wrangling *there* as the corruption of the virtues by original sin does *here*. Meanwhile, I am left with the Atheist on my hands. I do not want him. I have no use for him. I have no missionary zeal at all.[8] God is behaving with His usual outrageous lack of scruple. The man keeps on bothering about Miracles; he thinks Hall Caine's *Life of Christ* is the last word in Biblical criticism, and objects violently to the doctrine of Sin, the idea of a Perfect Man without any sex-life, and the ecclesiastical tyranny of the B.B.C. He is in the Home Guard, can't spell, and has a mind like a junk-shop. If he reads any of the books I have recommended, he will write me long and disorderly letters about them. It will go on for years. I cannot bear it. Two of the books are yours[9] – I only hope they will rouse him to fury. Then I shall hand him on to you. You like souls. I don't. God is simply taking advantage of the fact that I can't stand intellectual chaos, and it isn't fair. Anyhow, there aren't any up-to-date books about Miracles.[10]

The Hound of Heaven

People have stopped arguing about them. Why? Has Physics sold the pass? or is it merely that everybody is thinking in terms of Sociology and international Ethics? Please tell me what to do with this relic of the Darwinian age, who is wasting my time, sapping my energies and destroying my soul.

Yours indignantly,
Dorothy L. Sayers

---

8 Nevertheless the correspondence continued for at least another year and she even permitted him to call on her twice.

9 *Broadcast Talks* and *The Problem of Pain*. See her letter to L. T. Duff, 10 May 1943 and accompanying list.

10 C. S. Lewis' book, *Miracles*, was not published until 1947. He had preached a sermon on the subject in November 1942. A short version was printed in *The Guardian*, 2 October 1942. This was followed by an article in two instalments, "Dogma and the Universe", published in *The Guardian*, 19 and 26 March 1943. Walter Hooper thinks that D. L. S.' observation that "there aren't any up-to-date books about Miracles" may have encouraged Lewis to continue. (See pp. 343–344 of *C. S. Lewis: A Companion and Guide*.) In his reply to this letter, dated 17 May 1943, Lewis said, "I'm starting a book on Miracles".

[24 Newland Street
Witham
Essex]

TO THE REV. G. H. CROSSLAND[1]

18 May 1943

My good Sir,

I am quite well aware that wine, like tea and coffee, is poison when taken in excess.

It must be a great grief to you that Our Lord should have been so ill-informed, or so lacking in common, moral, and Christian sense, as to use it both for His sacrament and for His pleasure. What a pity He had not the advantage of being able to study Miss Baker's pamphlet on the subject! However, since I am a Christian and not a Mohammedan, I shall make so bold as to follow His example, despite any claims made on behalf of the Free Churches to know better than God Almighty....

Yours faithfully,

[Dorothy L. Sayers]

1 A Wesleyan Minister of Tunbridge Wells.

[24 Newland Street
Witham
Essex]

TO L. T. DUFF

16 June 1943

Dear Mr Duff,

Thank you very much for your letter. I am sure you will forgive me if I answer it this time rather briefly. If I were to deal with all your points exhaustively, I should have to write a small book, so I will leave you to deal with the other twenty-one books I have recommended. I think you will find that most of the points are dealt with in one or other of them.

But I do want to say just one thing. The "Gospel" or "Good News" is first and foremost a story — a "news-story" about something that happened. And it is important to remember just what the story is. It is not a story about a very good man who taught a good way of life and was killed, like Socrates. The story told by the Christian Faith is that God — the living energy that made and sustains the universe — once showed Himself openly in earthly history in the body and mind of a man; that, except for a few people who loved Him and learned to recognize Him for what He was, man hated God at sight and killed Him; but that death could not hold that living energy, which showed Its power by again reanimating the material form which It had made (as It made all things), before It passed out of human history into the eternity which It had never quitted.

If you remember exactly what the story is, you may see that your first objection cannot be answered in exactly the terms in which you have raised it. God has never said that if we believe in Him unpleasant things will not happen to us in this world. What He did was to suffer those things Himself. God-in-History prayed to God-in-Eternity that, if it were possible, the suffering might be avoided. But it was not possible, and He went through with it. The answer to the prayer in the Garden of Gethsemane was not the cancelling of the Crucifixion, but the Resurrection from the dead. God had to go through with it; and His promise is that He will take us through with Him as a part of His own living energy to the same triumphant eternity. The Christian Church shares consciously in this process, knowing what is happening to her, "filling up that which is lacking in the sufferings of Christ";[1] the rest of the world does the same, though unconsciously and without understanding. Consequently, prayer that just asks to be spared suffering is really a way of saying, "God, put me out of Your life and work – I don't want to go through the mill with You and my fellow-men". The only really *Christian* prayer is made on Christ's model: "O God, spare me if possible; but if not, I am ready to go through with it as You did". And sometimes that particular suffering can be spared; but at other times God says: "No; your suffering is needed as Mine was needed; you are called to share My cross – willingly, if you love and trust Me. I ask no more of you than I exacted of Myself; and you know where it is we are going together – through suffering and despair and death into life and power. What happened to Me in the few years of My manifestation in history is at once the supreme instance and the perpetual symbol of what man has been doing to God throughout all history. My historical body of mind and flesh I have dissipated again into the elements from which I made it. You are now my earthly body in which I show myself and go about in the world, and your way to the sharing of My life is to make your body as My body, your thoughts as My thoughts, your will as My will, your suffering and death as My suffering and death so that your resurrection in power will be as My resurrection in power."

So that "prayer" which is just a childish repetition of "Don't want", or a pagan incantation to drive away disaster, is not prayer in the Christian sense at all. A lot of it is just nonsense-talk: "Please God don't let anything

1 Who now rejoice in my sufferings for you and fill up that which remaineth of the afflictions of Christ in my flesh for His body's sake, which is the church. (Colossians, chapter 1, verse 24)

have any real consequences." And of course it is quite futile. The world is so made that things really happen and have real consequences, and the only way of altering that would be to unmake the world. In this world of time, Christ promises nothing but "blood, toil, tears and sweat"[2] – and "in the world of eternity life unlimited".

I am sending you a short article of mine,[3] in which "the story" is boiled down to its bones, so to speak; because so often in arguing and explaining, we lose sight of what the story actually is. It is the story of how man sent God to the gallows. Anything less startling than that isn't historic Christianity at all – it is only Christianity-and-water. The reason why God and man behaved like that has to do with sin, and I won't attempt to cope with that subject now – you will find it in the books I have suggested, especially in Whale's *Christian Doctrine* and Lewis' *Problem of Pain*. By the way, Mr Lewis has sent me an article of his on Miracles[4] which he hopes may come in useful. Please let me have it back some time, because it is the only copy I possess. Of course, in reading it, you have to remember the story – that Christ is God, the life and power that animates the whole universe. You can't fit the doctrine to a totally different kind of story.

Thank you for letting me know your background. It is pretty much what your previous letters led me to expect, and I think the choice of books is as good as I can make for you. What I find when reading a lot of books on a subject like theology is that one may wade through a lot of stuff, finding it meaningless or disagreeing with every word of it, and that then, suddenly, some phrase strikes one and one says, "Good Lord, yes! that means something, and now I begin to see what all the rest of the verbiage was about". And that means that one has found a way into the subject – the gap in the perimeter, so to speak, and when one is once inside one can fan out and mop up all the other positions from the back. But no two people find exactly the same way in, and that's why recommending books is such a job. You may lead one person up to what (for his equipment) is an absolutely unscalable intellectual escarpment, and only discover too late that he could have gone in quite easily over what (to you) looks like a quite impassable emotional bog. So, once again, if the first book you try does not, in the charming Quaker phrase, "speak to your condition", don't waste time getting angry with it, but put it aside and tap round the defences for a more assailable spot.

2 See letter to B. E. Nicolls, 12 May 1943, note.

3 "The Greatest Drama Ever Staged", published in pamphlet form by Hodder and Stoughton, 2 June 1938.

4 In his reply dated 17 May 1943, Lewis asked "Is the enclosed any help?" This was followed by a note dated 20 May: "Keep the magazine if it simplifies the matter, for I have the MS." This may have been his sermon on Miracles, published in the church magazine (the Church of St Jude on the Hill, London).

Of course, if none of it, after careful consideration, seems to make sense, you can fall back on your defensive line of "we are as we are and we can't help anything" but that doesn't seem a very cheerful doctrine, and it has the (to me) fatal defect of making nonsense of our ingrained sense of responsibility. Even the "blood and tears" of Christianity is more stimulating than that!

And you say you sometimes think that man may be just a disease in the universe. So, after all, you feel that there is something not quite right about man. Christianity is a trifle less pessimistic than you are. It doesn't say that man is the disease, but that he is diseased through and through; and it adds that the disease is curable. But look! the moment you say: "There's something wrong, there's a disease, and it's something to do with man" – then, it doesn't matter two hoots what you call it, *you have discovered what the Church means by sin*. Never mind whether you thought that was what the Church meant or not – she may have expressed herself badly in your hearing. But that is it. Whatever you may think about "sin" as a theory, you have discovered it for yourself as a fact.

And *of course* man is made of the dust of the earth, subject to the same chemical and mechanical and biological laws [as] his fellow-creatures, and of course his conceit is overweening and his pride intolerable; Christianity will agree heartily with you, and has been saying the same thing in no measured terms for centuries. The only thing for which man has any cause to reverence himself is that he has been so made as to be (in the phrase of a great Christian father[5]) *capax Dei*, "capable of God". However, I won't go on about this – already I have been much less "brief" than I meant to be. I will now leave you to wrestle with the angel of theology!

Please don't thank me for making out the book-list. I only hope you may find something there that "says something to you". If you do, I should be very grateful to know which book it is that has in any way stimulated or interested or cleared anything up for you, because people so often ask what they shall read on this subject and sometimes one doesn't know what sort of thing they will like.

Yours sincerely,

[Dorothy L. Sayers]

---

5 There are a number of uses of this phrase recorded in the Patrologia Latina. The most likely source is Hilary of Poitiers (315–367), who wrote the first Latin treatise on the Trinity (*De Trinitate*): "Si in judicii severitatem capax illa Dei Virgo ventura est…" (If that Virgin God-bearer is to come to the strictness of Judgement…).

Correspondence between D. L. S. and Mr Duff continued but not all the letters are extant. The continuation, between March and August 1944, will be found in the following volume.

[24 Newland Street
Witham
Essex]

TO THE REV. G. H. CROSSLAND
16 June 1943

Dear Sir,
You are extraordinarily evasive. Will you kindly either keep to the point or cease from controversy.

I will put to you two questions, and will trouble you to answer them in two words, or not at all.

1. "The Son of Man came eating and drinking and ye say, *Behold a gluttonous man and a wine-bibber.*"[1]

Do you agree with this criticism, Yes or No?

2. If the answer to the above is "Yes", then please state in one word whether you consider that Our Lord,

in drinking wine, showed Himself to be

(a) wicked

or

(b) ignorant

It is neither presumptuous, heretical, nor infidel to be an abstainer. But if you believe that Jesus was wholly God, then to condemn His conduct is presumptuous. If you believe that He was not wholly God, but only partly or in some respects divine, you are a heretic. If you think He was not God at all, you are an infidel.

Yours faithfully,
[Dorothy L. Sayers]

Pressure of work prevented me from dealing with your letter earlier.

---

1 Luke, chapter 7, verse 34.

[24 Newland Street
Witham
Essex]

TO STORM JAMESON[1]

21 June 1943

Dear Miss Storm Jameson,

I have been meaning for a long time to write to you.

First to say how very sorry I was to hear about your sister, secondly to express my satisfaction that the book[2] had gone so well in America, and thirdly to tell you (in case you had not noticed it in the papers) that a centre[3] for instructing intelligent professional people in the Christian religion has now in fact been opened at St. Anne's Church House, 57A Dean Street, Soho. One of the incumbents, Fr. Pat McLaughlin, is a very energetic young priest, whom I know very well, and it will, I think, be run in a vigorous and lively manner. They are having lectures from time to time, and I am, in fact, speaking there myself on Thursday evening about the Theatre. They are also open all the time for anybody who wants to come and ask questions and so on. I meant to send you one of their leaflets, but have most unfortunately mislaid it, but if you are still interested you could easily get in touch with them. Their 'phone number is Gerrard 5006.

With kind regards,
    Yours sincerely,
        [Dorothy L. Sayers]

1 See letter to her, 4 May 1942, note 1.
2 *London Calling*, edited by Storm Jameson (New York and London, Harper and Brothers, 1942), to which D. L. S. contributed a poem, "Lord, I thank thee". (See *Poetry of Dorothy L. Sayers*, ed. cit., pp. 123–129.)
3 The centre, known as the Society of St Anne, occupied a great deal of D. L. S.' time and energy during the last 14 years of her life.

24 Newland Street
Witham
Essex

TO HER SON

26 June 1943

Dear John,

Many thanks for your letter and birthday greetings – the enclosure which you mentioned was not enclosed, but from the context I take it to

have been something in the nature of a bill. I don't know whether it had
to do with some kind of extraordinary expenditure, as it's called, because
you didn't say; but on general principles I don't think it's a good thing for
me to anticipate your allowance by too long a period. If you get it a fortnight early, it merely means that the sum of money has to cover three and
a half months instead of three; and if one goes on along those lines one
soon finds one's self in a rather Micawberish state, financially speaking. So
try and arrange things to fit in with the proper [word missing] because
finance is pretty tight these days.

I know it's extremely difficult to keep one's mind alive when one's doing
other sorts of work. I can only say, "Do your best not to cultivate an
'interim-mentality,' because that's what people did in the last war, and it
led to all the troubles of the '20-30's. I am reminded of my daily woman,
who looks on the war-years as a period during which she's compelled by
circumstances to take care of pottery and hardware and looks forward
eagerly to the day when she may again light-heartedly smash plates and
burn the bottoms out of saucepans, knowing that she can always run out
to Woolworth's and replace them. (I haven't the heart to tell her that I
don't think that merry state of things is coming back, and that things will
be much better if it doesn't.)

As far as I can make out, finance and power are due for a divorce. This
seems to have happened already in Russia and (under rather different
conditions) only comparatively few people see that here, and probably still
fewer in America, where they are due for a few shocks. It's all very
exciting to watch, though a little unnerving when one sees that the reins
are mostly in the hands of people who don't know which way the horses
are going, so probably it's too much to expect that they should begin now.
All the same, I fancy Peter Drucker has got hold of the right end of the
stick. I thought so when I read *The End of Economic Man*, and *The Future of
Industrial Man*[1] confirms me in that opinion. The people who base their
utopias on the notion that markets are going to expand seem to me to be
talking like children. But of course, they may succeed in staving off the
inevitable for another twenty years and a third world-war. I don't know;
but be prepared accordingly! – Meanwhile, one does the necessary
amount of vegetation while the present conflict is got on with. We had
two strange Belgians to tea the other day. Their opinion of the French was
not printable. Of all the nations, France is going to be the most troublesome and unhappy after the War, and some of the people who know most
seem to think she is due for a really frightful civil war. Which is what
comes of saying that one will do and suffer anything rather than fight!

1 *The End of Economic Man*, 1939; *The Future of Industrial Man*, 1943.

The usual enantiodrame[2] in a particularly spectacular form. But, my God, it's enthralling to watch! The trouble is that one dare not – indeed cannot – remain merely a spectator of things, and that it's difficult to know precisely which part of the universal muddle one should prepare one's self to take active part in. I should like to be twenty years younger, with my present mind and attitude. But we never can have that, and that's the devil of it.

Your affectionate
D. L. F.

2 Interaction of opposites (from Greek, ευάντιος opposing, and δράμά spectacle).

[24 Newland Street
Witham
Essex]

TO MISS J. HODGSON[1]

8 July 1943

Dear Miss Hodgson,

I certainly agree that the Church's record is a bad one as regards the position of women, and I said so with some emphasis in the *Christendom* article to which you refer.

The question of admission to Holy Orders, however, leaves me cold. In any case, I think it is perfectly idiotic to start this particular hare at the present moment. One cannot possibly expect such a proposition to receive serious attention until the basic position (infinitely more important) is conceded; viz: that a woman possesses status as a human being, and that all her functions are not necessarily related to her sex.

As matters stand it is almost impossible to get the clergy to tackle the subject of the status of women, because they always think it is going to be something or other about Orders; and the agitation about this has only succeeded in side-tracking the dispute and confusing the issues. I think that to clamour for admission to the priesthood (whether or not it is desirable) is to throw the whole thing out of proportion; it is bound to look like just one more effort to get women into a paid profession, whereas the real controversy is about something much more fundamental. As for preaching and prophesying, I know to my cost that there is no difficulty whatever about doing *that* – the difficulty is to avoid it!

Quite apart from all this – where is the sense of introducing an

1 Identity unknown.

entirely new spanner into the works at a moment when the Churches seem a little more disposed than they have been for centuries to pull together and show some sort of united front? Can you conceive anything more likely to [affront] and alienate the Orthodox and Roman Communions or the more traditional parties in the Church of England? It's running your head against a stone wall to no purpose. And if "women who have made their mark in public life" are not going to attend to spiritual things until they see the chance of getting something out of it, their spirituality is such as the Church can very well dispense with. Do let us preserve some sense of proportion.

Yours sincerely,

    [Dorothy L. Sayers]

The following letter and the one which concludes the present volume, mark the beginning of a correspondence with Helmut Kuhn,[1] the interest and importance of which will further emerge in volume three.

                              [24 Newland Street
                              Witham
                              Essex]

TO HELMUT KUHN, ESQ.

c/o The University of North Carolina Press,
Chapel Hill,
North Carolina
U.S.A.
30 August 1943

Dear Mr. Kuhn,

    I have received from your publishers a copy of your book *Freedom Forgotten and Remembered*, with the request that I should "write and give

---

1 Helmut Kuhn (b.1899), philosopher, had undertaken to write a volume for "Bridgeheads". It was eventually published, first in German (*Begegnung mit dem Nichts; ein Versuch über die Existenzphilosophie*, Tübingen, 1950 and next in English, *Encounter with Nothingness: an Essay on Existentialism*, Methuen, 1951) but by then the series "Bridgeheads" had been discontinued. In 1949 D. L. S. was still sufficiently involved to ask C. S. Lewis if he would write an introduction to the English version, but he declined. A Foreword was written by Martin Jarrett-Kerr, C.R.

Helmut Kuhn, professor of Philosophy at Erlangen, had held a Chair of Philosophy also at the University of North Carolina (1928–1947) and at Emory University (1947–1949). His book *Freedom Forgotten and Remembered* was published in 1942. *A History of Esthetics*, co-authored by Katharine Everett Gilbert and Helmut Kuhn, was first published by Thames and Hudson in 1939 (revised and enlarged edition, 1956). *Christianity and Reason*, edited by Edward D. Myers (New York, Oxford University Press, 1951), a collection of papers read by the Guild of Scholars at the General Theological Seminary in New York, 5–7 December 1947, contains an article by Kuhn: "The Wisdom of the Greeks".

them my opinion of it". But I would rather write directly to you, so that I may at the same time thank you for the very kindly review you gave to *The Mind of the Maker* – in a periodical so learned that its very title makes me blush. It must have been only too obvious to you that my theology was amateurish and my philosophy extremely sketchy, and it was exceedingly kind of you to overlook the many faults of rash and inadequate terminology in which the book abounds, and to give it such generous and serious attention. I am glad you thought there was "something in it", as they say. There are parts of it which I could wish better expressed, and which I could do better now, having read more and consulted people. At the time I wrote it, I was rather cut off from books and consultation, and also rather distracted of mind, owing to the fact that the Battle of France was startling us all through the first chapters and the Battle of Britain whizzing round our heads during the conclusion. Not that that is any real excuse. One should preserve one's detachment; but as a matter of fact, one doesn't altogether.

Is your book being published over here?[2] I hope so, because there is a great deal in it that English people ought and need to understand. For example: the distinction you firmly draw between incidental brutalities in time of emergency and the calculated brutalities that are an integral part of the order they seek to enforce. The English as everybody knows, are rather muddled thinkers; and also (as everybody doesn't know) they are very easily abashed into self-criticism and scrupulosity. It's not really hypocrisy that makes us demand moral justification for what we do; it's really a rather childish feeling that we "want to be good", and can't get on if we are made to feel that we are hopelessly naughty.[3] That's why we are so much more lively and vigorous in defeat than in victory – because we feel pretty sure there's a moral justification for staying alive if possible. But when we are safe and powerful, we get uneasy, and begin to listen to the doctrinaire people who argue and scold, and say: "What right have we to oppose Hitler or set ourselves up as champions of liberty? We're just as bad. We put distinguished foreigners into internment camps with bad lavatory accommodation, we suppressed *The Daily Worker*, we suspended *habeas corpus*, we shot some people in India, we are uniformed and regimented up to the hilt, the police are empowered to pry into our store-cupboards and coal-cellars,[4] we rejoice in the bombing of Berlin and sometimes speak irritably about Jews – we might just as well be in Germany!" And then we get worried, having been taught to despise the method of

---

2 It was distributed by the Oxford University Press.

3 Cf. her article "They Tried to be Good", first published in *World Review*, November 1943, pp. 30–34; reprinted in *Unpopular Opinions*, Gollancz, 1946, pp. 97–105.

4 This was true during World War II.

argument which begins with *distinguo*,[5] and lose confidence and do silly
things.

You say there must be a true victory – "a real victor who believes in the
truth of his triumphant cause". You couldn't be more right – but that's
just where we are likely to come over all queer and lose grip. We do so dislike what we call "a bad winner" (meaning an ungenerous and boastful
winner) that we shall probably end by confusing the triumphant cause
with our triumphant selves, and so disown the triumph. This is a sort of
pride and egotism, in one way, but also it's a kind of disordered humility.
"The great question is whether any one individual or any one nation is
good enough to fight the good battle." That is important. In a sense, of
course, nobody is – but if God insisted on waiting till all His battles could
be fought with clean hands, He would have no soldiers at all. The fact is,
we have let our minds be taken captive by the Perfectionists and
Absolutists and Whole-hoggers who are obsessed with the notion that
there can be *absolute* perfection in human affairs. Therefore, having said
with St. Paul that we "are not meet to be apostles because we persecuted
the Church of God", we proceed to the conclusion not that we should
"labour more abundantly than them all", but that we are disqualified
from all apostolic function, and had better sit down and shut up.

You say that, after the war, existing ties and alliances should be
preserved and strengthened – we should build on, and extend, that which
already exists. Again, how right you are! And again, how the doctrinaire
perfectionists will insist on doing otherwise. You include the British
Commonwealth of Nations among the foundations to be built on. But
they will try, in the name of equality, or internationalism, or something,
to dissolve all such existing ties, and set up some [neopolitical ?] novelty
in their place – a Federation of Europe, or a rejuvenated League of
Nations, or some other fancy association of states without roots in heart
or history. It can't be done. Nothing will come of nothing. Nations are
realities, like families. Frontiers are made by geographical facts like mountains and rivers and soil and coal-mines. Nobody can draw random lines
over the map and say "Your loyalties begin at a place decided for you by
a committee of experts"; or "You mustn't have any loyalties except to
humanity-in-general".

Nor is it the slightest use – it's the most wicked mischief – to talk about
"abiding peace and lasting security". There's no such thing. Good God,
didn't we learn that last time? Then it was "No More War" – and that
slogan landed us in the biggest war ever. Now it's "No More Poverty" and
"No More Fear" – I know what horrid enantiodramas[6] of themselves the

5 Latin: I distinguish (used to present the points in mediaeval disputation).
6 She employs this unusual word also in her letter to John Anthony, dated 26 June 1943; see
   note 2.

slogans are going to issue in. The worst slogan of the lot is "No More Risk": that's the thing that makes people run away from freedom and land themselves in a total tyranny, with the risk of the gallows at every corner.

It's true that "the democracies" (as we agreed to call them for want of a better name) do really want and thrive on freedom. But the thing they want and instinctively fight for is not the thing they have become accustomed to *call* freedom. What popular speakers *call* "freedom" is nearly always the "freedom from" – and that's why we don't know how to explain ourselves when people point out that we, like every other [state], are obliged to impose certain restrictions on ourselves. Too much "freedom from" ends in leaving one no "freedom *to*" at all. If I am free from *all* bonds, even the right to bind myself, I am not free to believe in anything definite, to make any definite decision, even to love one person or thing more than another; and every daily choice becomes an agony, because there is no paramount claim to bind the will to a single course. That is where people begin to welcome regimentation, and find themselves more genuinely free in war than in peace – free to follow their fixed choice, without hesitation or conflicting claim.

Why should I say all this badly to you who know it already and have said it better? Only to tell you how passionately I agree with you, and because I want somebody to say it and go on saying it very loudly to our nation. The English are all right really. In a way they are protected by not being able to think too neatly, because, when a choice has to be made they make it instinctively without bothering too much about theoretical consistency. But they've got to the point where they can't plump out with their choice till they have their backs against the wall and must choose or perish. I don't want them to go further and get like France, which seems to have almost lost the power of choice. Even when she was right up against it, she didn't choose anything, and so far as one can see she isn't choosing yet. Not really. In some ways, the condition of France frightens me more than that of Germany. I think it's nearer to what we might become. Though I don't know. It's queer how, in any desperate emergency, the British do all think the same thing at bottom (though you wouldn't suppose it, seeing how violently they disagree in Parliament and the newspapers). But they do, though it needs the emergency to bring the essential agreement to the surface. I should think any outsider would wonder how the Government (knowing, as we didn't know, the non-existent state of our armament) dared to take the risk of going on in 1940. But if they hadn't there would have been such a howl of fury from one end of Britain to the other that they couldn't have faced it. (Fortunately Churchill was there to howl the loudest, and we were spared a General Election or a revolution with the Germans at Calais.)

This letter seems to be all about Britain – narrow and national. But I'm concerned about Britain. I think we have something valuable here, if the theorists and the tolerationists will stop bewildering us and let us hold on to it. But a lot of people in positions of importance seem to me to be looking in the wrong direction and flogging dead horses. I have a feeling that while they are concentrating on divorcing money from power (which is all right as far as it goes) they may lose sight of the fact that this doesn't mean abolishing power, but merely shifting the effective focus of power to some other quarter. Indeed, I think power has already evacuated the financial strong-hold and gone elsewhere, and that we are really doing mopping-up operations, under the impression that we are conducting a major campaign. Perhaps one never realizes where power is until the moment it is preparing to collapse. None of this is much to the point, I fear. All I really have to do is to express my appreciation of a very wise book, and to hope that it will be read, marked, and digested.

Yours very truly,

[Dorothy L. Sayers]

From the following letter it is apparent that John Anthony, then aged 19, was developing literary talent. He had written a play, which he sent to his mother for her comments.

Witham

TO HER SON

7 September 1943

Dear John,

"Return of post" – You're lucky, because in another day I shouldn't have been here. However, here it is, and I've added a fiver to make whoopee with.

Here also is the play, which I meant to read through again before commenting on. However –

You can write dialogue, and that is the most important thing. I mean you can write speakable lines that sound like speech and not like writing. Anybody who can do that has got the first necessity for writing plays. If they haven't got it, they usually don't acquire it.

Most of the faults you have seen quite well for yourself – notably the lack of action. The reason for putting a thing on the stage rather than in a novel is that the story may be seen in action. (This is one of those tiresome truisms which are none the less true because Aristotle said them in the year dot.) My feeling about the thing is that it could have been told just as well, if not better, in narrative form, which would have allowed the author to do some of the character-analysis "off", so to speak, instead of obliging the character to do so much undressing in public. The trouble about people explaining their own insides at such length is that they can scarcely help appearing the most appalling egotists – even if they were less egotistical than this bunch of people in fact are (is?). Of course Bernard Shaw can get away with plays that are all argument and no action, but how cunningly he manages to make things look like action even when they aren't! But he is a law to himself, anyhow, and nobody has ever yet succeeded in learning his trick of perpetual surprise.

The general atmosphere of the play seems to me a bit stuffy and old-fashioned. It's the kind of thing we had so much of after the last war, and which did so much to make this war inevitable. No character seems to have any conception of anything except as it happens to affect his private affairs – one almost expects somebody to say, like poor dear Neville Chamberlain, that it seems a terrible thing to be fighting about Czecho-Slovakia, a far-away country that most of us have never heard of. That, of course, is your affair – but dramatically speaking, I think you have fallen into the old trap of not giving the devil his due. If you are going to make a PLAY out of anti-war feeling, you get no real dramatic clash unless you give war the best spokesman possible. That's why (to go back to Shaw) the Grand Inquisitor's speech in *St Joan* is the most important and tremendous thing in the play, the focal point on which it all turns. It says everything that can be said on the "other" side, and in itself it is quite unanswerable – that is, it can only be answered in terms of emotion and action.

You've got the right idea about the Third Act – the idea of something that acts as a catalyst to precipitate the situation which has been saturated in the first two acts. But the thing doesn't quite run clear. There are two catalysts, and neither does quite what it should – Phyllis's affair with Michael and Michael's death. The latter is not really motivated by the action of the play – I think that's the snag in it. He has an air of being killed for the playwright's convenience, and this gives an air of unreality to the last scene. (Which is rather unreal anyhow, because, when people die or get killed, their families don't just sit around sneering at one another. They haven't time. It's all telephoning and writing letters, and making arrangements about whether one will have a private or a military funeral, or what.)

Technical details – You can't have a five-year-old child. Nobody under the age of twelve is allowed on the stage, so that about nine years old is about as young as you can expect your child-actor to impersonate. I don't think the child adds a great deal to the action; but if you must have her, you can make her a bit older, without greatly altering her attitude to life and war.

I'm not clear about the business with the clock in Act II. If it's really got to strike all eleven hours the actors will go mad – a grandfather tends to have rather a slow strike and it will distract the audience. It would be all right if Michael removed the striking weight before he started.

You might make Phyllis's position in the household a bit clearer at the start. Except for a vague mention of Chelsea there's no background to her until a long explanation is dragged in rather late.

You know, I fancy your real difficulty is in constructing a story. Many good playwrights have the same difficulty, and that's why so many of them, from Æschylus to Shakespeare and Shaw worked so much more freely with a ready-made plot. It might be good exercise to try – it means, in practice, finding motives for the action, instead of inventing an action to carry the motives –

Good luck to it,
    D. L. F.

In June of this year Dr Welch wrote to the Archbishop of Canterbury, the Most Revd Dr William Temple, to ask whether a Lambeth Doctorate in Divinity might be conferred on D. L. S. in consideration of The Man Born to be King. *He said: "My serious judgment is that these plays have done more for the preaching of the Gospel to the unconverted than any other single effort of the churches or religious broadcasting since the last war – that is a big statement, but my experience forces me to make it."*

Dr Temple, having consulted the Regius Professor of Divinity at Oxford,[1] wrote to ask if she would allow him to confer upon her the Degree of Doctor of Divinity, "in recognition of what I regard as the great value of your work especially The Man Born to be King *and* The Mind of the Maker." *He added that she would be the first woman to receive the Degree. She replied:*

---

1 The Rev. Oliver Chase Quick, M.A., D.D. (1885–1944), Regius Professor of Divinity in the University of Oxford from 1939 to 1943, author of *The Christian Sacraments*, 1927, *The Ground of Faith and the Chaos of Thought*, 1931, *The Doctrine of the Creed*, 1938, etc.

[24 Newland Street
Witham
Essex]

TO THE ARCHBISHOP OF CANTERBURY

7 September 1943

Your Grace,

Thank you very much indeed for the great honour you do me. I find it
very difficult to reply as I ought, because I am extremely conscious that I
don't deserve it. A Doctorate of Letters – yes; I have served Letters as
faithfully as I knew how. But I have only served Divinity, as it were, accidentally, coming to it as a writer rather than as a Christian person. A
Degree in Divinity is not, I suppose, intended as a certificate of sanctity,
exactly; but I should feel better about it if I were a more convincing kind
of Christian. I am never quite sure whether I really am one, or whether I
have only fallen in love with an intellectual pattern. And when one is able
to handle language it is sometimes hard to know how far one is under the
spell of one's own words.

Also, you know, I am just a common novelist and playwright. I may not
– in fact I almost certainly shan't – remain on the austere level of *The Man
Born to be King* and *The Mind of the Maker*. I can't promise not to break out
into something thoroughly secular, frivolous or unbecoming – adorned, if
the story requires it, with the language of the rude soldiery, or purple
passages descriptive of the less restrained and respectable passions. I
shouldn't like your first woman D.D. to create scandal, or give reviewers
cause to blaspheme.

My husband says, helpfully, that after all I could scarcely be more scandalous than Dean Swift! He also says (being military-minded) that I
should do as the Archbishop says and not argue. Perhaps he is right.
Probably I am only trying to keep a bolt-hole open into which I can
retreat, crying: "I never really committed myself to anything – I only
wrote books!" I don't know. I find it very difficult to tell where conscience
ends and pride, or cowardice, begins.

I expect I had better leave it to your judgement. If you tell me that I
ought to accept, I will. It is a very great honour, and I am deeply sensible
of it. I feel as though I had not expressed myself very gratefully, but I do
appreciate it very deeply and I thank you . . .

I shall be in Town from tomorrow till Saturday morning if you would
like me to come and see you or anything. My address is 24, Great James
St., W.C.1. Or I could come up at any time.

Yours very sincerely, and indeed gratefully,

[Dorothy L. Sayers]

The Archbishop replied that if she would prefer to receive a Doctorate in Letters he would readily agree to that, but assured her that a Doctorate in Divinity was not to be regarded as "a certificate in sanctity". A few days later, however, he wrote to say that the object he had in mind would not be quite fully met by a Doctorate in Letters and that he was hoping more than ever that she would agree to accept the D.D. Still uneasy, D. L. S. asked for a few more days in which to think the matter over.

[24 Newland Street
Witham
Essex]

TO THE ARCHBISHOP OF CANTERBURY

18 September 1943

Your Grace,

Thank you very much for your letter. I quite see that a D.Litt. wouldn't be the same thing from your point of view – I only mentioned it as the kind of thing I should have no qualms about accepting.[1]

I do still feel a little uneasy about it. Will Your Grace forgive me and not think I am making a silly and ostentatious fuss if I ask for two or three days more in which to consider? I seem to be behaving very ungraciously, but I can't help feeling horribly like the jay in peacock's feathers, with a touch of Judas Iscariot.

Yours very sincerely,
[Dorothy L. Sayers]

1 She did accept a Doctorate in Letters from Durham University in 1950.

Having consulted several friends, among them probably Muriel St Clare Byrne and Marjorie Barber, whose opinion she often sought, D. L. S. decided not to accept the Lambeth Doctorate in Divinity.

[24 Newland Street
Witham
Essex]

TO THE ARCHBISHOP OF CANTERBURY

24 September 1943]

Your Grace,

Thank you very much for your letter. I have been thinking the matter over very carefully and have consulted, confidentially, one or two people whose advice I thought would be valuable, and have come to the conclusion that it would be better for me not to accept the D.D. My consultants all felt on the whole the same way about it, though not all for the same reasons. (If you cared to have their names, I am sure they would readily explain to you why their judgement supported my instinctive feeling about it.)

Quite apart from my reluctance to sail under anything that might appear to be false colours, there are certain practical considerations. The first, and perhaps the most cogent from the Church's point of view is this: that any good I can do in the way of presenting the Christian Faith to the common people is bound to be hampered and impeded the moment I carry any sort of ecclesiastical label. In the present peculiar state of public opinion, it is the "outsider" with neither dog-collar nor professional standing in the Church who can sometimes carry the exterior defensive positions by the mere shock of a surprise assault; but the power to do this depends largely upon remaining a free-lance. The moment one becomes one of the regular "religious gang", or (in the elegant phrase used by the *Daily Herald*) "the pet of the bishops", everything one says is heavily discounted. That is why I have lately been refusing to appear on the platform at religious meetings, or to sign protests and manifestoes – the oftener one's name appears in such contexts, the less weight it carries.

Also, knowing the world of journalism as I have only too much reason to do, I think we might find ourselves up against some very disagreeable publicity. It is, I think, your generous intention that the recognition given to my work should be publicly known. But women are "news", in a way that men are not, and peculiarly subject to the attentions of the sensational press – some of which does not love me very much. There might well be some rather disagreeable comments, impossible to refute or argue about,[1] whose [barb] would stick, ranging from, "Thriller-writer Dorothy Sayers, having made Christ a best-seller to the tune of 30,000 copies, has been rewarded with a D.D." to "This not very seemly farce, dealing cynically and light-heartedly with divorce (or what not) is by Miss Dorothy Sayers, D.D., and will probably make the Archbishop rather sorry that he ever . . ." and so forth. And to the extent that this might happen, and that one would not wish it to happen, there would always be a sort of interior inhibition in the handling of secular work. I know, of course, that there is nothing to prevent the writing of detective stories – mostly a very innocuous form of entertainment; but there would always be the strain of an obligation to *be* innocuous and refrain from giving offence, and that is a strain under which no writer can work properly.

---

1 It is possible that she also thought that the discovery by a journalist of her son's existence would cause embarrassment.

By all means say to those people who have been demanding that "something should be done about" the author of the books that you have offered her a Degree, and that she has, with a deep sense of appreciation, thought it nevertheless better to decline the honour. I understand very well, I think, the purpose you had in mind – and indeed I have often felt, and said, that it would be a good thing and helpful to the work of what it is fashionable to call the Lay Apostolate, if their books could receive some form of official recognition – not in order to reward the writer so much as to establish the orthodoxy of his doctrine. As it is, the reader is only too apt to suppose that Christianity interestingly presented is not historical Christianity at all, but a new "interpretation" deriving from the author's individual taste and fancy. (As, only too often, it is.) But I would suggest, with submission, that the best way would be to accord recognition, not so much to the workman as to the work. If, for example, the Church had something analogous to the power of the French Academy to "couronner" the actual book, when it appeared to be both orthodox and valuable to God's work. I am not thinking of anything quite like a medal or a "prize", but something which would act both as a "nihil obstat" and as a mark of honour – which would say, in effect, "This book, though readable and even exciting, stands within the Catholic tradition, and the Church commends it". This should satisfy any writer who was not making Divinity his life-work, and would also be of some guidance to the reader (who at present is in some uncertainty about what is and is not "in the tradition"); while the Church would not have committed herself to approving any subsequent errors and extravagances into which the amateur theologian might (through sin or ignorance) so easily fall. (I often wonder what the Popes think of the FID. DEF.[2] on English coins, and if they ponder on the rashness which conferred that title on Henry VIII!)

But all this is by the way. I hope very much that Your Grace will understand why, after very careful deliberation, I have come to the conclusion that I must refuse the very great honour offered to me, and will believe that I have done so in no ungrateful spirit.

Yours very sincerely,

[Dorothy L. Sayers]

---

2 Latin: *Fidei Defensor*, Defender of the Faith.

The Archbishop replied on 30 September:

I am extremely grateful for your most kind letter. I think I do fully understand the situation; indeed you have persuaded me that if I were in your position I should have reached your conclusion. Meanwhile I am still glad that I made the proposal and that you are willing for me to mention it to some of those who have been eager that the Church should show some real recognition of the great value of your plays and also the book *The Mind of the Maker*.

[24 Newland Street
Witham
Essex]

TO DR HELMUT KUHN
2 December 1943

Dear Dr Kuhn,
Thank you very much for your kind letter. I will certainly recommend *Freedom Forgotten and Remembered* whenever I can find an opportunity. My difficulty up to now was that I didn't know whether it was yet on sale in this country, but I can now refer people to the O.U.P. I gather, from what you say, that they do not publish, but only distribute it; that may account for the fact that I have not seen it reviewed over here. I will prod my friends at the Press and see what they are doing about it.

As regards England: I know we are a tiresome, irritating and insolent people. But the point is that we are *here*. Chosen race or not, we are the bridgehead into Europe. That is no virtue of ours: God (or Nature, or Geography, or Circumstances, or whatever abstraction it is fashionable to personify)[1] put this island in this place for the affliction of European dictators; the Napoleon who can seize it and hold it can bolt the door of the Continent and cock snoots at the New World.. Therefore, love us or hate us, it is best to keep us in good heart lest in our place you get seven devils worse than the first. What I am afraid of is that constant nagging and criticism may in the end wear down our confidence by making us over-critical of ourselves. This time (as the Duke of Wellington, or somebody, said) it was "a damned near thing".

1 Cf. letter to Father Herbert Kelly, 4 December 1937 and note 8.

I am venturing to send you an article[2] I wrote, in a popular style for a popular paper – legitur, non laudatur[3] – which you may use to infuriate your victims further. If you can pardon the necessary vulgarity of its style, it will show you what it is I am afraid of, and why I eagerly welcome any voice from overseas which is ready to praise, or cheer, or interpret, or explain us, or in fact do anything but scold.

As for Mr Gandhi, all I can say is that if he is half Jesus, he is not the half that died for the sins of the world, for he has always been particular to see that his passion stopped short of the cross. India is a difficulty – what national unity she has is of our making. She is not a country but a sub-continent; the job of unifying her is like the job of unifying Europe, and that is a thing that nobody has found very easy. I think, perhaps, one reason why it appears to Americans easier than it is is that though in the States you have a population of many races and creeds living in harmony together, they have been torn up from their European or Asiatic roots. In India and in Europe they are still living on their roots with all their age-old loyalties still in full life and strength. The parallel case is not so much what America has done with her immigrant Swedes, Danes, Chinese, Japs, Irish, Germans – not even what she has done with her negroes, but what she has done with her Red Indians. Perhaps (I don't know) it is a sign of grace in us that our rule should produce subject peoples bursting with energy and national self-consciousness and eager to throw off our yoke and run things for themselves. Whatever else we have stupidly or cruelly done, we have not let the roots of India wither. Nor has the Welsh root withered after seven centuries of English domination.

I know what people will say about this: "All tyrannies unite the subjugated people against them. There is no difference between Hitler in Europe and the British in India". Yet that would be true only if we saw Hitler eagerly fostering Polish national feeling, earnestly endeavouring to compose differences between Croat and Slovene, and bestowing on the conquered countries precisely those educational facilities and political institutions which would provide them with arguments and weapons against him. But a result so often obscures the road by which it was reached: the Allies are all in uniform, therefore they must have abandoned freedom *just like the Germans*; Poland and India both want to be independent, therefore the one must have been treated as badly as the other, *and with the same intention*. It is not true; but if we hear it said often enough and loudly enough, we shall begin to believe it ourselves. Because there is enough plausibility in it to make us doubt our own good faith.

2 "They Tried to be Good", first published in *World Review*, November 1943, pp. 30–34; later published in *Unpopular Opinions*.
3 Latin: to be read, not praised.

I don't think the British worry about outside criticism very much, provided that it does not ally itself with what you so rightly call "the subtler temptations that, finding us in our privacy, break our wills by confusing our minds". But the mind, especially the British mind, is very easily confused, and in the years between the wars something very benumbing did happen to our will. I am sure that what I have said in my article about "scrupulosity" is true. It was only when Hitler appeared at the Channel Ports that we began to think better of ourselves. We were like the pessimistic philosopher in Chesterton's *Manalive*[4], who doubted whether life was worth living. Whereupon, you remember, the gentleman with the pistol chased him out to the extreme end of a gargoyle and keeping him in that precarious position forced him to repeat:

> I thank the goodness and the grace,
> That on my birth have smiled,
> And perched me in the curious place,
> A happy Christian child.

So here we are, perched in this very anxious place at the edge of Europe, between the Dictator and the Deep Sea, and we've jolly well got to feel happy and Christian about it, or else, as they say on your side, Curtains for us. Another letter all about England. But the awful thing is that nations can really go under. It did happen in France. And upon my soul I don't know why it didn't happen here. Perhaps for no reason except that we are an island. Perhaps because we had got to that place in the mind when one says: "Here stand I; God helping me, I can no other."[5]

Meanwhile, having discovered where your book is to be got, I will purchase several copies as Christmas presents for my friends.

With all good wishes for the New Year (I expect this letter will arrive too late for Christmas),

Yours sincerely,
[Dorothy L. Sayers]

4 Published in 1912.
5 A translation of the statement by Martin Luther at the Diet of Worms, 18 April 1521.

And so, in the short space of seven years, having already
achieved world renown as an author of detective
novels, Dorothy L. Sayers had become, as a result of
her plays, articles and speeches, a figure of
influence and significance both in her own country and abroad.
This extraordinary development had occurred
so rapidly that she herself was
disconcerted by it and scarcely knew which direction
her work should now take.

The unexpected direction it did take and the consequences
which arose are the subject of
letters contained in the next two volumes.

Appendix

Particulars of the birth of John Anthony

ↅↅↅↅↅↅ

In my biography, *Dorothy L.Sayers: Her Life and Soul*, and in the Notes to the first volume of her *Letters*, the account of the circumstances concerning the birth of Dorothy L. Sayers' son, John Anthony Fleming, were per force incomplete, owing to lack of information. Particulars have since come to hand which clarify a good deal that was left unexplained. Above all, the mystery as to why she chose Southbourne, Hampshire[1] for the place of birth is now solved.

William White, John Anthony's father, was born in the Isle of Man on 14 June 1892. His mother died at his birth and his father, the Rev. Henry Gattan White, vicar of Kirk St Ann, Ramsey[2], died four years later. Thereafter William was brought up by his father's sister, Dot White, who lived near Wakefield in Yorkshire. In 1907, at the age of 15, he was sent to Denstone College, a public school near Uttoxeter in North Staffordshire, where he became a member of Lowe House. Denstone College, of which the foundation stone was laid in 1868, is the Senior School of the Woodard Corporation in the Midlands. Situated to the south of the Peak District, it commands views of rolling countryside of great beauty. The original school buildings, dedicated in 1873, were designed by Hubert Carpenter and the chapel is recognized as one of the finest of its kind in the country. For three years, until he left in 1910, William received an excellent education in this privileged environment. The school was strong in Latin and Greek and held a distinguished record of scholarships to Oxford and Cambridge. In 1907, the year William entered the school, a young enthusiastic French master, F. S. Whitmore, joined the staff. He also

---

1 Now part of Dorset,
2 He was curate at Kirk Ballough, Ramsey from 1870 to 1877 and vicar at Kirk St Ann from 1878 to 1894, retiring two years before his death.

organized productions of Shakespeare, in which William enjoyed taking part.[3]

Soon after leaving school William White applied for a post as clerk in Coutts Bank, 440 The Strand, London, where he began work on 21 October 1912 at a salary of £100 a year. In his spare time he took up motorcycling and learned to fly. He resigned for war service on 24 April 1916, by which time his salary had risen to £132. During his time in the Army he was on half pay from the bank.

He joined the Royal Engineers (Motor Cyclists Section) as a Pioneer and was subsequently promoted Corporal. He saw active service in France as a despatch rider and was himself mentioned in despatches. As a result of Mr Whitmore's teaching he had learned to speak French fluently. This qualified him to serve for a period as an interpreter. He was for some time attached to General Headquarters Staff, and later to a Field Survey Company in the neighbourhood of Arques. He was never wounded but was in hospital at one time with trench fever. He was demobilized on 15 September 1919 and returned to Coutts Bank at a salary of £156. He resigned from this post on 1 May 1920.[4]

He decided next to try his fortune in the fast developing motor trade. In 1914, in London, he had married Beatrice Mary Wilson (1881–1964), herself the daughter of a clergyman. They had one daughter, Valerie, born in 1915. In his attempt to make a living he moved from place to place, his family sometimes joining him as he took short-lived jobs in various parts of the country. They once spent a year with his aunt, Dot White, in the town in Yorkshire where he was brought up. In 1922 they were living in Southbourne, in an attic flat of a house belonging to Mrs White's brother ("Rollestone", 91 Southbourne Road), and William went to London alone to try to find work, returning to visit his wife and daughter at weekends. He took a room with friends in the flat above Dorothy's, at 24 Great James Street.

It was there that Dorothy got to know him, as she relates in a letter to her mother dated 18 December 1922. She describes him as "a poor devil who has been staying with the people above me, and whom I chummed up with one weekend, finding him left lonely...."[5] She invited him to spend Christmas at her father's Rectory in Christchurch, Cambridgeshire, and they rode down together on his motorcycle. The tone of this letter and of subsequent references to him in letters home do not suggest that Dorothy was then aware that Bill, as she called him,[6] was married. She said that he

---

3   I am indebted to Mr M. K. Swales, Hon. Secretary of the Old Denstonian Club, for information about Denstone College.
4   I thank Ms Tracey Earl, Archivist of Coutts and Co., for this information.
5   See *The Letters of Dorothy L. Sayers: 1899–1936*, pp. 197–198.
6   His wife called him "Willy"

had "not a red cent or a roof" and from later letters it appears that she often provided meals for him and lent him money.

He accompanied her to theatres, dances and dinners. She introduced him to her friends and he escorted her to a staff dance at Benson's. He told his wife about these outings and also about another girl who took an interest in him but assured her that these relationships were "strictly Platonic". His wife did her best to believe him.

Dorothy and Bill became lovers and in the Spring of 1923 Dorothy found that she was pregnant. It may be that only then did Bill admit to Dorothy that he was married. His next move was surprising.. He asked his wife to come to London to celebrate the anniversary of their wedding. The following morning he told her that Dorothy was pregnant, saying "She is in a state about it, not wanting her father to know or to lose her job". He added: "I know you will help her." Mrs White's response was still more surprising. Out of compassion and perhaps also in an attempt to save her marriage, she agreed to help.

On the day she and Dorothy met they went round together to Bill's flat (he was then living off Theobalds Road) and they found him with another girl. Dorothy said to Mrs White: "He's like a child in a power-house, starting off machinery regardless of results. No woman on earth could hold him." She told Mrs White that she had never intended the pregnancy to occur and promised that if only she could be helped through the birth she would never see Bill again and would put the baby into the care of foster parents.[7] In return Mrs White invited Dorothy to come to Southbourne during the last stages of her pregnancy. She took a room for her at a guest house and arranged for her brother, Dr Murray Richmond Osborne Wilson, L.R.C.P., M.R.C.S., to attend the birth, which took place at Tuckton Lodge, a nursing-home in Ilford Lane, Southbourne. It was not revealed to Dr Wilson that he had been engaged to deliver his brother-in-law's child.

Valerie was then eight years old. Looking back 73 years, from 1997 to 1924, she remembers "a very large woman swathed in flowing garments" sitting beside the fire "in long earnest conversations" with her mother. Mrs White, whose own daughter had been born when she was 35, was in a position to give sympathetic encouragement to Dorothy, a primipara aged 30. A sisterly bond may have developed between them during this period: they both loved the same charming but unreliable man. Mrs White pledged to keep the baby's existence a secret and did so until after Dorothy's death in December 1957. Then, on 10 March 1958 she wrote a

---

7 Dorothy and Bill did, however, keep in touch for some time after the birth of John Anthony. See my biography, *Dorothy L. Sayers: Her Life and Soul* and her letters to Ivy Shrimpton and John Cournos in *The Letters of Dorothy L. Sayers: 1899–1936*.

letter to her daughter, at last revealing to her that she had a half-brother.[8]

Mrs White agreed to occupy Dorothy's flat in Great James Street during her absence, and, in order to lend credibility to the pretence that Dorothy was still living there, to send on letters to her and to post hers from London. Valerie, who accompanied her mother, remembers the flat clearly, in particular a cat called Agag, whose name Dorothy told her meant "he who treads lightly". She recalls also that there was a large supply of children's books in the flat. It is said that Bill joined them there occasionally.

About four years later, Mrs White, without preamble or explanation, informed her daughter that she had divorced her husband. She did not cite Dorothy as co-respondent; this was not necessary, as Bill continued to be involved with other women. Valerie never saw her father from then on. Nevertheless, she remembers him as a charming person. She recalls sitting on his knee while he taught her French. He showed her how to fly a kite and bought her instalments of Arthur Mee's *Children's Encyclopaedia*. He took particular care that she should speak English correctly. After the divorce he is said to have gone to live in the north of England. It is not known whether he married again or when or where he died.

This new information clarifies many points but some questions remain unanswered. Dorothy's letters to Ivy Shrimpton and particularly those to John Cournos draw a different picture in some respects. One puzzling matter is her off-hand reference to Mrs White in her letter to Ivy Shrimpton when she had returned to London after leaving the baby in her care:

> I was a bit weary yesterday, because I came home to find that the fool I'd let my flat to had locked up the keys inside the flat....[9]

This is a surprisingly ungracious (and uncharacteristic) comment about someone who had shown her so much kindness.

Another puzzling problem is Dorothy's delay in writing to her cousin Ivy to ask if she would be willing to foster the baby. Why did she wait so long – in the event two days before the birth? Had she perhaps agreed to give the baby up to someone else, advised possibly by Dr Wilson, and then changed her mind at the last moment? This seems the most likely explanation. If so, it sheds new light on Dorothy's attitude towards her child.

There are still dark patches in this period of her life. Perhaps she could not have explained them herself. They contrast strangely with the woman she later became, the woman revealed in her mature writings and in the

---

8 Some of the details in this account have been drawn from this letter. For further details I am indebted to Valerie (Mrs S. V. O. Napier) and to her daughter, Ms. F. M. Crawford. Both Mrs Napier and Ms Crawford remember Mrs White as an exceptionally kind and gentle person.

9 See *The Letters of Dorothy L. Sayers: 1899-1936*, p.209.

remarkable letters contained in this volume.

There is a touching post-script. In 1991 Mrs Napier decided at last to try to make contact with her half-brother. She wrote as follows:[10]

Dear Anthony,

Perhaps I should have written this letter thirty years ago when I first heard of your existence; I could have contacted you earlier, but didn't wish to cause any embarrassment.

I've recently read Brabazon's biography of your mother (whom I knew when I was a small child), and thought you might be interested to know a bit more about your father, William White (Bill).

Bill was not the common, ill-educated little clerk he was made out to be in the book. Both my mother and yours agreed that he was a "charming rotter"! His father was a clergyman in the Isle of Man, and Bill had been well educated at Denstone [College], and was a good Shakespearian actor during his school-days. He spoke good French, and was always crazy about cars and motor-bikes. He was a despatch rider in France during the First War, being himself mentioned in despatches. Afterwards he returned to his employment at Coutts Bank, having put most of my mother's money into several motor businesses, with varying success.

After Dorothy died my mother wrote me a detailed letter (which I still have) about the circumstances of your birth. She had been married to Bill since 1914. I was born the following year.

We lived in a flat in the Southbourne house of my uncle, Dr Murray Wilson. At Bill's request (!) my mother arranged for her brother to attend Dorothy at the Tuckton Nursing Home, during which time my mother and I stayed at the [Great] James Street flat, in order to forward letters, to prevent Dorothy's parents discovering her absence from London. I have memories of long discussions between the two women, but did not understand the situation.

My parents divorced later and Bill went to live in the north of England....There are no relations left from my own generation; and that is why I should like to get in touch with you; we do have something in common!

I do hope you don't find my letter "embarrassing or distressful" (your words).[11] After all these years I certainly don't, and, if you are willing, I should like to get to know you better – I always missed not having a brother....

This letter was sent c/o the publishers, Victor Gollancz Ltd. It was returned unopened. John Anthony had been dead for seven years.

B.R.

10 Published with the permission of Mrs Valerie Napier, who retains the copyright.
11 Quoted from Brabazon.

Index

❧❧❧